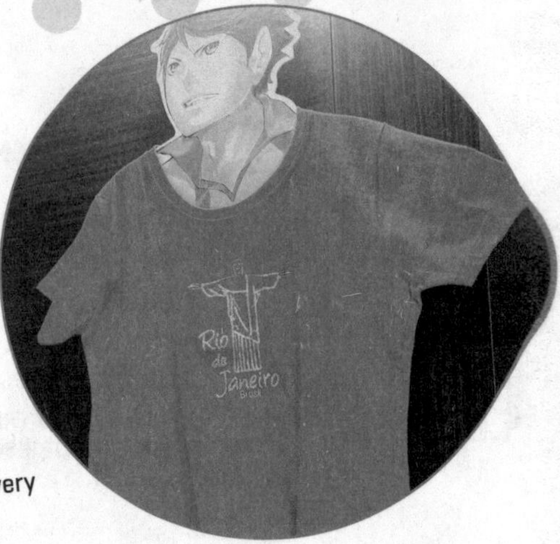
Rio
Janeiro

Thank you very much for purchasing *Haikyu!!* volume 44! I was watching a real-life V.League game while I was working when I caught myself thinking, "Why am I going to all the trouble of drawing this volleyball game on paper? People can just go watch it themselves!" I was very confused.

HARUICHI FURUDATE began his manga career when he was 25 years old with the one-shot *Ousama Kid* [King Kid], which won an honorable mention for the 14th Jump Treasure Newcomer Manga Prize. His first series, *Kiben Gakuha, Yotsuya Sensei no Kaidan* [Philosophy School, Yotsuya Sensei's Ghost Stories], was serialized in *Weekly Shonen Jump* in 2010. In 2012, he began serializing *Haikyu!!* in *Weekly Shonen Jump*, where it became his most popular work to date.

HAIKYU!!

VOLUME 44
SHONEN JUMP Manga Edition

Story and Art by
HARUICHI FURUDATE

Translation  **ADRIENNE BECK**
Touch-Up Art & Lettering ❷ **ERIKA TERRIQUEZ**
Design ❸ **JULIAN [JR] ROBINSON**
Editor ❹ **MARLENE FIRST**

HAIKYU!! © 2012 by Haruichi Furudate
All rights reserved.
First published in Japan in 2012 by SHUEISHA Inc., Tokyo.
English translation rights arranged by SHUEISHA Inc.

The stories, characters and incidents mentioned
in this publication are entirely fictional.

Printed in Canada

Published by VIZ Media, LLC
P.O. Box 77010
San Francisco, CA 94107

10 9 8 7 6 5 4 3 2 1
First printing, May 2021

 **VIZ MEDIA**
viz.com

SHONEN JUMP

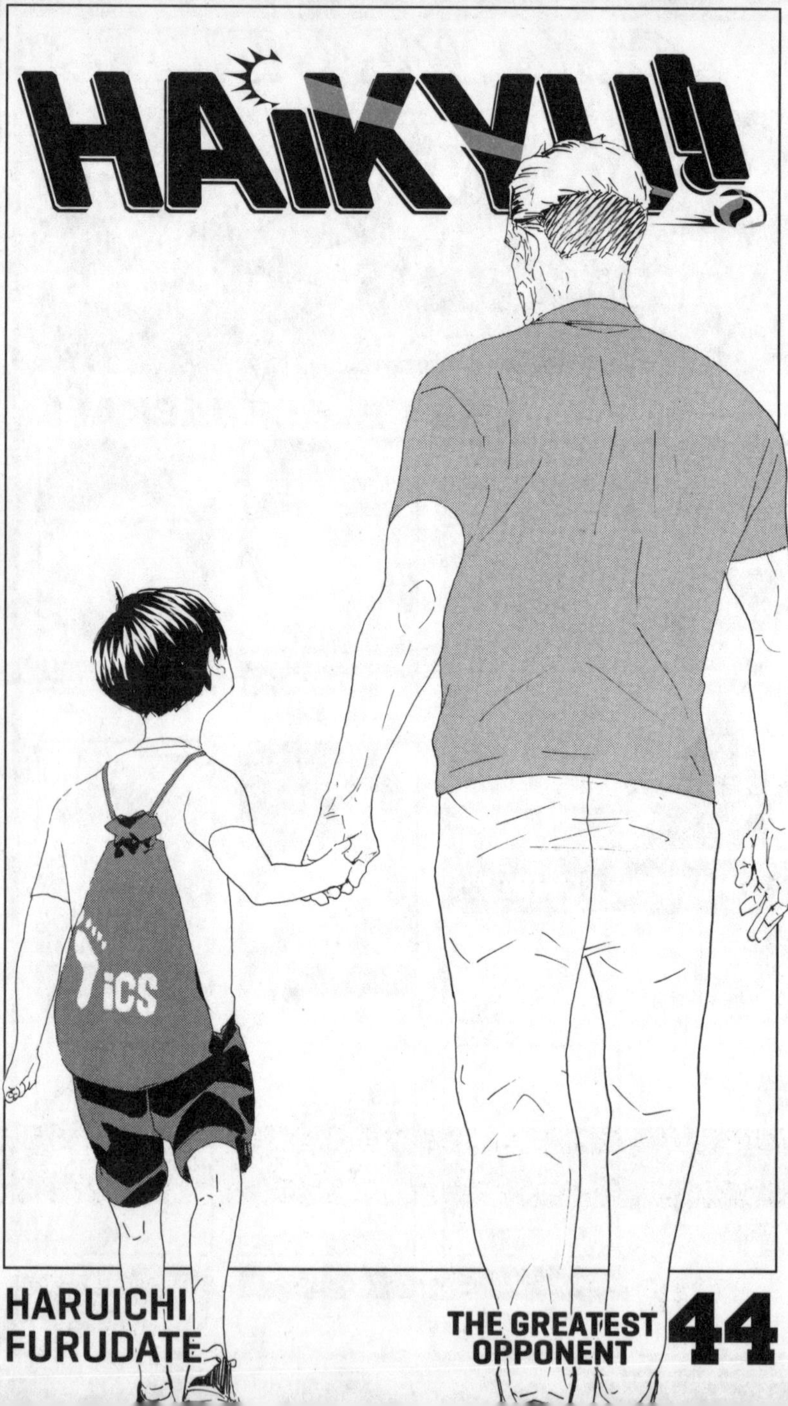
HAIKYU!!
iCS

HARUICHI
FURUDATE

THE GREATEST
OPPONENT

44

CHARACTERS

2018 - 2019 Season

V.LEAGUE MEN'S Division 1

SCHWEIDEN ADLERS Vs MSBY BLACK JACKALS

in SENDAI

MSBY BLACKJACKALS

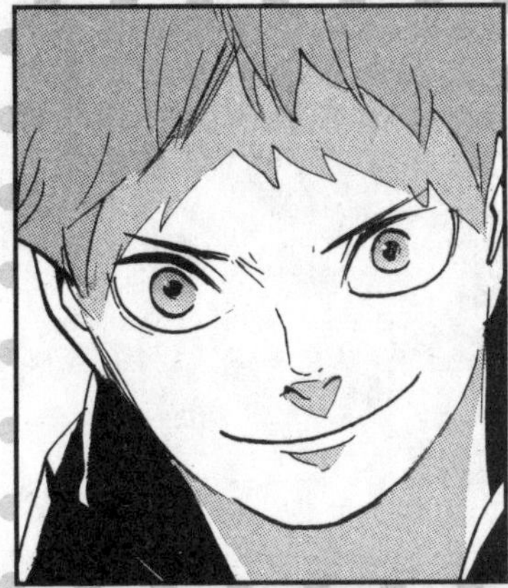

SHOYO HINATA (22)

OP / 5'7"

Trained in beach volleyball in Brazil before joining the V.League in Japan.

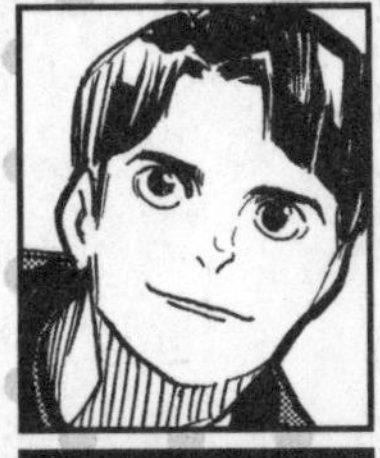

ADRIAH THOMAS (27)

MB / 6'7"

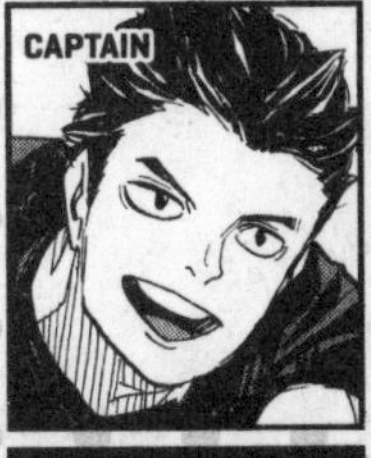
CAPTAIN

SHUGO MEIAN (29)

MB / 6'5"

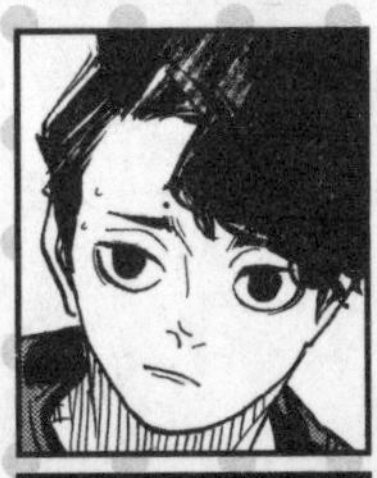

KIYOOMI SAKUSA (22)

OH / 6'4"

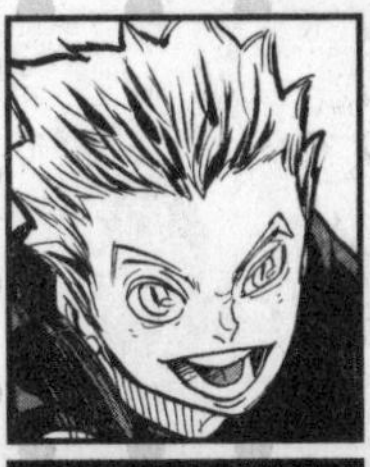

KOTARO BOKUTO (24)

OH / 6'3"

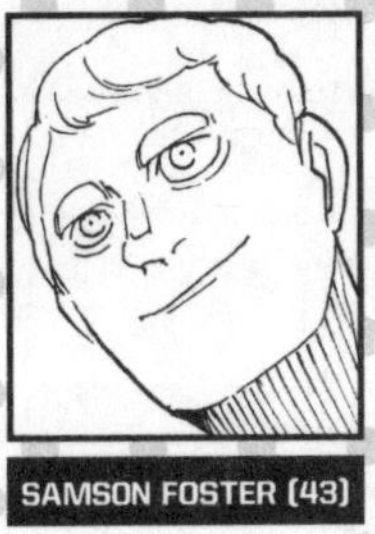

SAMSON FOSTER (43)

HEAD COACH

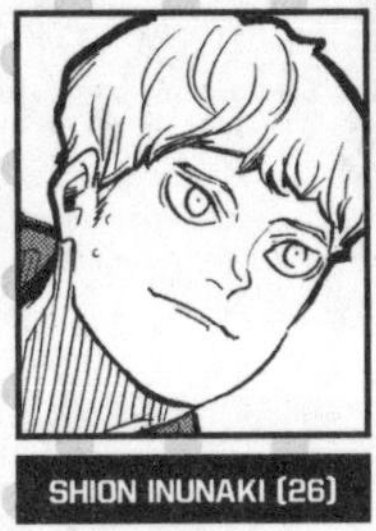

SHION INUNAKI (26)

L / 5'9"

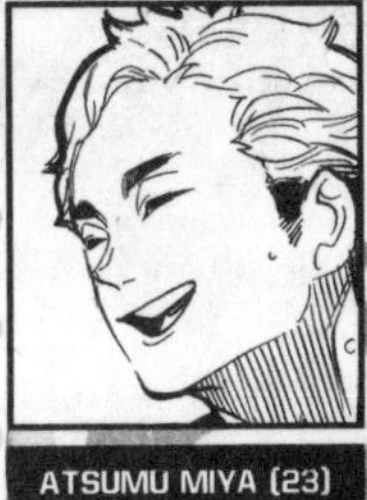

ATSUMU MIYA (23)

S / 6'2"

Schweiden ADLERS

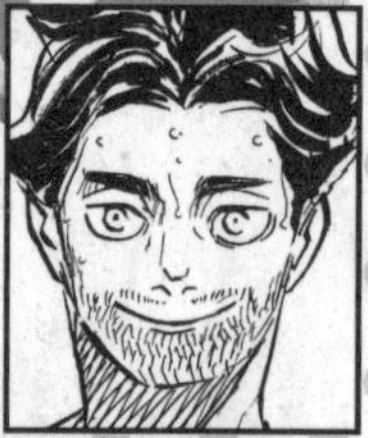

NICOLAS ROMERO (30)

OH / 6'3"

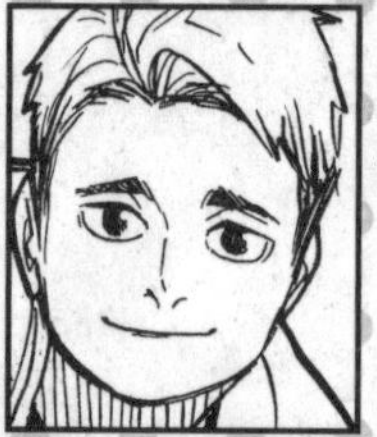

TATSUTO SOKOLOV (25)

MB / 6'7"

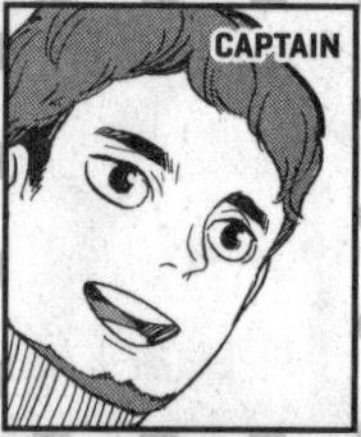
CAPTAIN

FUKURO HIRUGAMI (29)

MB / 6'6"

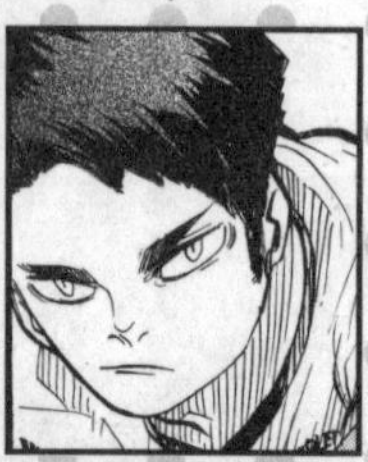

WAKATOSHI USHIJIMA (24)

OP / 6'4"

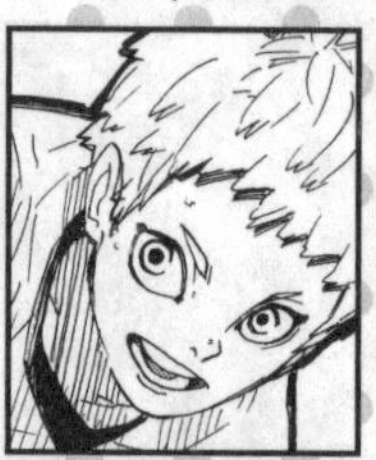

KORAI HOSHIUMI (23)

OH / 5'8"

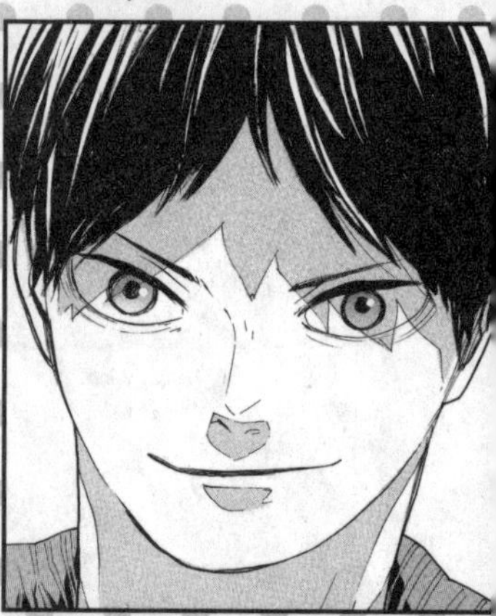

TOBIO KAGEYAMA (21)

S / 6'2"

He advanced straight into the V.League after graduation, putting up eye-popping stats as a teenage rookie.

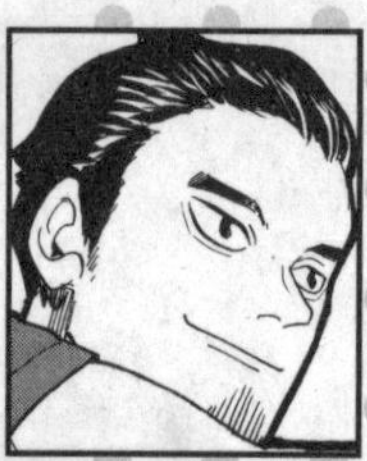

BANJO SUZAKU (46)

HEAD COACH

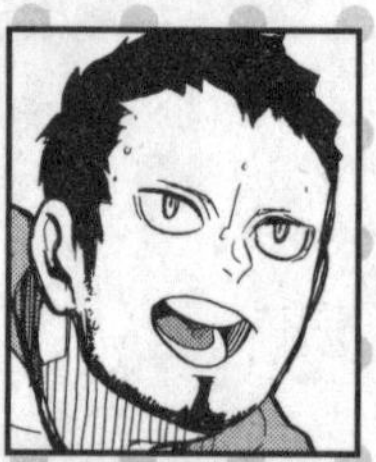

TOSHIRO HEIWAJIMA (28)

L / 5'9"

Ever since he saw the legendary player known as "the Little Giant" compete at the national volleyball finals, Shoyo Hinata has been aiming to be the best volleyball player ever! He decides to join the volleyball club at his middle school and gets to play in an official tournament during his third year. His team is crushed by a team led by volleyball prodigy Tobio Kageyama, also known as "the King of the Court." Swearing revenge on Kageyama, Hinata graduates middle school and enters Karasuno High School, the school where the Little Giant played. However, upon joining the club, he finds out that Kageyama is there too! The two of them bicker constantly, but they bring out the best in each other's talents and become a powerful combo. But when they make it to the Spring Tournament in their first year of high school, Hinata develops a fever and gets benched. His regrets are engraved in his memory as he watches Karasuno get eliminated. Six years later, Hinata finally returns to Japan after spending two years playing beach volleyball in Brazil. He joins the V.League, and his debut pro game is against Kageyama and his team! It's the Black Jackals versus the Adlers, their rosters stacked with names like Ushijima, Hoshiumi, Atsumu Miya, Bokuto and Sakusa—"the Monster Generation." What will the crowd think of a fully trained Hinata? Will he prove that he truly is "the Greatest Decoy"?

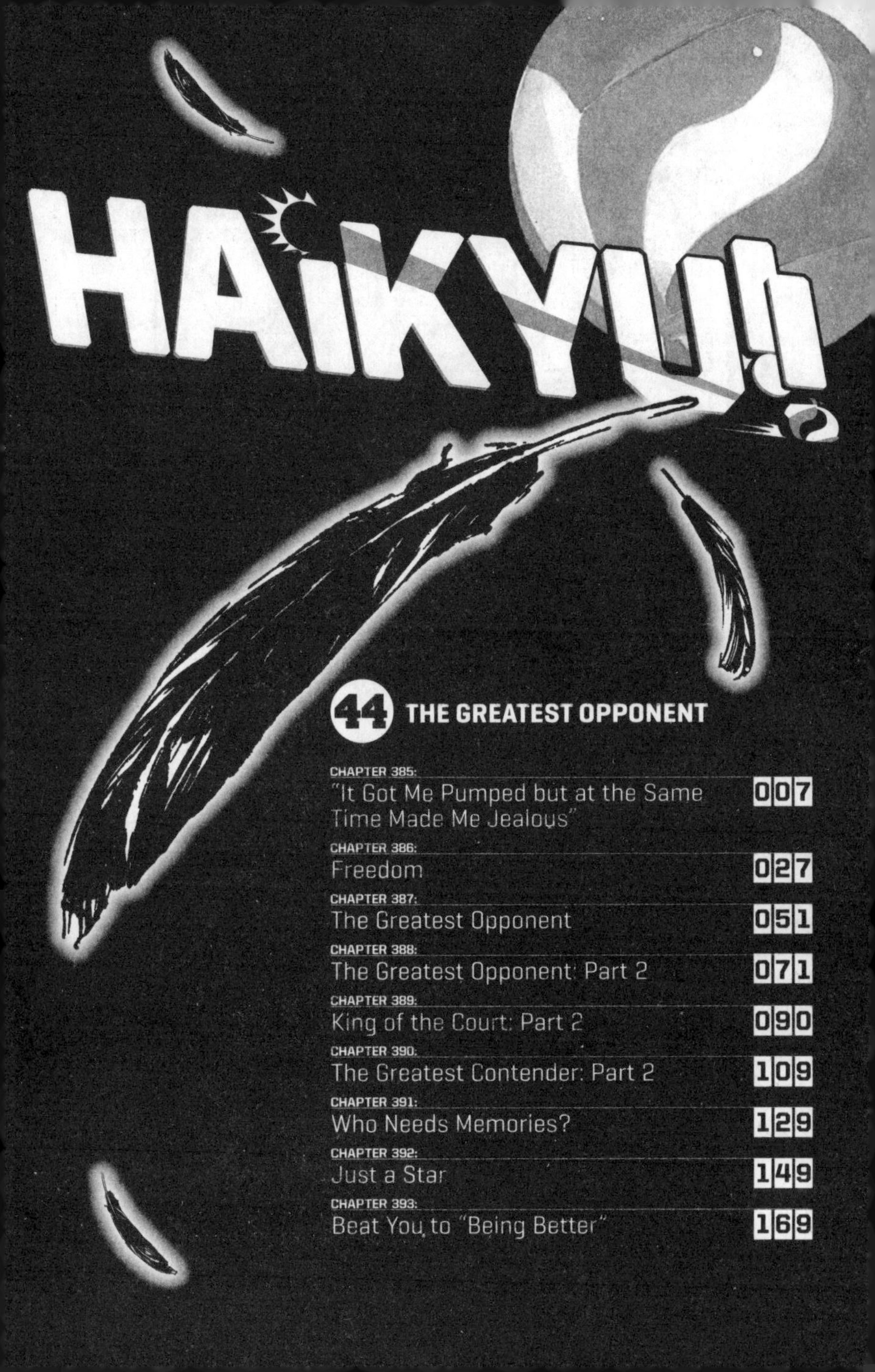
HAIKYU!!

44 THE GREATEST OPPONENT

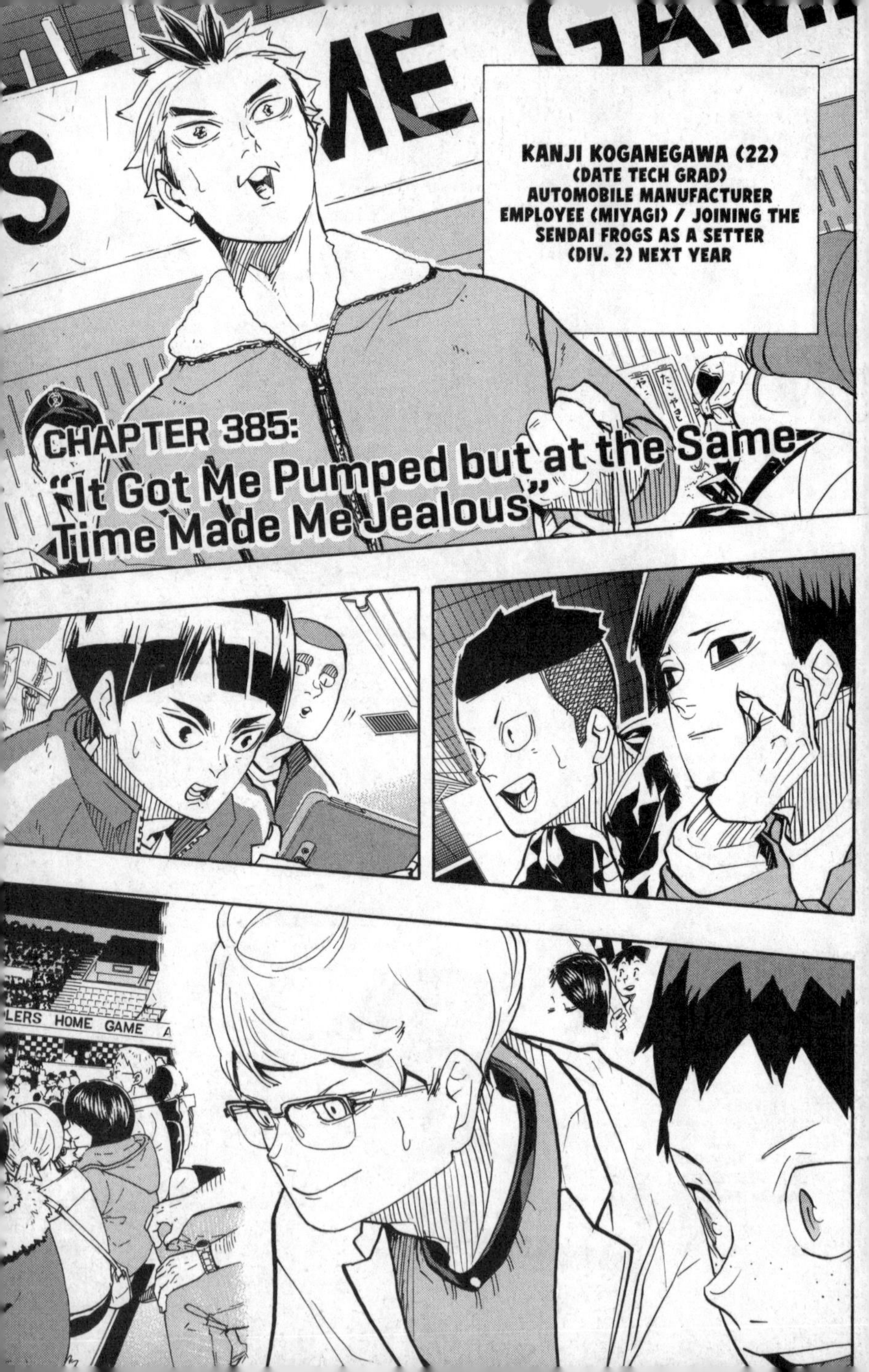
KANJI KOGANEGAWA (22)
(DATE TECH GRAD)
AUTOMOBILE MANUFACTURER
EMPLOYEE (MIYAGI) / JOINING THE
SENDAI FROGS AS A SETTER
(DIV. 2) NEXT YEAR
CHAPTER 385:
"It Got Me Pumped but at the Same Time Made Me Jealous"
LERS HOME GAME

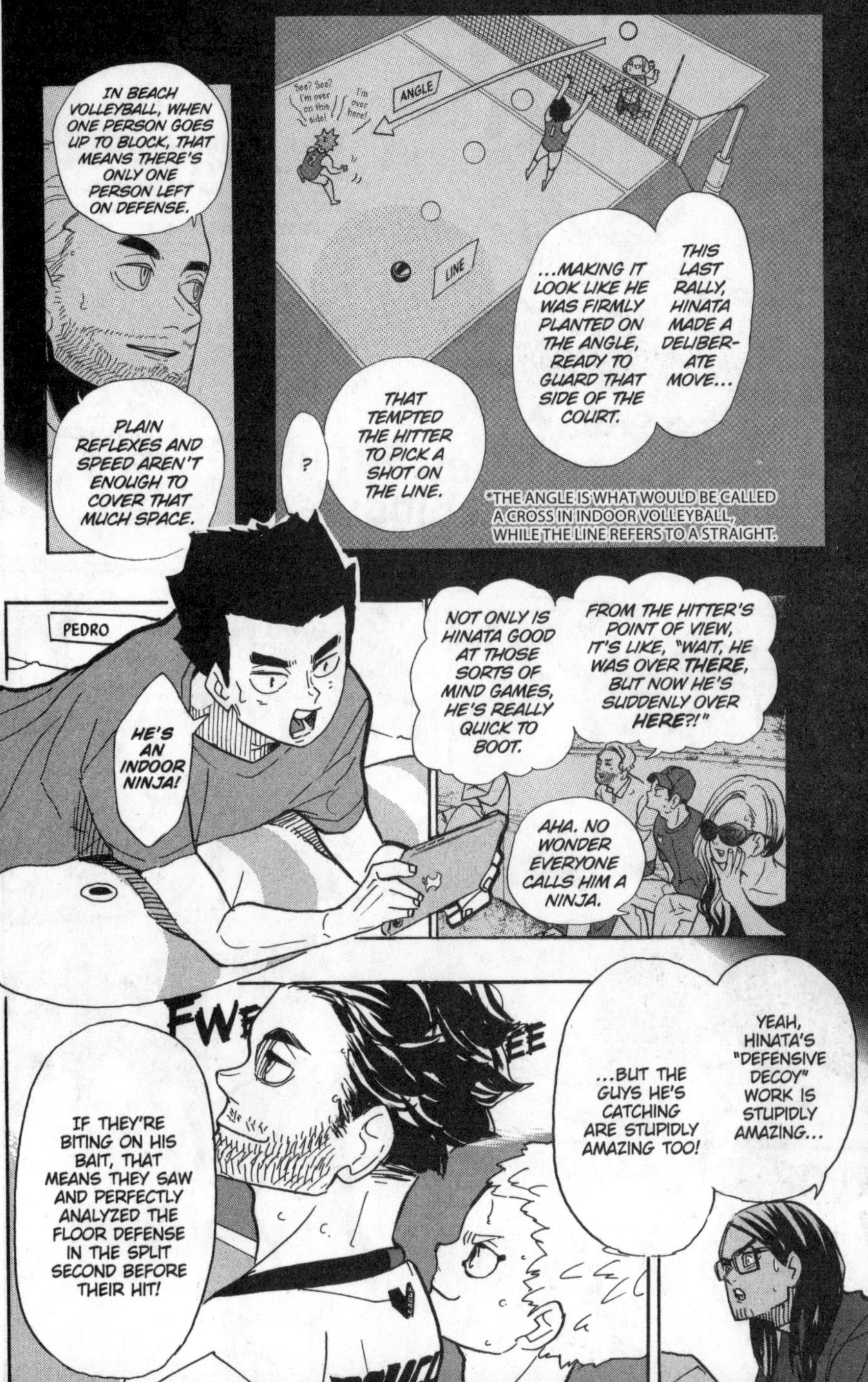
THIS LAST RALLY, HINATA MADE A DELIBERATE MOVE...
...MAKING IT LOOK LIKE HE WAS FIRMLY PLANTED ON THE ANGLE, READY TO GUARD THAT SIDE OF THE COURT.
I'm over here!
See? See? I'm over on this side!
ANGLE
LINE
THAT TEMPTED THE HITTER TO PICK A SHOT ON THE LINE.
?
*THE ANGLE IS WHAT WOULD BE CALLED A CROSS IN INDOOR VOLLEYBALL, WHILE THE LINE REFERS TO A STRAIGHT.
IN BEACH VOLLEYBALL, WHEN ONE PERSON GOES UP TO BLOCK, THAT MEANS THERE'S ONLY ONE PERSON LEFT ON DEFENSE.
PLAIN REFLEXES AND SPEED AREN'T ENOUGH TO COVER THAT MUCH SPACE.
FROM THE HITTER'S POINT OF VIEW, IT'S LIKE, "WAIT, HE WAS OVER THERE, BUT NOW HE'S SUDDENLY OVER HERE?!"
NOT ONLY IS HINATA GOOD AT THOSE SORTS OF MIND GAMES, HE'S REALLY QUICK TO BOOT.
AHA. NO WONDER EVERYONE CALLS HIM A NINJA.
PEDRO
HE'S AN INDOOR NINJA!
YEAH, HINATA'S "DEFENSIVE DECOY" WORK IS STUPIDLY AMAZING...
...BUT THE GUYS HE'S CATCHING ARE STUPIDLY AMAZING TOO!
IF THEY'RE BITING ON HIS BAIT, THAT MEANS THEY SAW AND PERFECTLY ANALYZED THE FLOOR DEFENSE IN THE SPLIT SECOND BEFORE THEIR HIT!

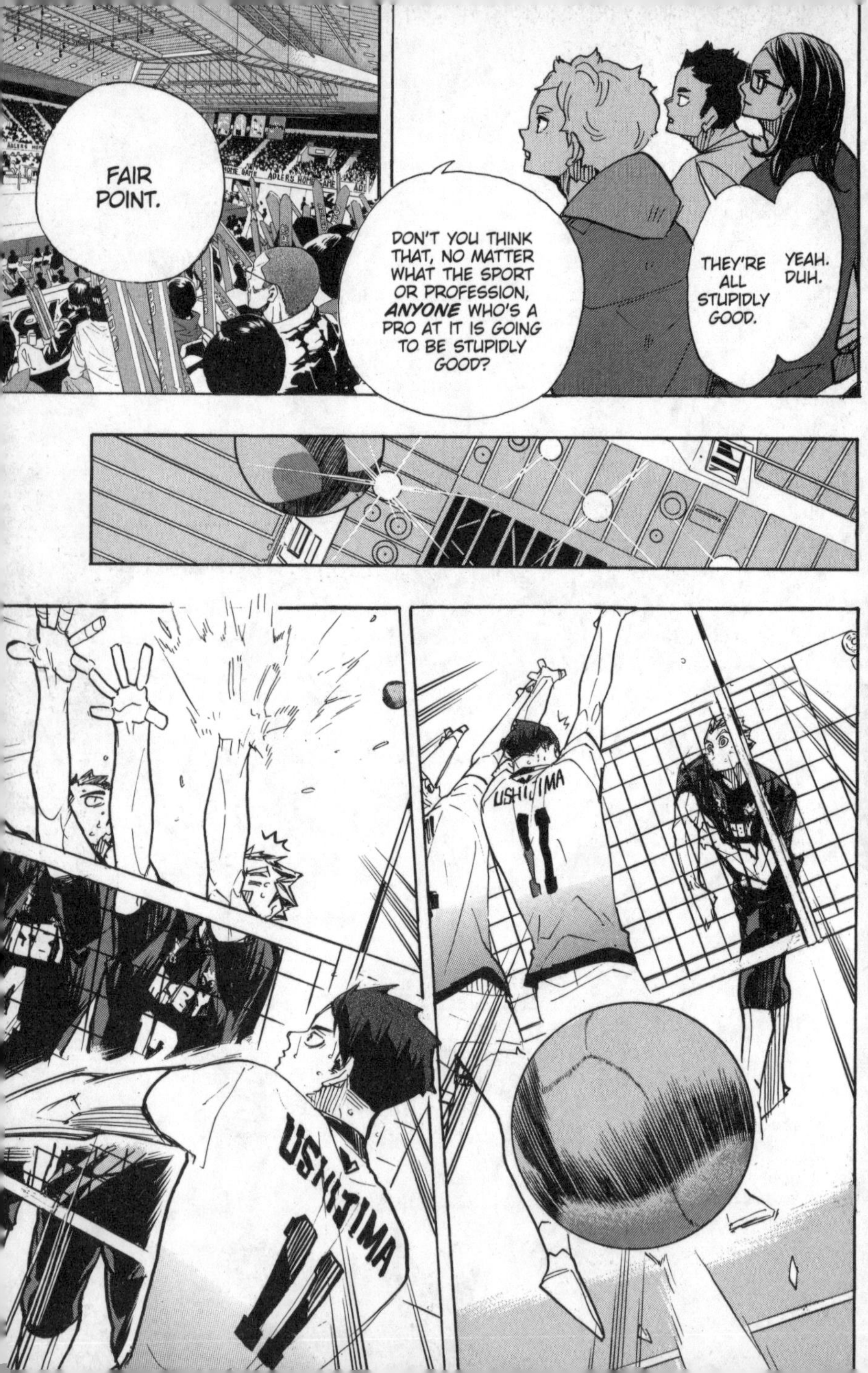
YEAH. DUH.
THEY'RE ALL STUPIDLY GOOD.
DON'T YOU THINK THAT, NO MATTER WHAT THE SPORT OR PROFESSION, ANYONE WHO'S A PRO AT IT IS GOING TO BE STUPIDLY GOOD?
FAIR POINT.

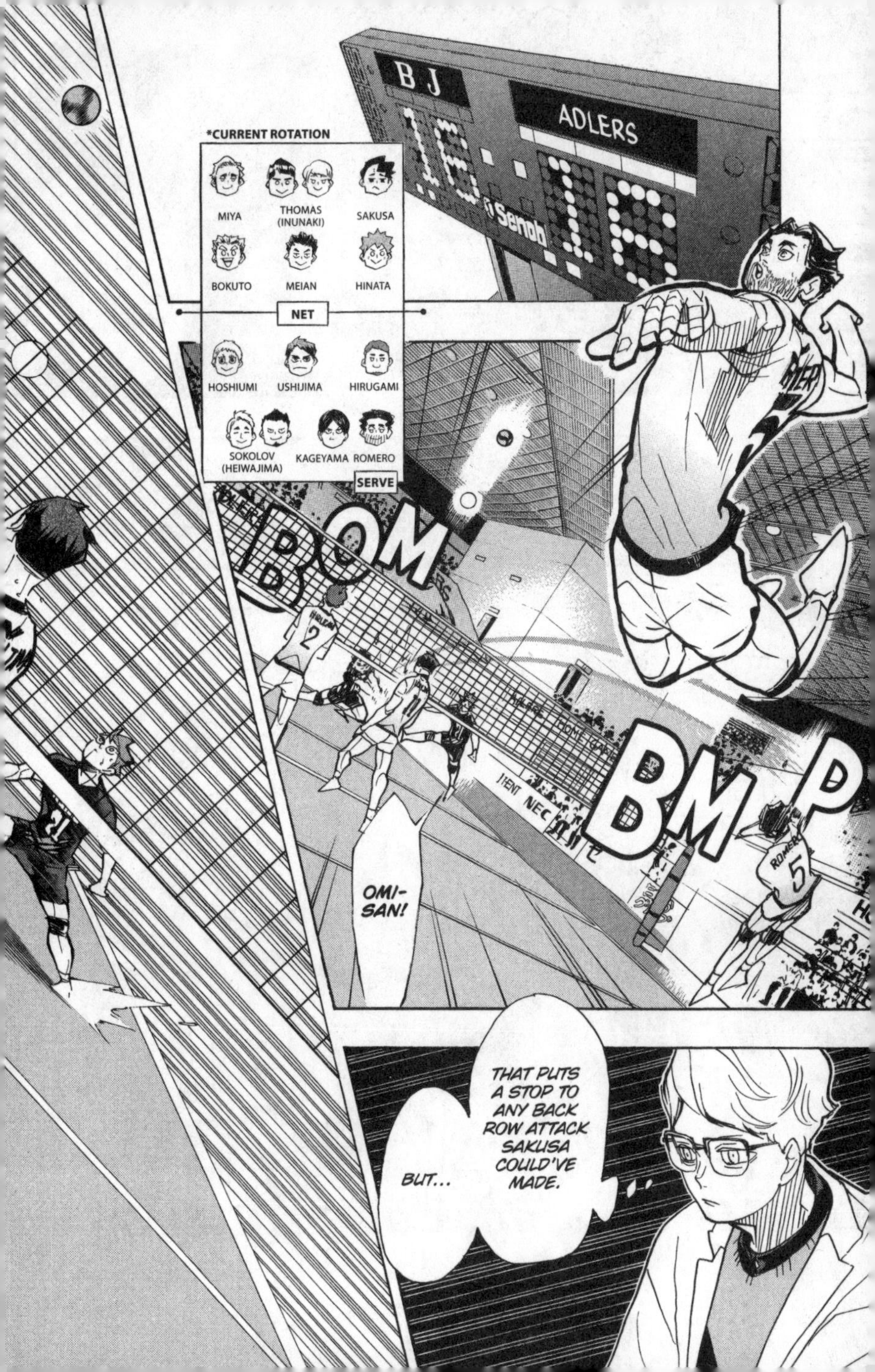
B J
ADLERS
*CURRENT ROTATION
MIYA
THOMAS (INUNAKI)
SAKUSA
BOKUTO
MEIAN
HINATA
NET
HOSHIUMI
USHIJIMA
HIRUGAMI
SOKOLOV (HEIWAJIMA)
KAGEYAMA
ROMERO
SERVE
BOM
BMP
OMI-SAN!
THAT PUTS A STOP TO ANY BACK ROW ATTACK SAKUSA COULD'VE MADE.
BUT...

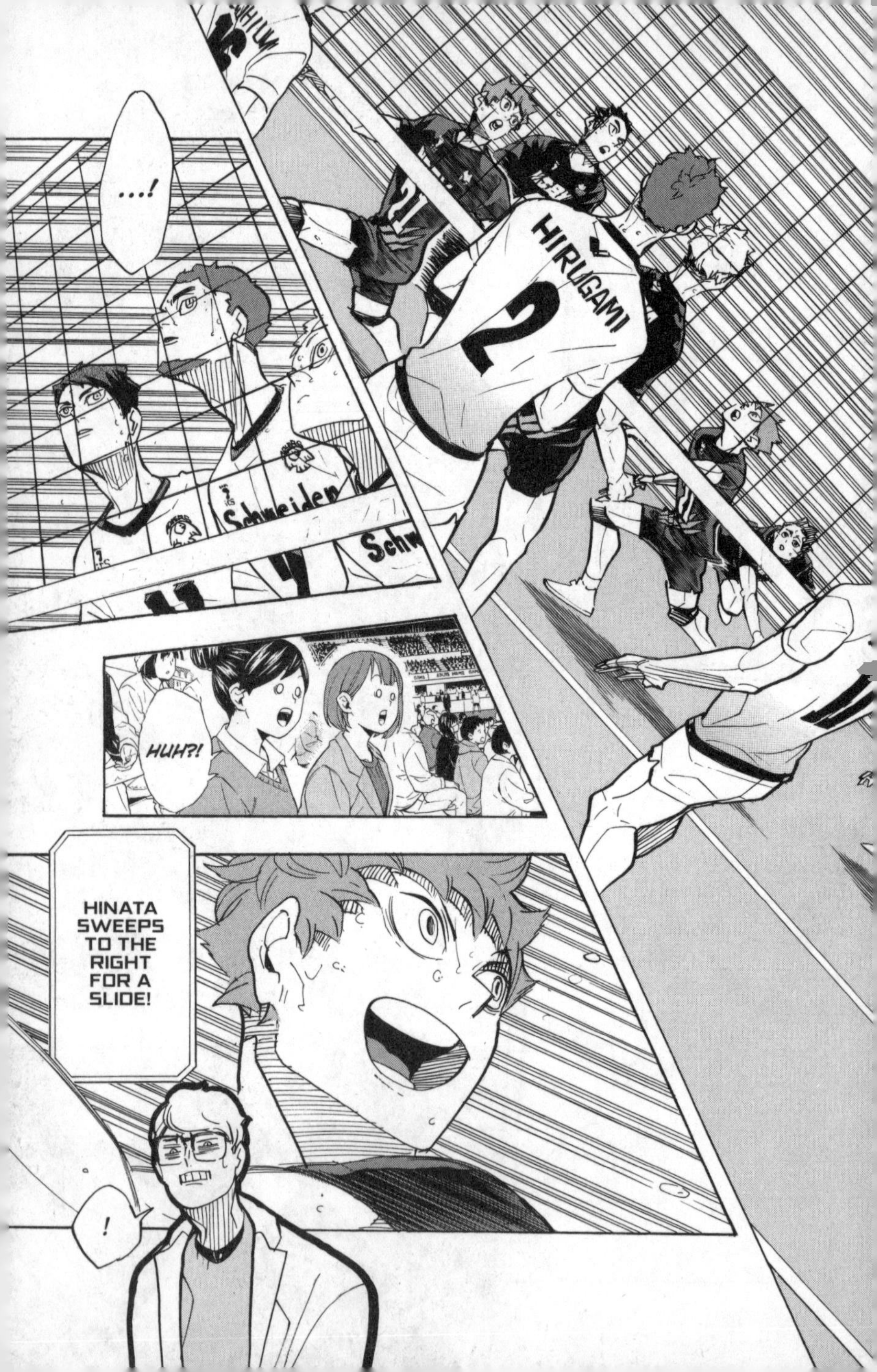
...!
HUH?!
HINATA SWEEPS TO THE RIGHT FOR A SLIDE!
!

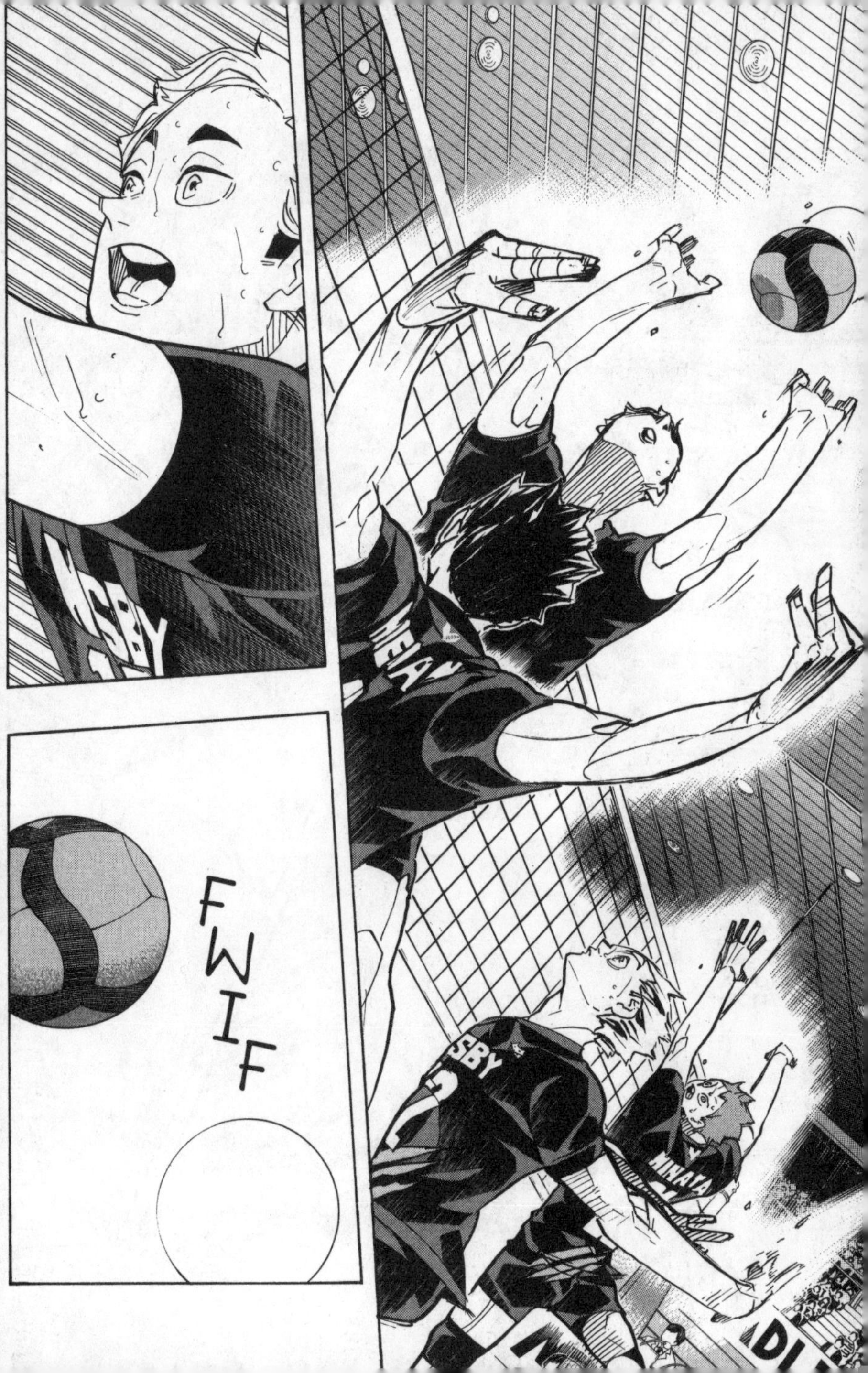
FWIF

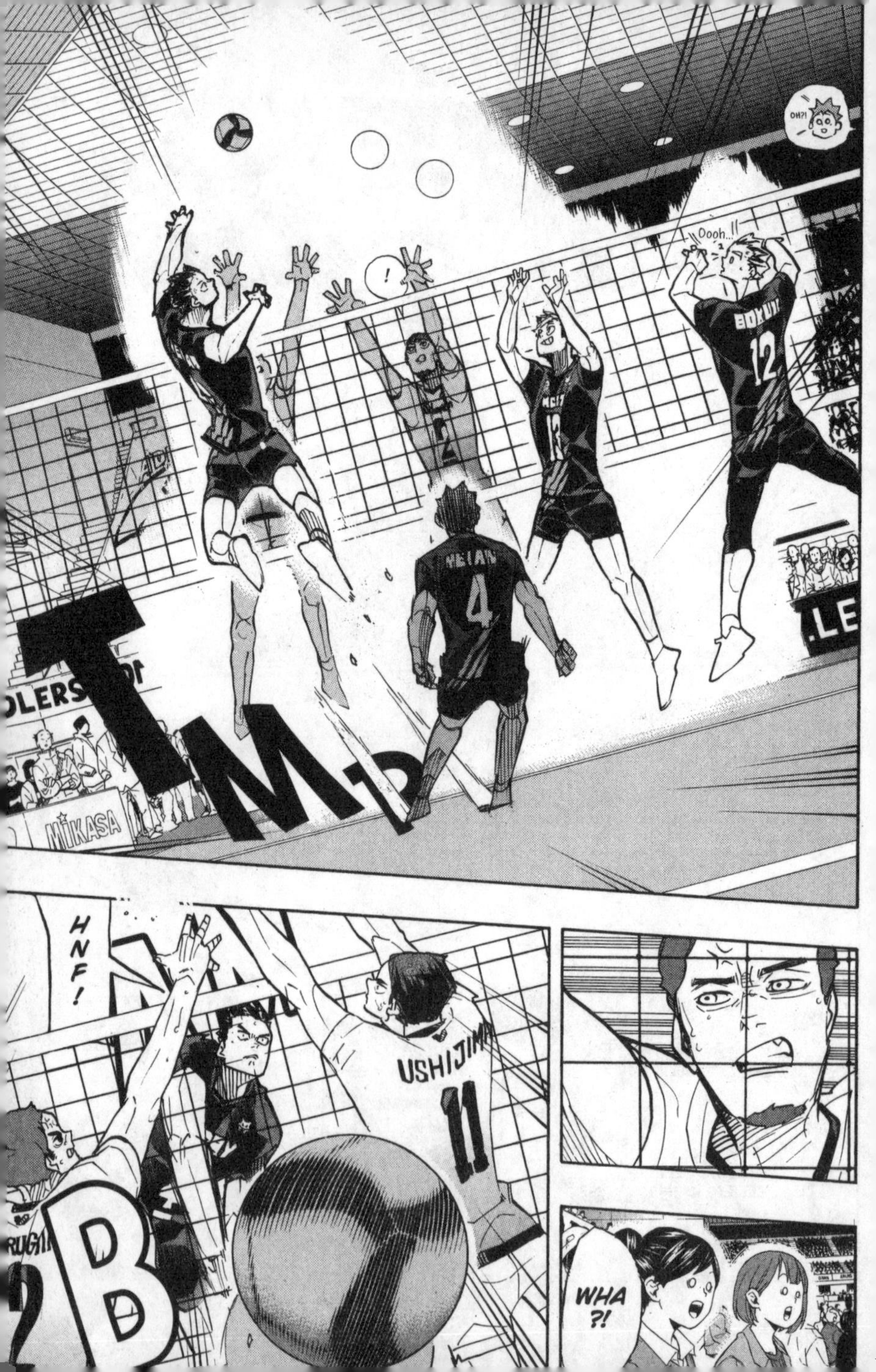
OH?!
Oooh...!!
!
WHA ?!
HNF!
USHIJIMA

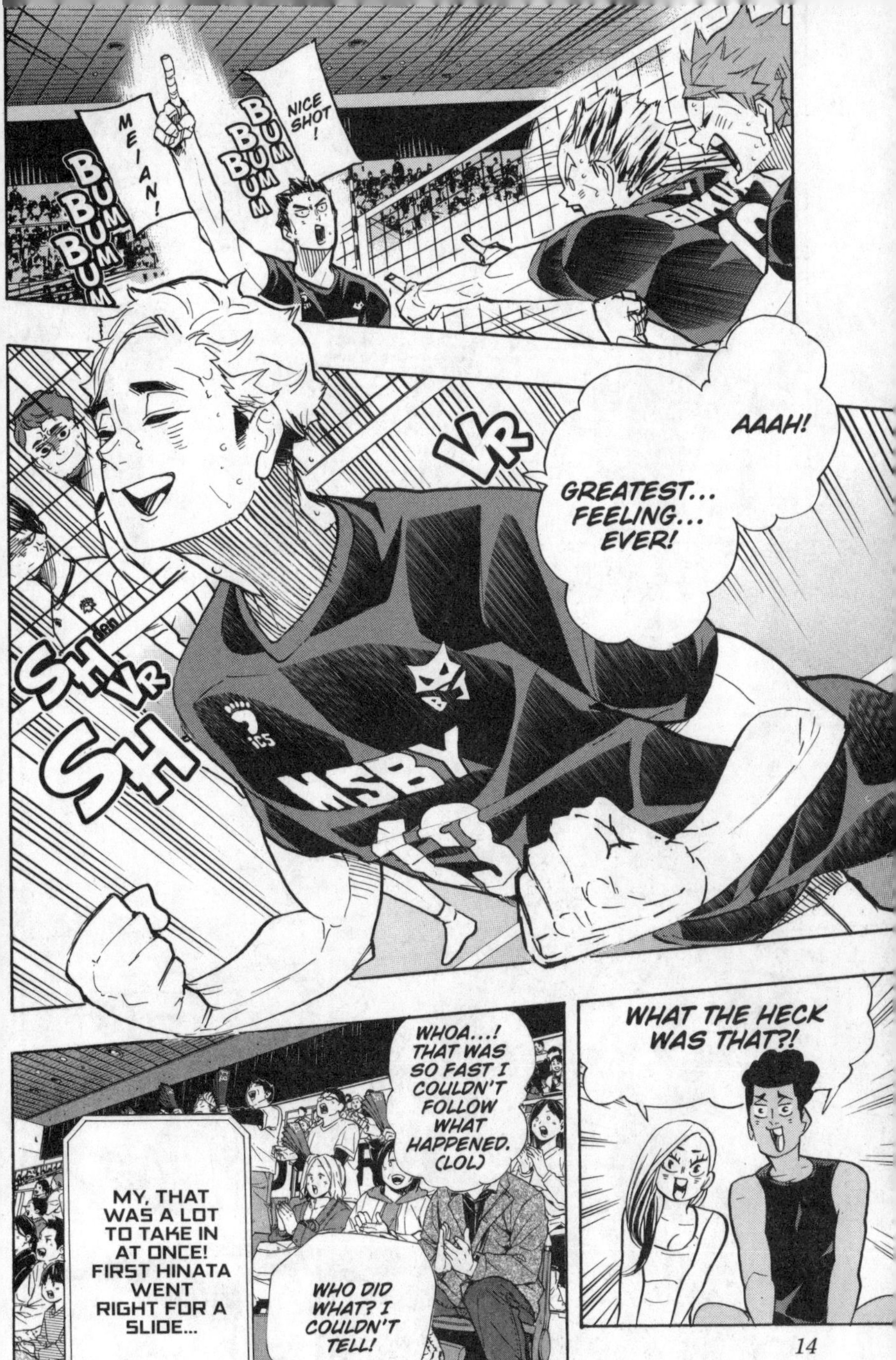
NICE SHOT!
BUMBUMBUM
MEIAN!
BUMBUMBUM
AAAH!
GREATEST... FEELING... EVER!
VR
SHVR
SH
WHAT THE HECK WAS THAT?!
WHOA...! THAT WAS SO FAST I COULDN'T FOLLOW WHAT HAPPENED. (LOL)
MY, THAT WAS A LOT TO TAKE IN AT ONCE! FIRST HINATA WENT RIGHT FOR A SLIDE...
WHO DID WHAT? I COULDN'T TELL!

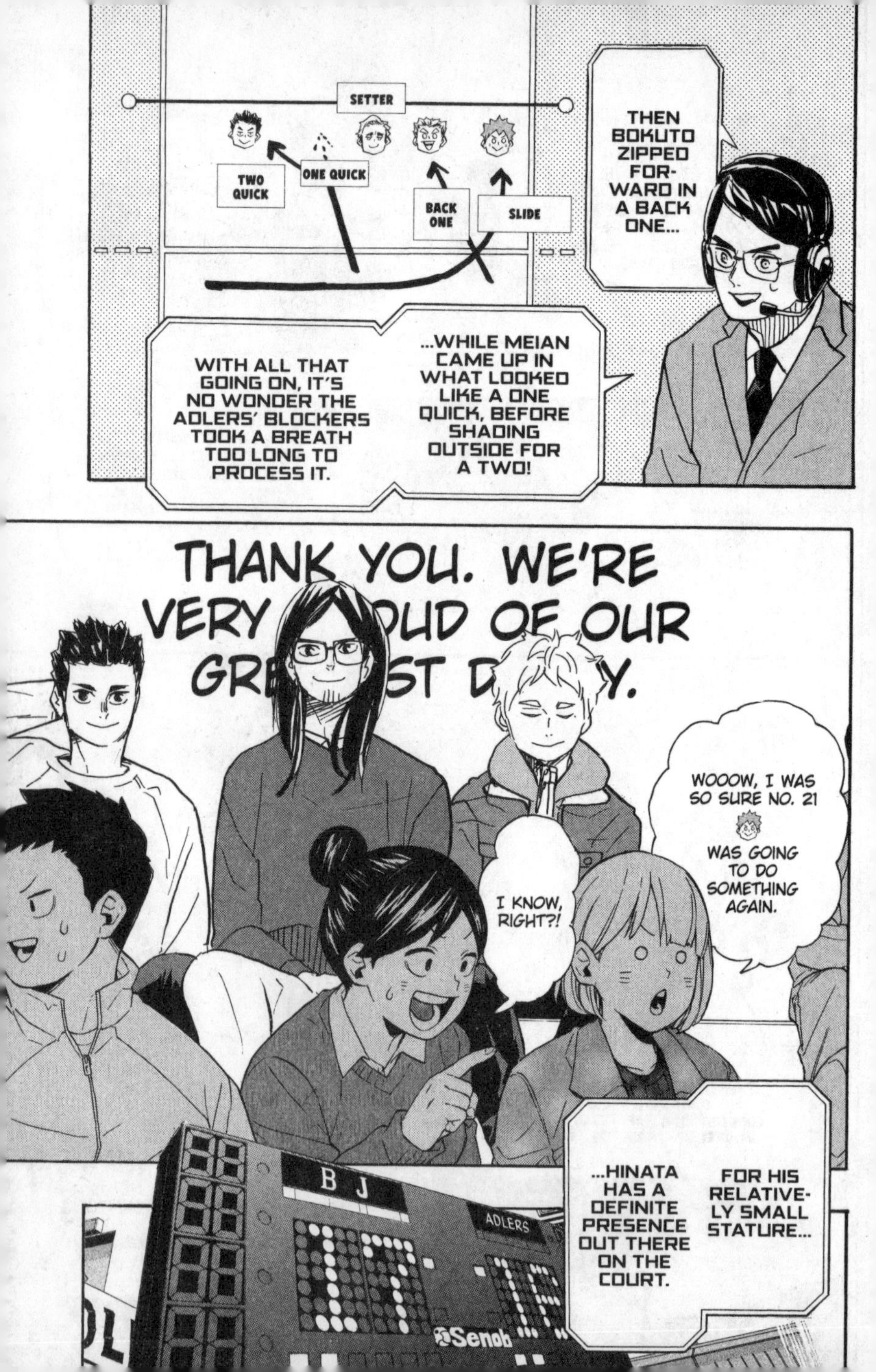
THEN BOKUTO ZIPPED FOR-WARD IN A BACK ONE...
...WHILE MEIAN CAME UP IN WHAT LOOKED LIKE A ONE QUICK, BEFORE SHADING OUTSIDE FOR A TWO!
WITH ALL THAT GOING ON, IT'S NO WONDER THE ADLERS' BLOCKERS TOOK A BREATH TOO LONG TO PROCESS IT.
SETTER
TWO QUICK
ONE QUICK
BACK ONE
SLIDE
THANK YOU. WE'RE
WOOOW, I WAS SO SURE NO. 21 WAS GOING TO DO SOMETHING AGAIN.
I KNOW, RIGHT?!
FOR HIS RELATIVE-LY SMALL STATURE...
...HINATA HAS A DEFINITE PRESENCE OUT THERE ON THE COURT.
B J
ADLERS
Senob

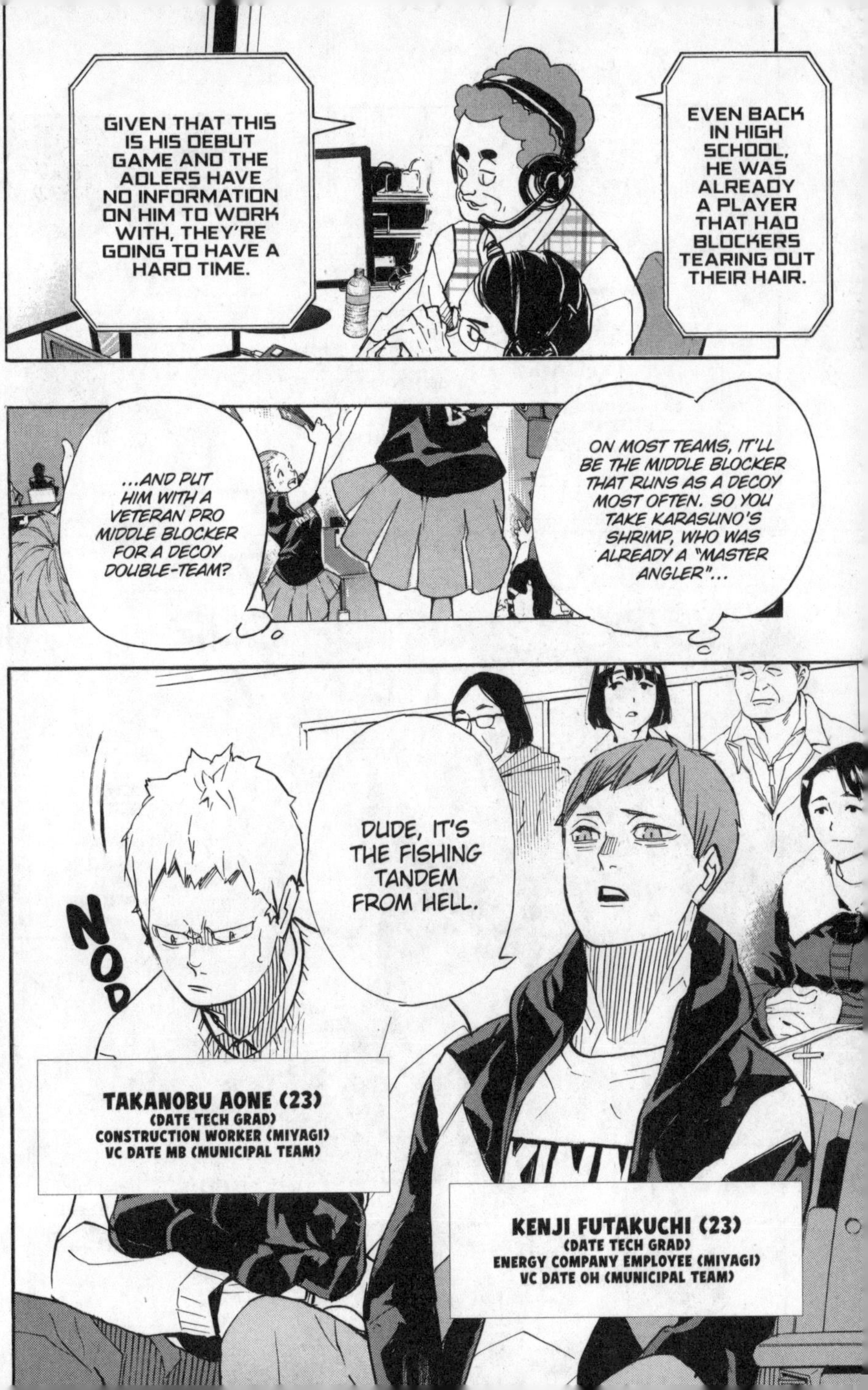
EVEN BACK IN HIGH SCHOOL, HE WAS ALREADY A PLAYER THAT HAD BLOCKERS TEARING OUT THEIR HAIR.
GIVEN THAT THIS IS HIS DEBUT GAME AND THE ADLERS HAVE NO INFORMATION ON HIM TO WORK WITH, THEY'RE GOING TO HAVE A HARD TIME.
ON MOST TEAMS, IT'LL BE THE MIDDLE BLOCKER THAT RUNS AS A DECOY MOST OFTEN. SO YOU TAKE KARASUNO'S SHRIMP, WHO WAS ALREADY A "MASTER ANGLER"...
...AND PUT HIM WITH A VETERAN PRO MIDDLE BLOCKER FOR A DECOY DOUBLE-TEAM?
DUDE, IT'S THE FISHING TANDEM FROM HELL.
NOD
TAKANOBU AONE (23) (DATE TECH GRAD) CONSTRUCTION WORKER (MIYAGI) VC DATE MB (MUNICIPAL TEAM)
KENJI FUTAKUCHI (23) (DATE TECH GRAD) ENERGY COMPANY EMPLOYEE (MIYAGI) VC DATE OH (MUNICIPAL TEAM)

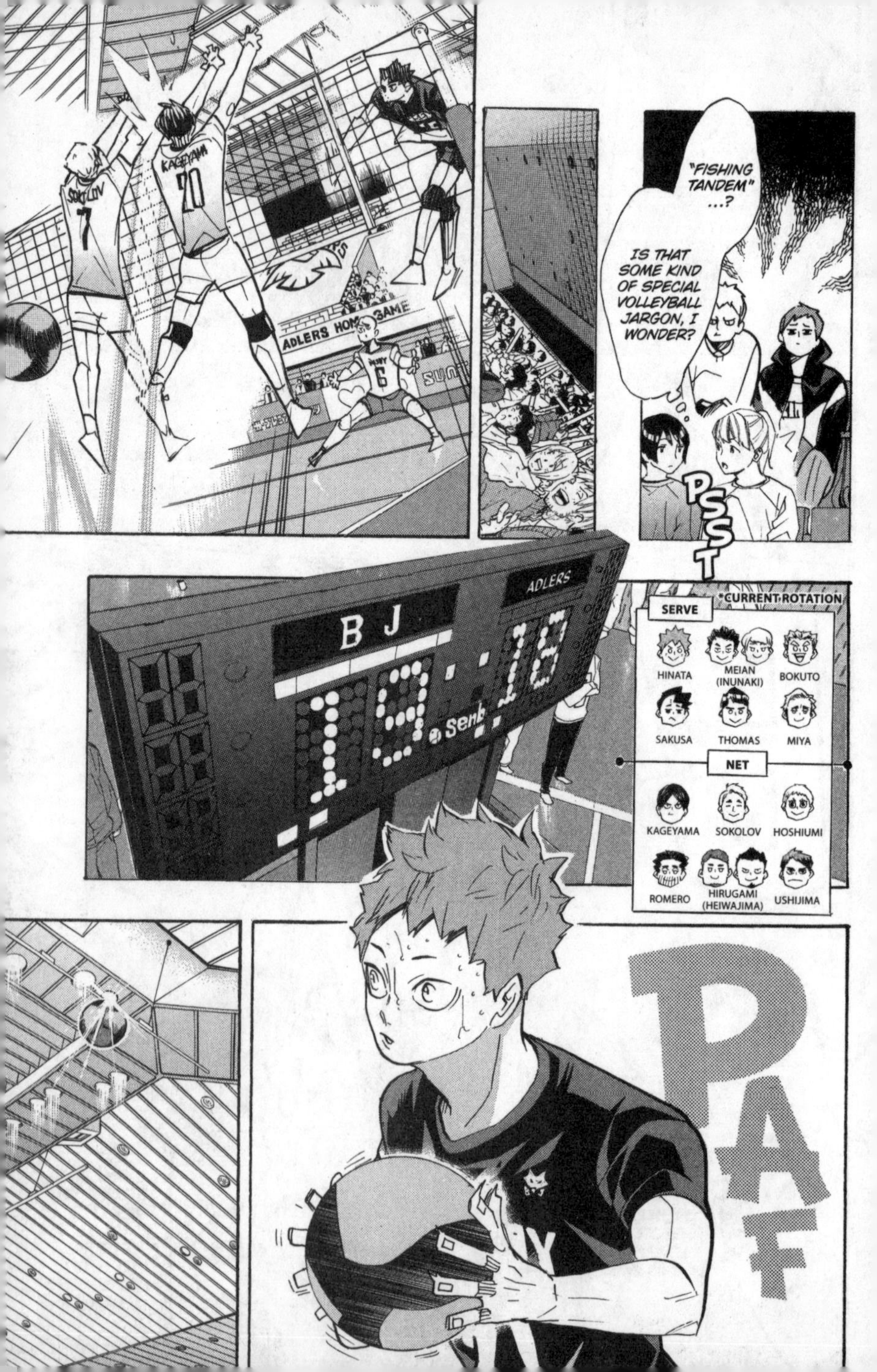

"FISHING TANDEM" ...?
IS THAT SOME KIND OF SPECIAL VOLLEYBALL JARGON, I WONDER?
PSST
KAGEYAMA 20
SOKOLOV 7
ADLERS HOME GAME
*CURRENT ROTATION
SERVE
HINATA
MEIAN (INUNAKI)
BOKUTO
SAKUSA
THOMAS
MIYA
NET
KAGEYAMA
SOKOLOV
HOSHIUMI
ROMERO
HIRUGAMI (HEIWAJIMA)
USHIJIMA
ADLERS
B J
19
18
PAF

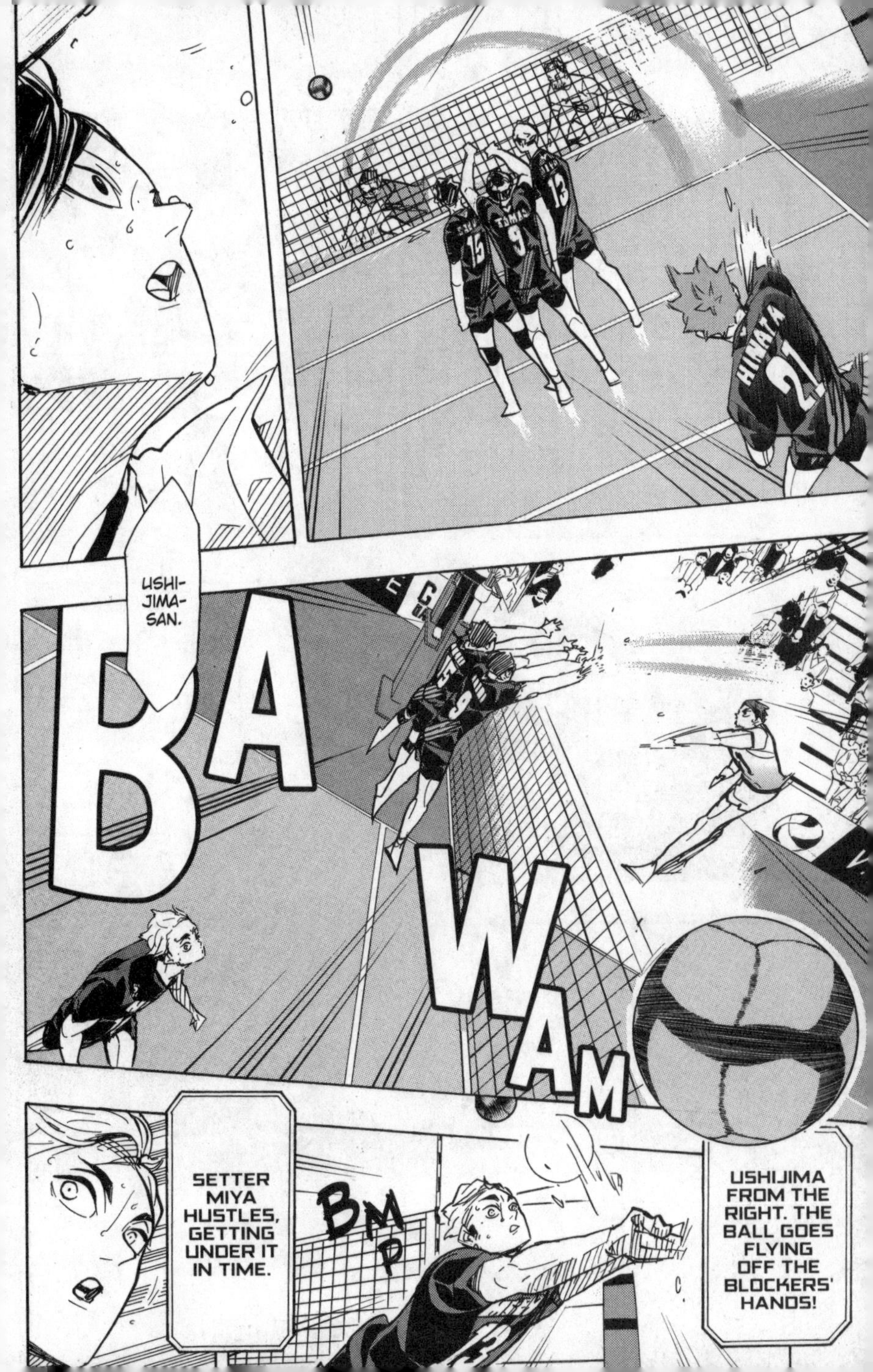
USHIJIMA-SAN.
BAWAM
USHIJIMA FROM THE RIGHT. THE BALL GOES FLYING OFF THE BLOCKERS' HANDS!
BMP
SETTER MIYA HUSTLES, GETTING UNDER IT IN TIME.

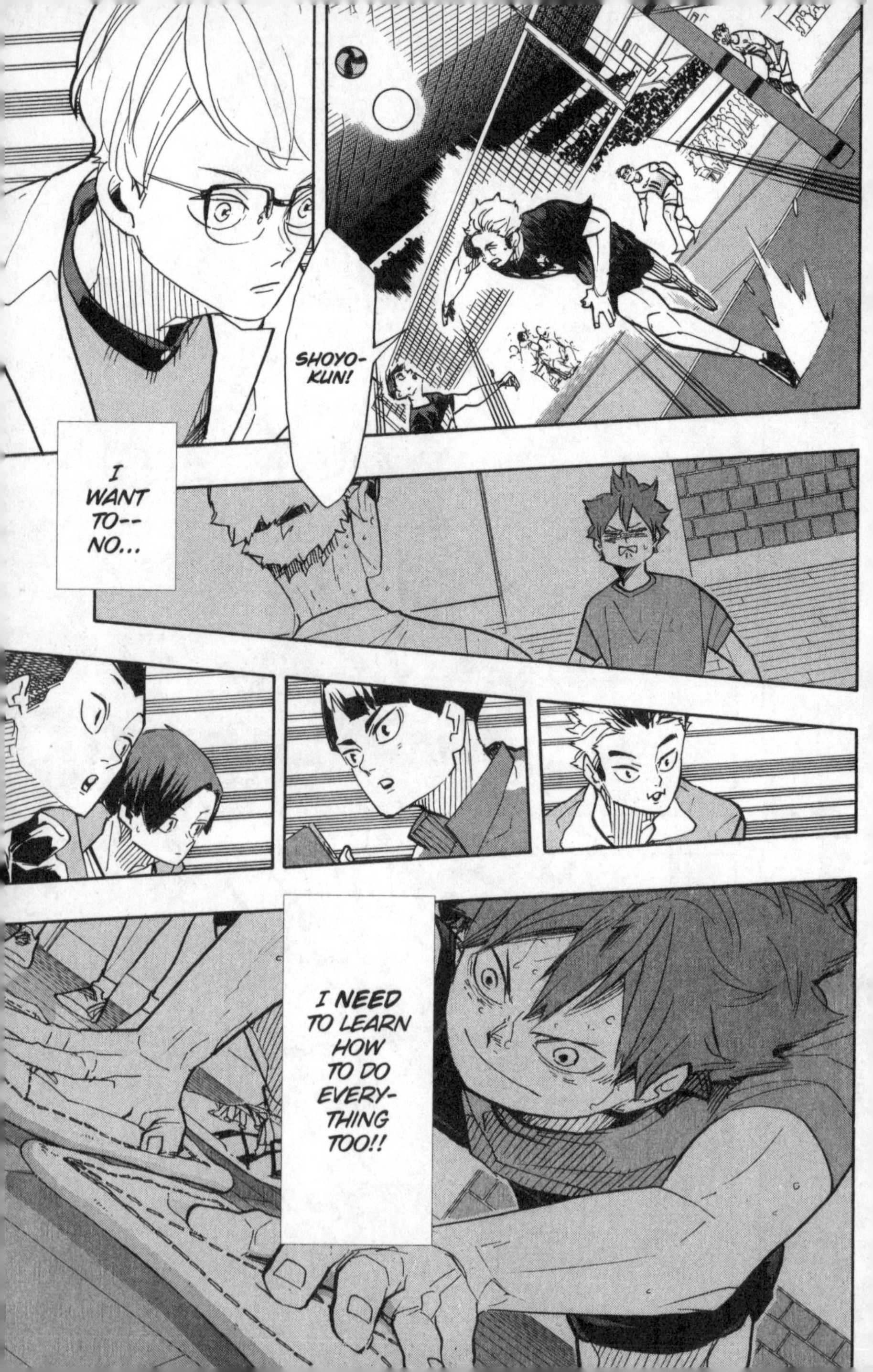
SHOYO-KUN!
I WANT TO-- NO...
I NEED TO LEARN HOW TO DO EVERYTHING TOO!!

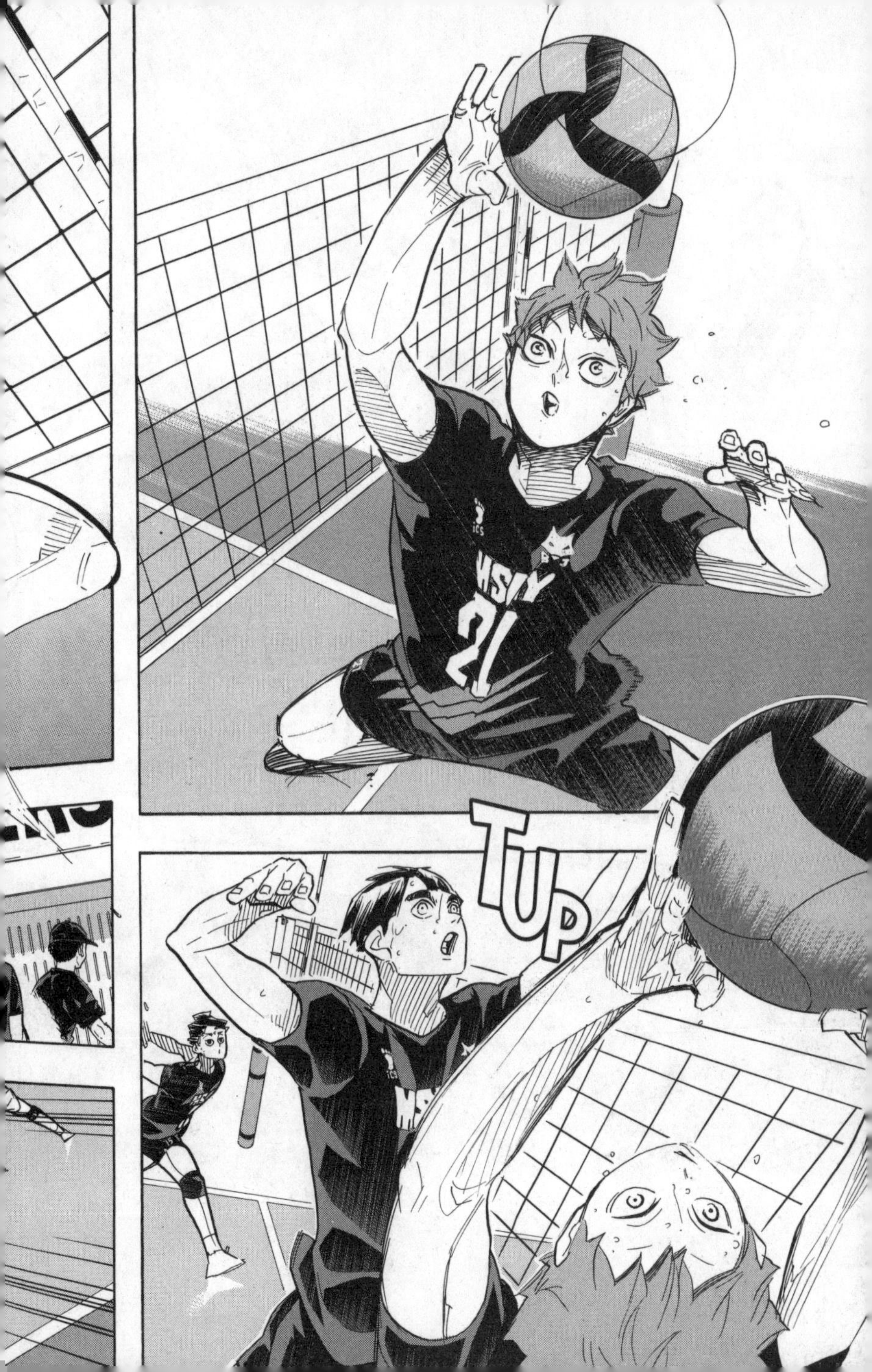
TUP

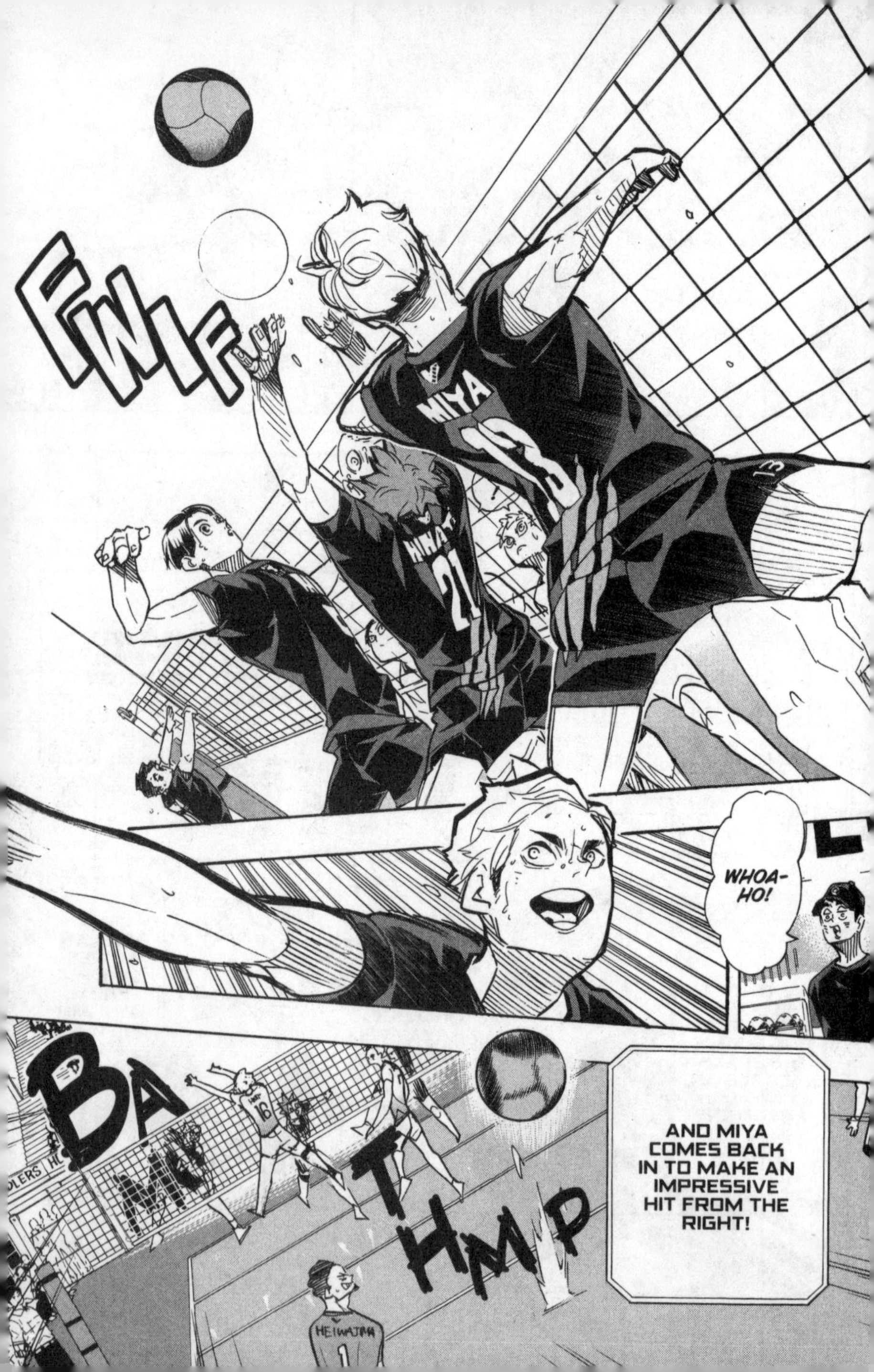
FWIP
WHOA-HO!
AND MIYA COMES BACK IN TO MAKE AN IMPRESSIVE HIT FROM THE RIGHT!
BAM
THMP

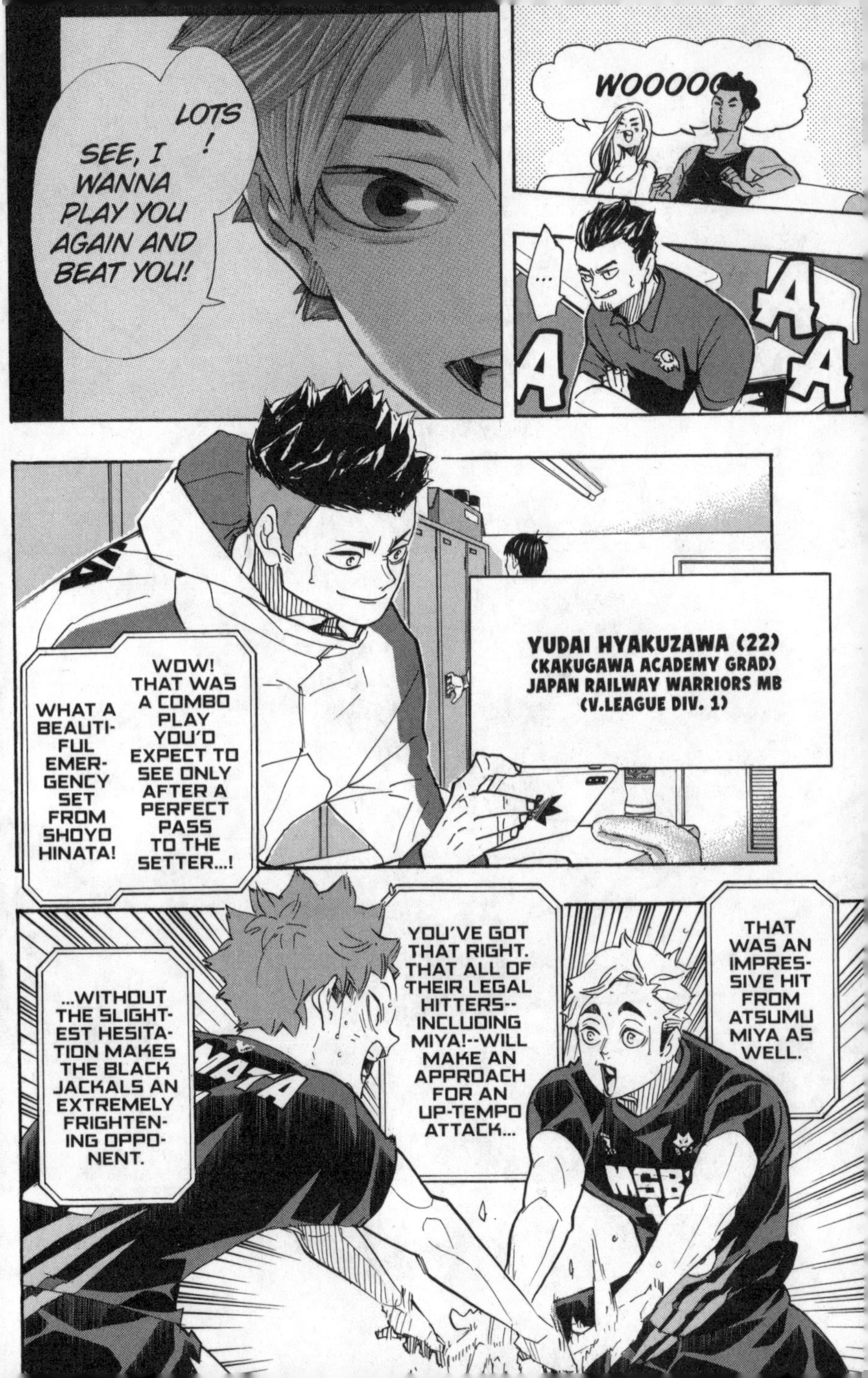
WOOOOO
...
AAAA
SEE, I WANNA PLAY YOU AGAIN AND BEAT YOU!
LOTS!
YUDAI HYAKUZAWA (22) (KAKUGAWA ACADEMY GRAD) JAPAN RAILWAY WARRIORS MB (V.LEAGUE DIV. 1)
WOW! THAT WAS A COMBO PLAY YOU'D EXPECT TO SEE ONLY AFTER A PERFECT PASS TO THE SETTER...!
WHAT A BEAUTIFUL EMERGENCY SET FROM SHOYO HINATA!
THAT WAS AN IMPRESSIVE HIT FROM ATSUMU MIYA AS WELL.
YOU'VE GOT THAT RIGHT. THAT ALL OF THEIR LEGAL HITTERS--INCLUDING MIYA!--WILL MAKE AN APPROACH FOR AN UP-TEMPO ATTACK...
...WITHOUT THE SLIGHTEST HESITATION MAKES THE BLACK JACKALS AN EXTREMELY FRIGHTENING OPPONENT.

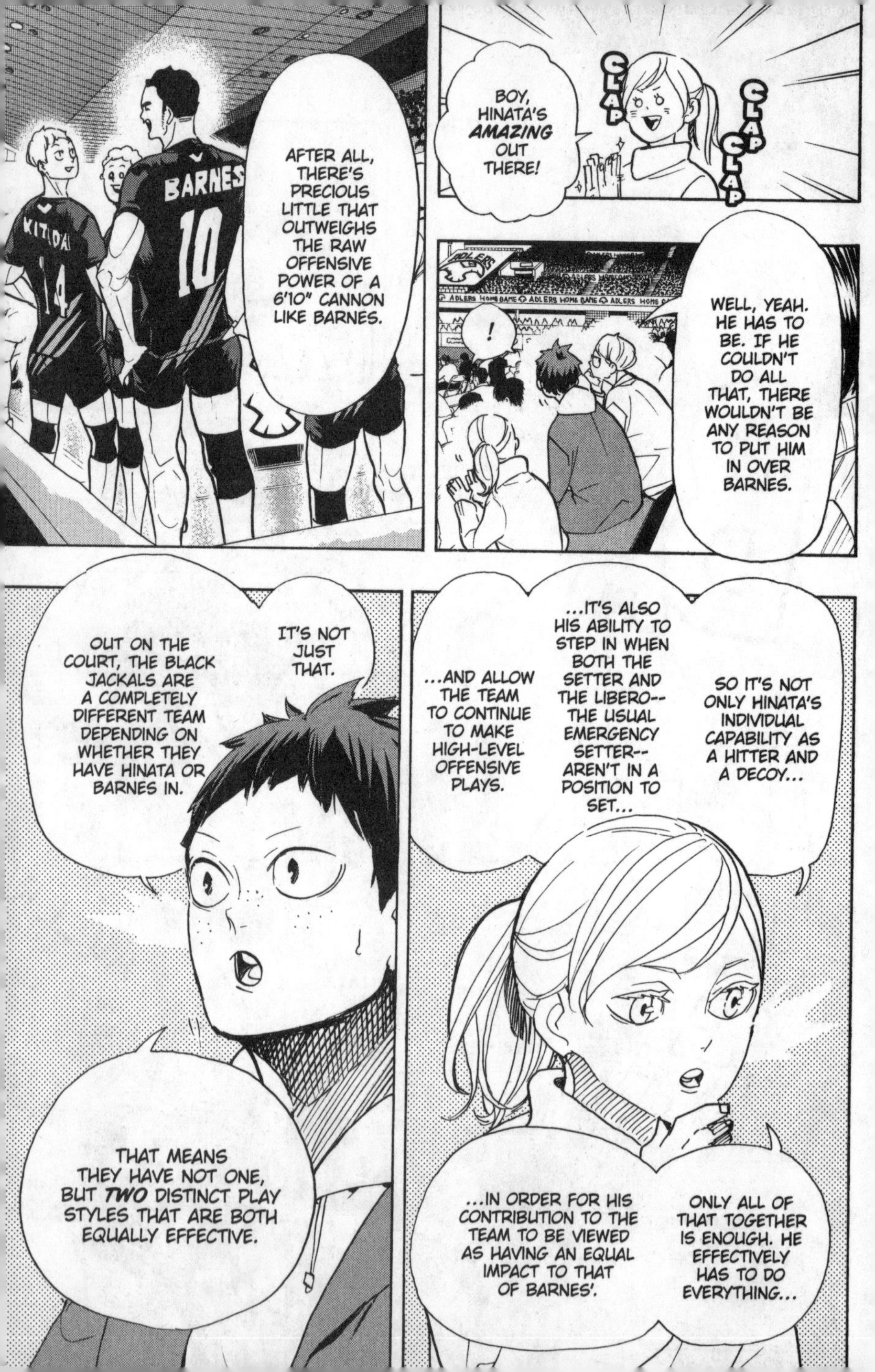
CLAP
CLAP
CLAP
CLAP
BOY, HINATA'S *AMAZING* OUT THERE!
ADLERS
ADLERS HOME GAME ADLERS HOME GAME ADLERS HOME GA
!
WELL, YEAH. HE HAS TO BE. IF HE COULDN'T DO ALL THAT, THERE WOULDN'T BE ANY REASON TO PUT HIM IN OVER BARNES.
BARNES
10
14
AFTER ALL, THERE'S PRECIOUS LITTLE THAT OUTWEIGHS THE RAW OFFENSIVE POWER OF A 6'10" CANNON LIKE BARNES.
SO IT'S NOT ONLY HINATA'S INDIVIDUAL CAPABILITY AS A HITTER AND A DECOY...
...IT'S ALSO HIS ABILITY TO STEP IN WHEN BOTH THE SETTER AND THE LIBERO--THE USUAL EMERGENCY SETTER--AREN'T IN A POSITION TO SET...
...AND ALLOW THE TEAM TO CONTINUE TO MAKE HIGH-LEVEL OFFENSIVE PLAYS.
ONLY ALL OF THAT TOGETHER IS ENOUGH. HE EFFECTIVELY HAS TO DO EVERYTHING...
...IN ORDER FOR HIS CONTRIBUTION TO THE TEAM TO BE VIEWED AS HAVING AN EQUAL IMPACT TO THAT OF BARNES'.
IT'S NOT JUST THAT.
OUT ON THE COURT, THE BLACK JACKALS ARE A COMPLETELY DIFFERENT TEAM DEPENDING ON WHETHER THEY HAVE HINATA OR BARNES IN.
THAT MEANS THEY HAVE NOT ONE, BUT *TWO* DISTINCT PLAY STYLES THAT ARE BOTH EQUALLY EFFECTIVE.

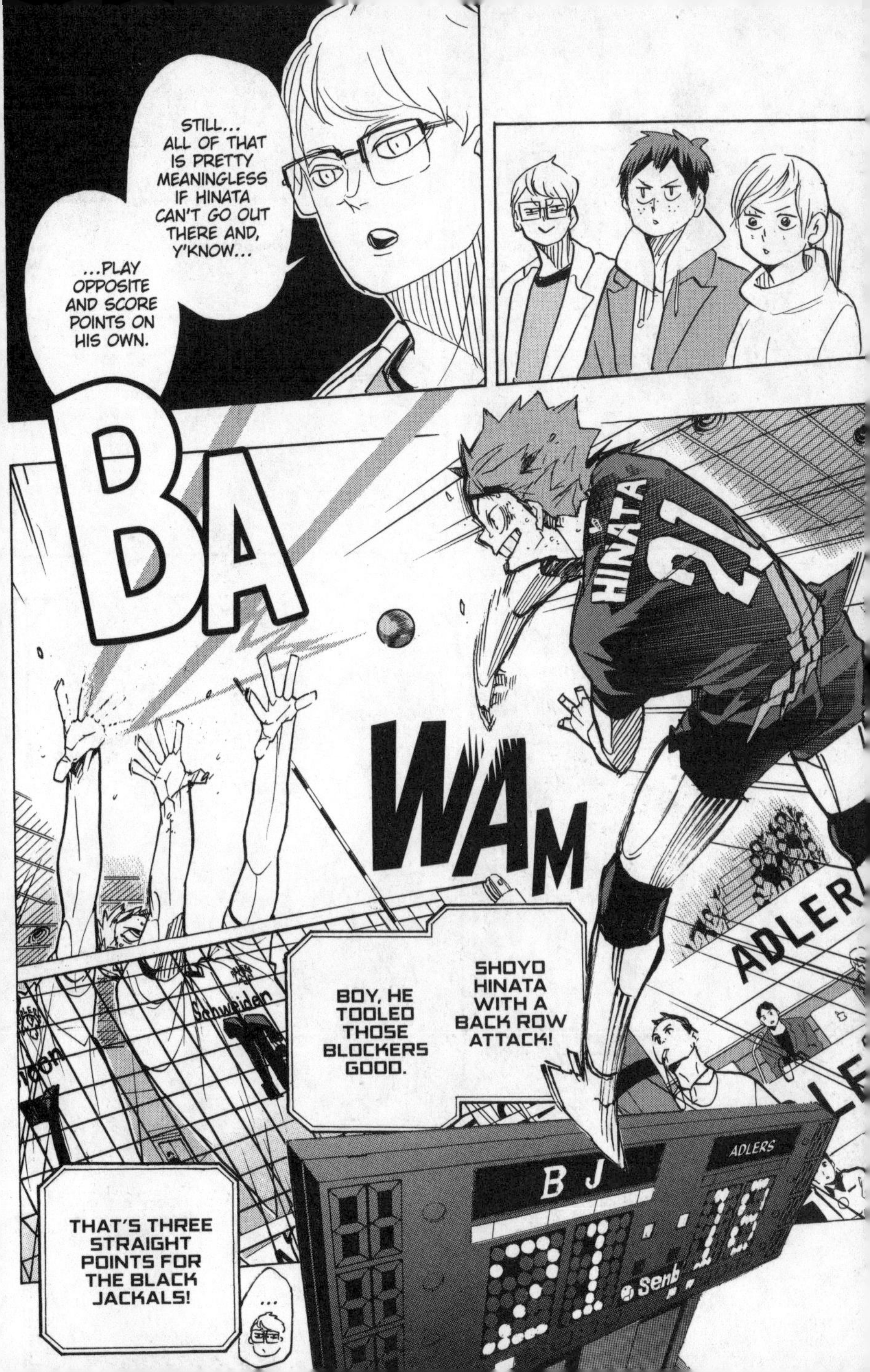
STILL... ALL OF THAT IS PRETTY MEANINGLESS IF HINATA CAN'T GO OUT THERE AND, Y'KNOW...
...PLAY OPPOSITE AND SCORE POINTS ON HIS OWN.
BA
WAM
HINATA 21
ADLER
SHOYO HINATA WITH A BACK ROW ATTACK!
BOY, HE TOOLED THOSE BLOCKERS GOOD.
Schweiden
ADLERS
B J
THAT'S THREE STRAIGHT POINTS FOR THE BLACK JACKALS!
...

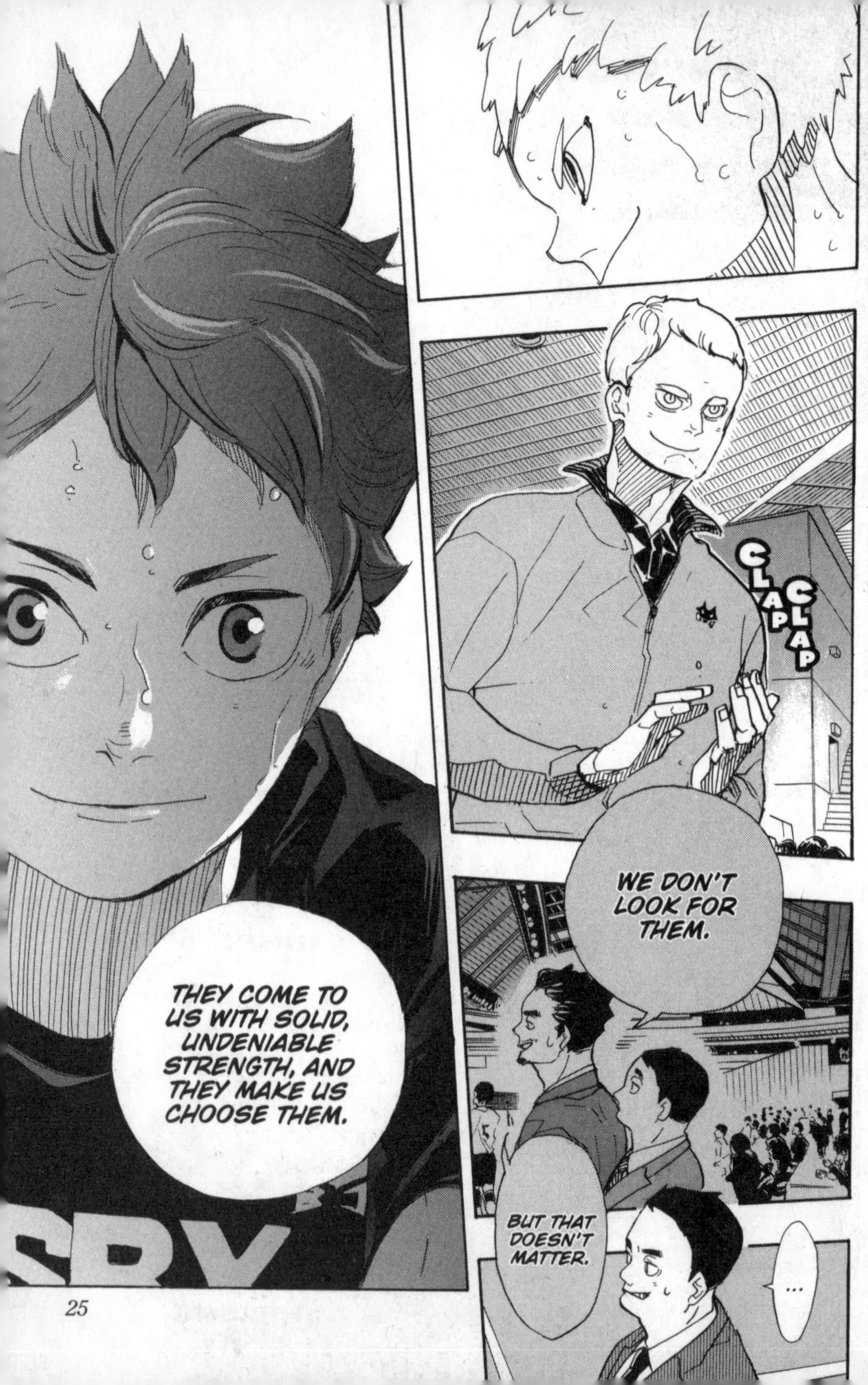
CLAP CLAP
WE DON'T LOOK FOR THEM.
BUT THAT DOESN'T MATTER.
...
THEY COME TO US WITH SOLID, UNDENIABLE STRENGTH, AND THEY MAKE US CHOOSE THEM.

SHUGO MEIAN (29)

MSBY BLACK JACKALS

POSITION: MIDDLE BLOCKER
HEIGHT: 6'5"
WEIGHT: 190 LBS.

ABILITY PARAMETERS
(5-POINT SCALE)

POWER (5)

SPEED (4)

JUMPING (3)

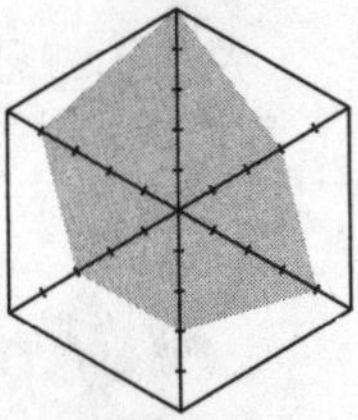

TECHNIQUE (3)

STAMINA (4)

INTELLIGENCE (3)

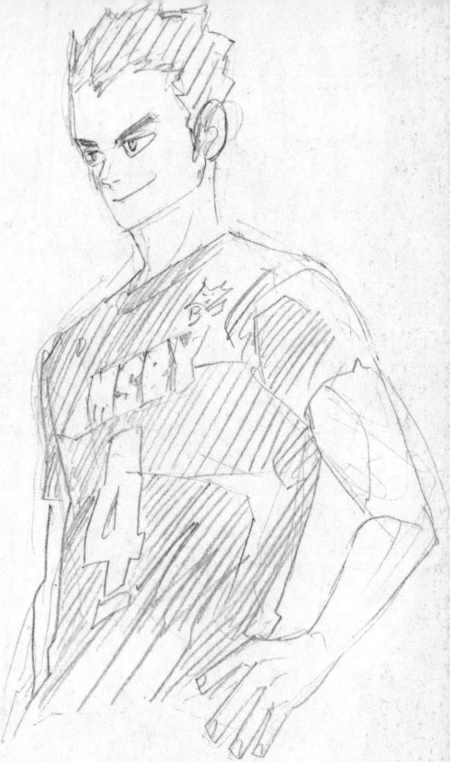

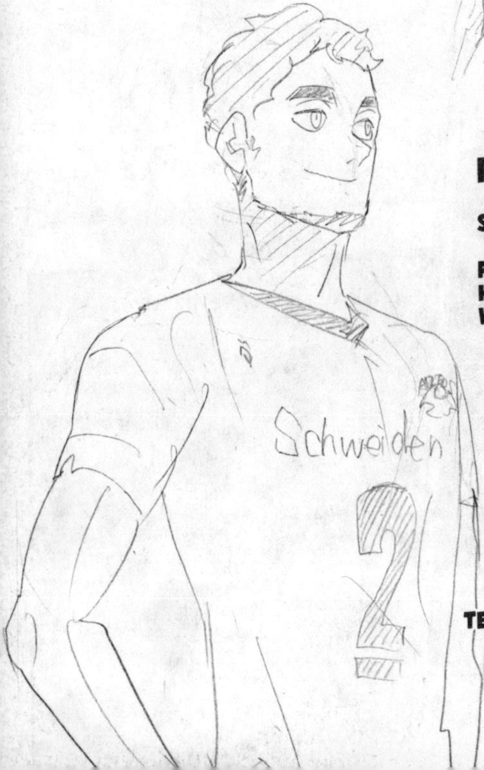
Schweiden

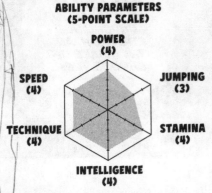

FUKURO HIRUGAMI (29)

SCHWEIDEN ADLERS

POSITION: MIDDLE BLOCKER
HEIGHT: 6'6"
WEIGHT: 186 LBS.

ABILITY PARAMETERS
(5-POINT SCALE)

POWER (4)

SPEED (4)

JUMPING (3)

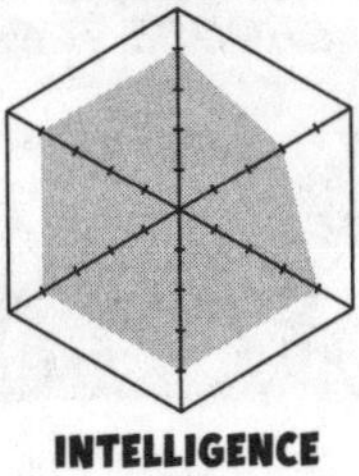

TECHNIQUE (4)

STAMINA (4)

INTELLIGENCE (4)

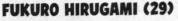

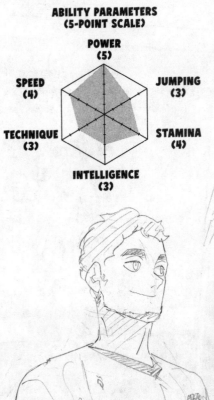

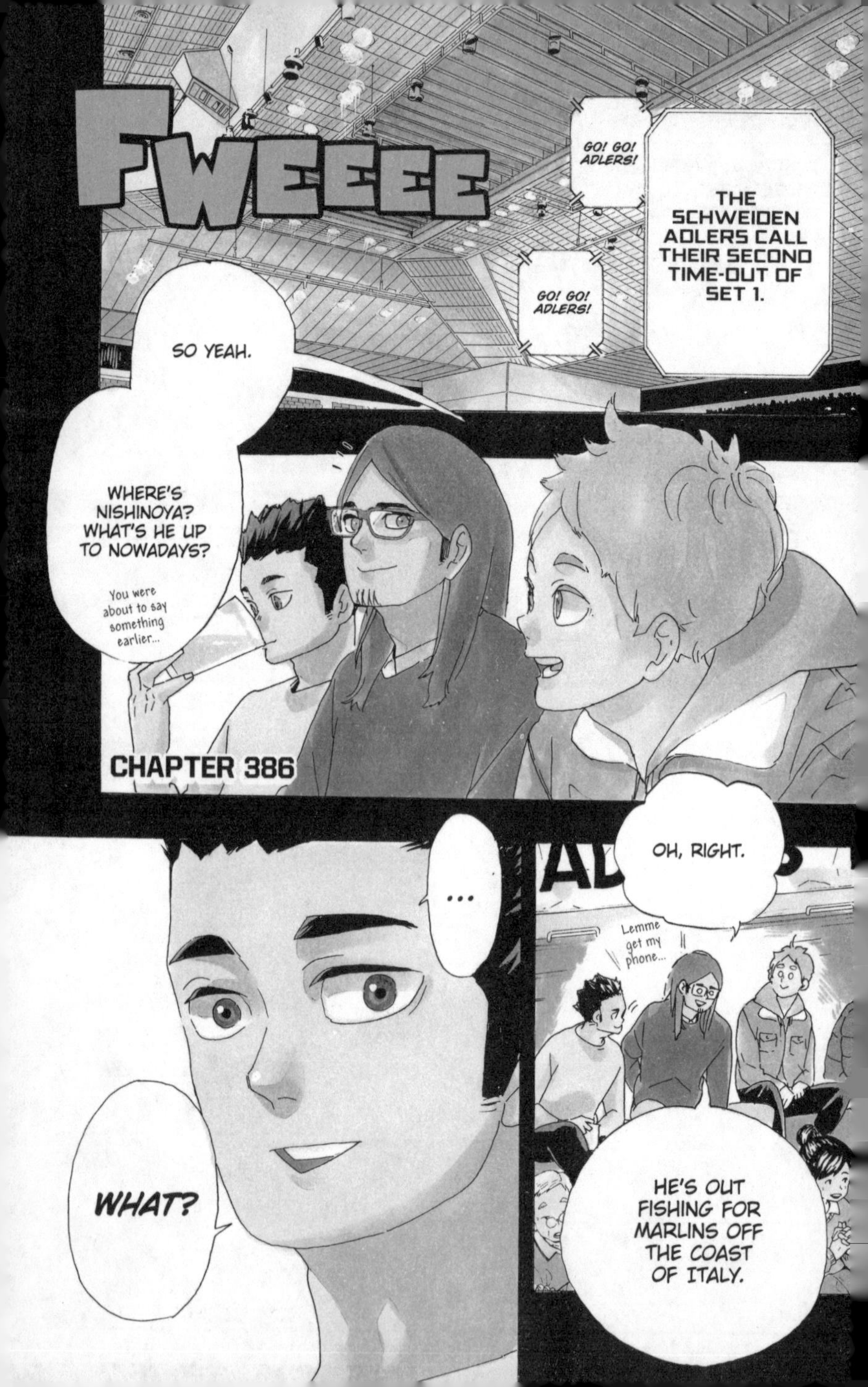
GO! GO! ADLERS!
THE SCHWEIDEN ADLERS CALL THEIR SECOND TIME-OUT OF SET 1.
GO! GO! ADLERS!
FWEEEE
SO YEAH.
WHERE'S NISHINOYA? WHAT'S HE UP TO NOWADAYS?
You were about to say something earlier...
CHAPTER 386
OH, RIGHT.
Lemme get my phone...
HE'S OUT FISHING FOR MARLINS OFF THE COAST OF ITALY.
...
WHAT?

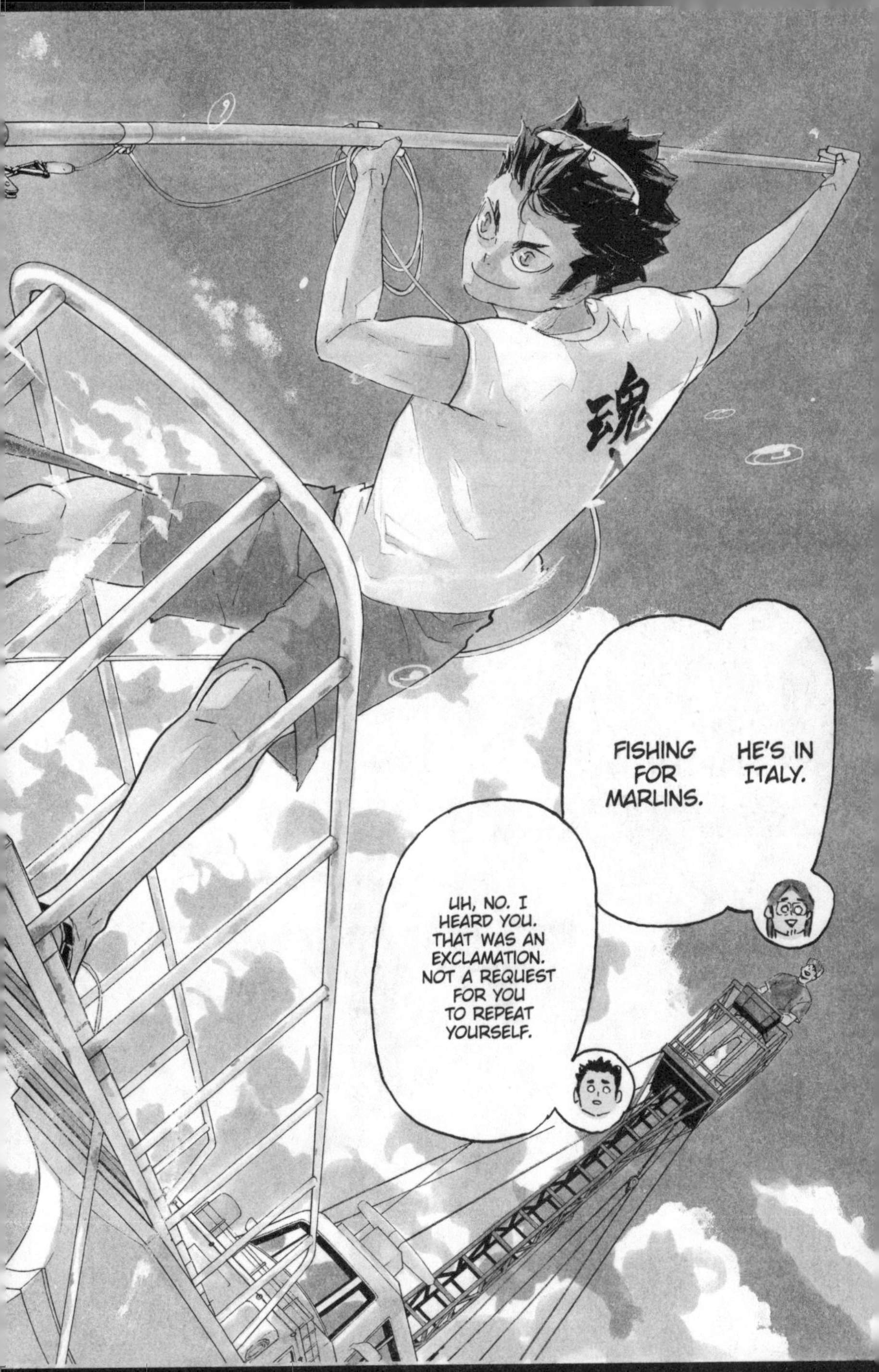
HE'S IN ITALY.
FISHING FOR MARLINS.
UH, NO. I HEARD YOU. THAT WAS AN EXCLAMATION. NOT A REQUEST FOR YOU TO REPEAT YOURSELF.

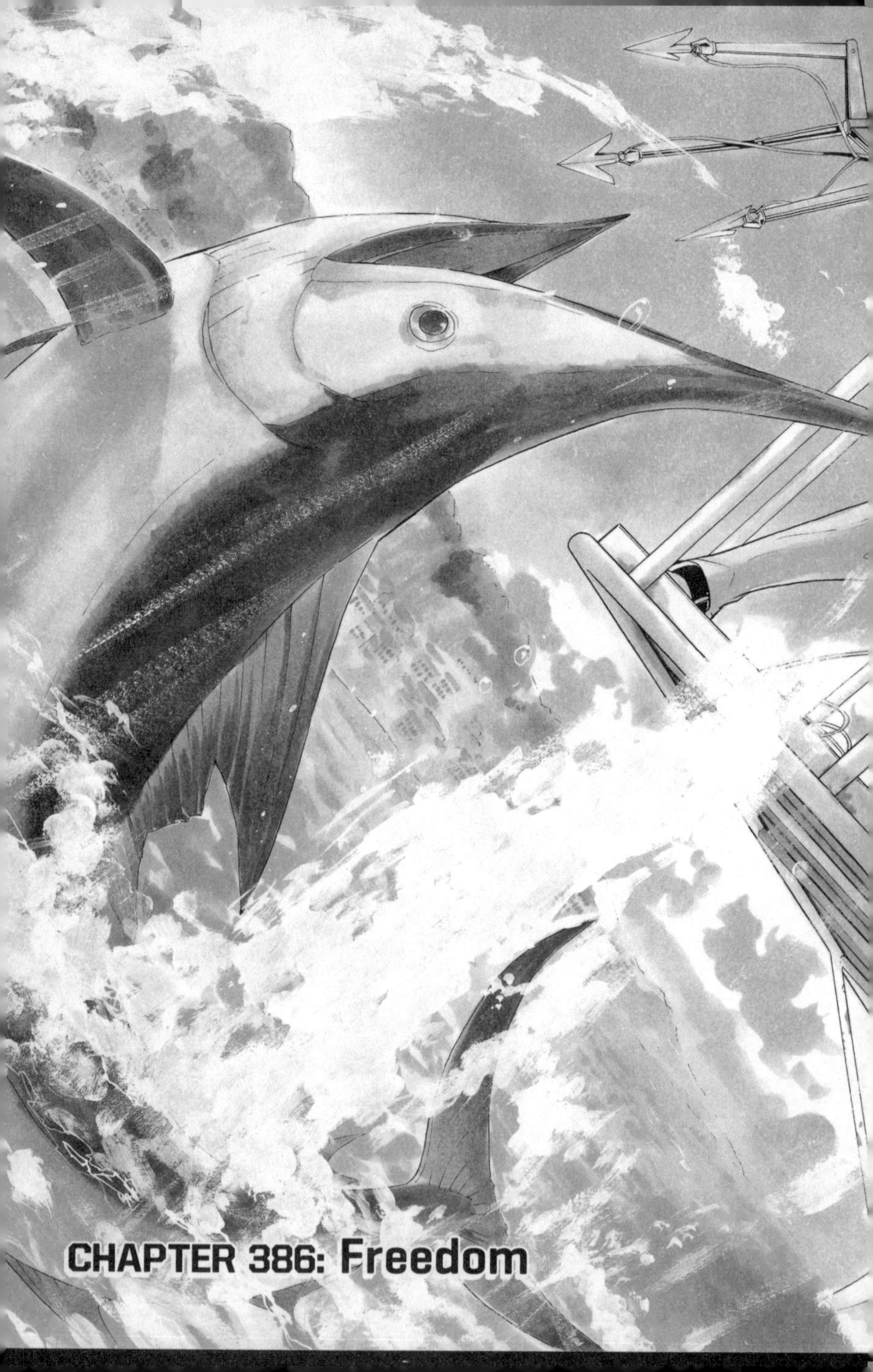
CHAPTER 386: Freedom

HAIKYU!!

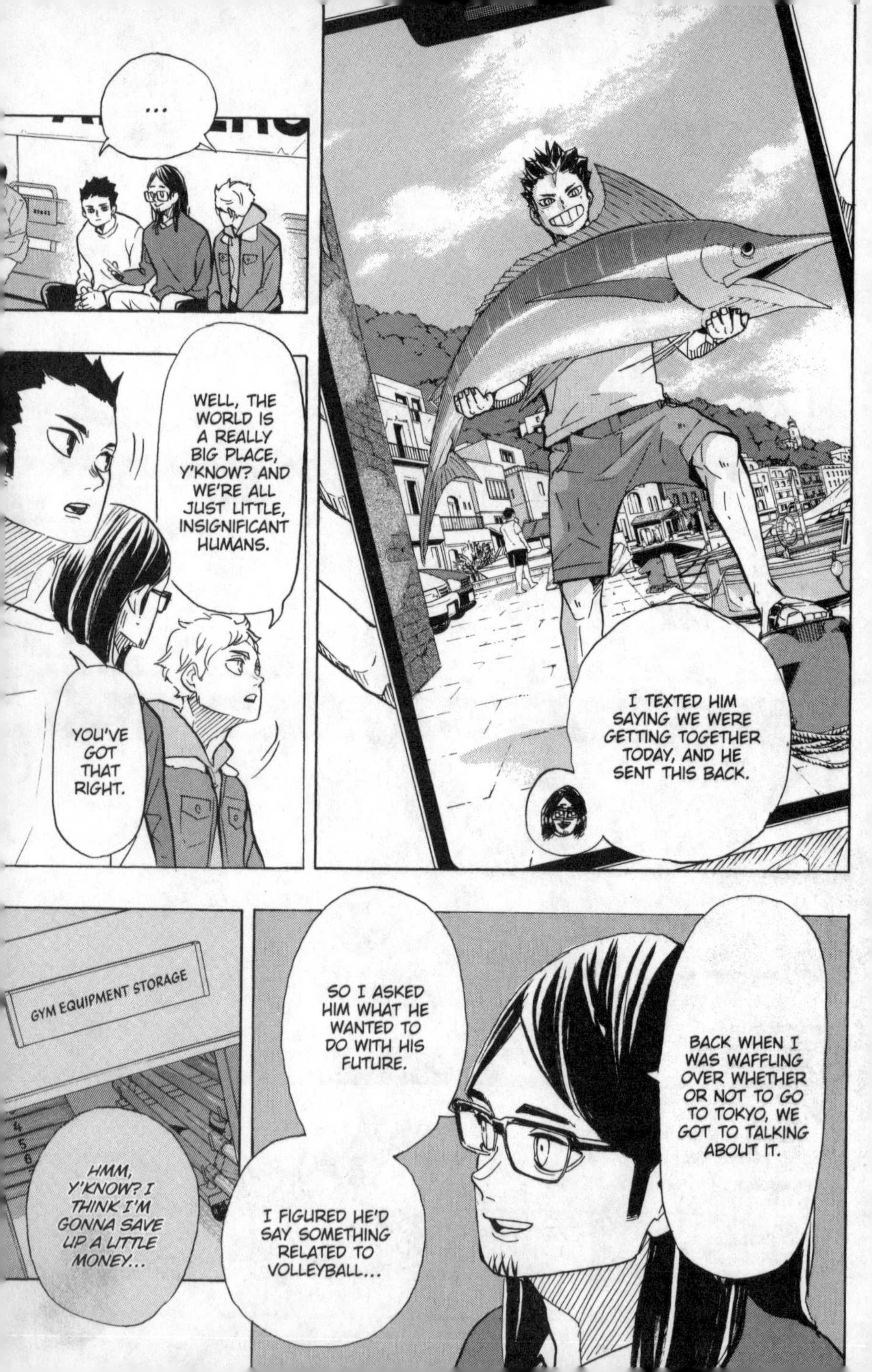
I TEXTED HIM SAYING WE WERE GETTING TOGETHER TODAY, AND HE SENT THIS BACK.
...
WELL, THE WORLD IS A REALLY BIG PLACE, Y'KNOW? AND WE'RE ALL JUST LITTLE, INSIGNIFICANT HUMANS.
YOU'VE GOT THAT RIGHT.
BACK WHEN I WAS WAFFLING OVER WHETHER OR NOT TO GO TO TOKYO, WE GOT TO TALKING ABOUT IT.
SO I ASKED HIM WHAT HE WANTED TO DO WITH HIS FUTURE.
I FIGURED HE'D SAY SOMETHING RELATED TO VOLLEYBALL...
GYM EQUIPMENT STORAGE
HMM, Y'KNOW? I THINK I'M GONNA SAVE UP A LITTLE MONEY...

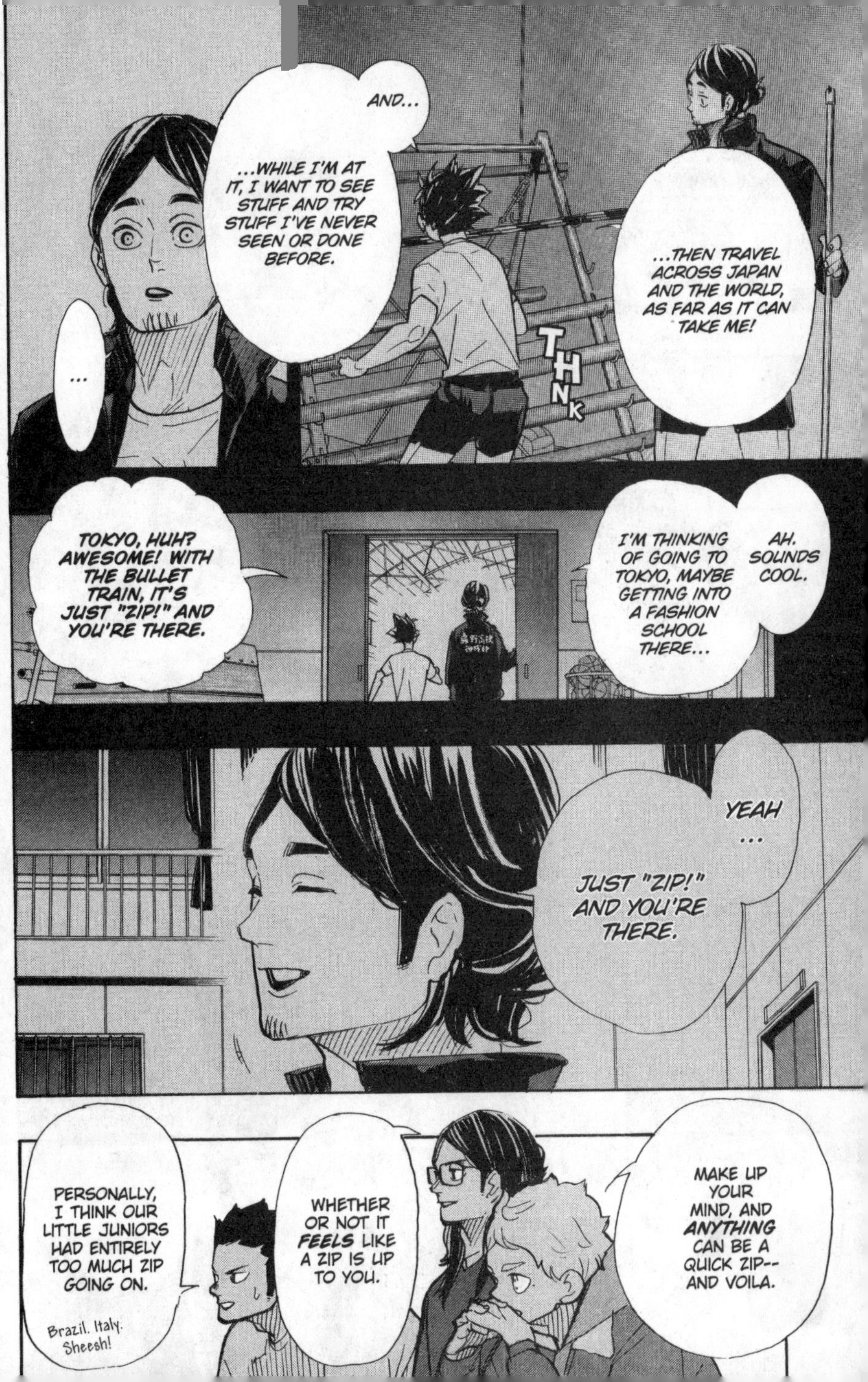
...THEN TRAVEL ACROSS JAPAN AND THE WORLD, AS FAR AS IT CAN TAKE ME!
THNK
AND...
...WHILE I'M AT IT, I WANT TO SEE STUFF AND TRY STUFF I'VE NEVER SEEN OR DONE BEFORE.
...
I'M THINKING OF GOING TO TOKYO, MAYBE GETTING INTO A FASHION SCHOOL THERE...
AH. SOUNDS COOL.
TOKYO, HUH? AWESOME! WITH THE BULLET TRAIN, IT'S JUST "ZIP!" AND YOU'RE THERE.
YEAH...
JUST "ZIP!" AND YOU'RE THERE.
MAKE UP YOUR MIND, AND **ANYTHING** CAN BE A QUICK ZIP-- AND VOILA.
WHETHER OR NOT IT **FEELS** LIKE A ZIP IS UP TO YOU.
PERSONALLY, I THINK OUR LITTLE JUNIORS HAD ENTIRELY TOO MUCH ZIP GOING ON.
Brazil. Italy. Sheesh!

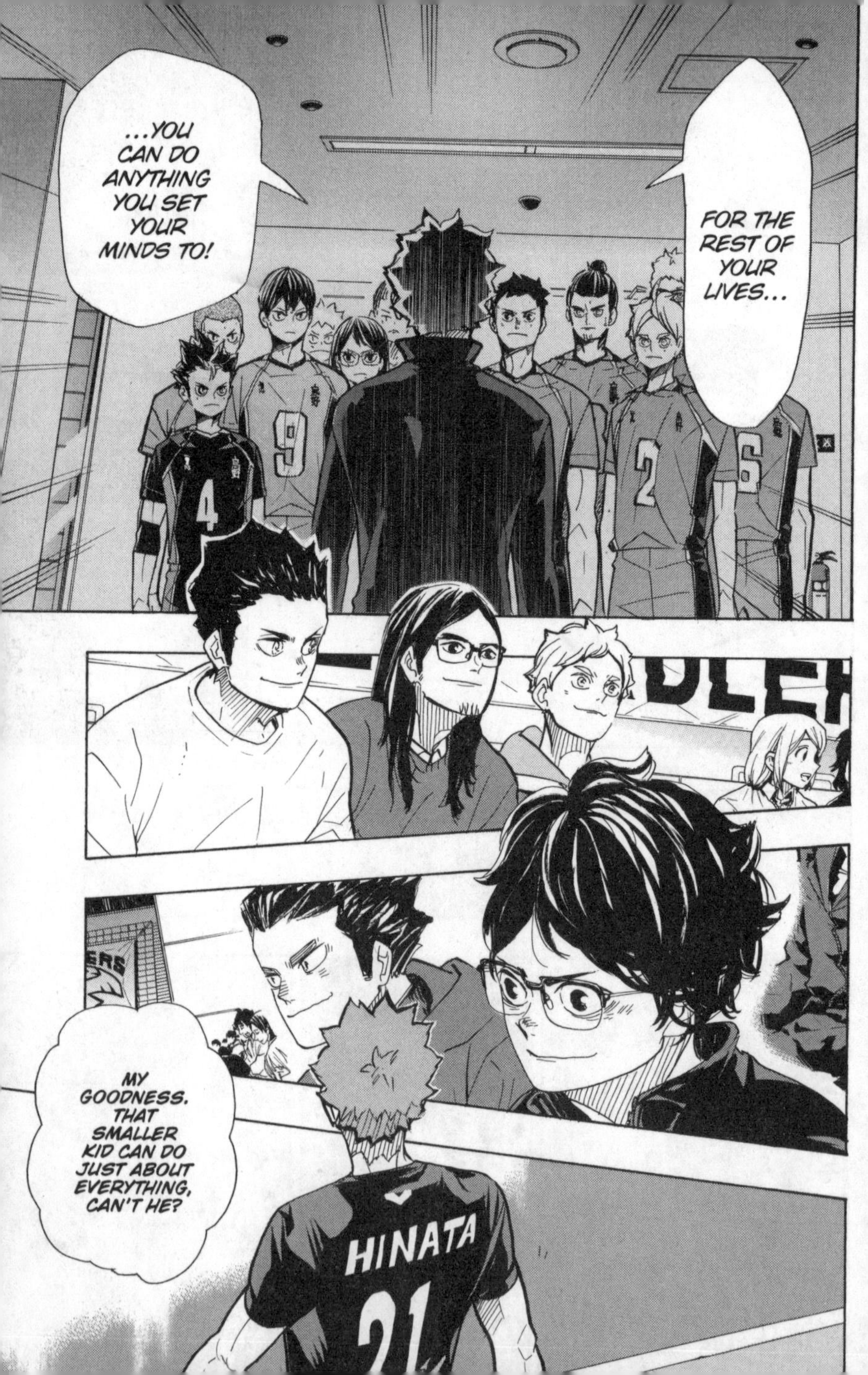
FOR THE REST OF YOUR LIVES...
...YOU CAN DO ANYTHING YOU SET YOUR MINDS TO!
MY GOODNESS. THAT SMALLER KID CAN DO JUST ABOUT EVERYTHING, CAN'T HE?
HINATA
21

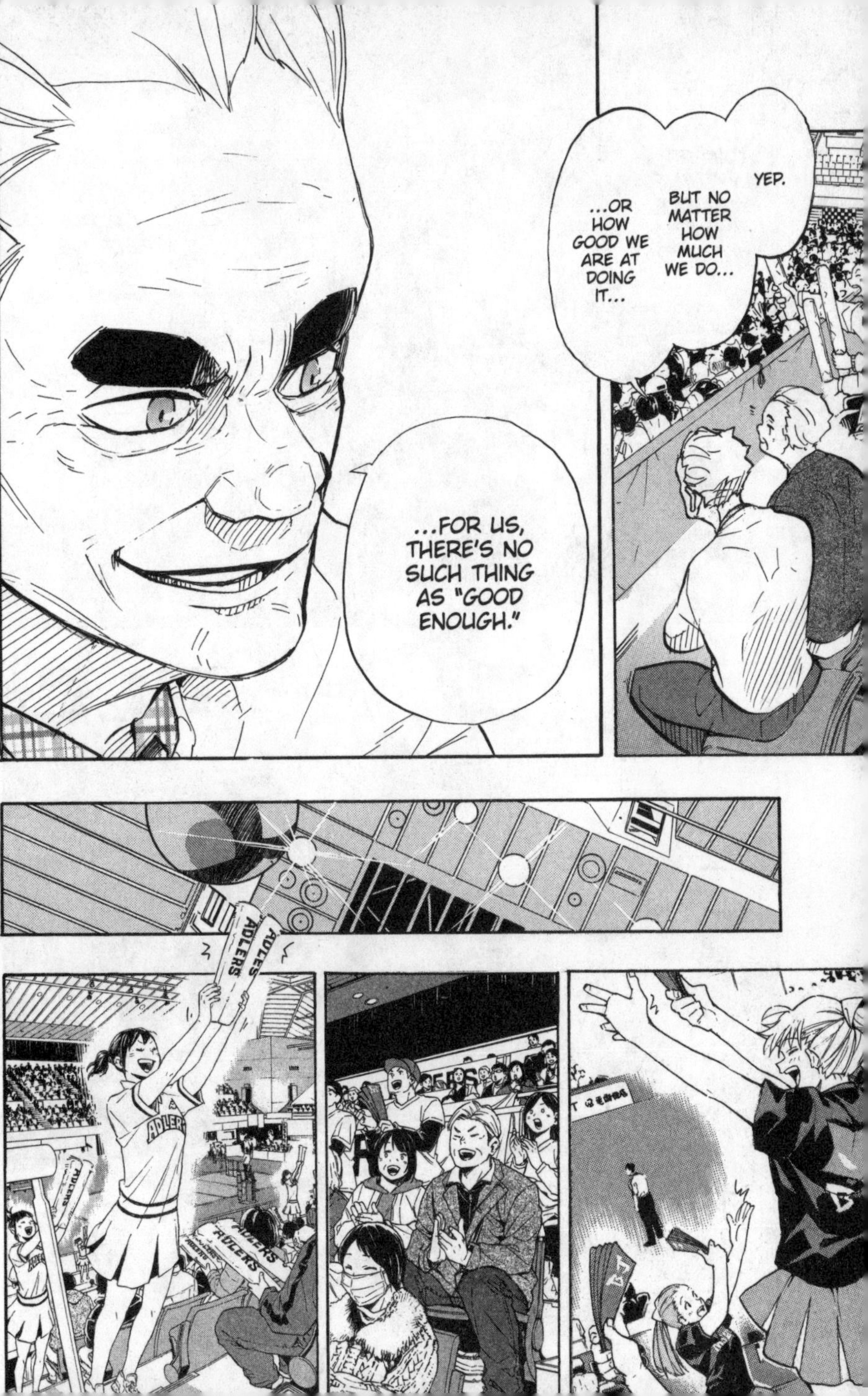
YEP.
BUT NO MATTER HOW MUCH WE DO...
...OR HOW GOOD WE ARE AT DOING IT...
...FOR US, THERE'S NO SUCH THING AS "GOOD ENOUGH."
ADLERS
ADLERS

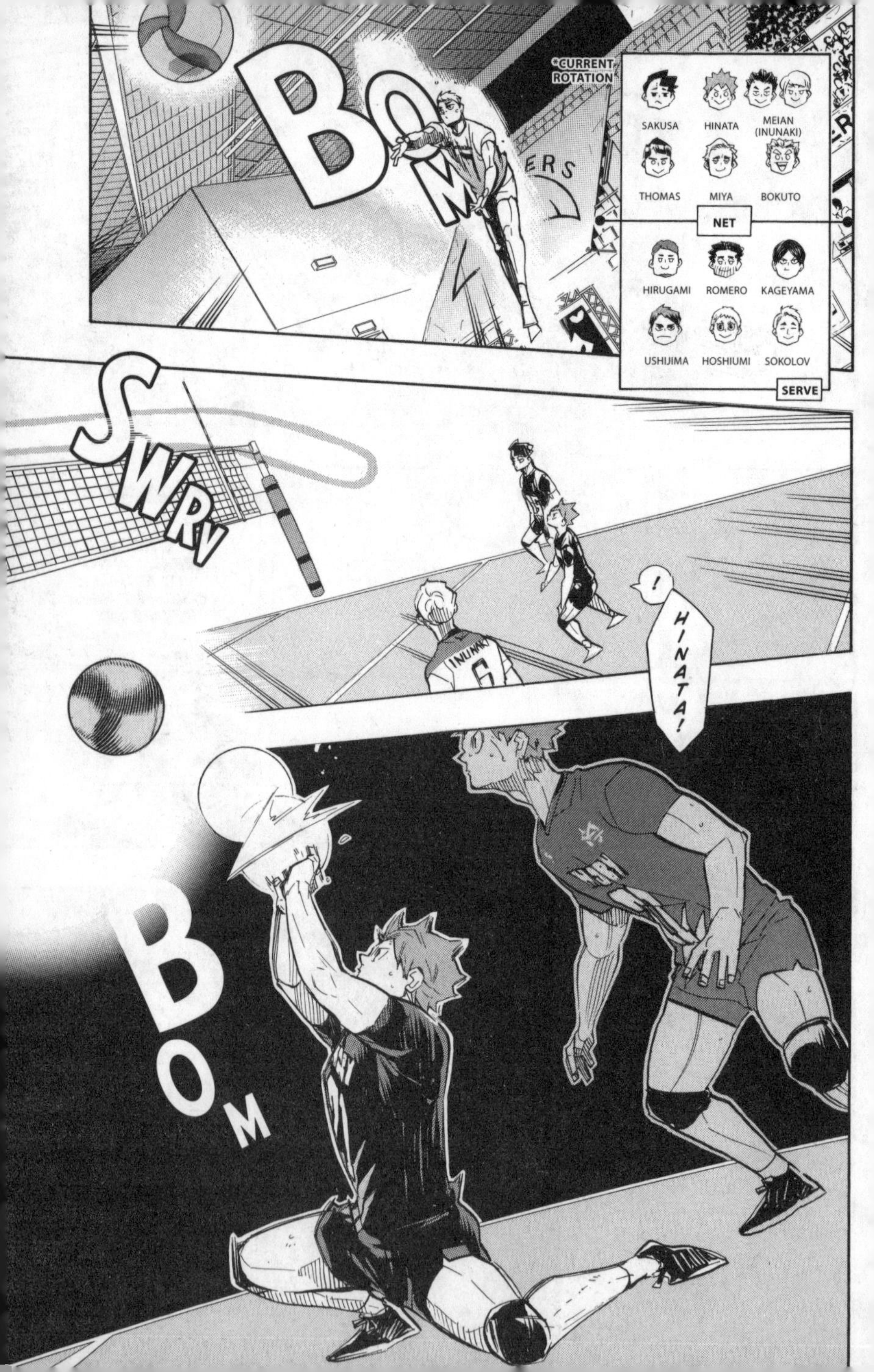
BOOM
*CURRENT ROTATION
SAKUSA
HINATA
MEIAN (INUNAKI)
THOMAS
MIYA
BOKUTO
NET
HIRUGAMI
ROMERO
KAGEYAMA
USHIJIMA
HOSHIUMI
SOKOLOV
SERVE
SWRV
!
HINATA!
BOOM

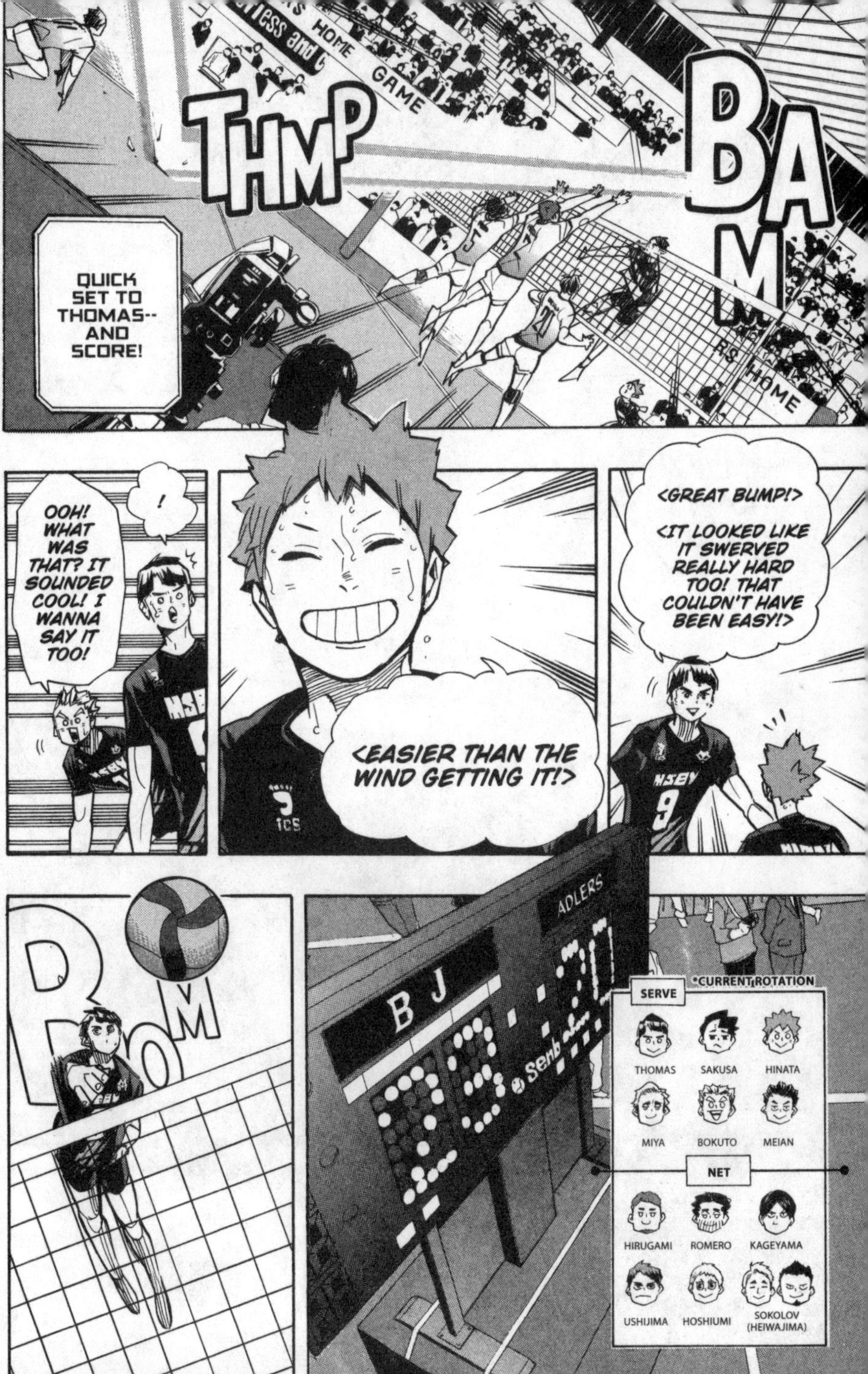
BAM
THMP
QUICK SET TO THOMAS-- AND SCORE!
<GREAT BUMP!>
<IT LOOKED LIKE IT SWERVED REALLY HARD TOO! THAT COULDN'T HAVE BEEN EASY!>
<EASIER THAN THE WIND GETTING IT!>
!
OOH! WHAT WAS THAT? IT SOUNDED COOL! I WANNA SAY IT TOO!
ADLERS
BJ
*CURRENT ROTATION
SERVE
THOMAS
SAKUSA
HINATA
MIYA
BOKUTO
MEIAN
NET
HIRUGAMI
ROMERO
KAGEYAMA
USHIJIMA
HOSHIUMI
SOKOLOV (HEIWAJIMA)
BOOM

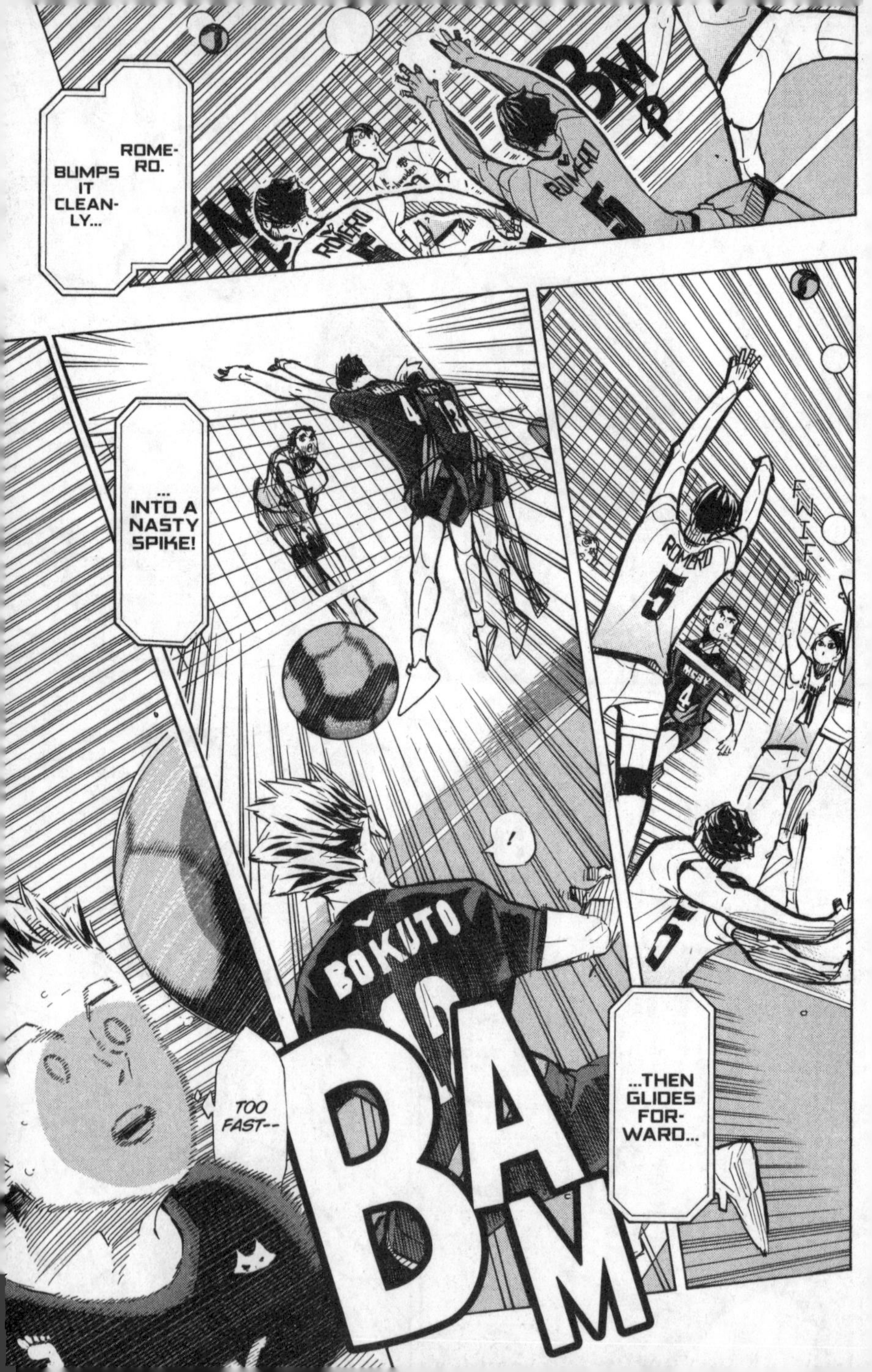

BMP
ROMERO. BUMPS IT CLEANLY...
...THEN GLIDES FORWARD...
...INTO A NASTY SPIKE!
!
TOO FAST--
BAM

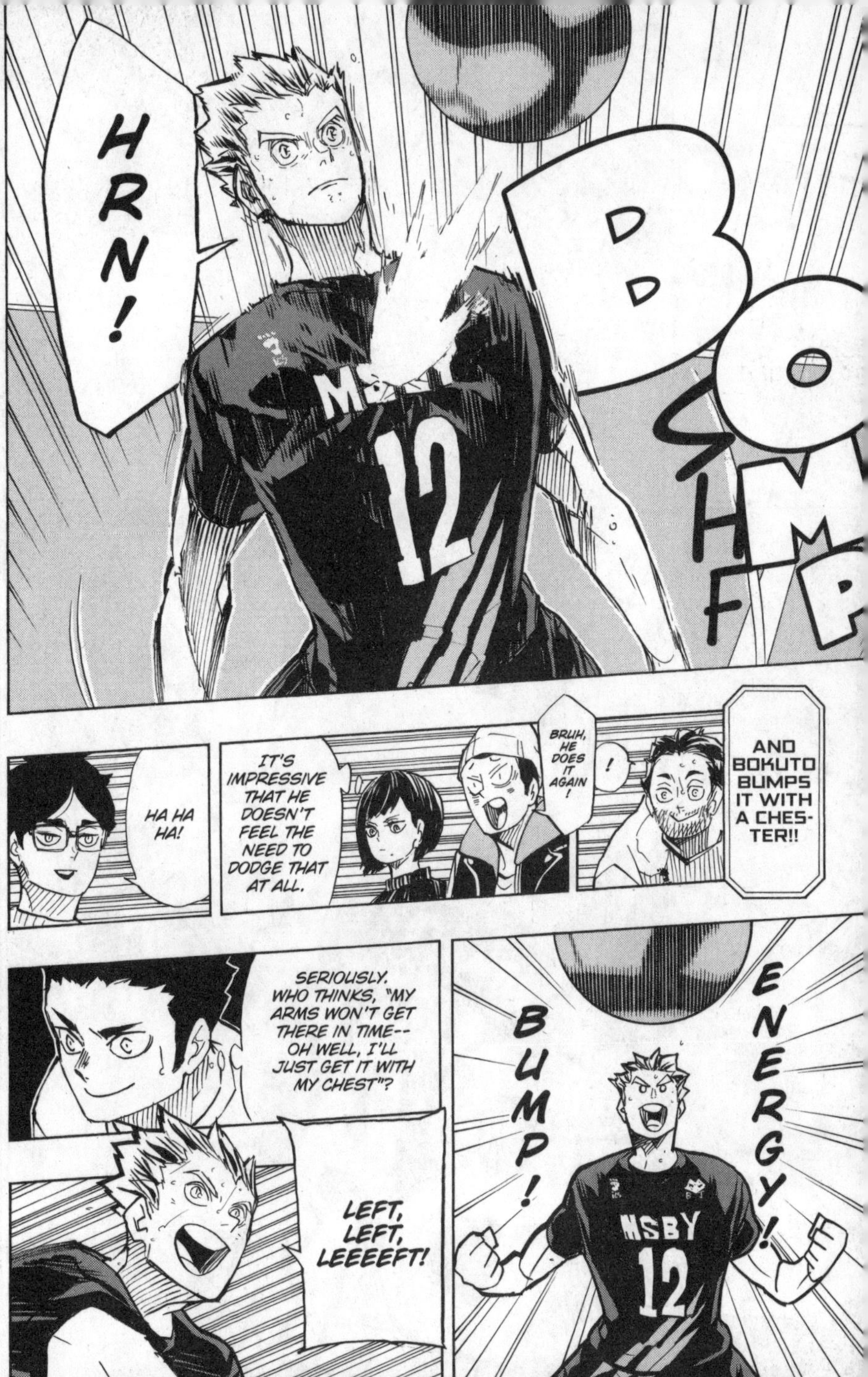
HRN!
AND BOKUTO BUMPS IT WITH A CHESTER!!
BRUH, HE DOES IT AGAIN!
!
IT'S IMPRESSIVE THAT HE DOESN'T FEEL THE NEED TO DODGE THAT AT ALL.
HA HA HA!
ENERGY!
BUMP!
SERIOUSLY. WHO THINKS, "MY ARMS WON'T GET THERE IN TIME-- OH WELL, I'LL JUST GET IT WITH MY CHEST"?
LEFT, LEFT, LEEEEFT!

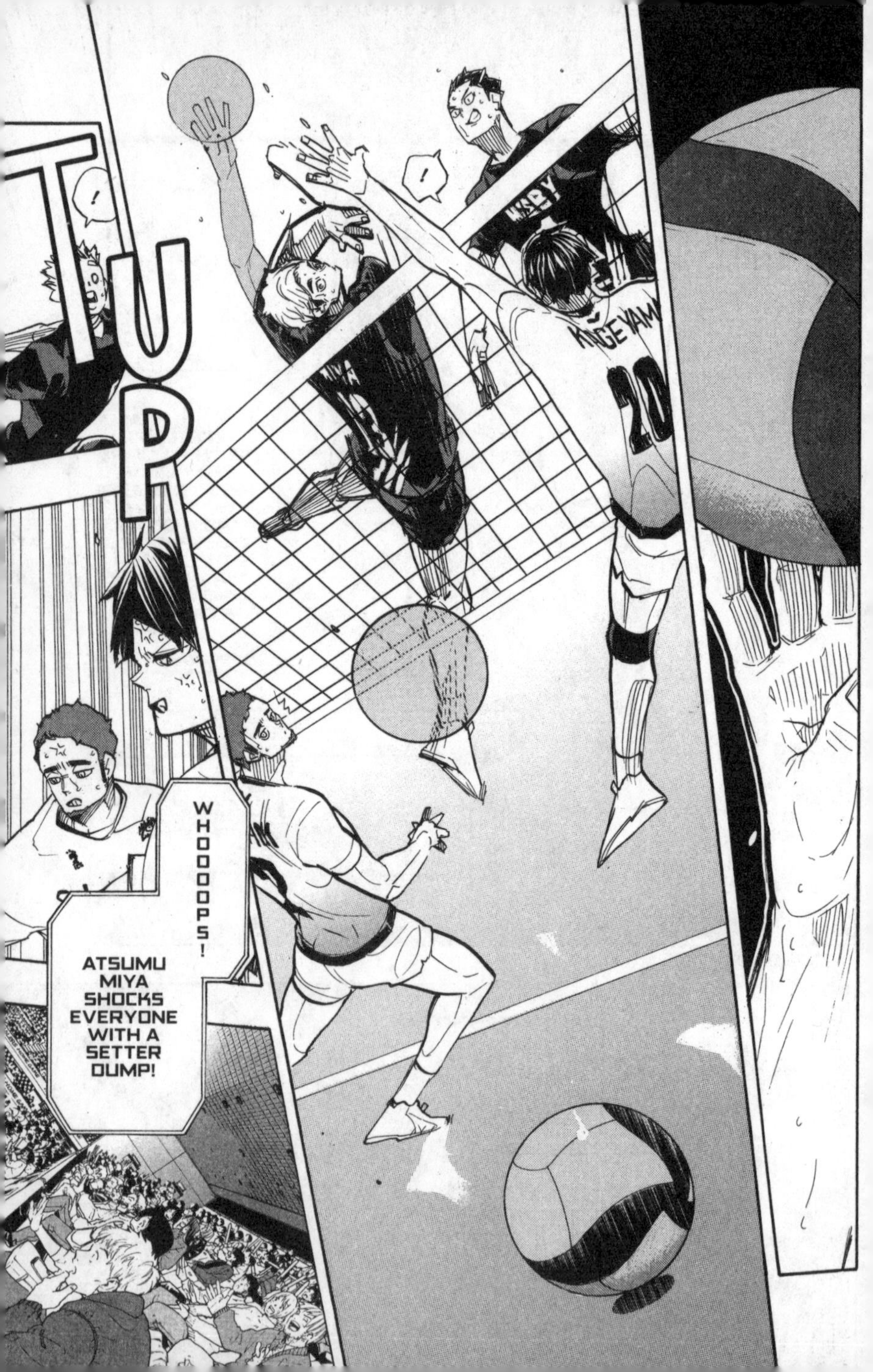
!
!
TUP
WHOOOOOPS!
ATSUMU MIYA SHOCKS EVERYONE WITH A SETTER DUMP!

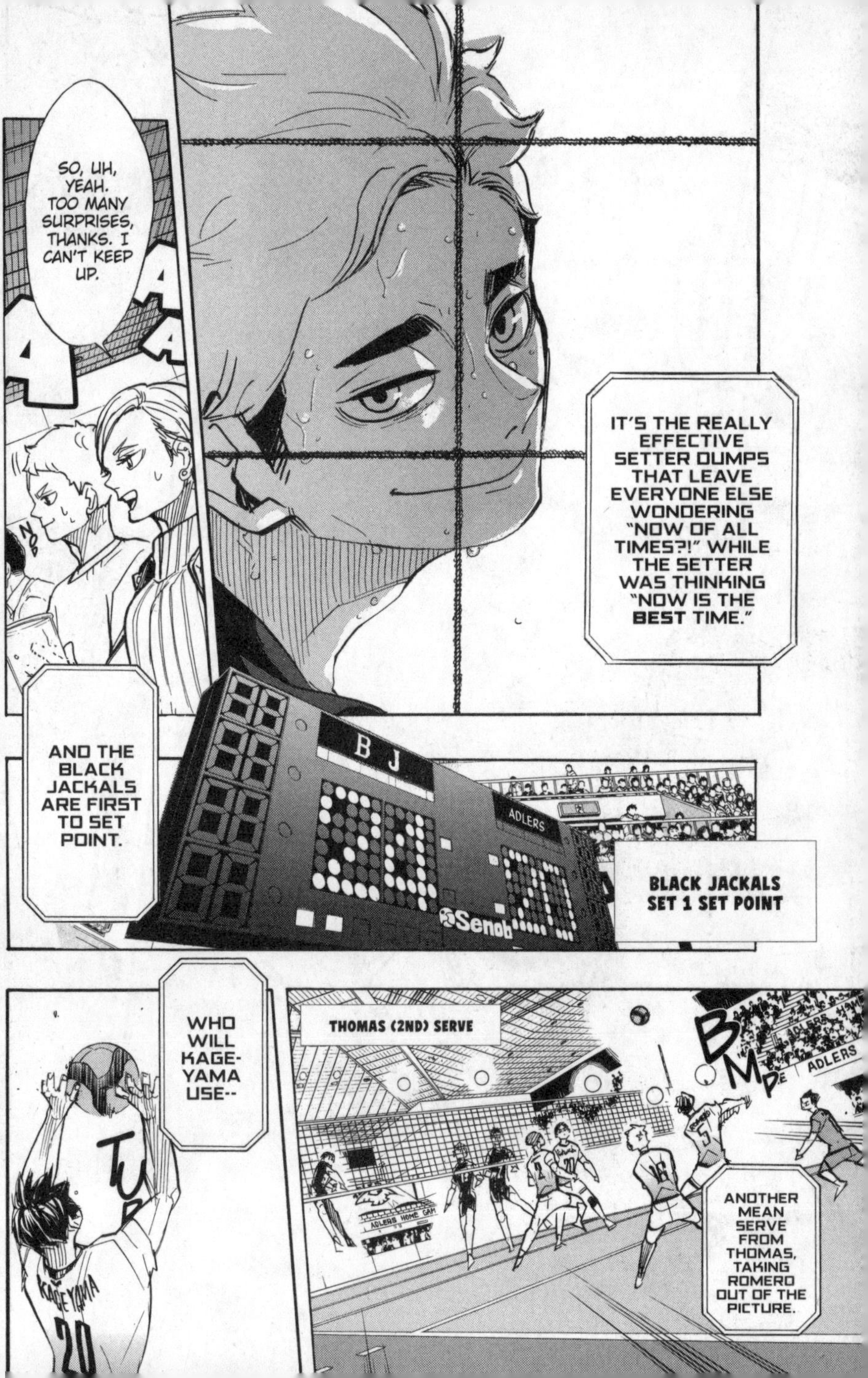
IT'S THE REALLY EFFECTIVE SETTER DUMPS THAT LEAVE EVERYONE ELSE WONDERING "NOW OF ALL TIMES?!" WHILE THE SETTER WAS THINKING "NOW IS THE BEST TIME."
SO, UH, YEAH. TOO MANY SURPRISES, THANKS. I CAN'T KEEP UP.
A A A
NOD
BLACK JACKALS SET 1 SET POINT
AND THE BLACK JACKALS ARE FIRST TO SET POINT.
BJ
ADLERS
Senob
THOMAS (2ND) SERVE
BMP
ADLERS
ANOTHER MEAN SERVE FROM THOMAS, TAKING ROMERO OUT OF THE PICTURE.
WHO WILL KAGE-YAMA USE--
TUP
KAGEYAMA
20

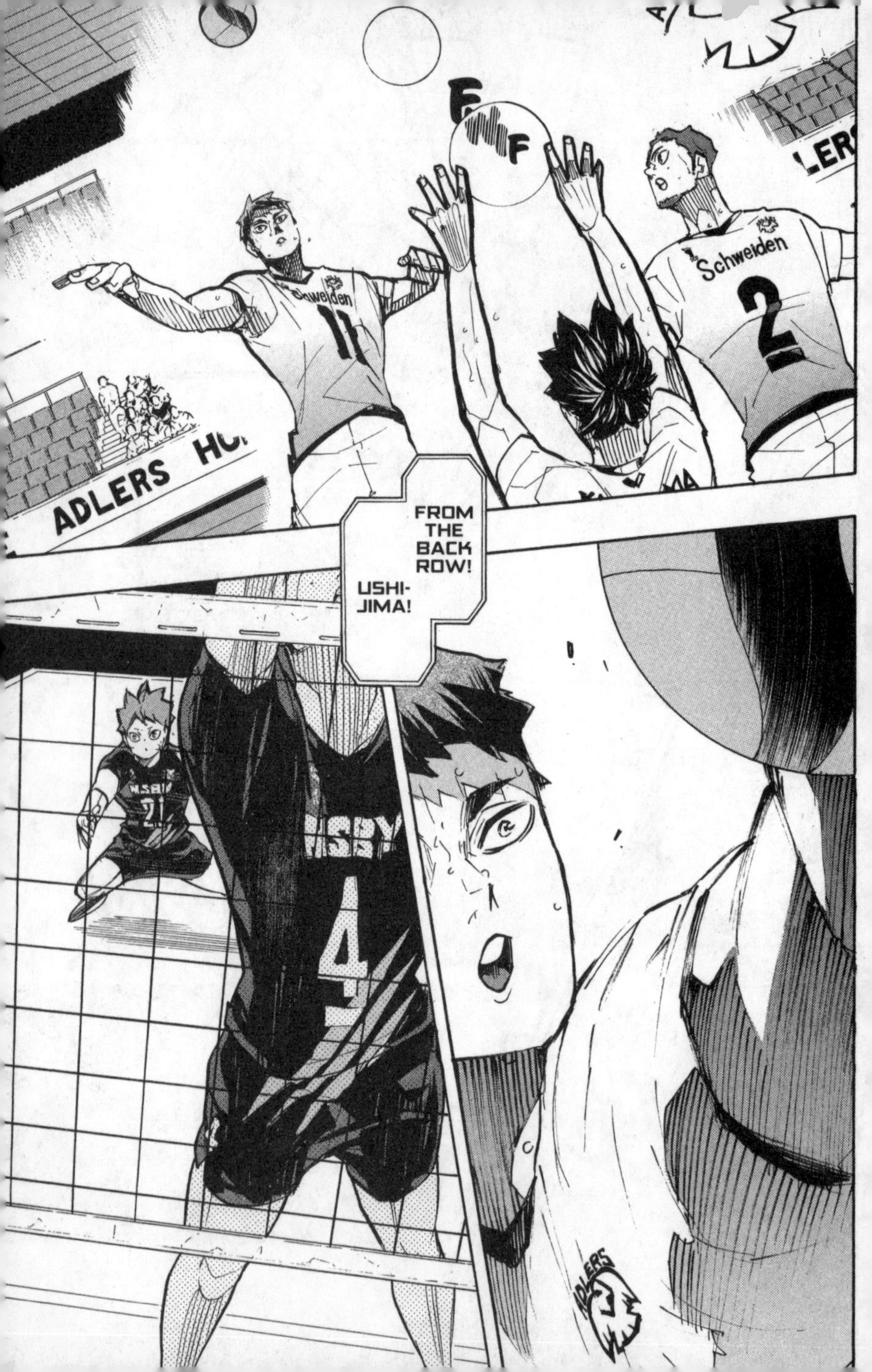
FFF
FROM THE BACK ROW!
USHI-JIMA!

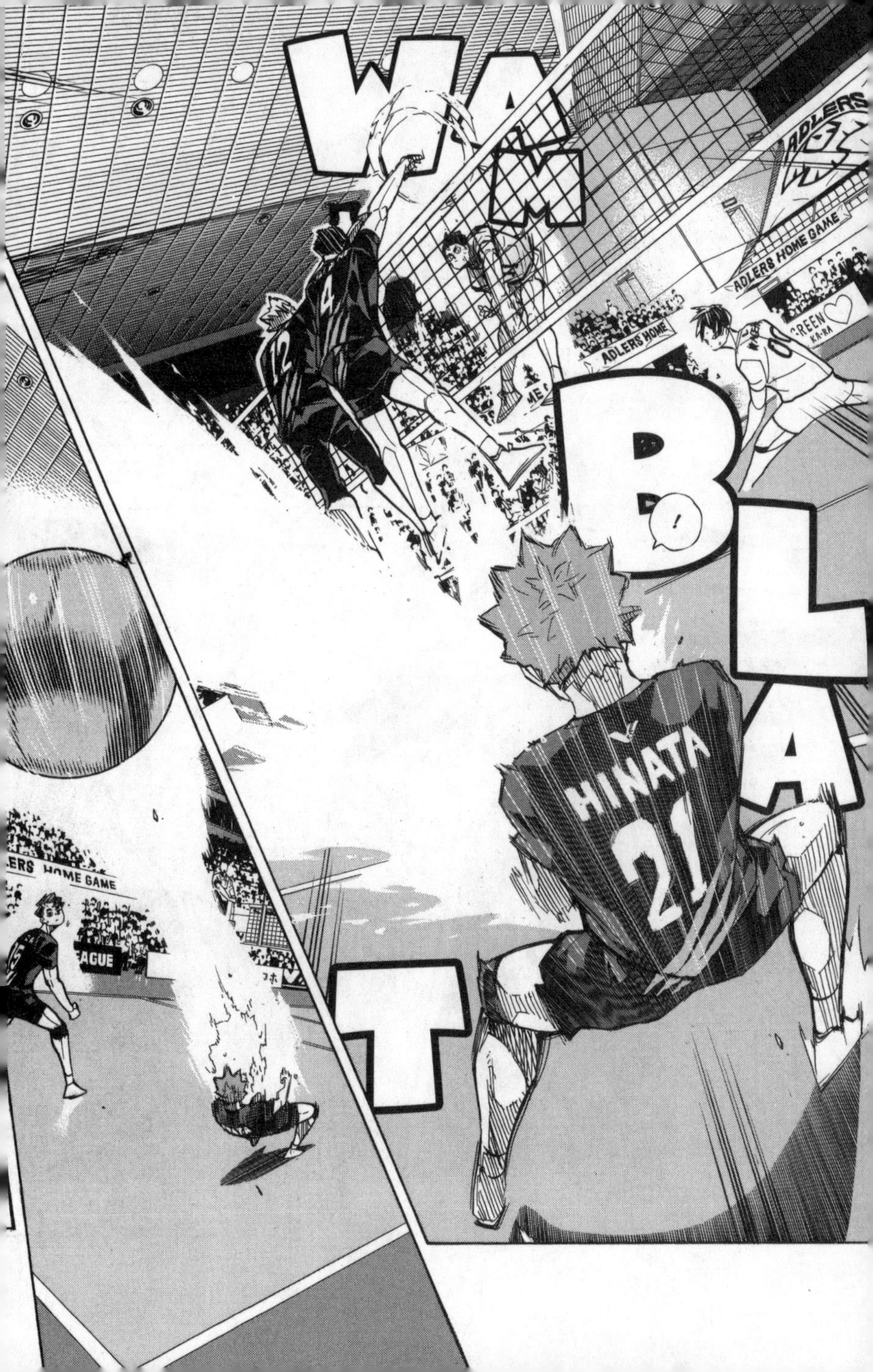
WHAM
ADLERS
ADLERS HOME GAME
ADLERS HOME GAME
ADLERS HOME
GREEN
BLAST
!
HINATA
21
LERS HOME GAME
AGUE

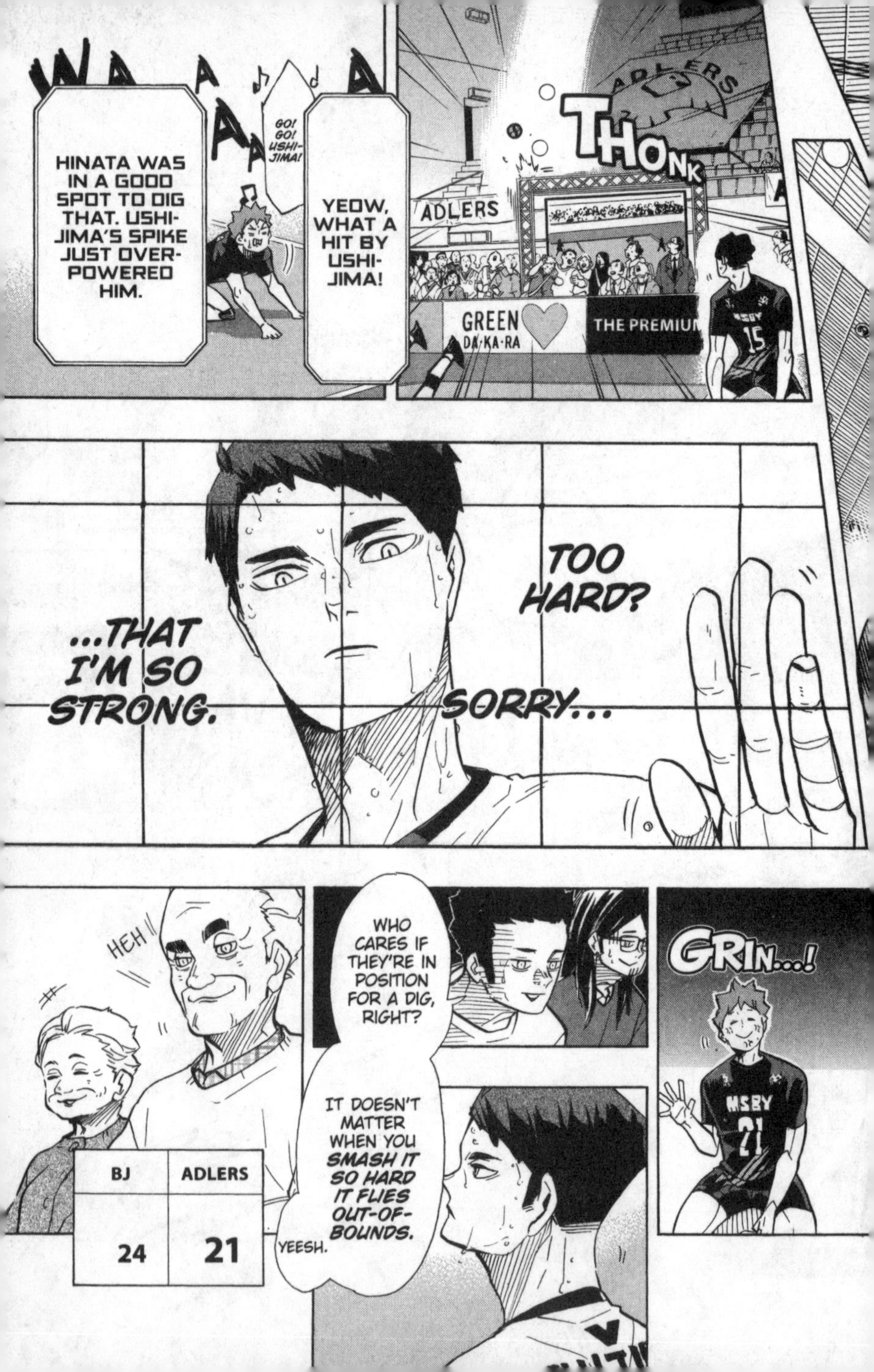
WAAAA
THONK
ADLERS
ADLERS
GREEN DA-KA-RA
THE PREMIUM
MSBY 15
YEOW, WHAT A HIT BY USHIJIMA!
GO! GO! USHIJIMA!
HINATA WAS IN A GOOD SPOT TO DIG THAT. USHIJIMA'S SPIKE JUST OVERPOWERED HIM.
TOO HARD?
SORRY...
...THAT I'M SO STRONG.
GRIN...!
MSBY 21
WHO CARES IF THEY'RE IN POSITION FOR A DIG, RIGHT?
IT DOESN'T MATTER WHEN YOU SMASH IT SO HARD IT FLIES OUT-OF-BOUNDS.
YEESH.
HEH
BJ 24
ADLERS 21

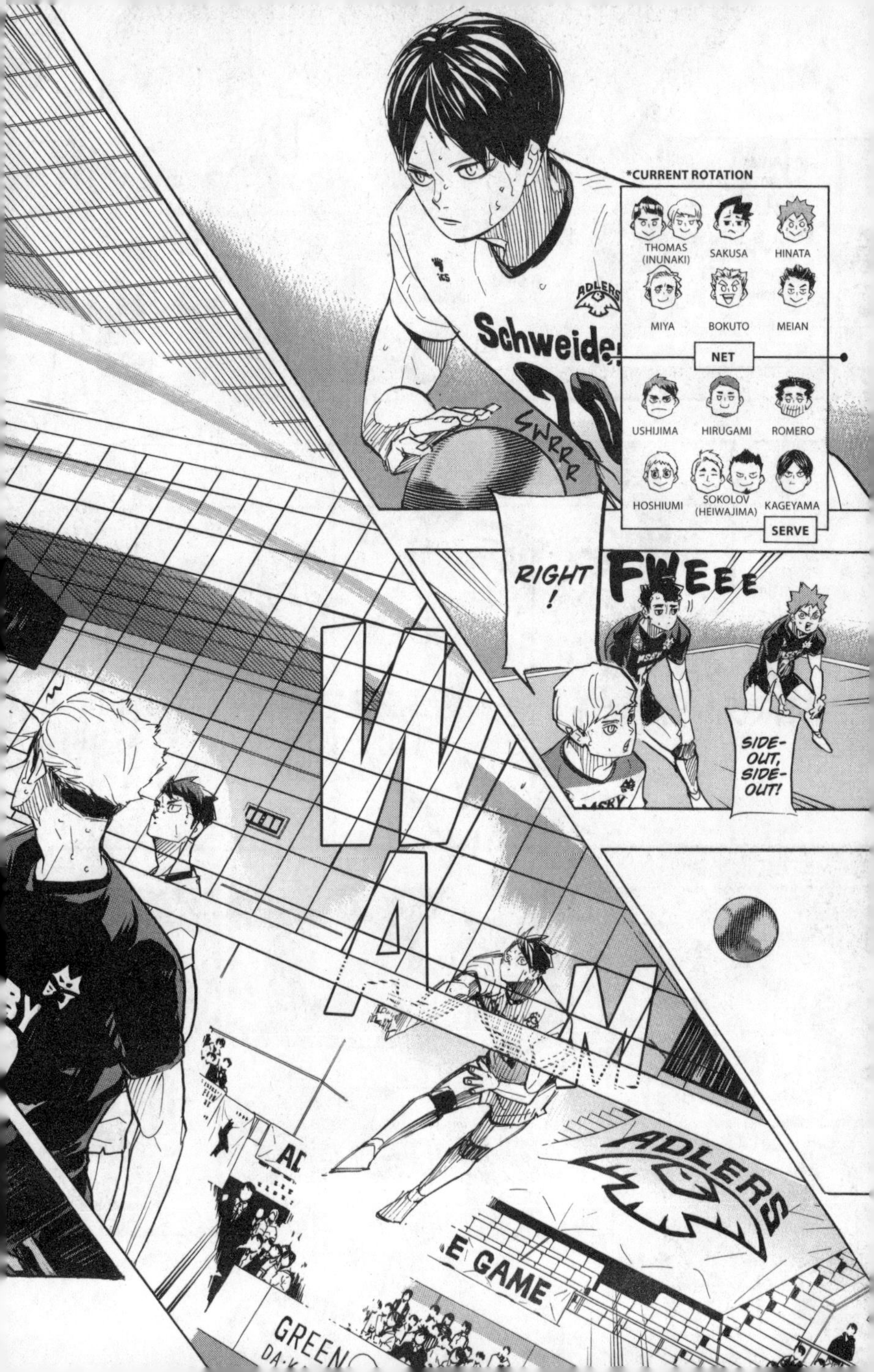

ADLERS
Schweiden
SWRRR
*CURRENT ROTATION
THOMAS (INUNAKI)
SAKUSA
HINATA
MIYA
BOKUTO
MEIAN
NET
USHIJIMA
HIRUGAMI
ROMERO
HOSHIUMI
SOKOLOV (HEIWAJIMA)
KAGEYAMA
SERVE
RIGHT!
FWEEE
SIDE-OUT, SIDE-OUT!
WHAM
ADLERS
E GAME
GREEN

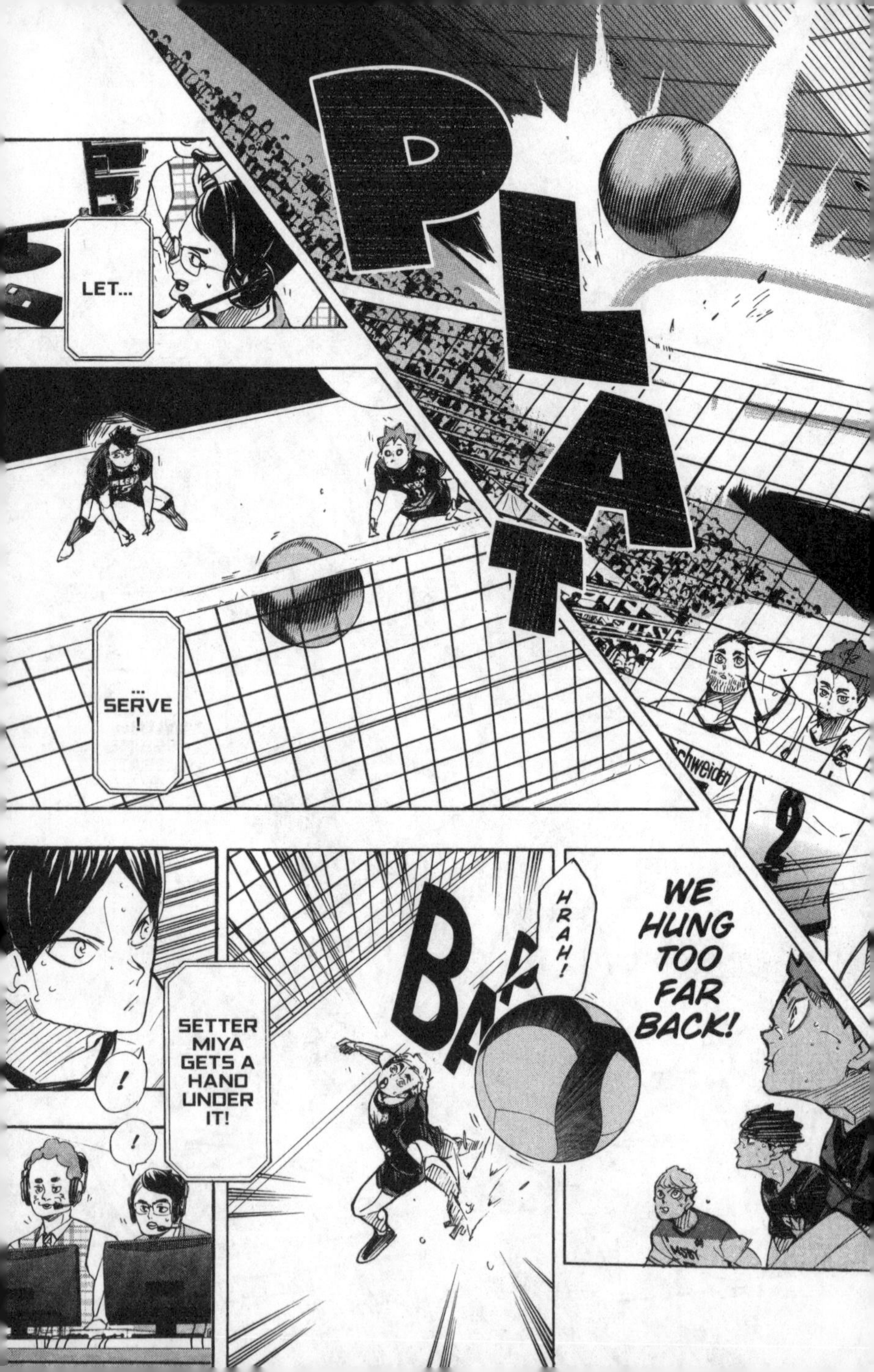
PLAT
LET...
... SERVE!
WE HUNG TOO FAR BACK!
HRAH!
BAP
SETTER MIYA GETS A HAND UNDER IT!
!
!

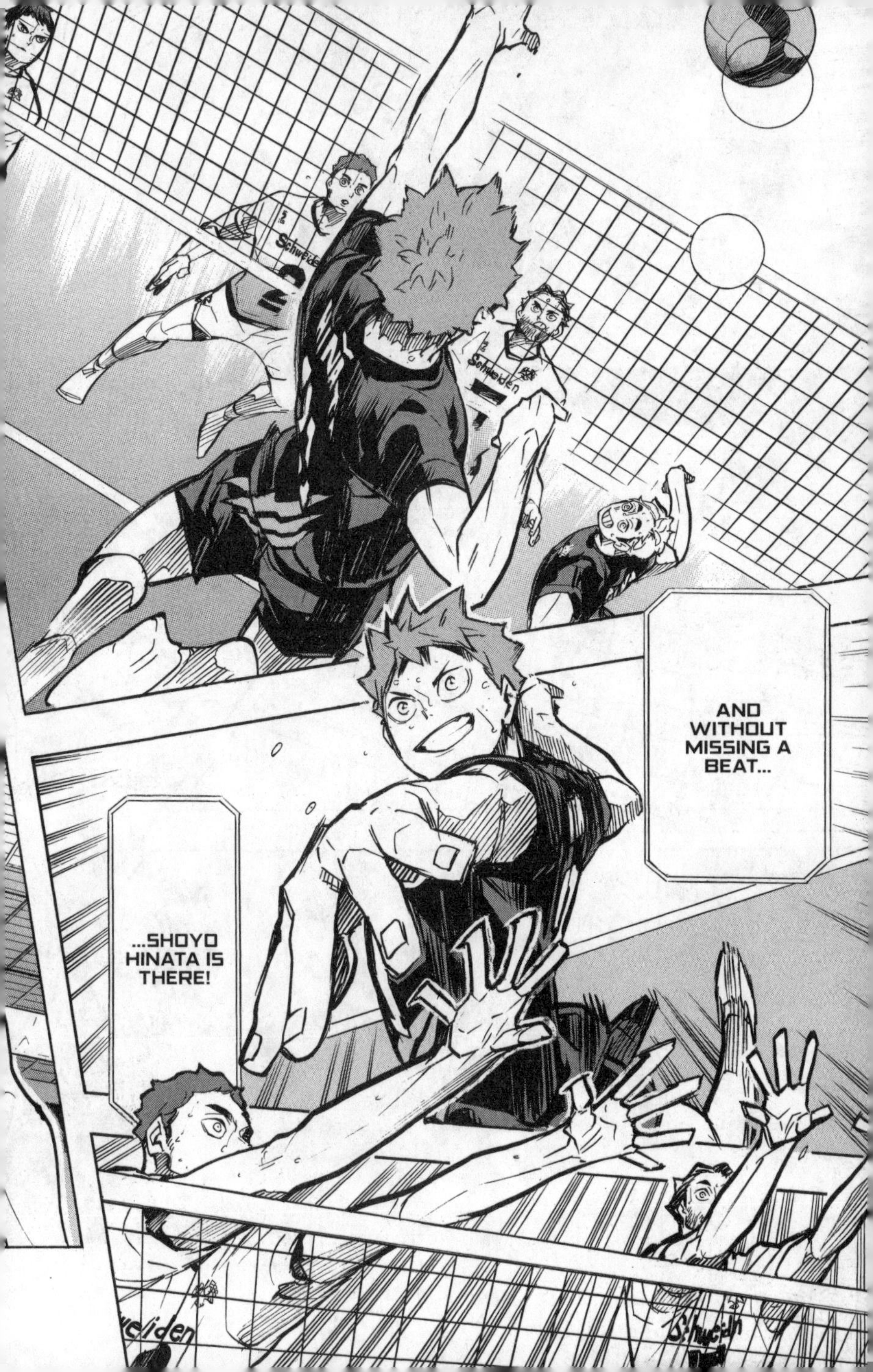
AND WITHOUT MISSING A BEAT...
...SHOYO HINATA IS THERE!

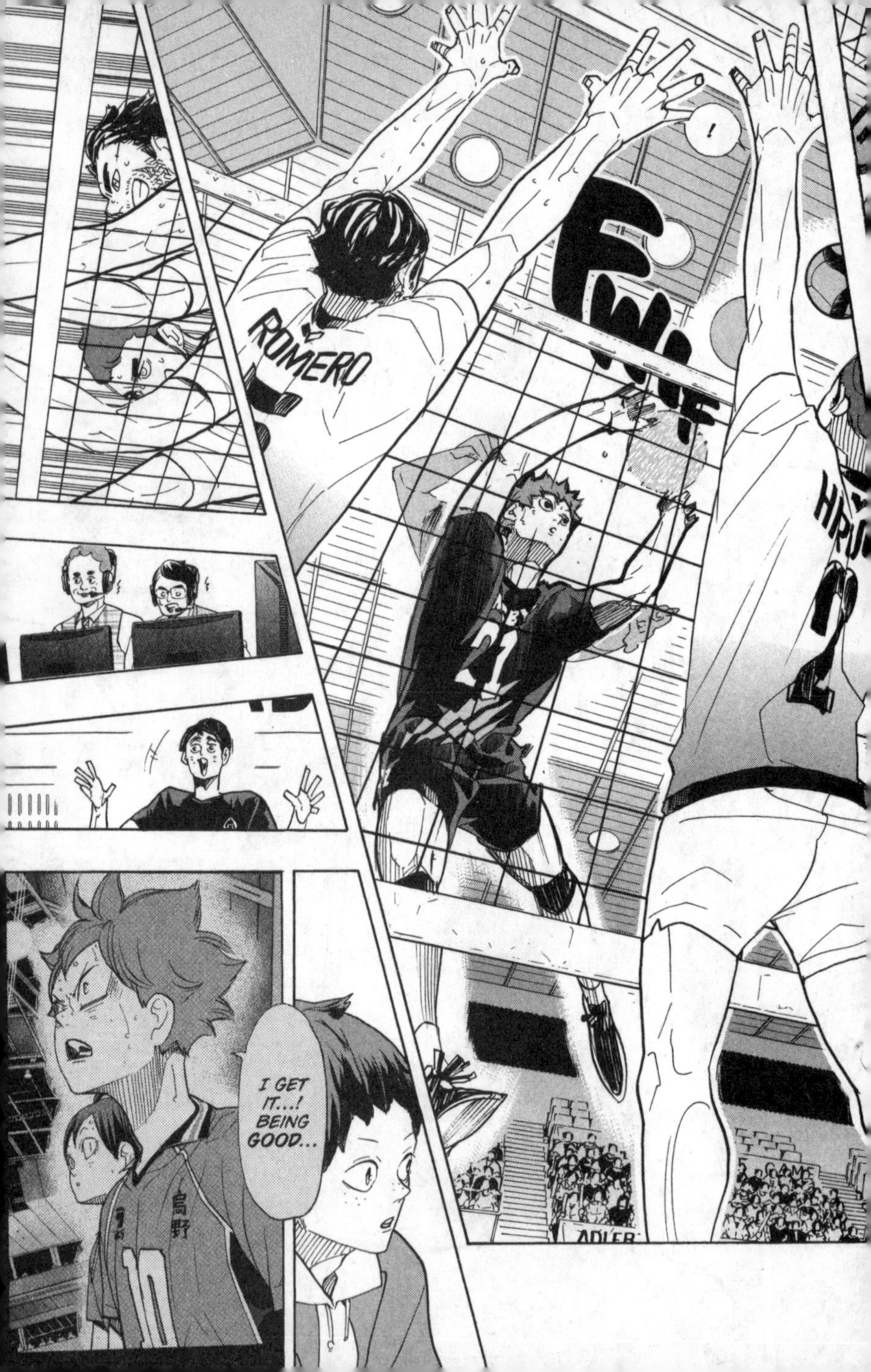
!
ROMERO
I GET IT...! BEING GOOD...
ADLER

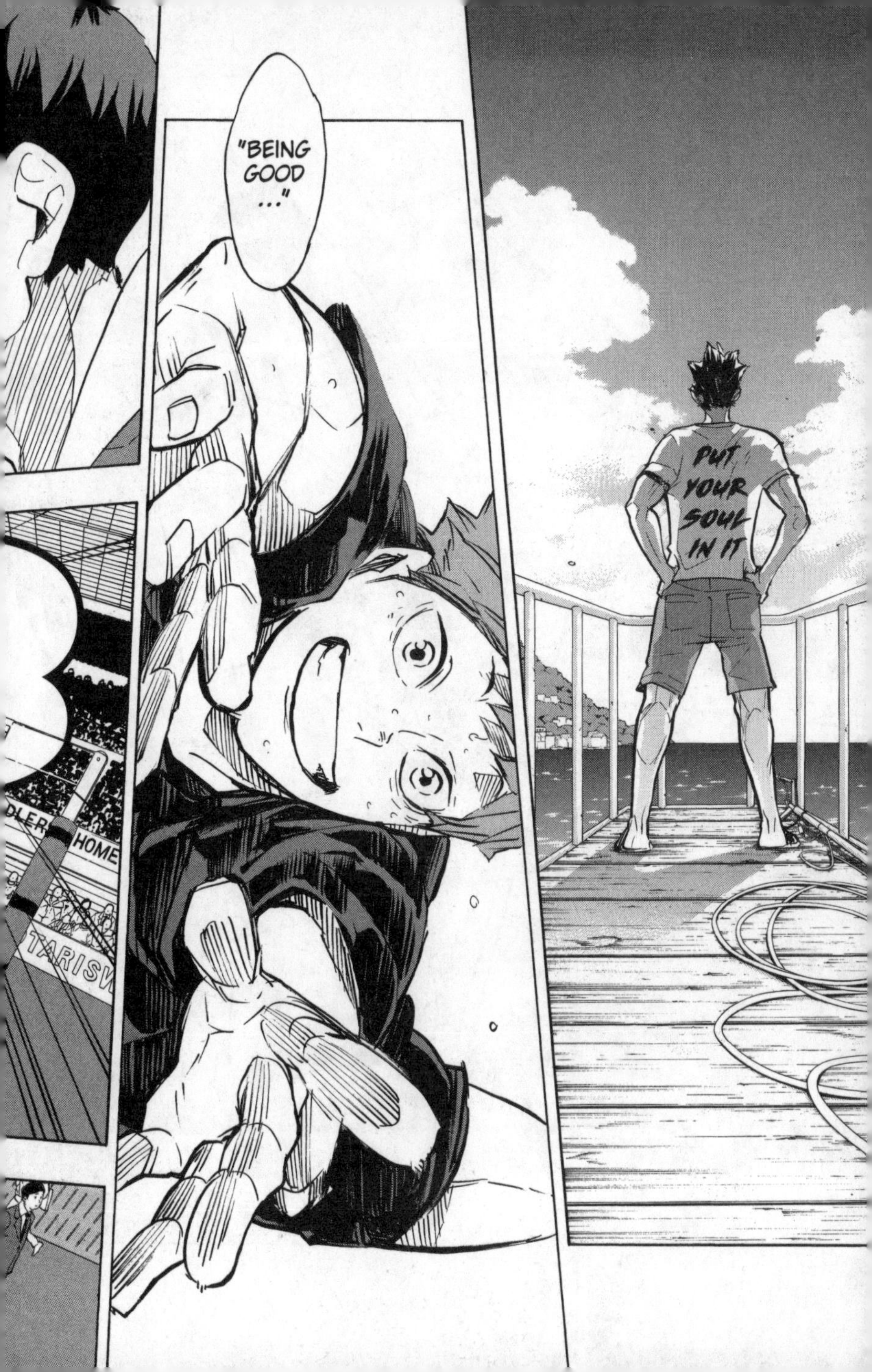
PUT YOUR SOUL IN IT
"BEING GOOD ..."
HOME

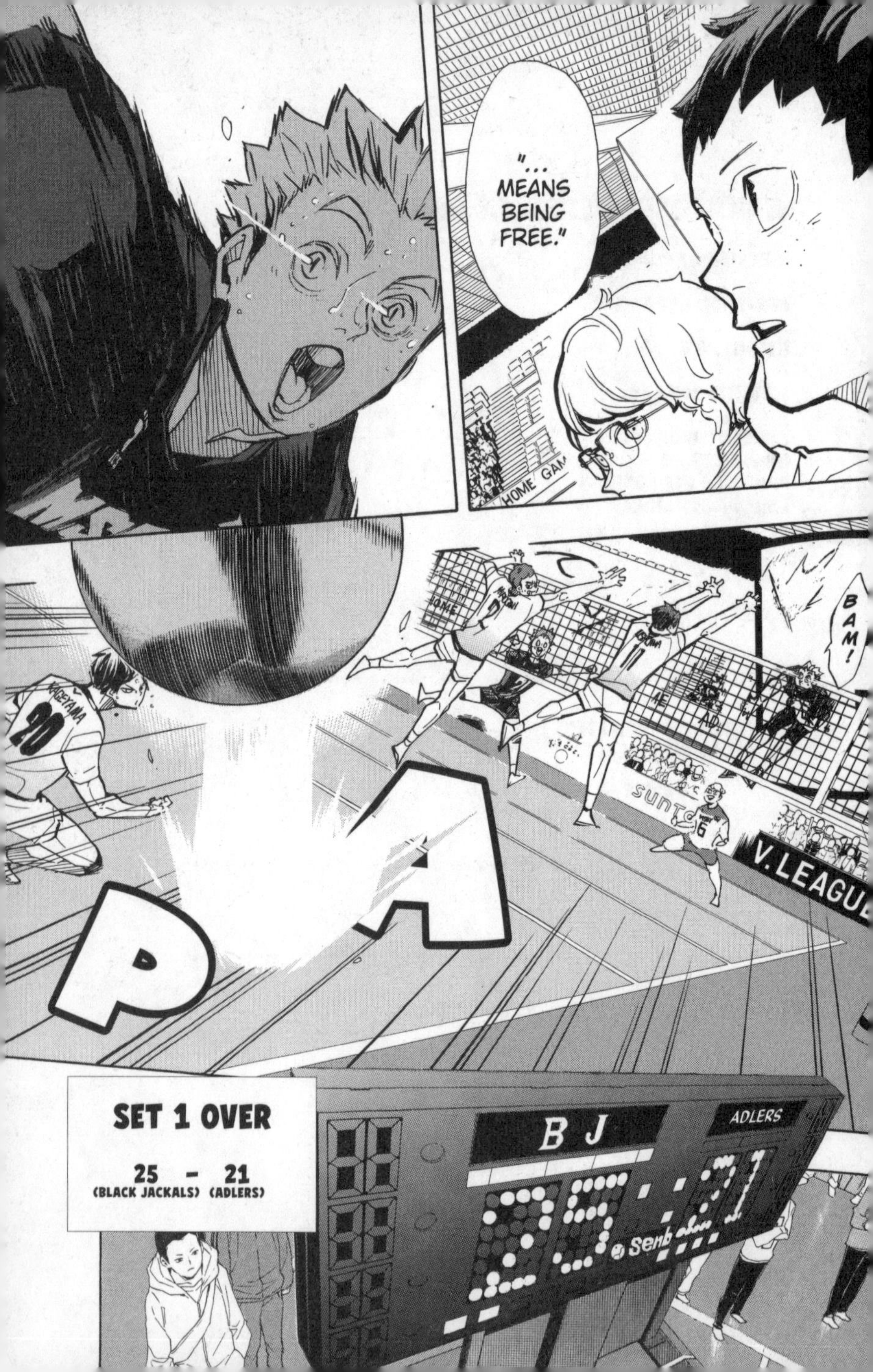
"... MEANS BEING FREE."
HOME GAM
BAM!
V.LEAGUE
KAGEYAMA
P
A
SET 1 OVER
25 – 21
(BLACK JACKALS) (ADLERS)
B J
ADLERS

WAKATOSHI USHIJIMA (24)

SHWEIDEN ADLERS

POSITION: OPPOSITE

HEIGHT: 6'4"

WEIGHT: 200 LBS.

**CURRENT WORRY:
HE WANTS TO
PRACTICE HIS FOREIGN
LANGUAGES MORE.**

**ABILITY PARAMETERS
(5-POINT SCALE)**

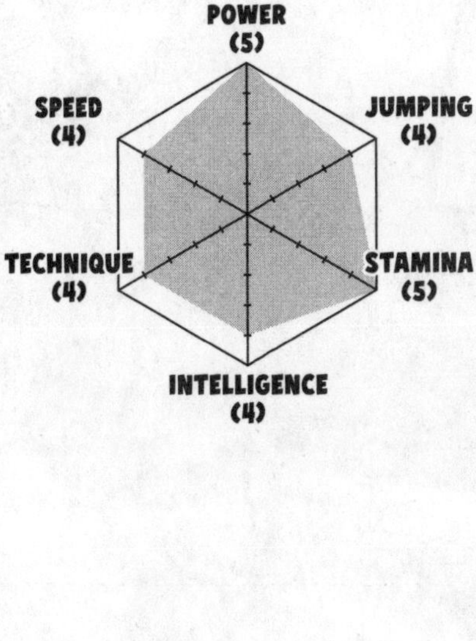
POWER
(5)
JUMPING
(4)
STAMINA
(5)
INTELLIGENCE
(4)
TECHNIQUE
(4)
SPEED
(4)

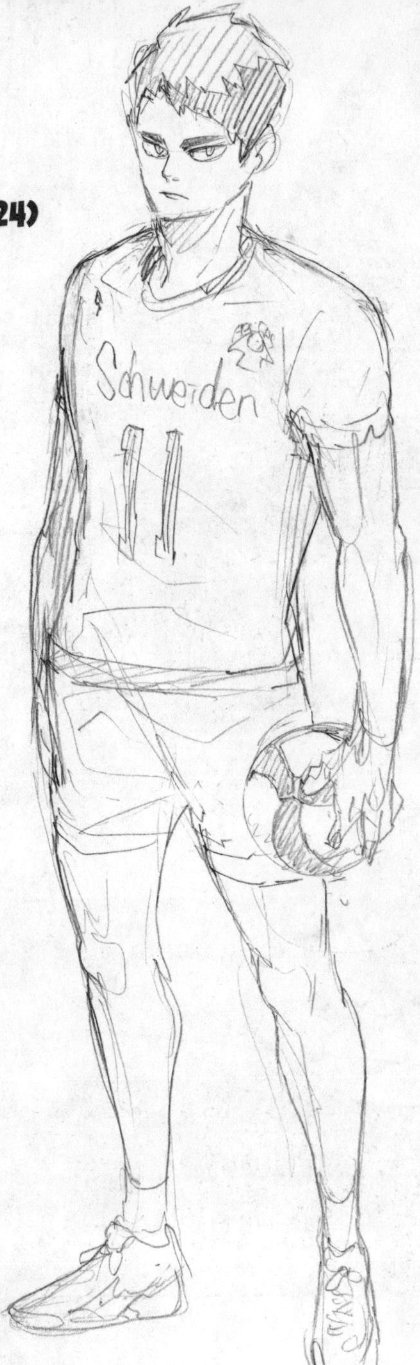
Schweiden
11

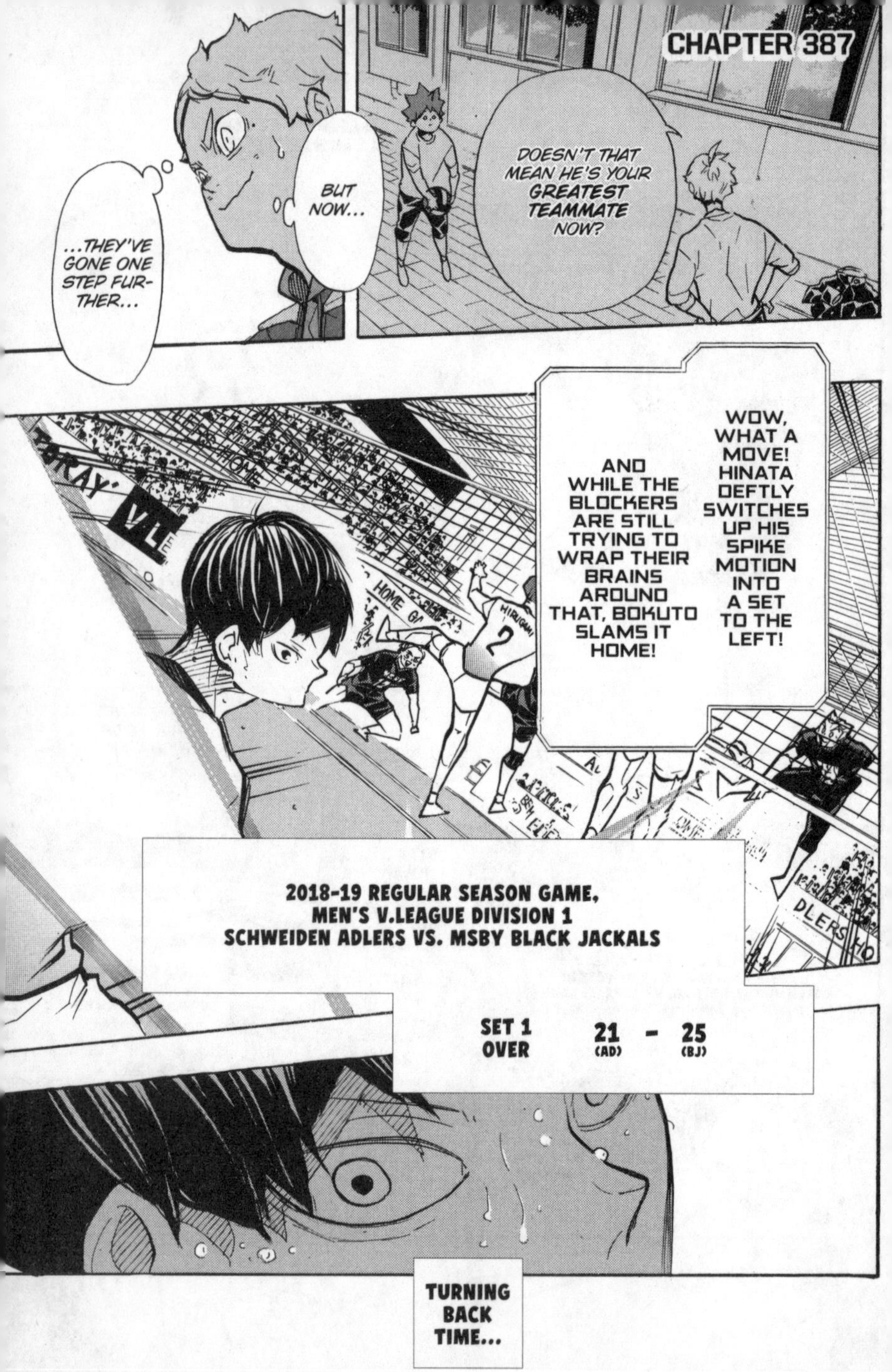
CHAPTER 387
DOESN'T THAT MEAN HE'S YOUR GREATEST TEAMMATE NOW?
BUT NOW...
...THEY'VE GONE ONE STEP FURTHER...
WOW, WHAT A MOVE! HINATA DEFTLY SWITCHES UP HIS SPIKE MOTION INTO A SET TO THE LEFT!
AND WHILE THE BLOCKERS ARE STILL TRYING TO WRAP THEIR BRAINS AROUND THAT, BOKUTO SLAMS IT HOME!
2018-19 REGULAR SEASON GAME, MEN'S V.LEAGUE DIVISION 1
SCHWEIDEN ADLERS VS. MSBY BLACK JACKALS
SET 1 OVER 21 (AD) - 25 (BJ)
TURNING BACK TIME...

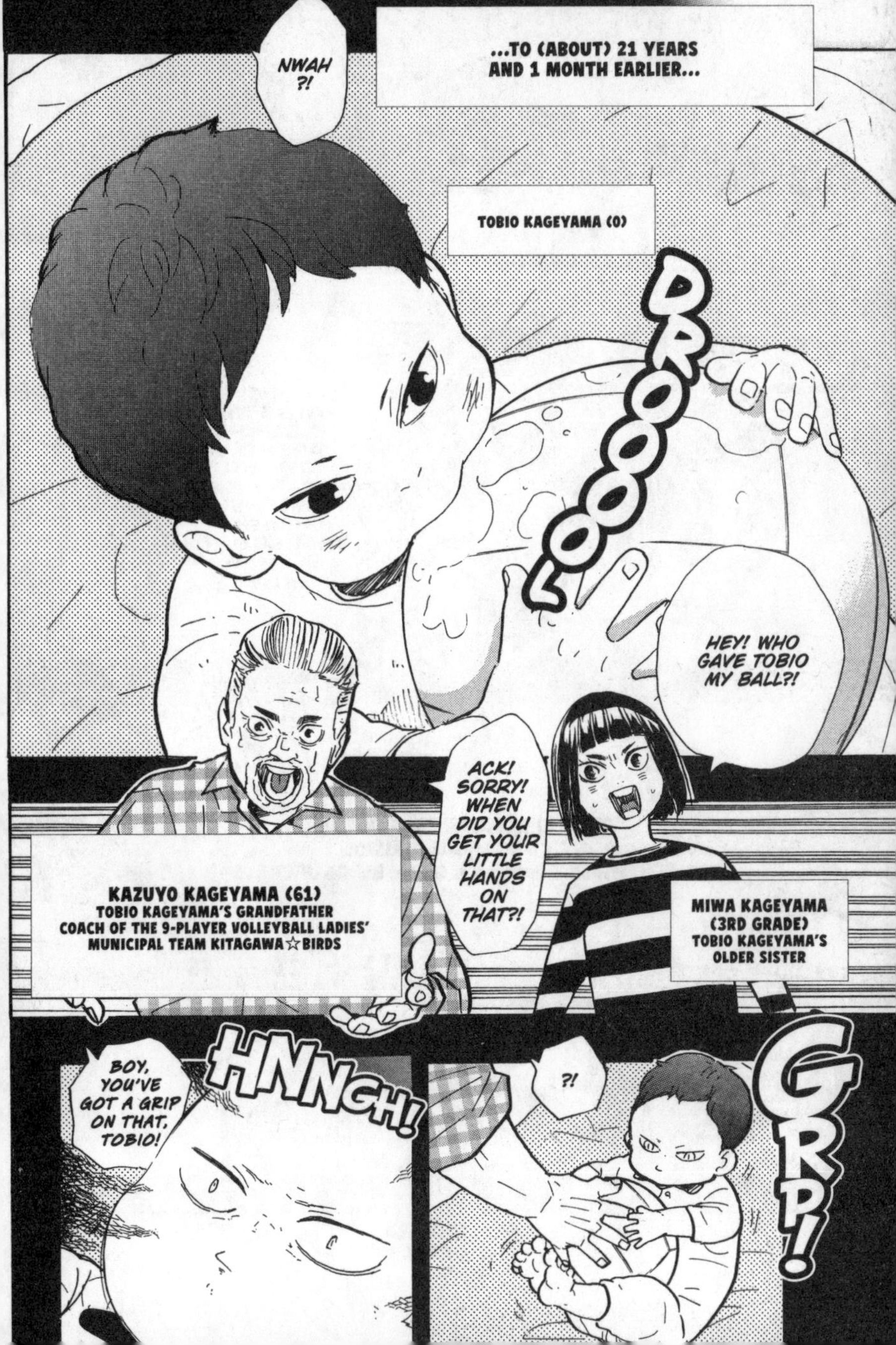
...TO (ABOUT) 21 YEARS AND 1 MONTH EARLIER...
NWAH ?!
TOBIO KAGEYAMA (0)
DROOOOL
HEY! WHO GAVE TOBIO MY BALL?!
ACK! SORRY! WHEN DID YOU GET YOUR LITTLE HANDS ON THAT?!
MIWA KAGEYAMA (3RD GRADE) TOBIO KAGEYAMA'S OLDER SISTER
KAZUYO KAGEYAMA (61) TOBIO KAGEYAMA'S GRANDFATHER COACH OF THE 9-PLAYER VOLLEYBALL LADIES' MUNICIPAL TEAM KITAGAWA☆BIRDS
GRP!
?!
HNNGH!
BOY, YOU'VE GOT A GRIP ON THAT, TOBIO!

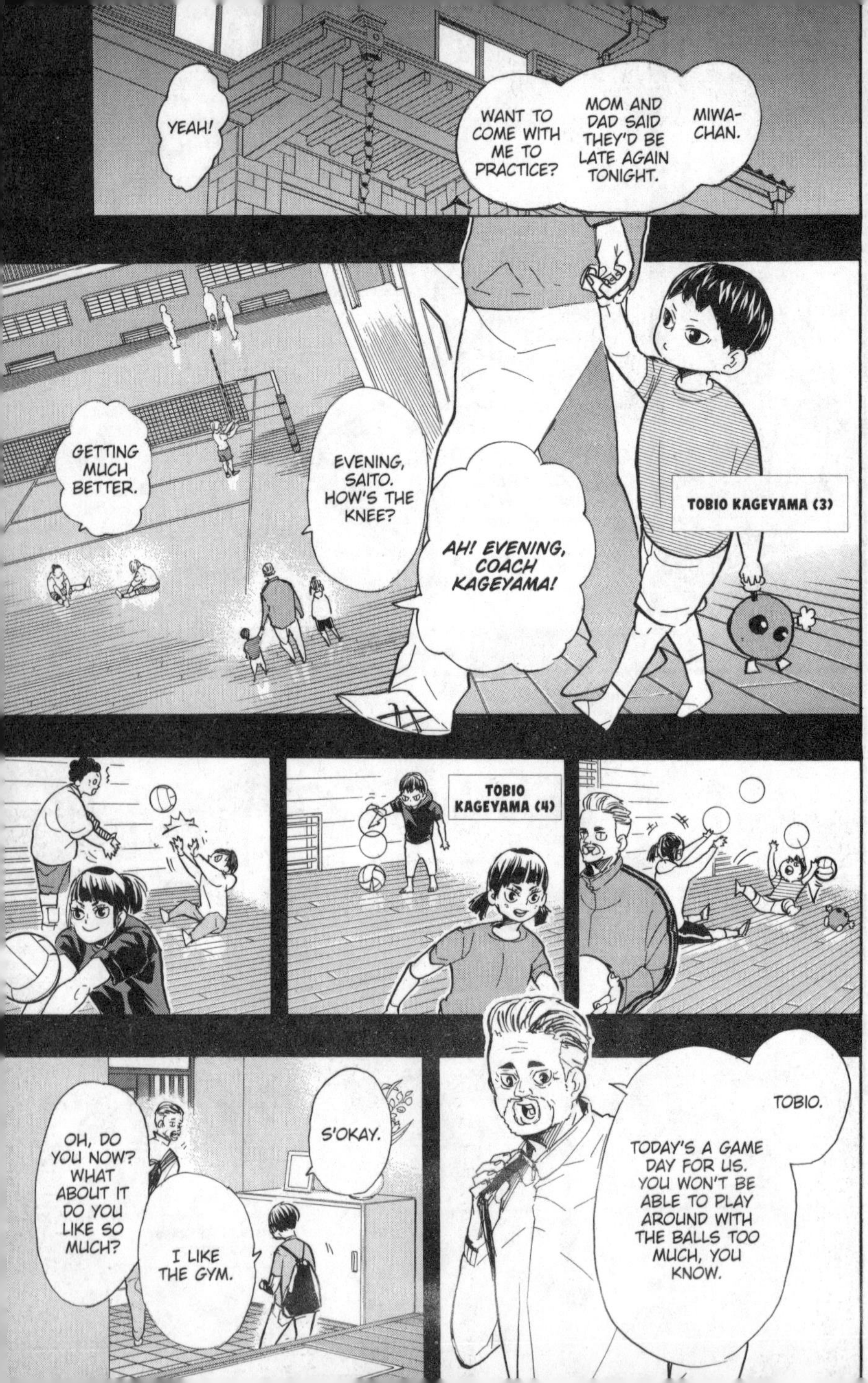
MIWA-CHAN.
MOM AND DAD SAID THEY'D BE LATE AGAIN TONIGHT.
WANT TO COME WITH ME TO PRACTICE?
YEAH!
TOBIO KAGEYAMA (3)
AH! EVENING, COACH KAGEYAMA!
EVENING, SAITO. HOW'S THE KNEE?
GETTING MUCH BETTER.
TOBIO KAGEYAMA (4)
TOBIO.
TODAY'S A GAME DAY FOR US. YOU WON'T BE ABLE TO PLAY AROUND WITH THE BALLS TOO MUCH, YOU KNOW.
S'OKAY.
I LIKE THE GYM.
OH, DO YOU NOW? WHAT ABOUT IT DO YOU LIKE SO MUCH?

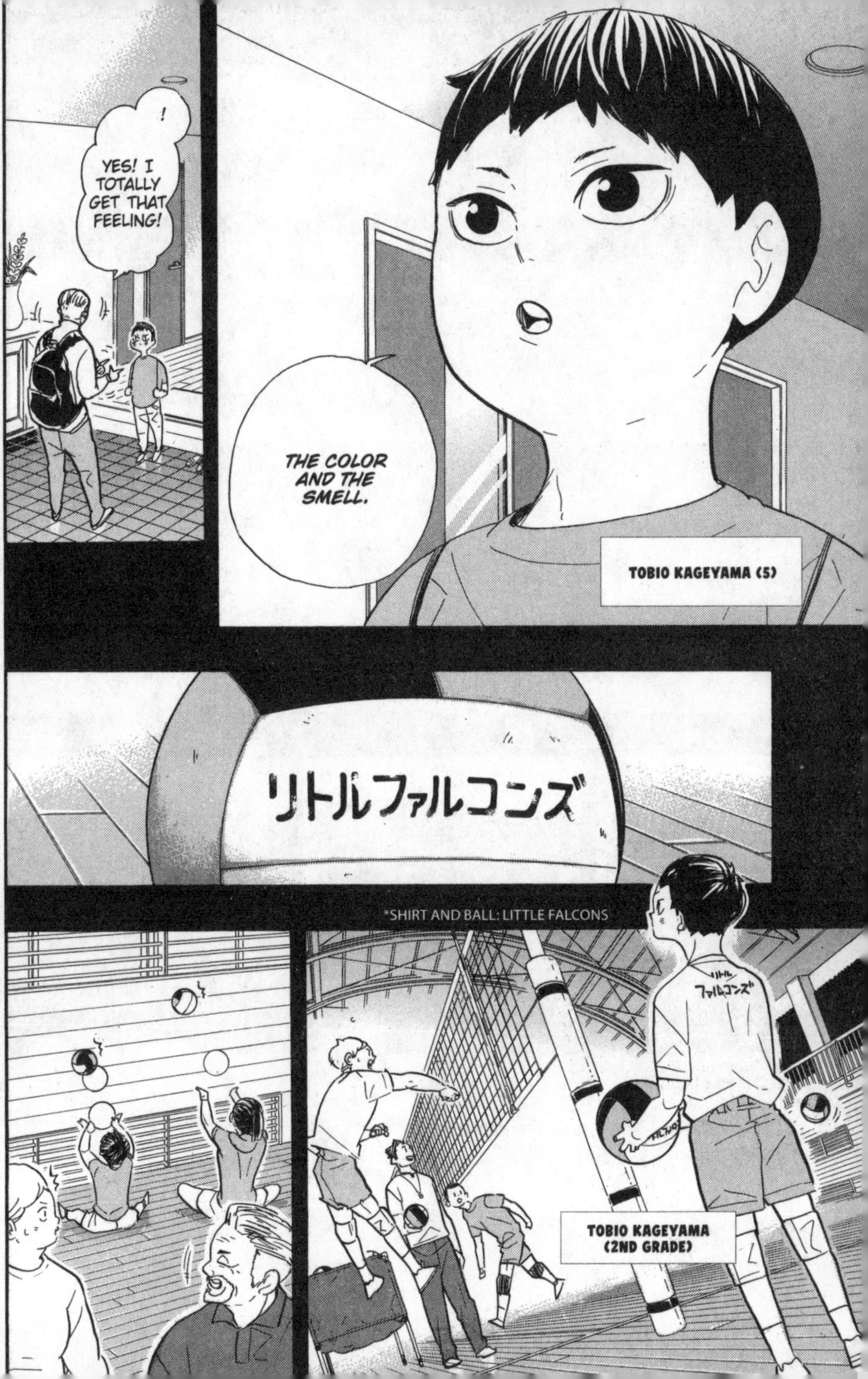
THE COLOR AND THE SMELL.
TOBIO KAGEYAMA (5)
!
YES! I TOTALLY GET THAT FEELING!
リトルファルコンズ
*SHIRT AND BALL: LITTLE FALCONS
リトル ファルコンズ
TOBIO KAGEYAMA (2ND GRADE)

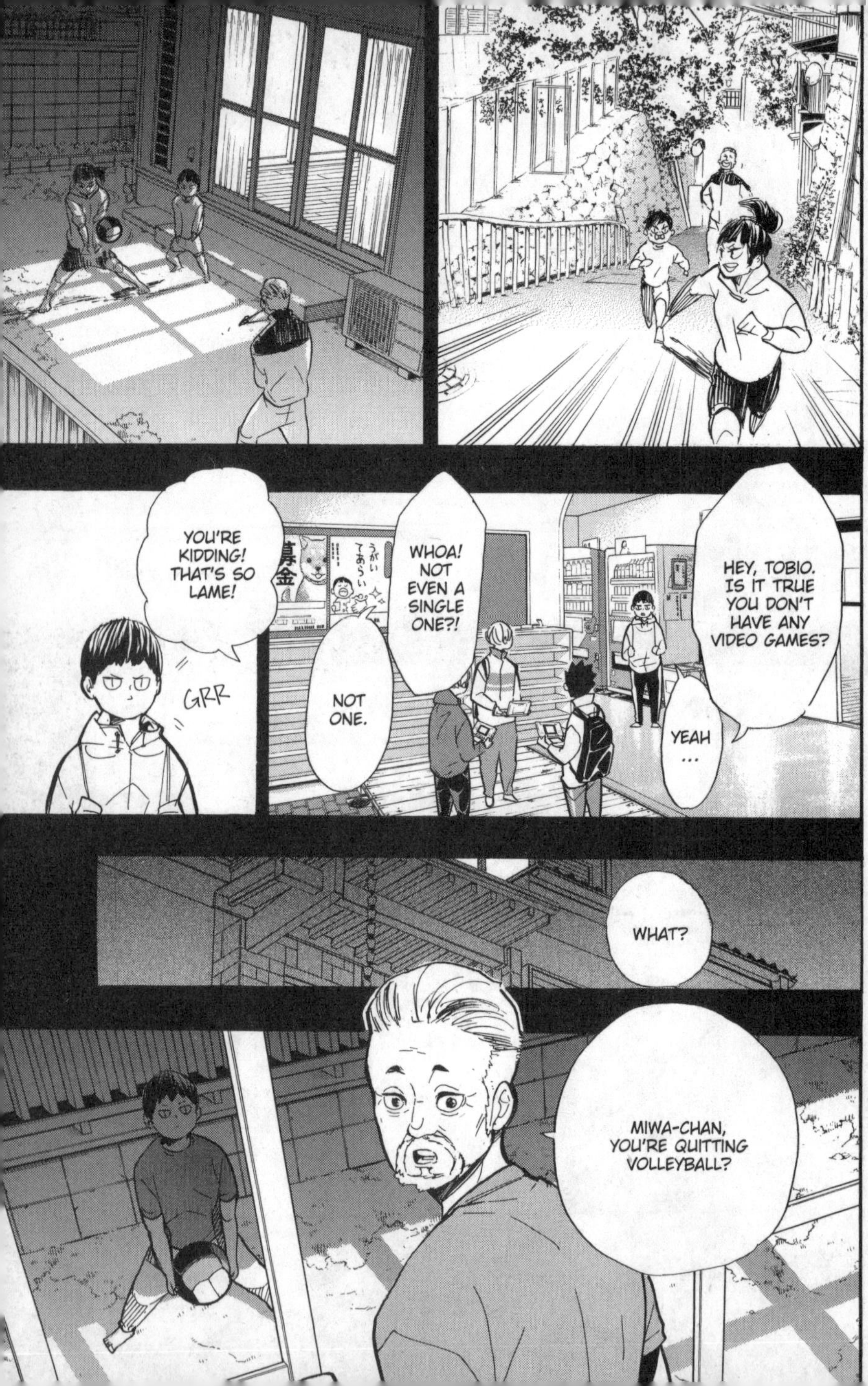
HEY, TOBIO. IS IT TRUE YOU DON'T HAVE ANY VIDEO GAMES?
YEAH...
WHOA! NOT EVEN A SINGLE ONE?!
NOT ONE.
うがい てあらい
YOU'RE KIDDING! THAT'S SO LAME!
GRR
WHAT?
MIWA-CHAN, YOU'RE QUITTING VOLLEYBALL?

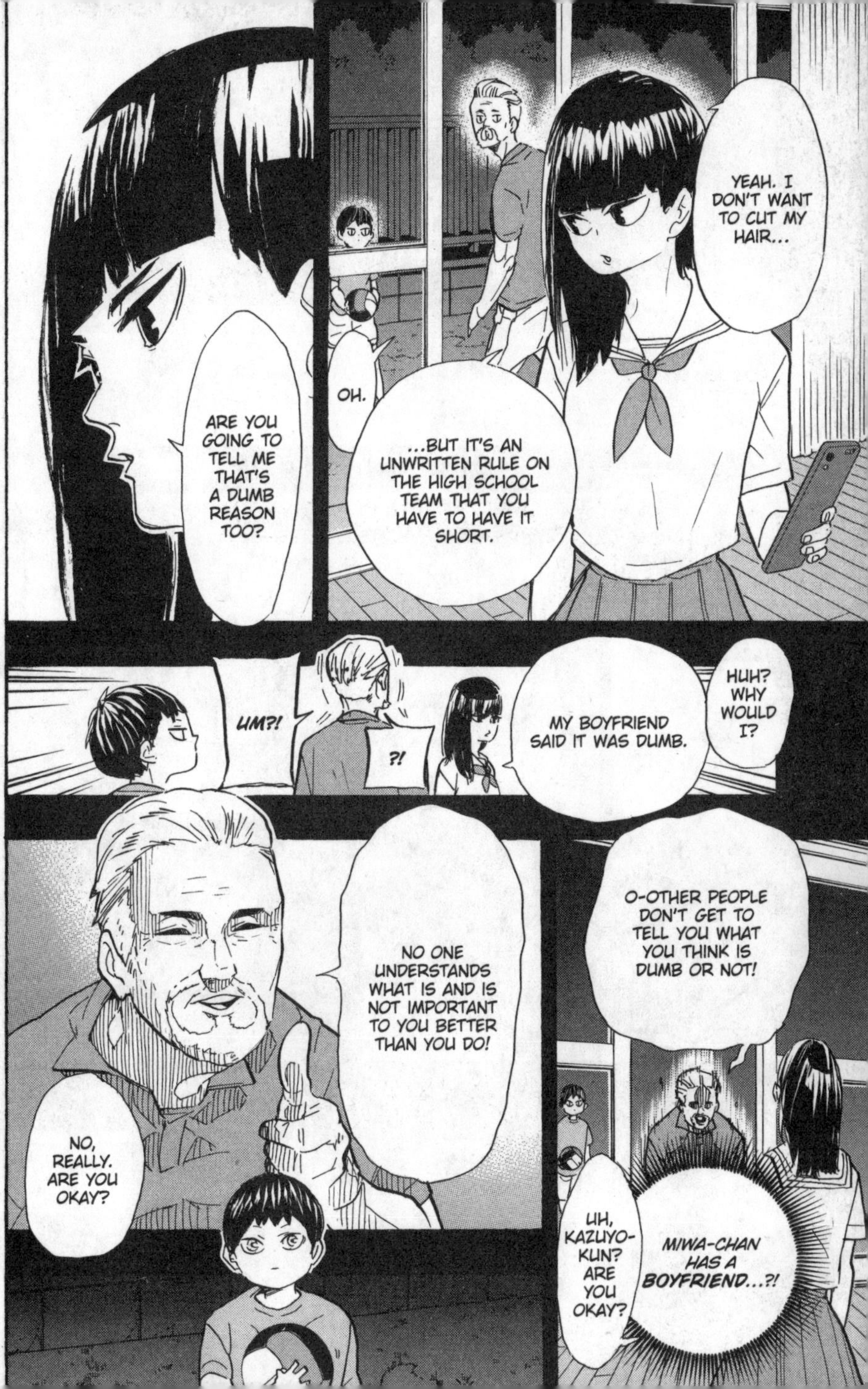
YEAH. I DON'T WANT TO CUT MY HAIR...
...BUT IT'S AN UNWRITTEN RULE ON THE HIGH SCHOOL TEAM THAT YOU HAVE TO HAVE IT SHORT.
OH.
ARE YOU GOING TO TELL ME THAT'S A DUMB REASON TOO?
HUH? WHY WOULD I?
MY BOYFRIEND SAID IT WAS DUMB.
?!
UM?!
O-OTHER PEOPLE DON'T GET TO TELL YOU WHAT YOU THINK IS DUMB OR NOT!
MIWA-CHAN HAS A BOYFRIEND...?!
UH, KAZUYO-KUN? ARE YOU OKAY?
NO ONE UNDERSTANDS WHAT IS AND IS NOT IMPORTANT TO YOU BETTER THAN YOU DO!
NO, REALLY. ARE YOU OKAY?

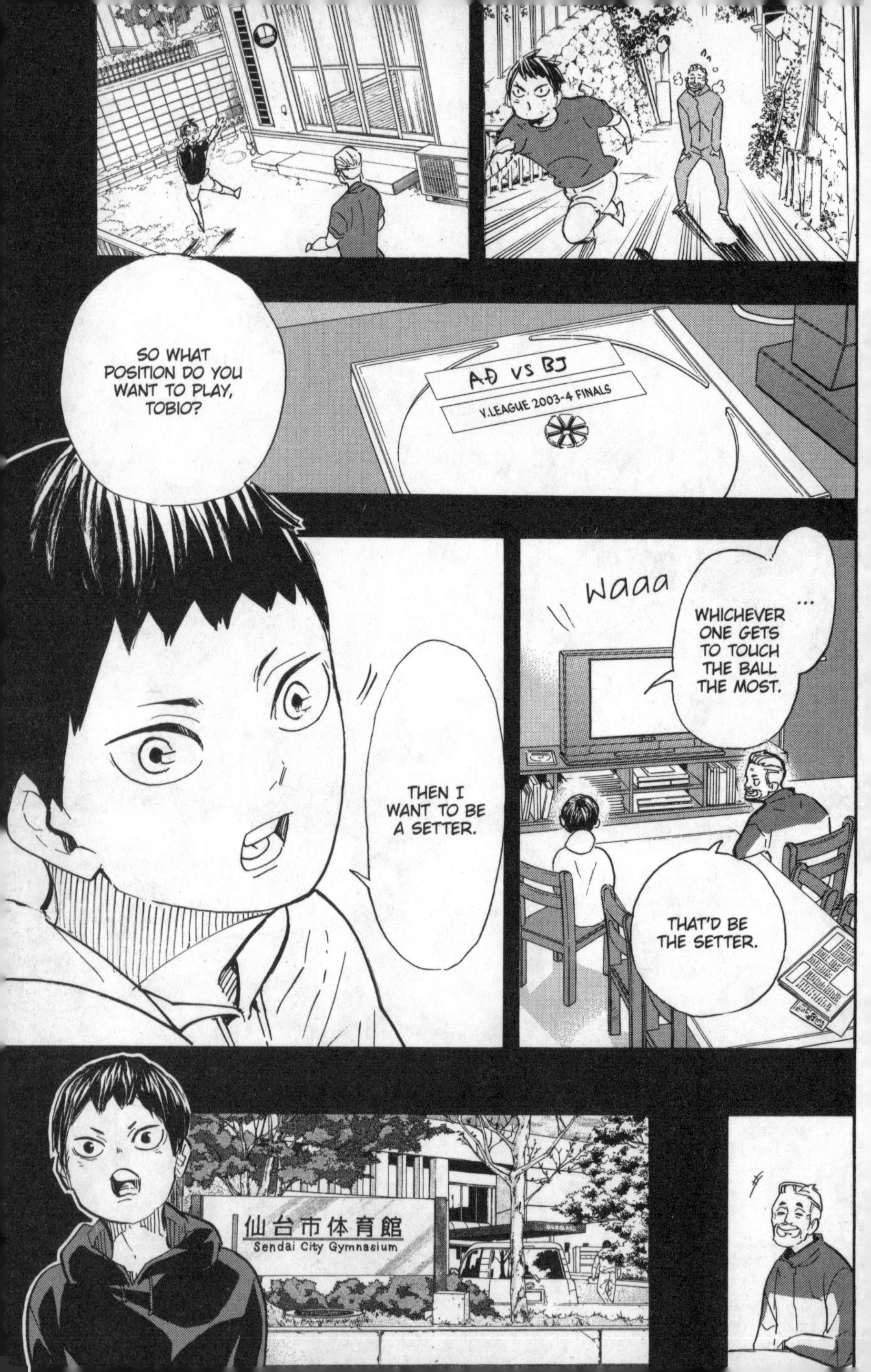
AÐ vs BJ
V.LEAGUE 2003-4 FINALS
SO WHAT POSITION DO YOU WANT TO PLAY, TOBIO?
Waaa
... WHICHEVER ONE GETS TO TOUCH THE BALL THE MOST.
THAT'D BE THE SETTER.
THEN I WANT TO BE A SETTER.
仙台市体育館
Sendai City Gymnasium

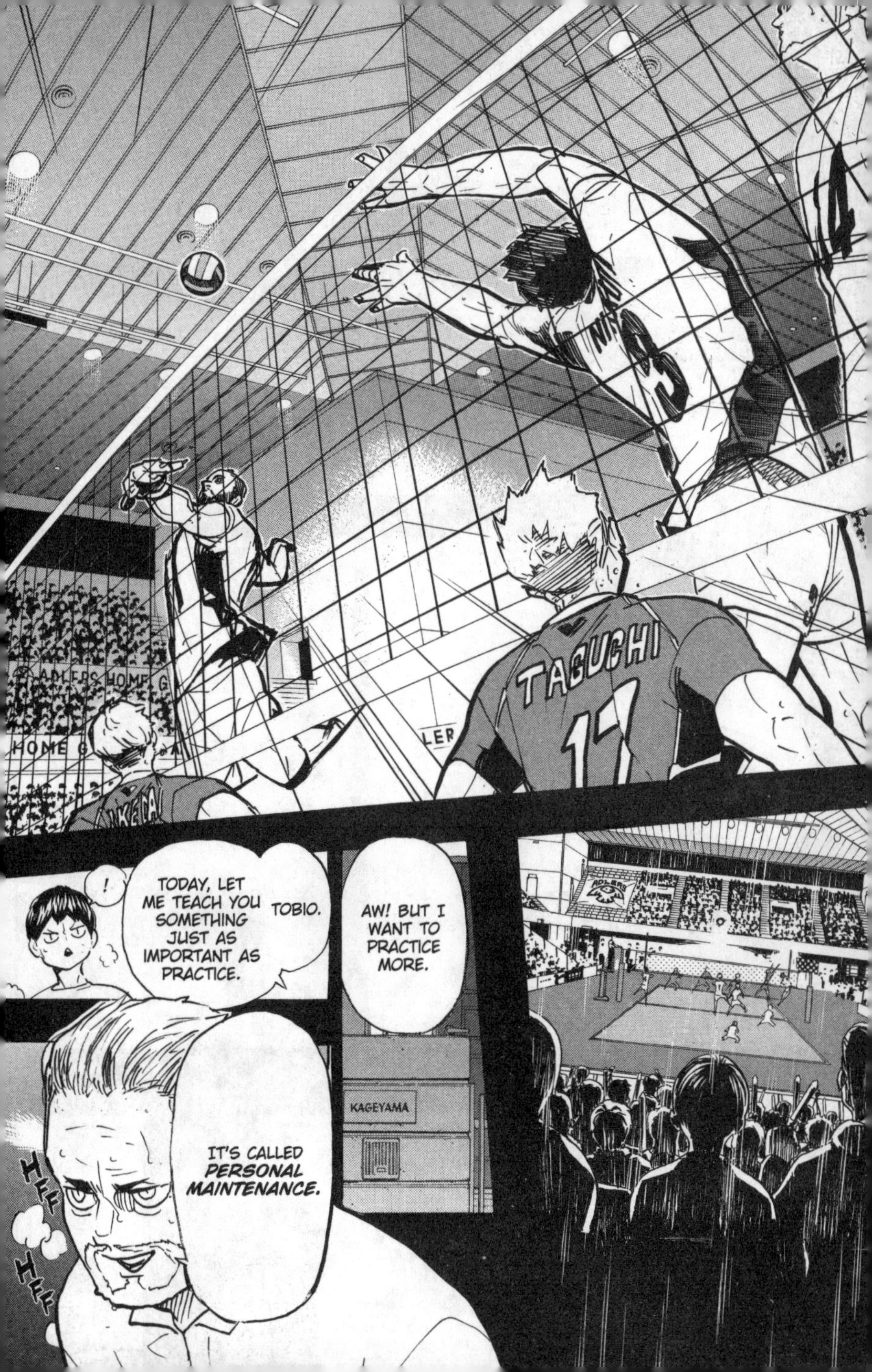
TAGUCHI
ADLERS
AW! BUT I WANT TO PRACTICE MORE.
KAGEYAMA
TOBIO.
TODAY, LET ME TEACH YOU SOMETHING JUST AS IMPORTANT AS PRACTICE.
!
IT'S CALLED *PERSONAL MAINTENANCE.*
HFF
HFF

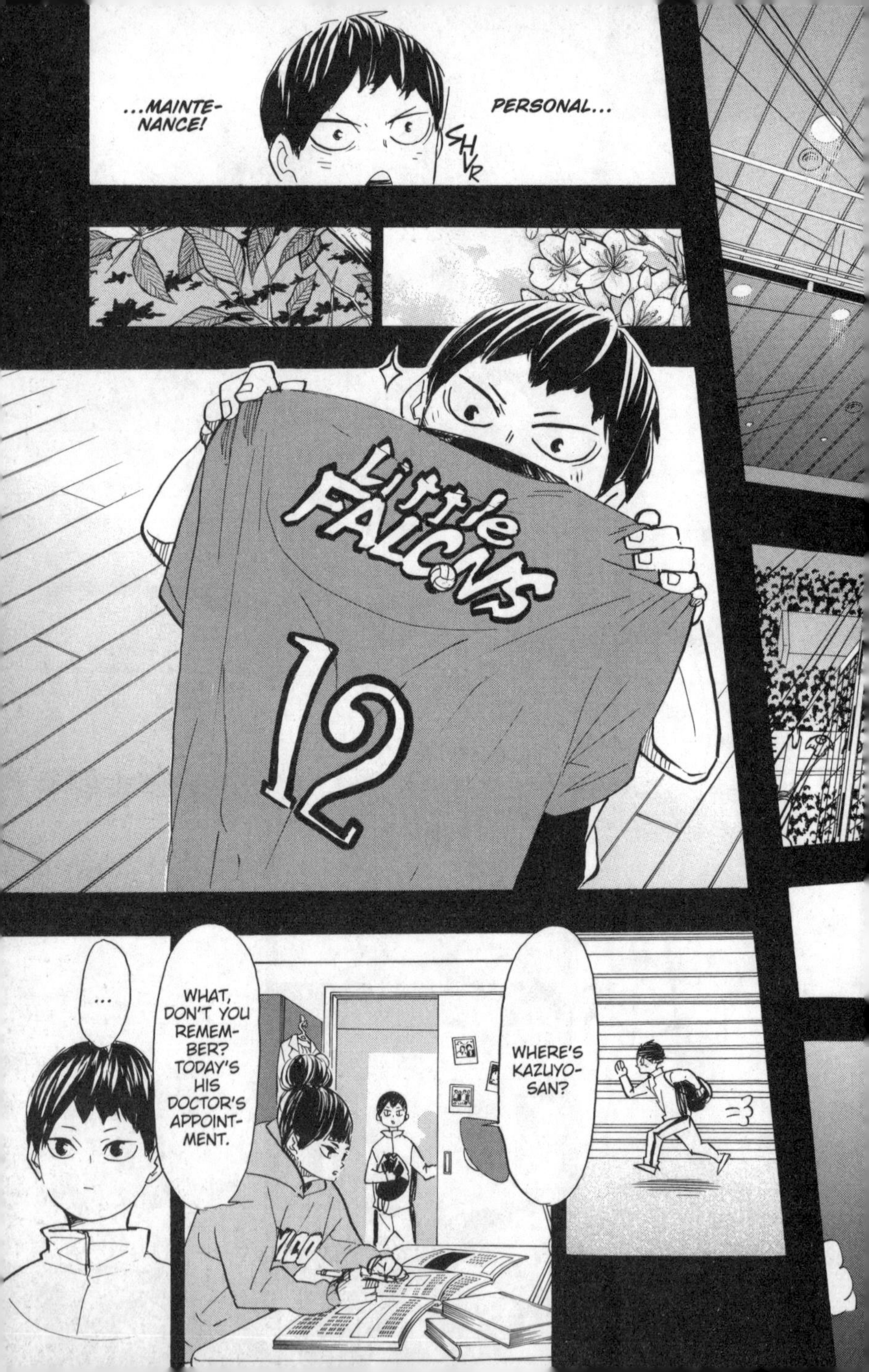
PERSONAL...
SHVR
...MAINTE-NANCE!
Little FALCONS
12
WHERE'S KAZUYO-SAN?
WHAT, DON'T YOU REMEMBER? TODAY'S HIS DOCTOR'S APPOINTMENT.
...

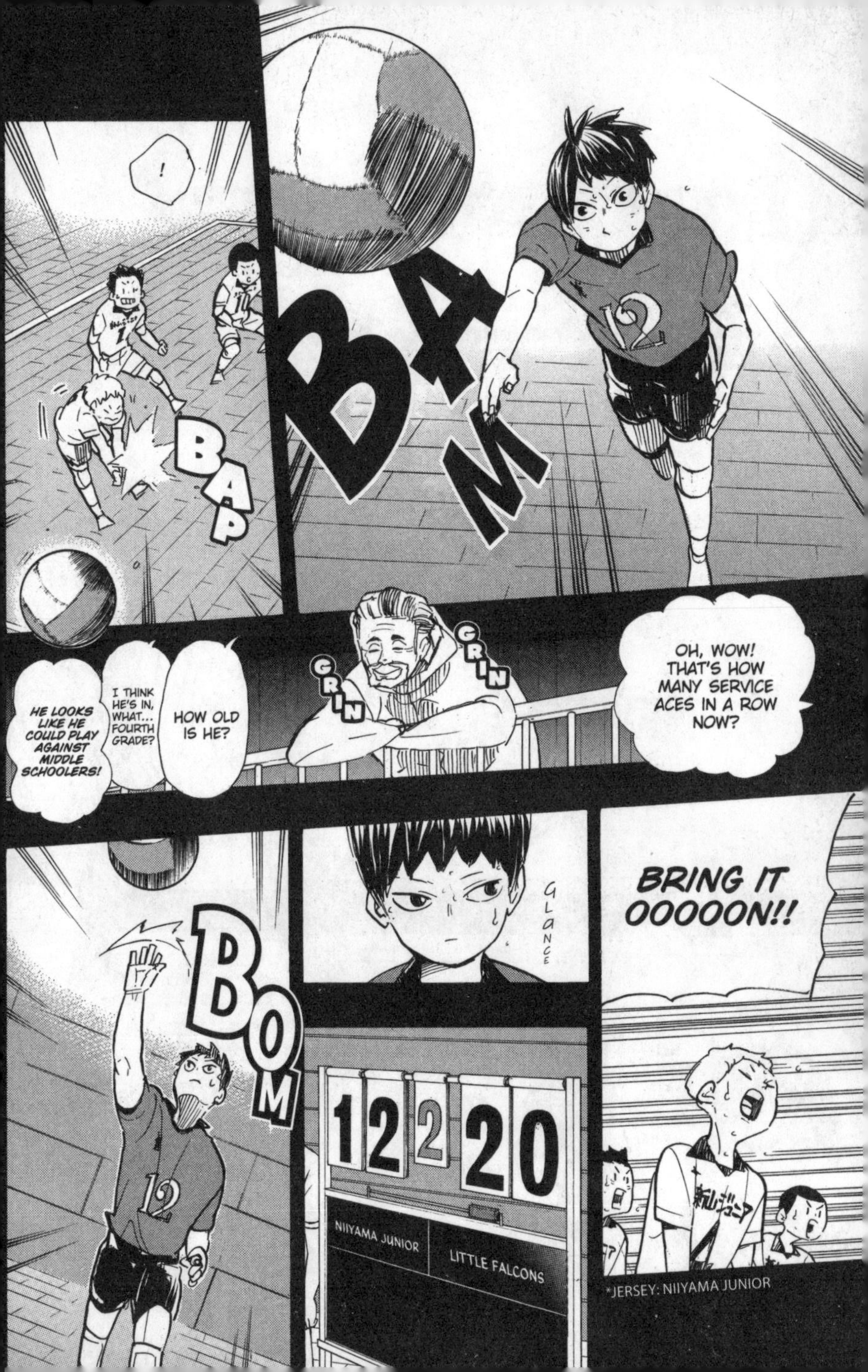
BAM
!
BAP
OH, WOW! THAT'S HOW MANY SERVICE ACES IN A ROW NOW?
GRIN
GRIN
HOW OLD IS HE?
I THINK HE'S IN, WHAT... FOURTH GRADE?
HE LOOKS LIKE HE COULD PLAY AGAINST MIDDLE SCHOOLERS!
BRING IT OOOOON!!
*JERSEY: NIIYAMA JUNIOR
GLANCE
12 2 20
NIIYAMA JUNIOR
LITTLE FALCONS
BOM

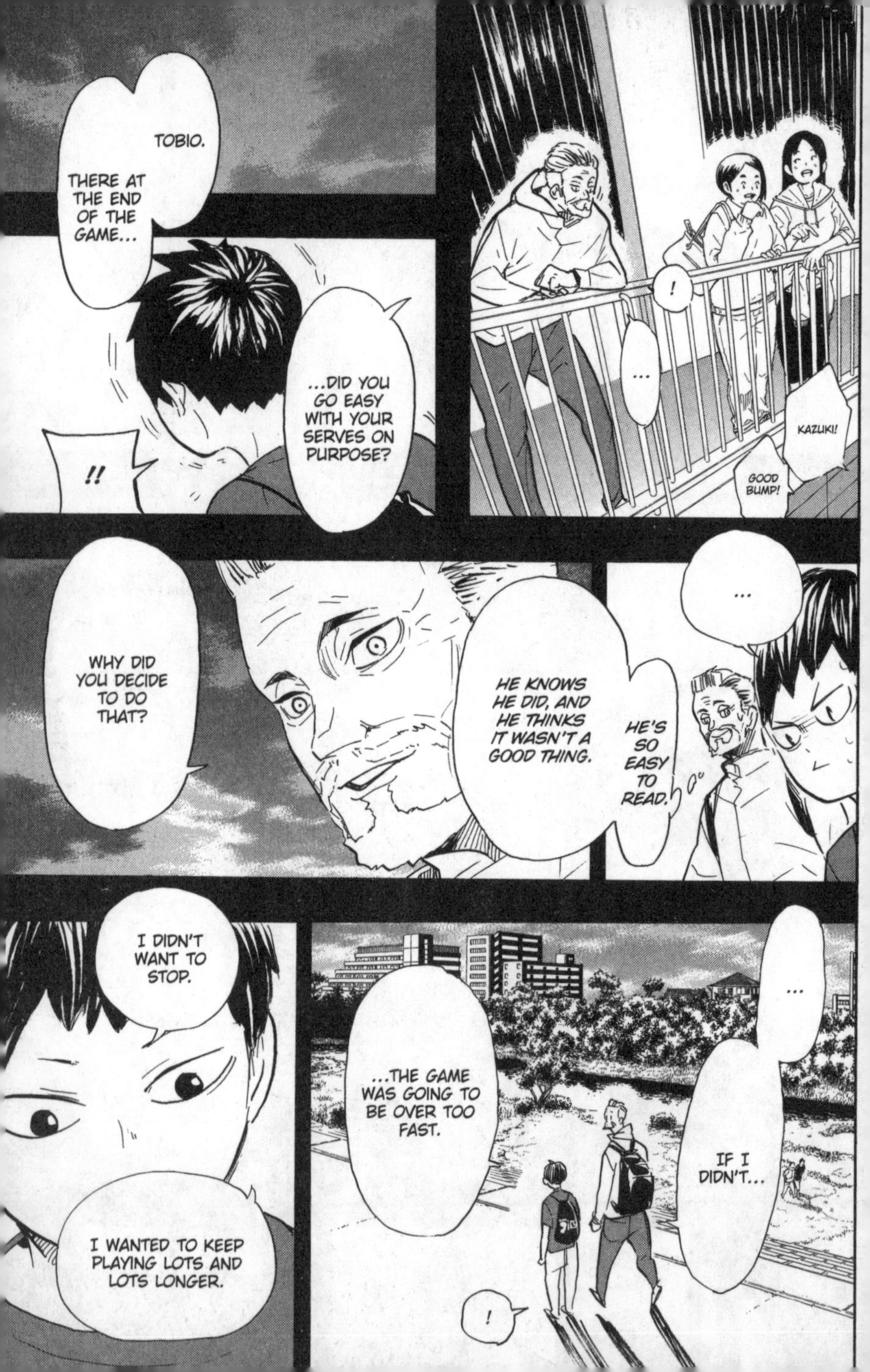
KAZUKI!
GOOD BUMP!
!
...
TOBIO.
THERE AT THE END OF THE GAME...
!!
...DID YOU GO EASY WITH YOUR SERVES ON PURPOSE?
...
HE'S SO EASY TO READ.
HE KNOWS HE DID, AND HE THINKS IT WASN'T A GOOD THING.
WHY DID YOU DECIDE TO DO THAT?
...
IF I DIDN'T...
...THE GAME WAS GOING TO BE OVER TOO FAST.
!
I DIDN'T WANT TO STOP.
I WANTED TO KEEP PLAYING LOTS AND LOTS LONGER.

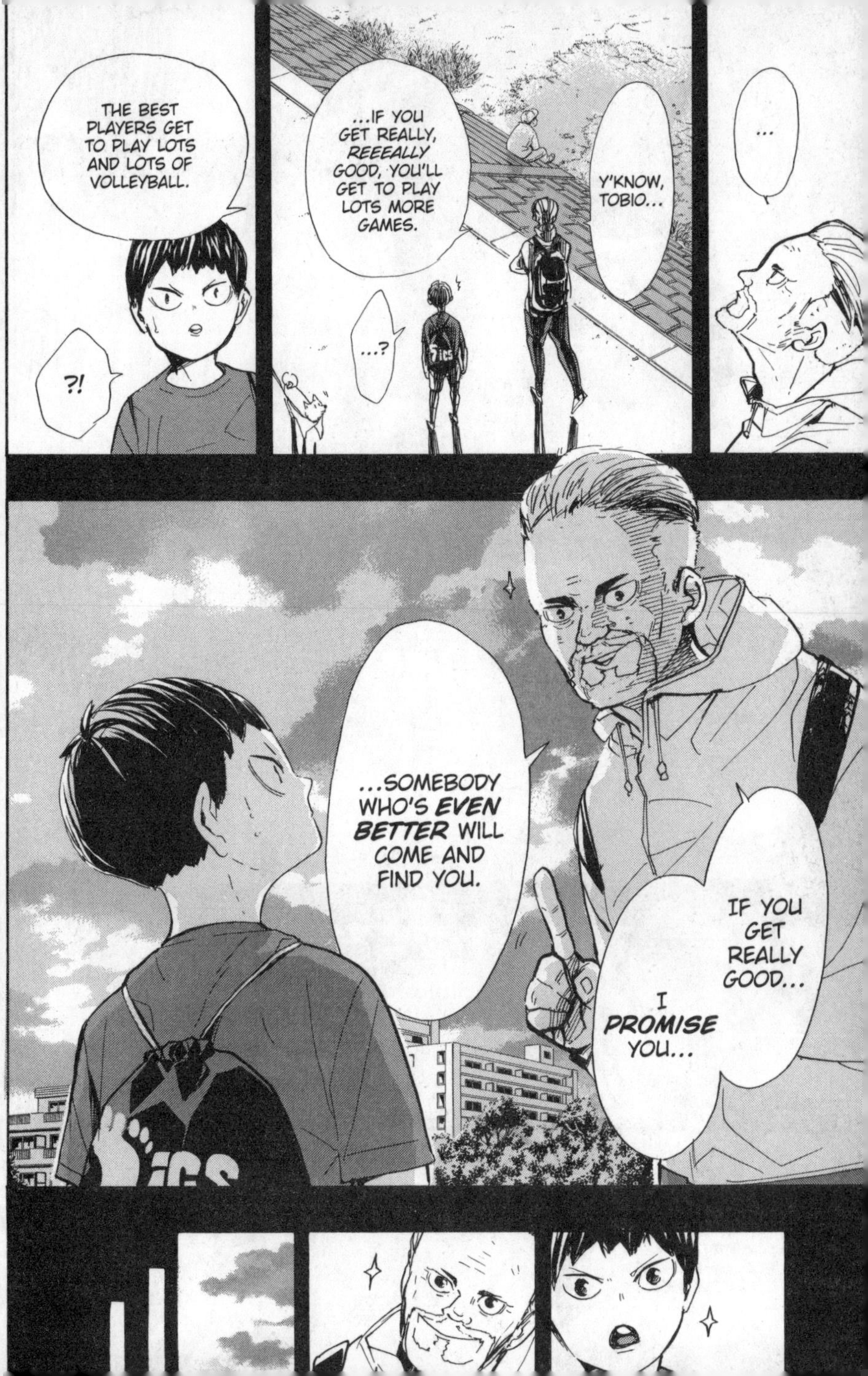
...
Y'KNOW, TOBIO...
...IF YOU GET REALLY, REEEALLY GOOD, YOU'LL GET TO PLAY LOTS MORE GAMES.
...?
THE BEST PLAYERS GET TO PLAY LOTS AND LOTS OF VOLLEYBALL.
?!
IF YOU GET REALLY GOOD...
I PROMISE YOU...
...SOMEBODY WHO'S EVEN BETTER WILL COME AND FIND YOU.

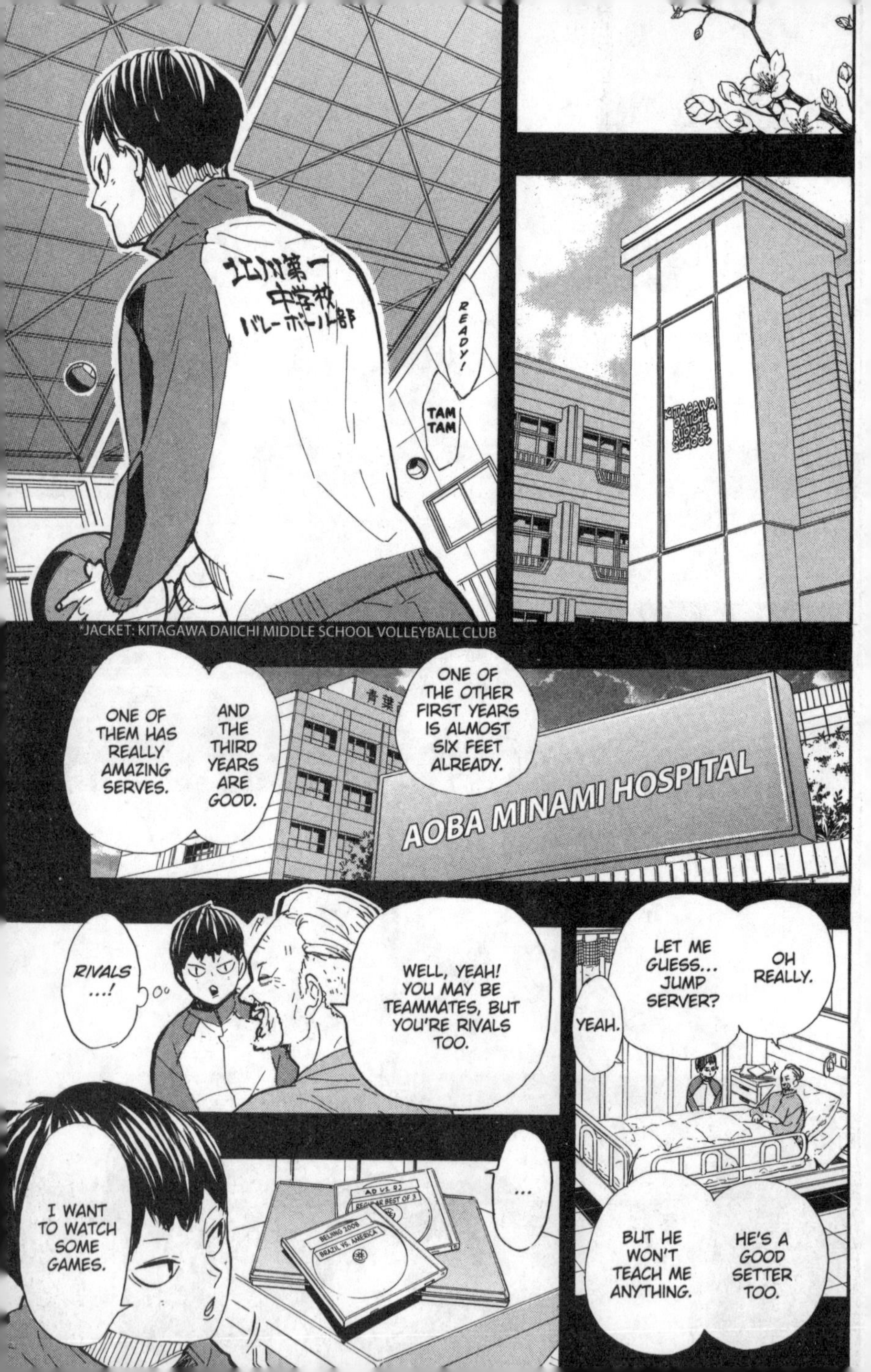
KITAGAWA DAIICHI MIDDLE SCHOOL
北川第一 中学校 バレーボール部
READY!
TAM TAM
*JACKET: KITAGAWA DAIICHI MIDDLE SCHOOL VOLLEYBALL CLUB
ONE OF THE OTHER FIRST YEARS IS ALMOST SIX FEET ALREADY.
AND THE THIRD YEARS ARE GOOD.
ONE OF THEM HAS REALLY AMAZING SERVES.
AOBA MINAMI HOSPITAL
OH REALLY.
LET ME GUESS... JUMP SERVER?
YEAH.
HE'S A GOOD SETTER TOO.
BUT HE WON'T TEACH ME ANYTHING.
WELL, YEAH! YOU MAY BE TEAMMATES, BUT YOU'RE RIVALS TOO.
RIVALS ...!
...
AD VS. BJ
REGULAR BEST OF 3
BEIJING 2008
BRAZIL VS. AMERICA
I WANT TO WATCH SOME GAMES.

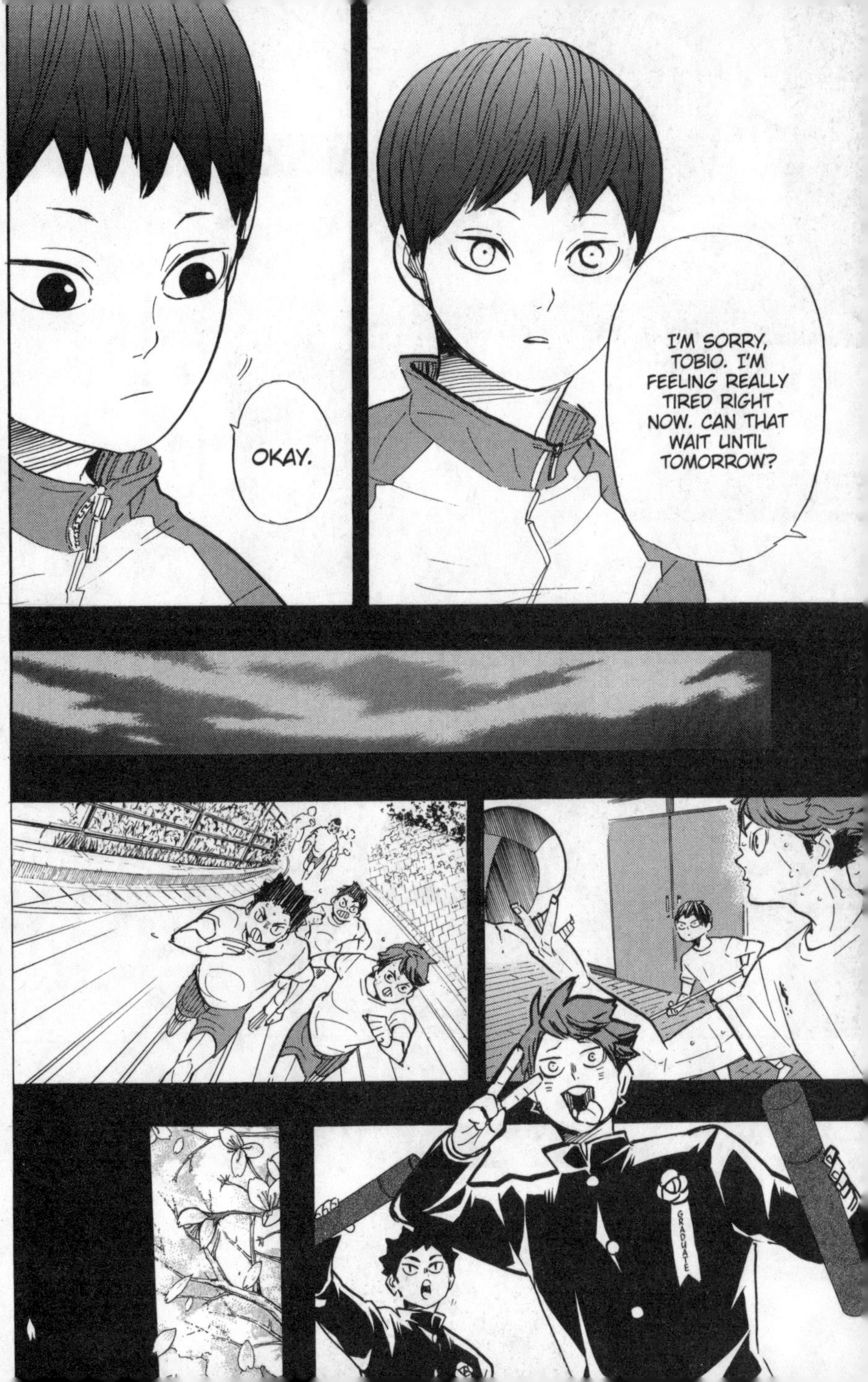
I'M SORRY, TOBIO. I'M FEELING REALLY TIRED RIGHT NOW. CAN THAT WAIT UNTIL TOMORROW?
OKAY.
GRADUATE

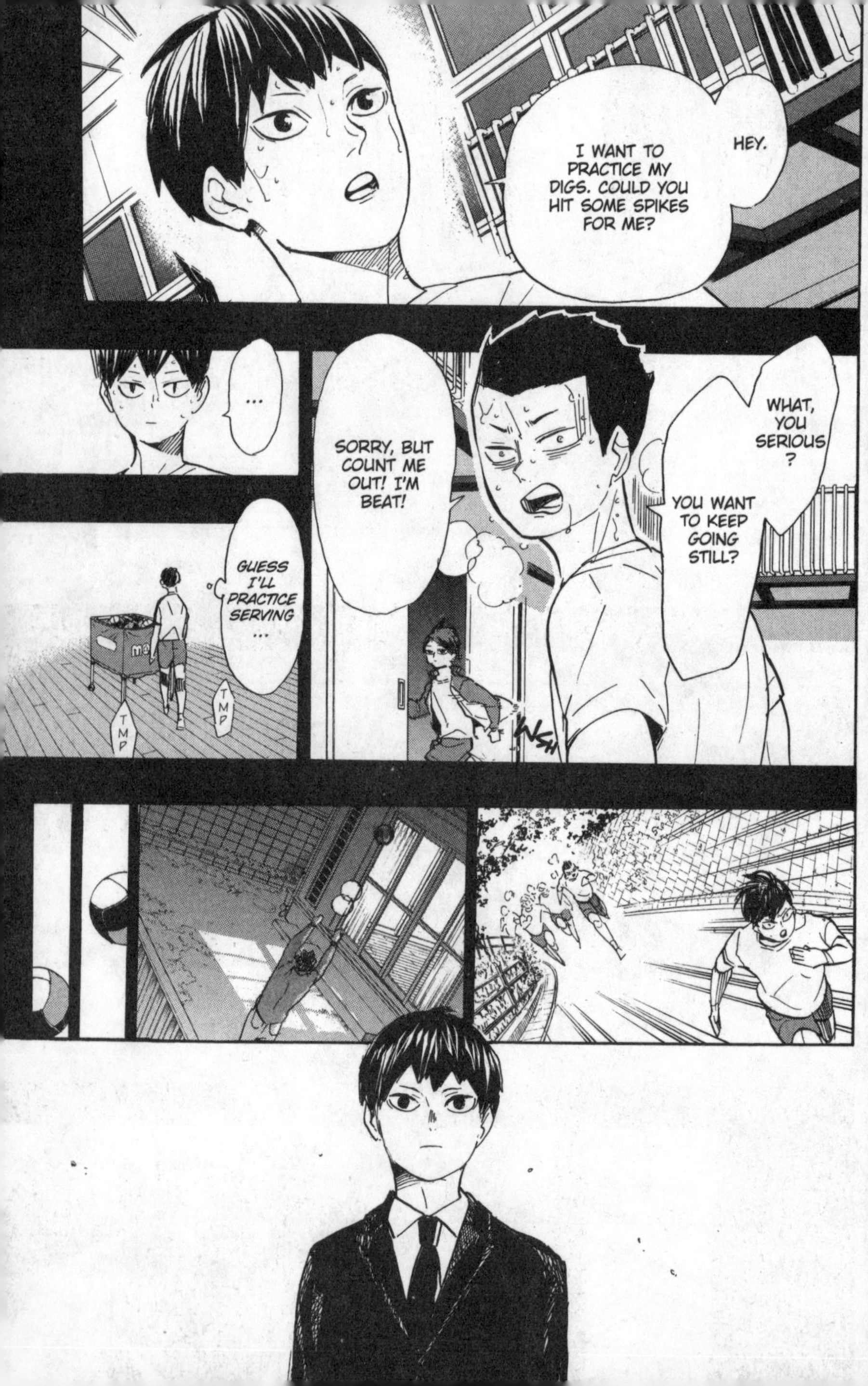
HEY.
I WANT TO PRACTICE MY DIGS. COULD YOU HIT SOME SPIKES FOR ME?
WHAT, YOU SERIOUS?
YOU WANT TO KEEP GOING STILL?
SORRY, BUT COUNT ME OUT! I'M BEAT!
WSH
...
GUESS I'LL PRACTICE SERVING...
TMP
TMP

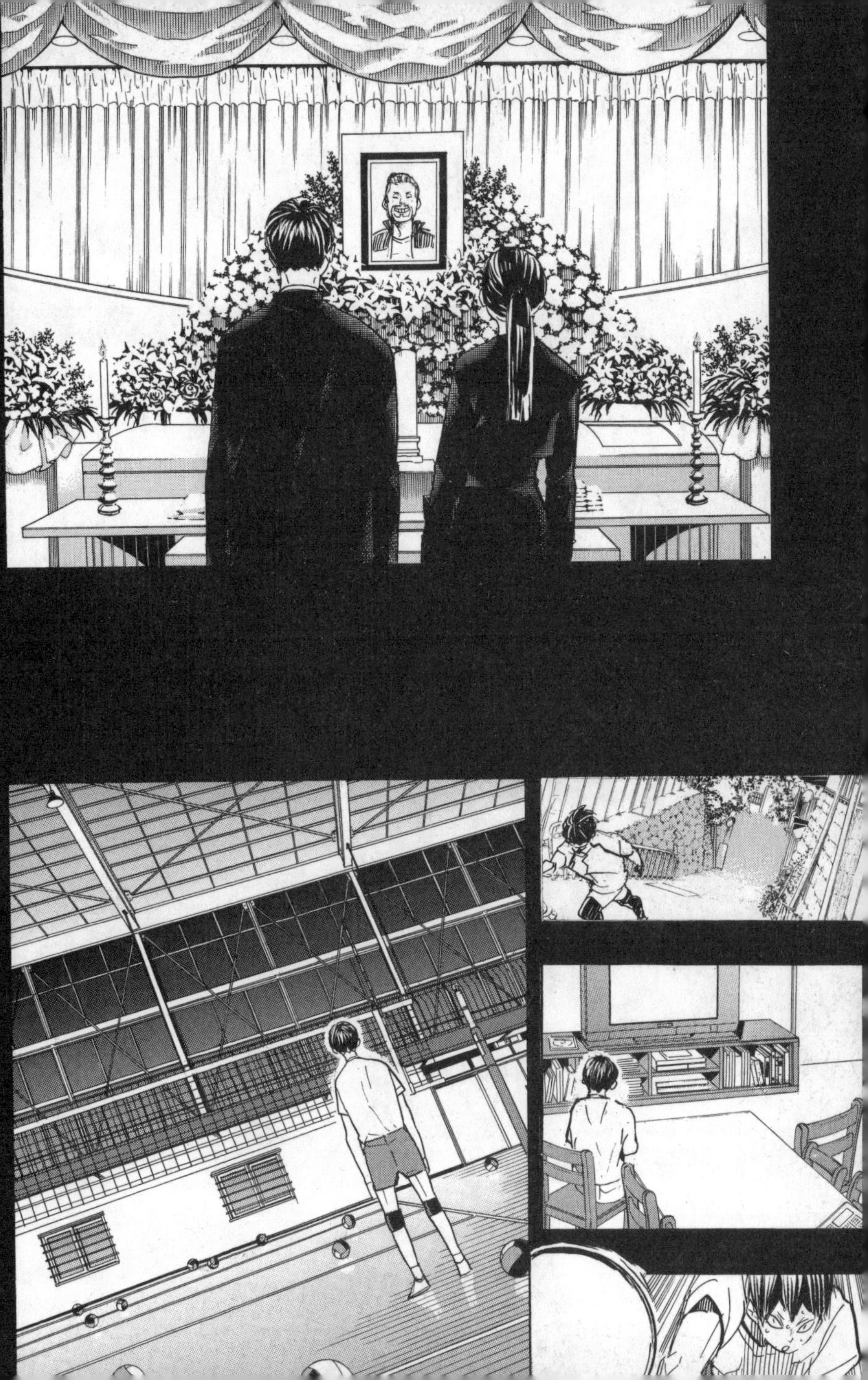

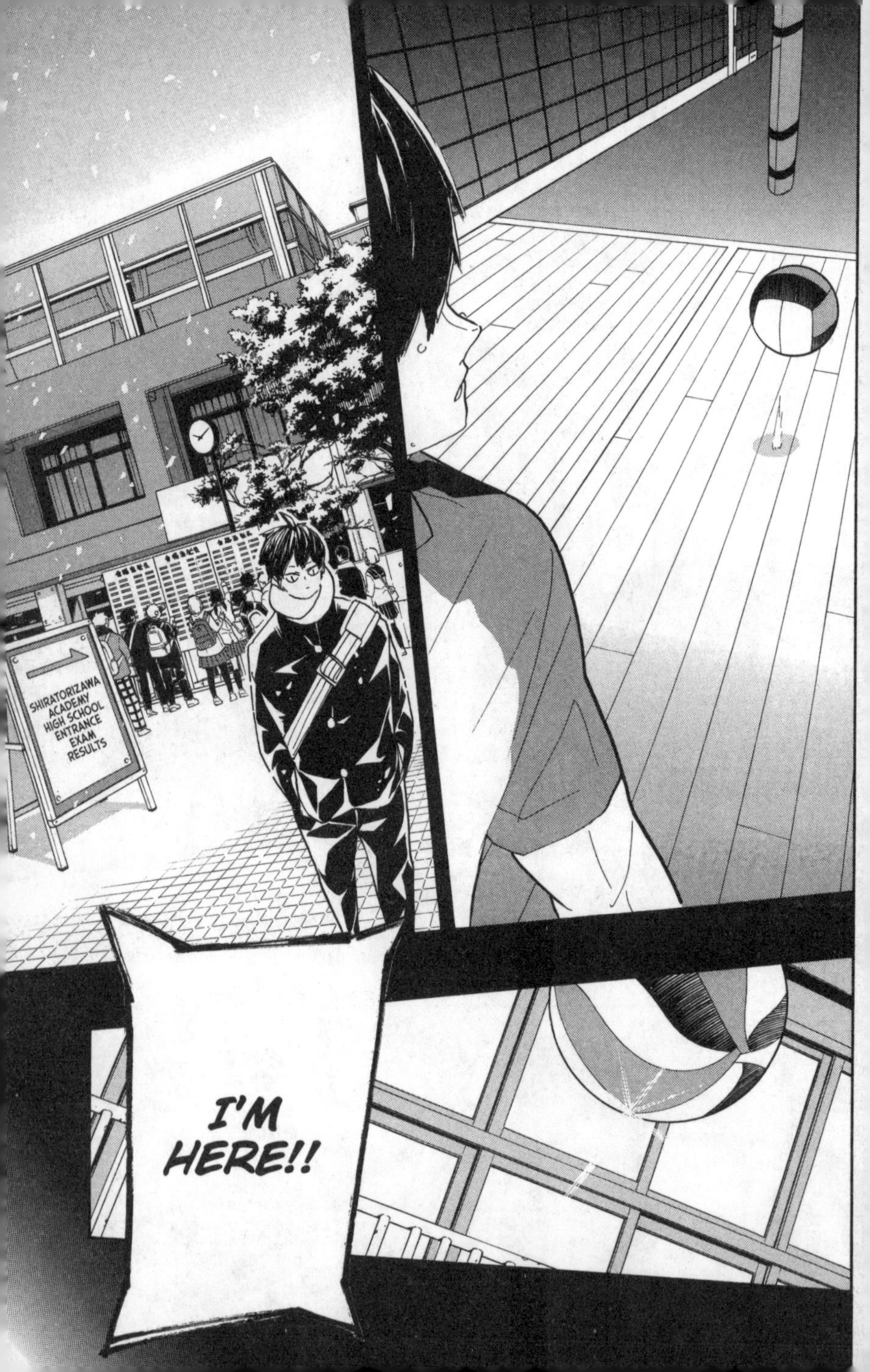
SHIRATORIZAWA ACADEMY HIGH SCHOOL ENTRANCE EXAM RESULTS
I'M HERE!!

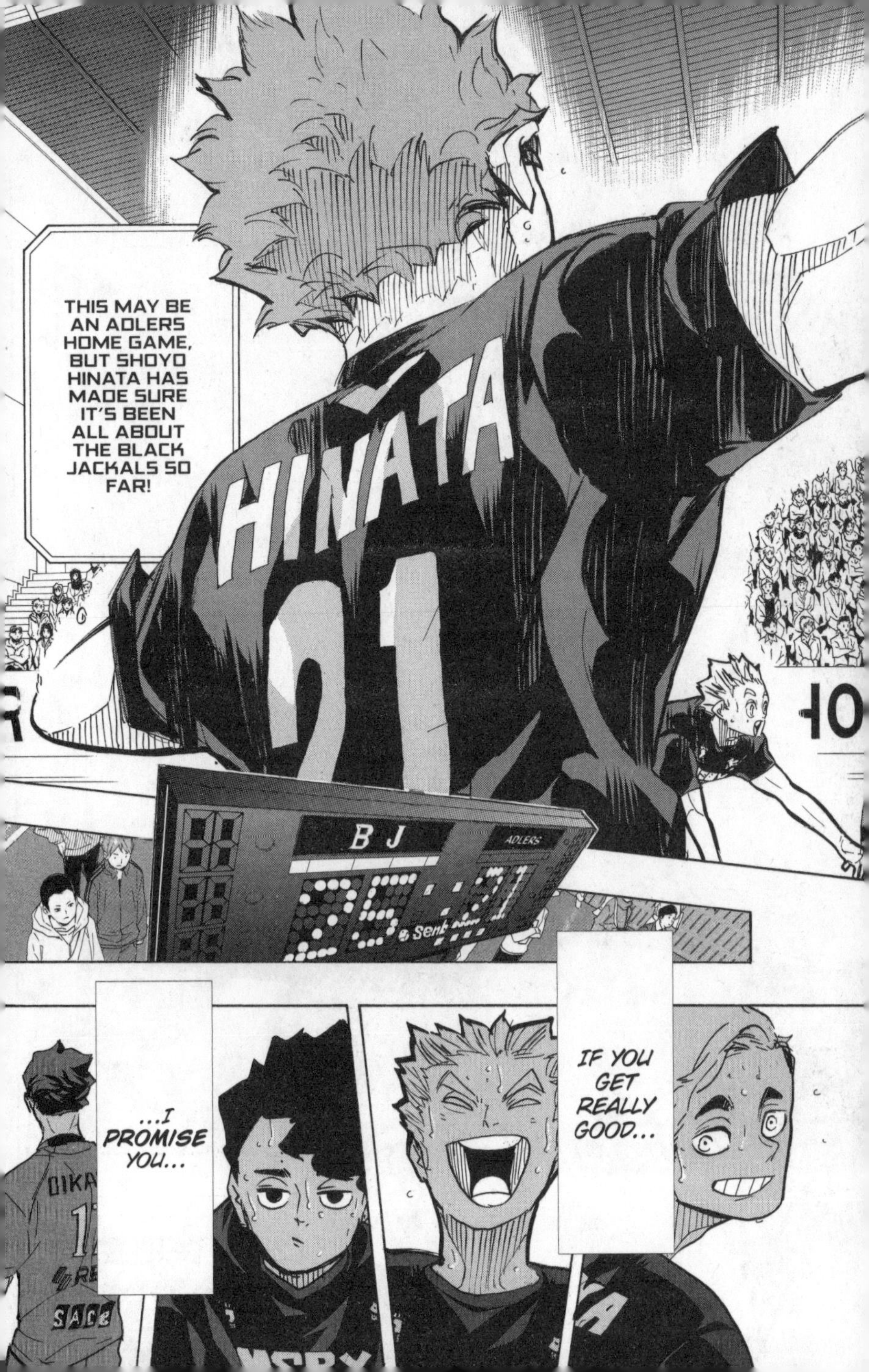
THIS MAY BE AN ADLERS HOME GAME, BUT SHOYO HINATA HAS MADE SURE IT'S BEEN ALL ABOUT THE BLACK JACKALS SO FAR!
B J
ADLERS
IF YOU GET REALLY GOOD...
...I PROMISE YOU...

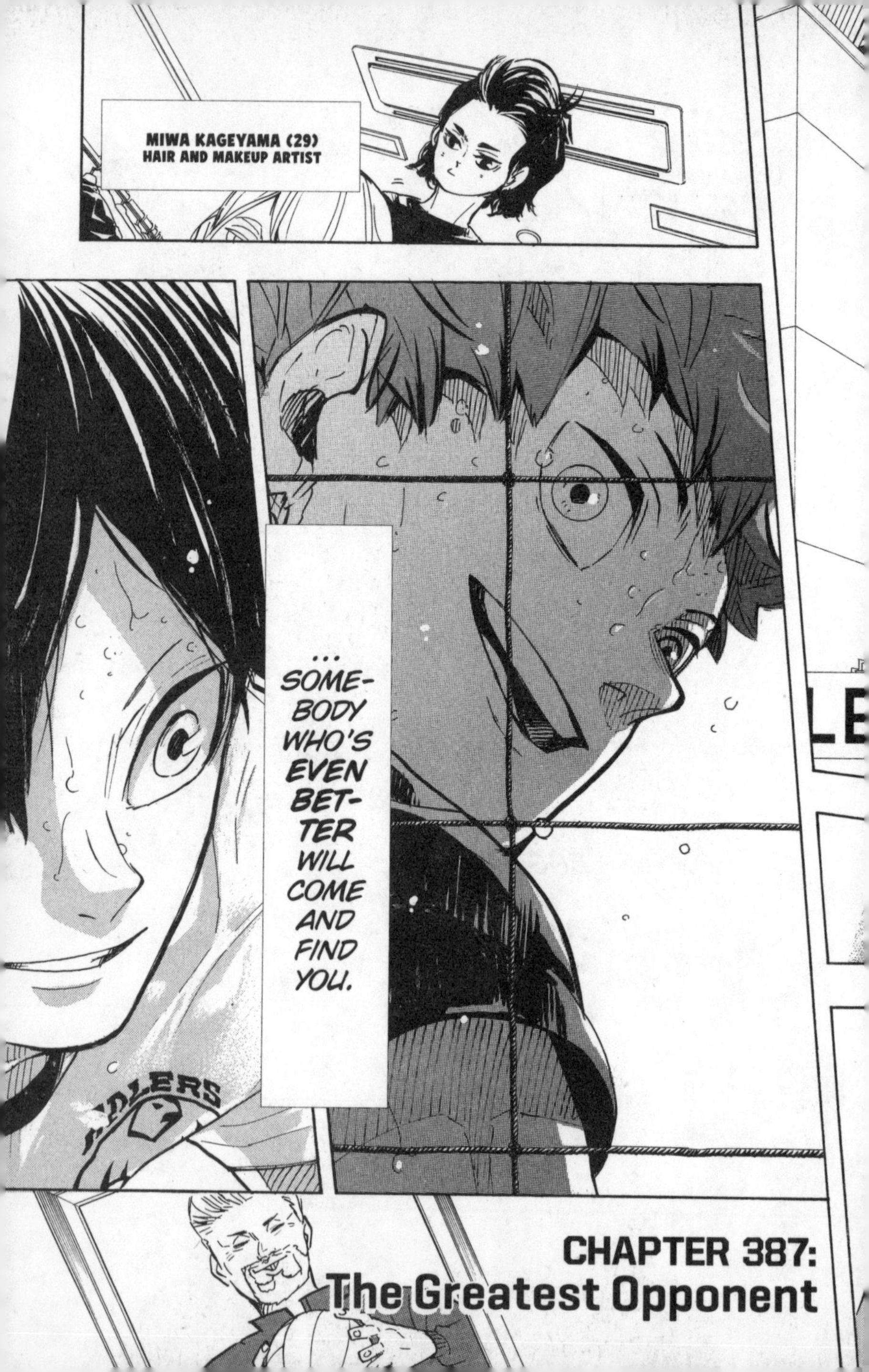
MIWA KAGEYAMA (29)
HAIR AND MAKEUP ARTIST
...SOME-BODY WHO'S EVEN BET-TER WILL COME AND FIND YOU.
CHAPTER 387:
The Greatest Opponent

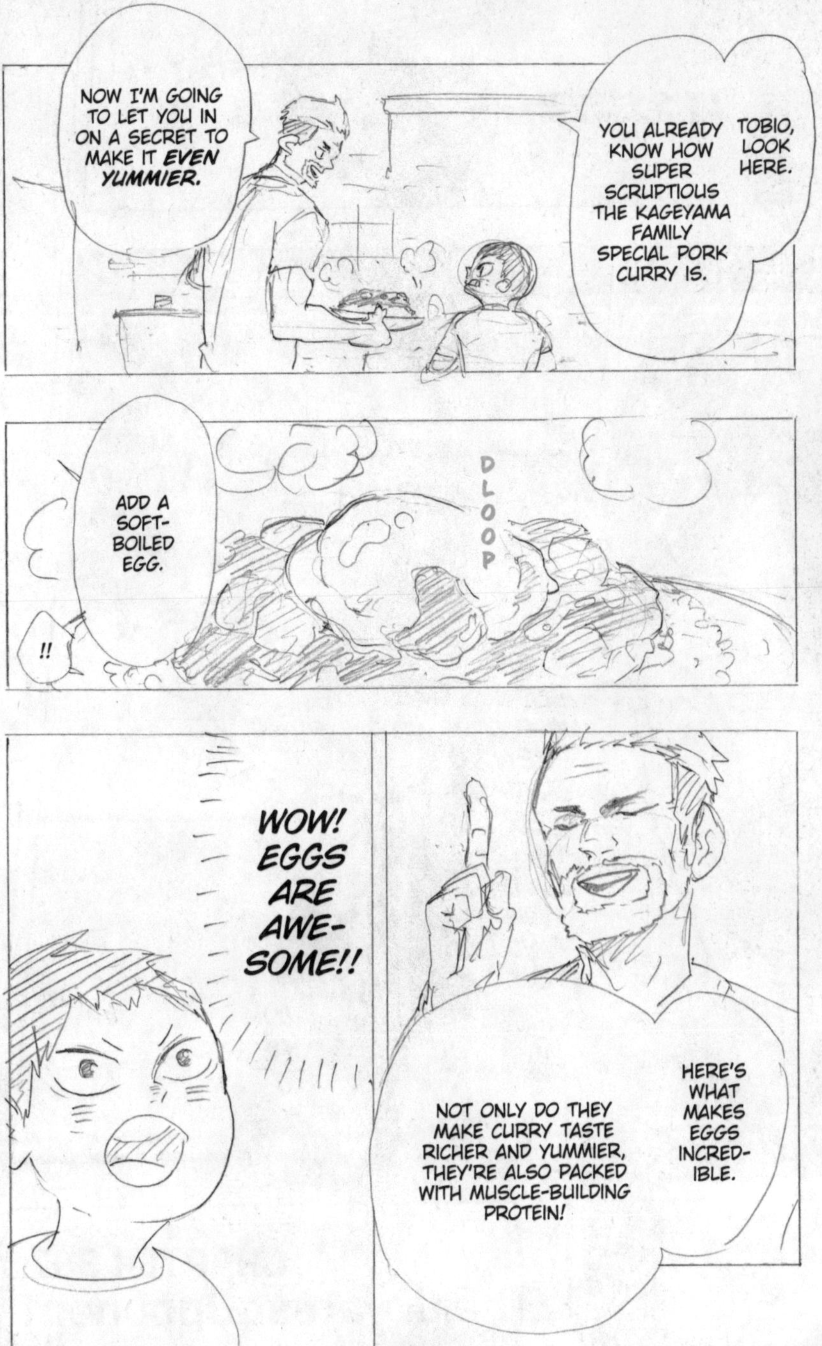
TOBIO, LOOK HERE.
YOU ALREADY KNOW HOW SUPER SCRUPTIOUS THE KAGEYAMA FAMILY SPECIAL PORK CURRY IS.
NOW I'M GOING TO LET YOU IN ON A SECRET TO MAKE IT *EVEN YUMMIER.*
DLOOP
ADD A SOFT-BOILED EGG.
!!
HERE'S WHAT MAKES EGGS INCRED-IBLE.
NOT ONLY DO THEY MAKE CURRY TASTE RICHER AND YUMMIER, THEY'RE ALSO PACKED WITH MUSCLE-BUILDING PROTEIN!
WOW! EGGS ARE AWE-SOME!!

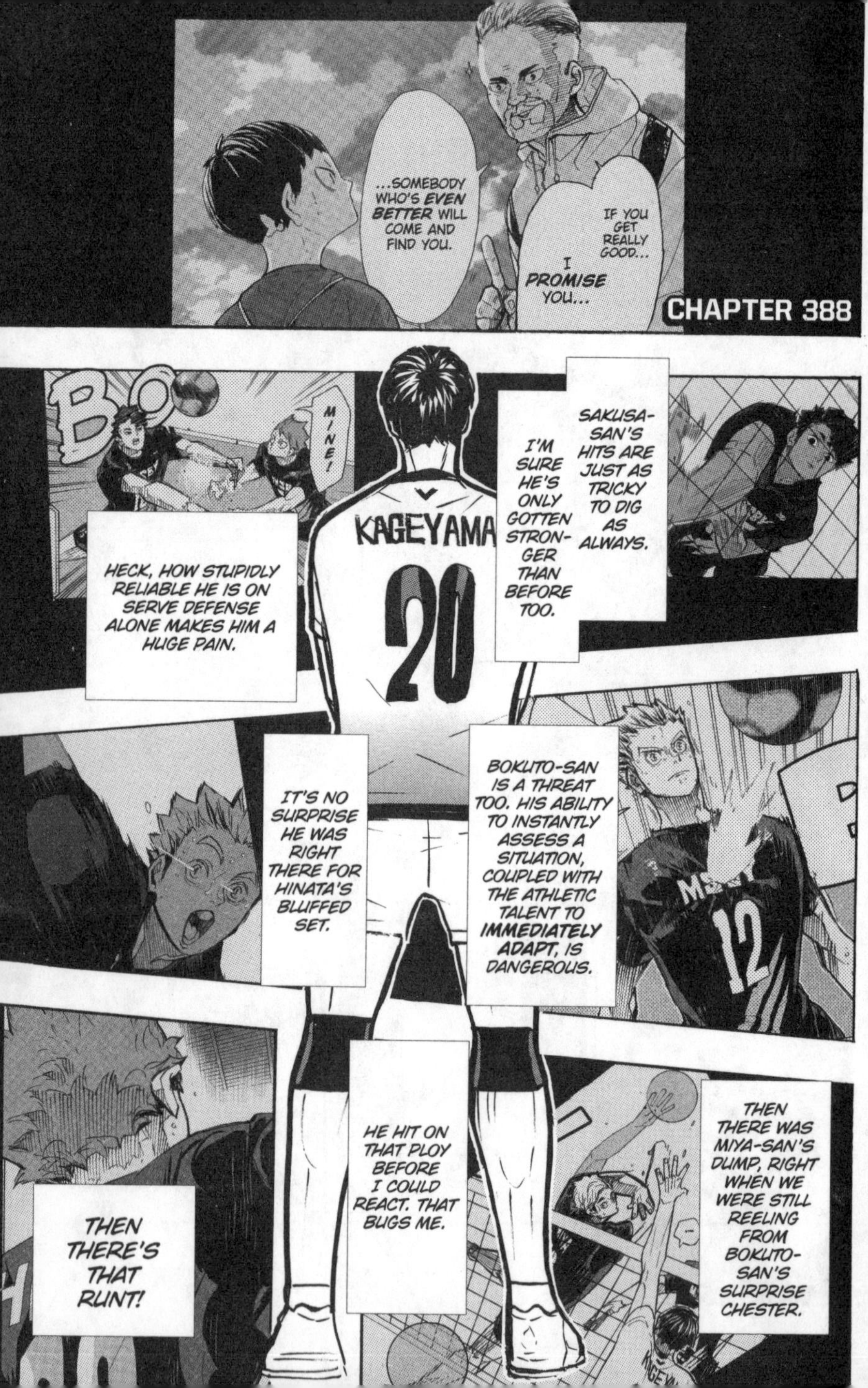
CHAPTER 388
IF YOU GET REALLY GOOD...
I PROMISE YOU...
...SOMEBODY WHO'S EVEN BETTER WILL COME AND FIND YOU.
SAKUSA-SAN'S HITS ARE JUST AS TRICKY TO DIG AS ALWAYS.
I'M SURE HE'S ONLY GOTTEN STRONGER THAN BEFORE TOO.
KAGEYAMA
20
BO
MINE!
HECK, HOW STUPIDLY RELIABLE HE IS ON SERVE DEFENSE ALONE MAKES HIM A HUGE PAIN.
BOKUTO-SAN IS A THREAT TOO. HIS ABILITY TO INSTANTLY ASSESS A SITUATION, COUPLED WITH THE ATHLETIC TALENT TO IMMEDIATELY ADAPT, IS DANGEROUS.
12
IT'S NO SURPRISE HE WAS RIGHT THERE FOR HINATA'S BLUFFED SET.
THEN THERE WAS MIYA-SAN'S DUMP, RIGHT WHEN WE WERE STILL REELING FROM BOKUTO-SAN'S SURPRISE CHESTER.
HE HIT ON THAT PLOY BEFORE I COULD REACT. THAT BUGS ME.
THEN THERE'S THAT RUNT!

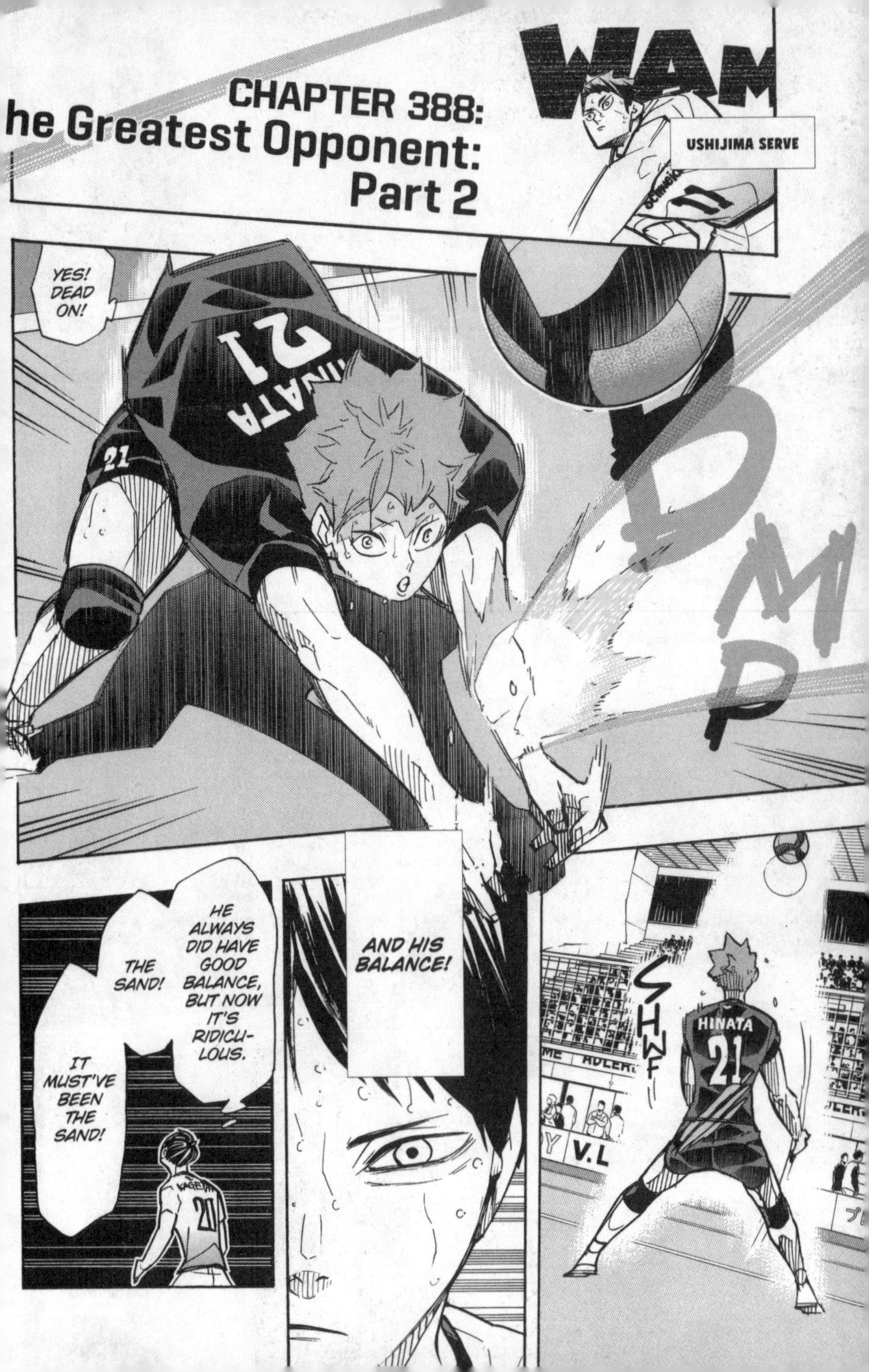
CHAPTER 388:
he Greatest Opponent:
Part 2
WAM
USHIJIMA SERVE
DMP
YES! DEAD ON!
SHWF
AND HIS BALANCE!
HE ALWAYS DID HAVE GOOD BALANCE, BUT NOW IT'S RIDICULOUS.
THE SAND!
IT MUST'VE BEEN THE SAND!

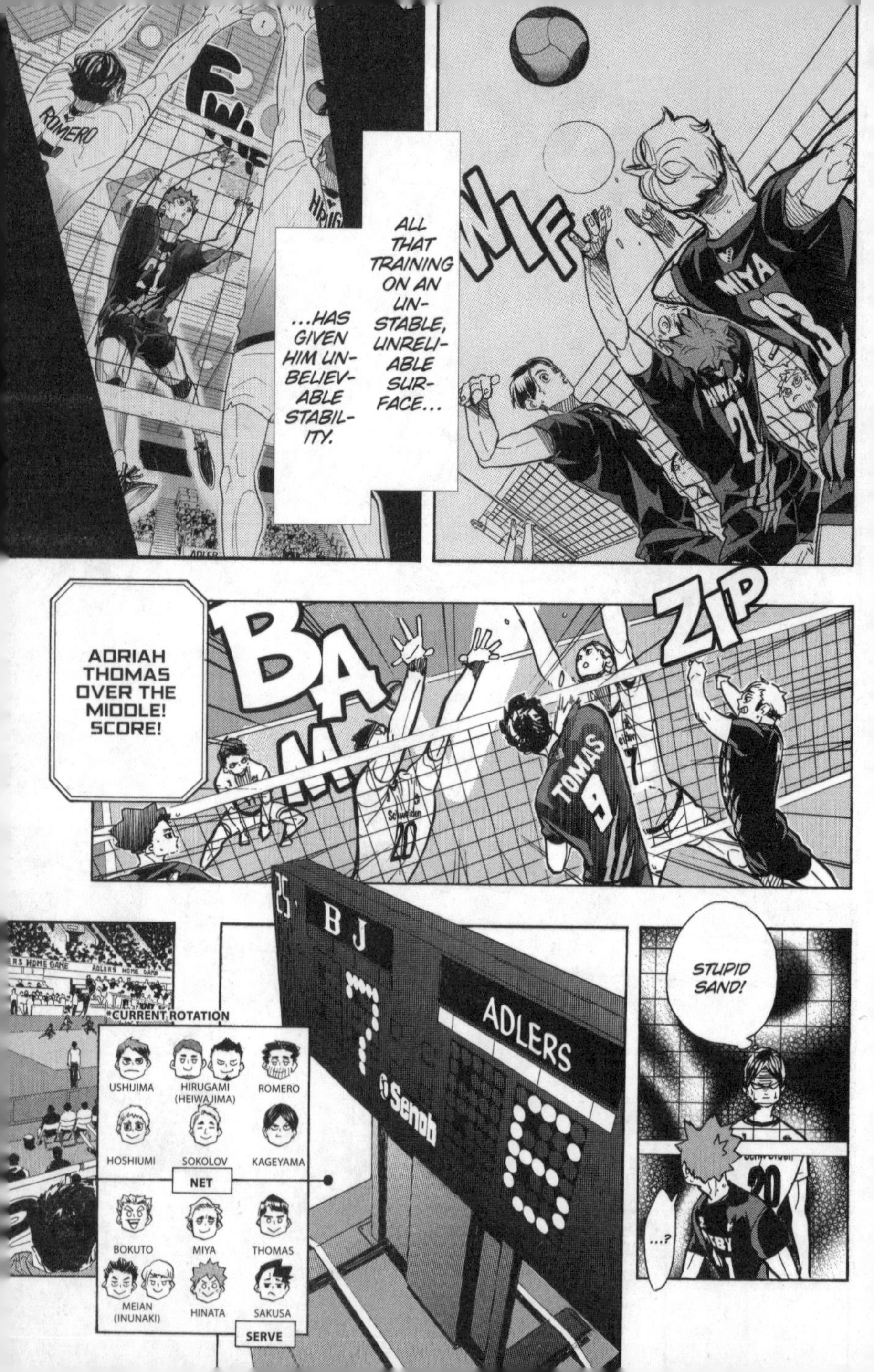

WIF
ALL THAT TRAINING ON AN UN-STABLE, UNRELI-ABLE SUR-FACE...
...HAS GIVEN HIM UN-BELIEV-ABLE STABIL-ITY.
MIYA
ROMERO
ZIP
BAM
ADRIAH THOMAS OVER THE MIDDLE! SCORE!
TOMAS
STUPID SAND!
...?
BJ
ADLERS
Senoh
*CURRENT ROTATION
USHIJIMA
HIRUGAMI (HEIWAJIMA)
ROMERO
HOSHIUMI
SOKOLOV
KAGEYAMA
NET
BOKUTO
MIYA
THOMAS
MEIAN (INUNAKI)
HINATA
SAKUSA
SERVE

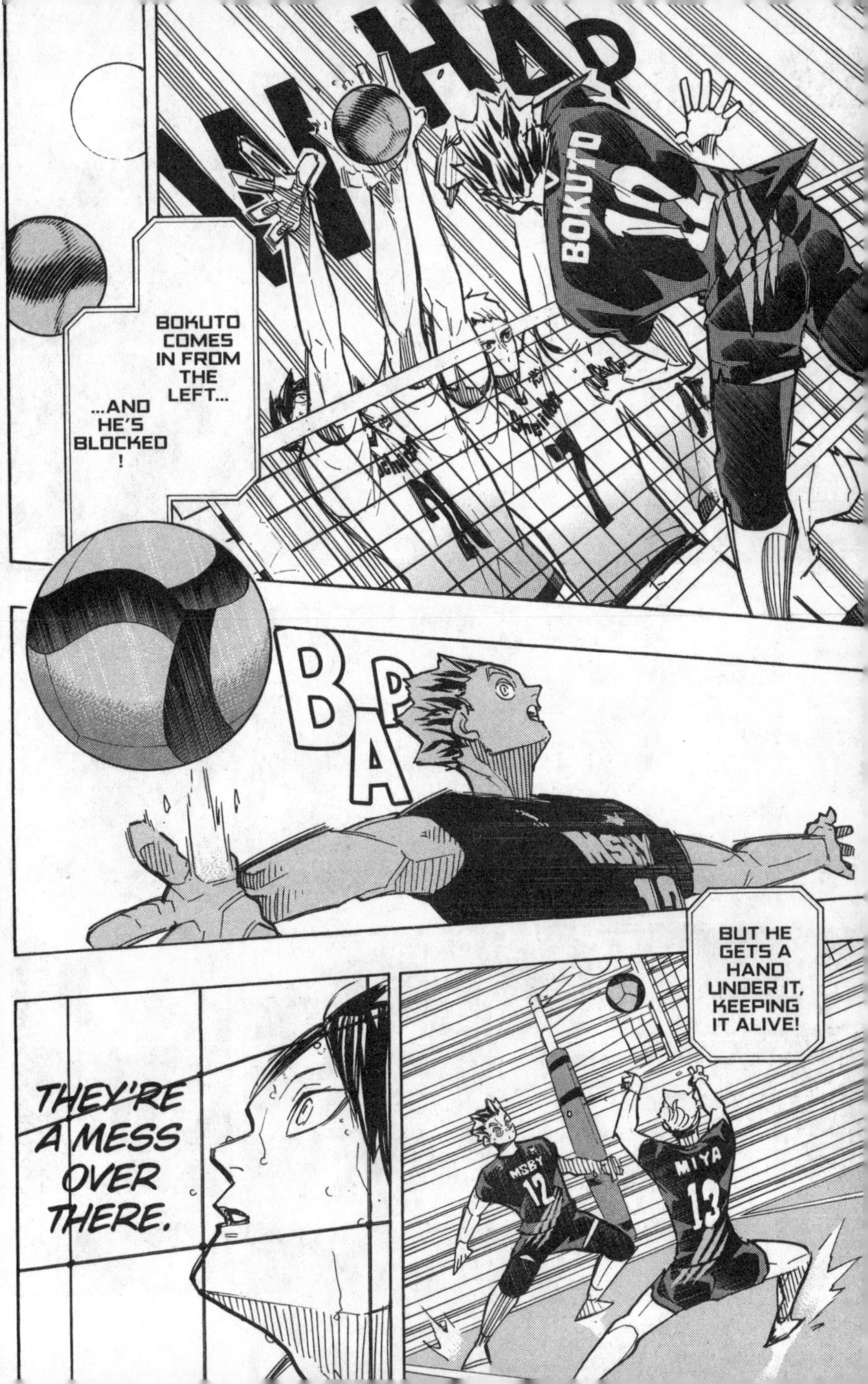
WHAP
BOKUTO COMES IN FROM THE LEFT...
...AND HE'S BLOCKED!
BAP
BUT HE GETS A HAND UNDER IT, KEEPING IT ALIVE!
THEY'RE A MESS OVER THERE.

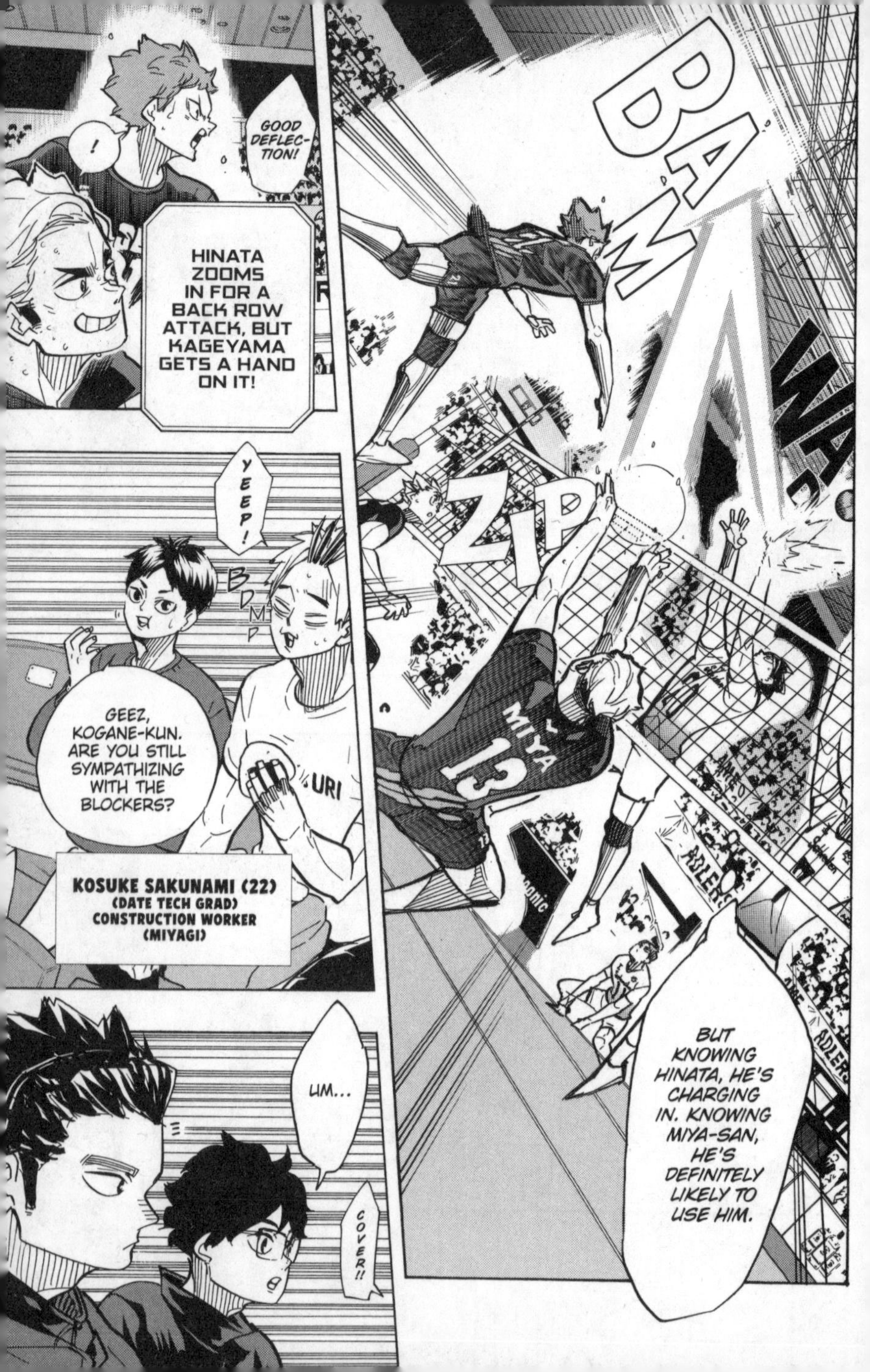
BAM
WA
ZIP
BUT KNOWING HINATA, HE'S CHARGING IN. KNOWING MIYA-SAN, HE'S DEFINITELY LIKELY TO USE HIM.
GOOD DEFLECTION!
!
HINATA ZOOMS IN FOR A BACK ROW ATTACK, BUT KAGEYAMA GETS A HAND ON IT!
YEEP!
BDMP
GEEZ, KOGANE-KUN. ARE YOU STILL SYMPATHIZING WITH THE BLOCKERS?
KOSUKE SAKUNAMI (22) (DATE TECH GRAD) CONSTRUCTION WORKER (MIYAGI)
UM...
COVER!!

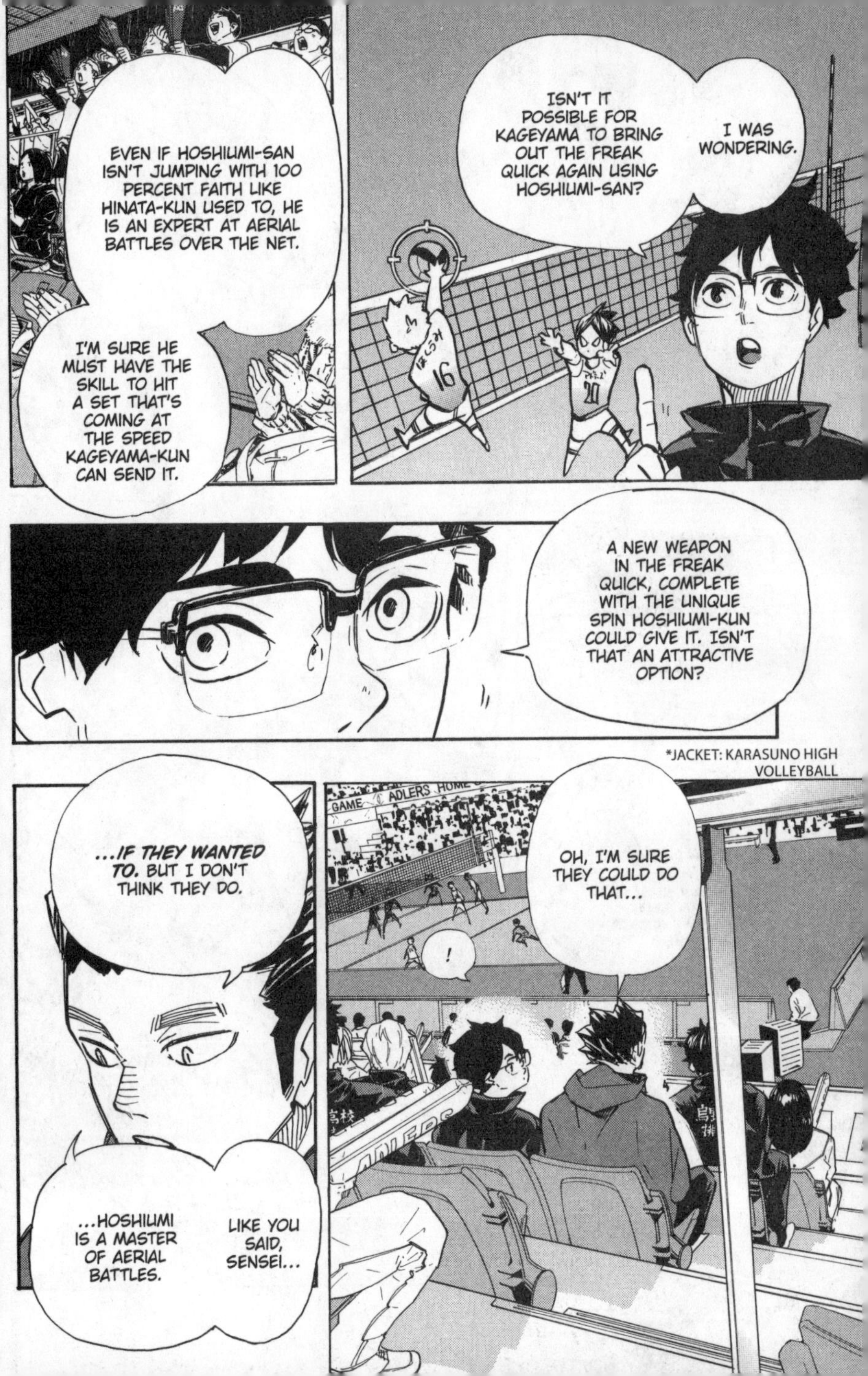

I WAS WONDERING.
ISN'T IT POSSIBLE FOR KAGEYAMA TO BRING OUT THE FREAK QUICK AGAIN USING HOSHIUMI-SAN?
EVEN IF HOSHIUMI-SAN ISN'T JUMPING WITH 100 PERCENT FAITH LIKE HINATA-KUN USED TO, HE IS AN EXPERT AT AERIAL BATTLES OVER THE NET.
I'M SURE HE MUST HAVE THE SKILL TO HIT A SET THAT'S COMING AT THE SPEED KAGEYAMA-KUN CAN SEND IT.
A NEW WEAPON IN THE FREAK QUICK, COMPLETE WITH THE UNIQUE SPIN HOSHIUMI-KUN COULD GIVE IT. ISN'T THAT AN ATTRACTIVE OPTION?
*JACKET: KARASUNO HIGH VOLLEYBALL
OH, I'M SURE THEY COULD DO THAT...
!
...IF THEY WANTED TO. BUT I DON'T THINK THEY DO.
LIKE YOU SAID, SENSEI...
...HOSHIUMI IS A MASTER OF AERIAL BATTLES.

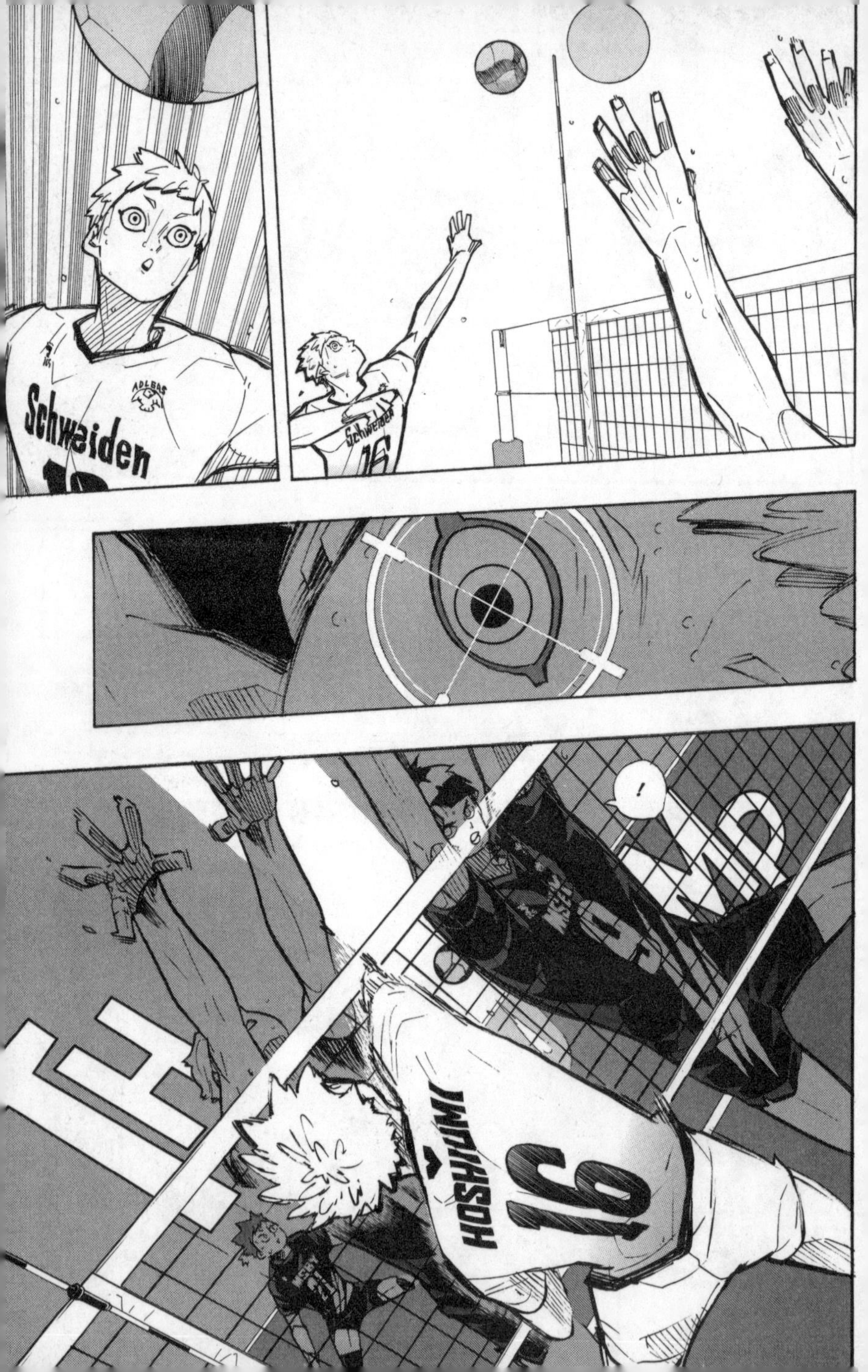
Schweiden
!

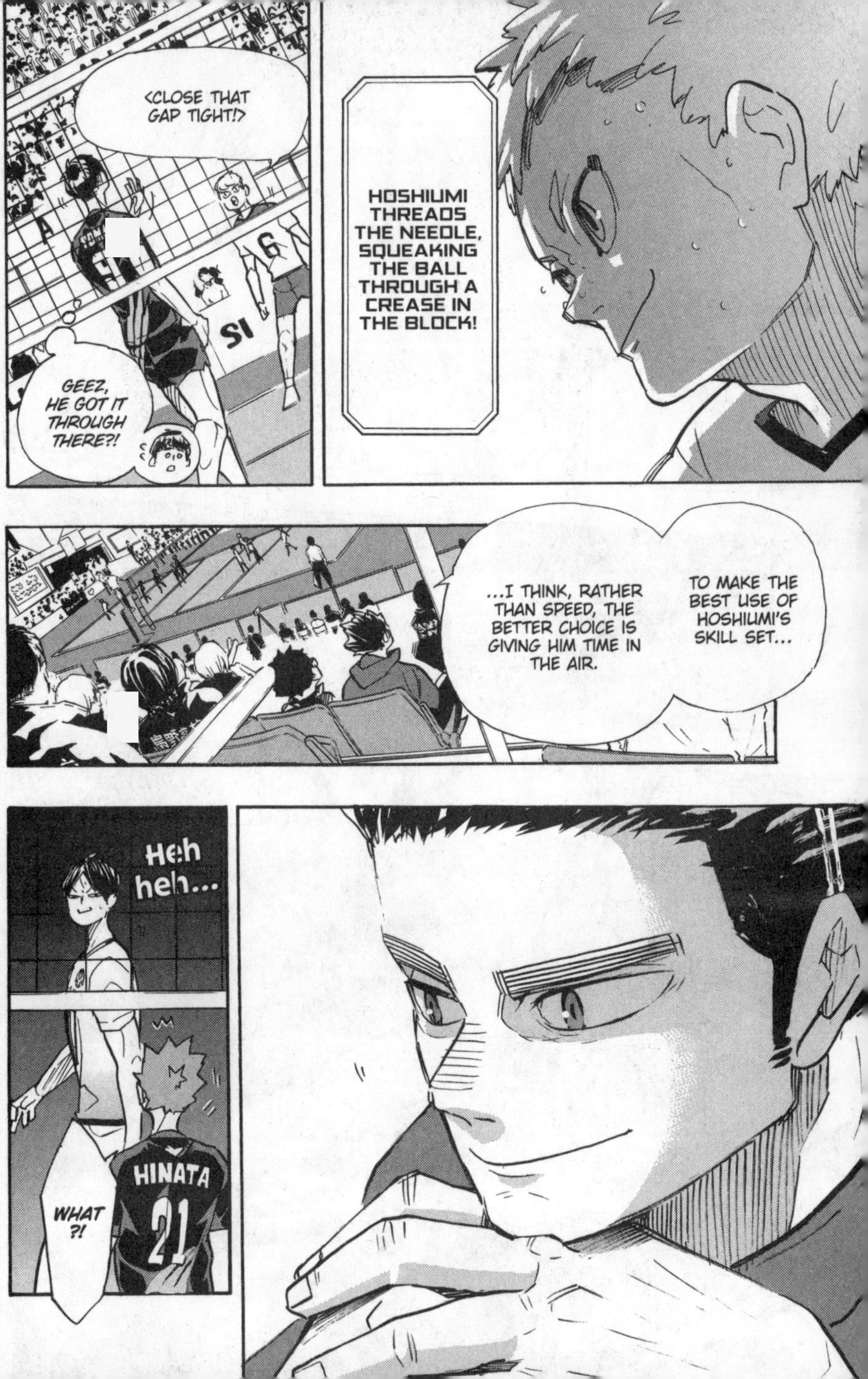
HOSHIUMI THREADS THE NEEDLE, SQUEAKING THE BALL THROUGH A CREASE IN THE BLOCK!
<CLOSE THAT GAP TIGHT!>
GEEZ, HE GOT IT THROUGH THERE?!
TO MAKE THE BEST USE OF HOSHIUMI'S SKILL SET...
...I THINK, RATHER THAN SPEED, THE BETTER CHOICE IS GIVING HIM TIME IN THE AIR.
Heh heh...
HINATA
21
WHAT ?!

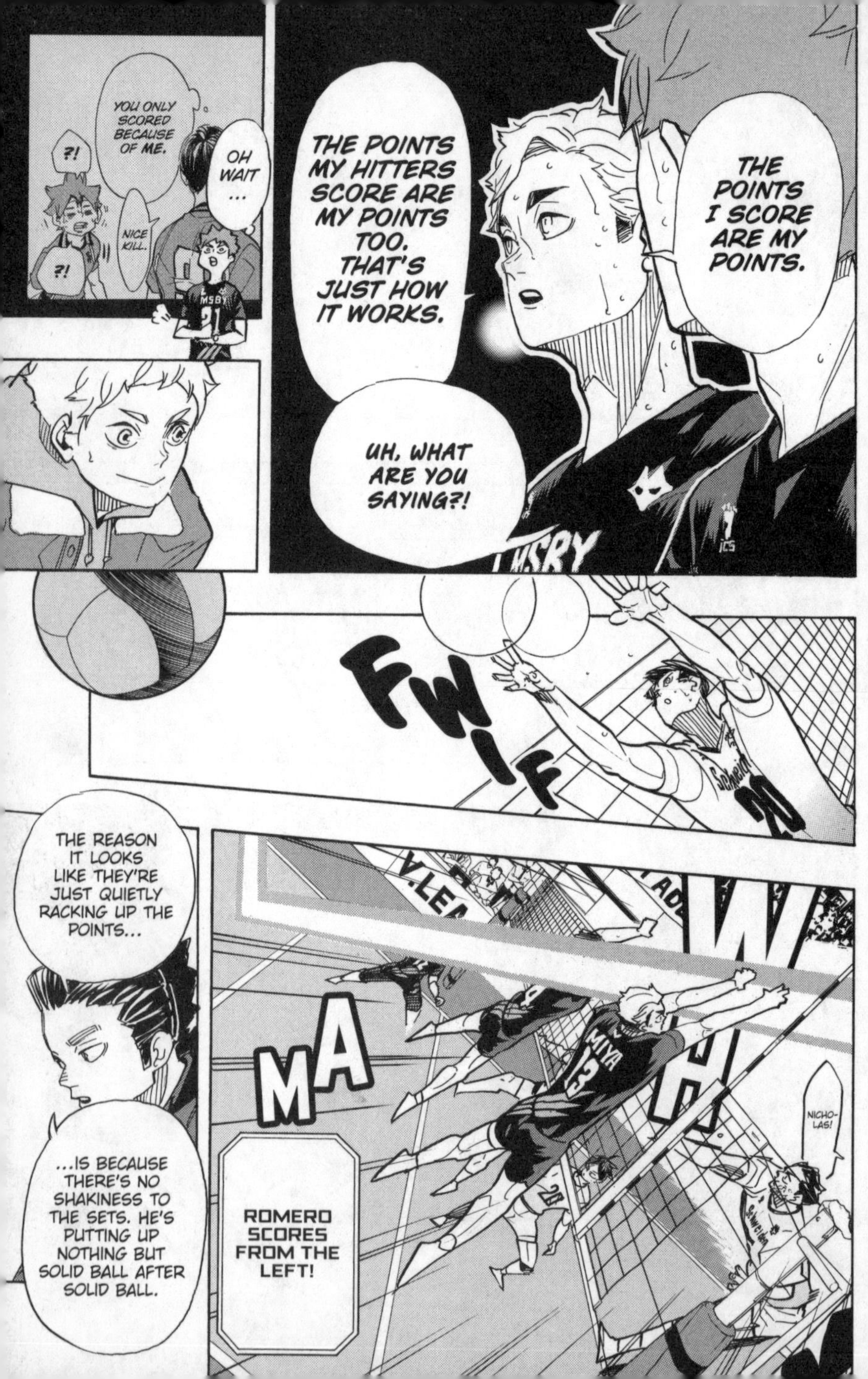
THE POINTS I SCORE ARE MY POINTS.
THE POINTS MY HITTERS SCORE ARE MY POINTS TOO. THAT'S JUST HOW IT WORKS.
UH, WHAT ARE YOU SAYING?!
YOU ONLY SCORED BECAUSE OF ME.
OH WAIT ...
NICE KILL.
?!
?!
FWIF
WHAM
NICHO-LAS!
ROMERO SCORES FROM THE LEFT!
THE REASON IT LOOKS LIKE THEY'RE JUST QUIETLY RACKING UP THE POINTS...
...IS BECAUSE THERE'S NO SHAKINESS TO THE SETS. HE'S PUTTING UP NOTHING BUT SOLID BALL AFTER SOLID BALL.

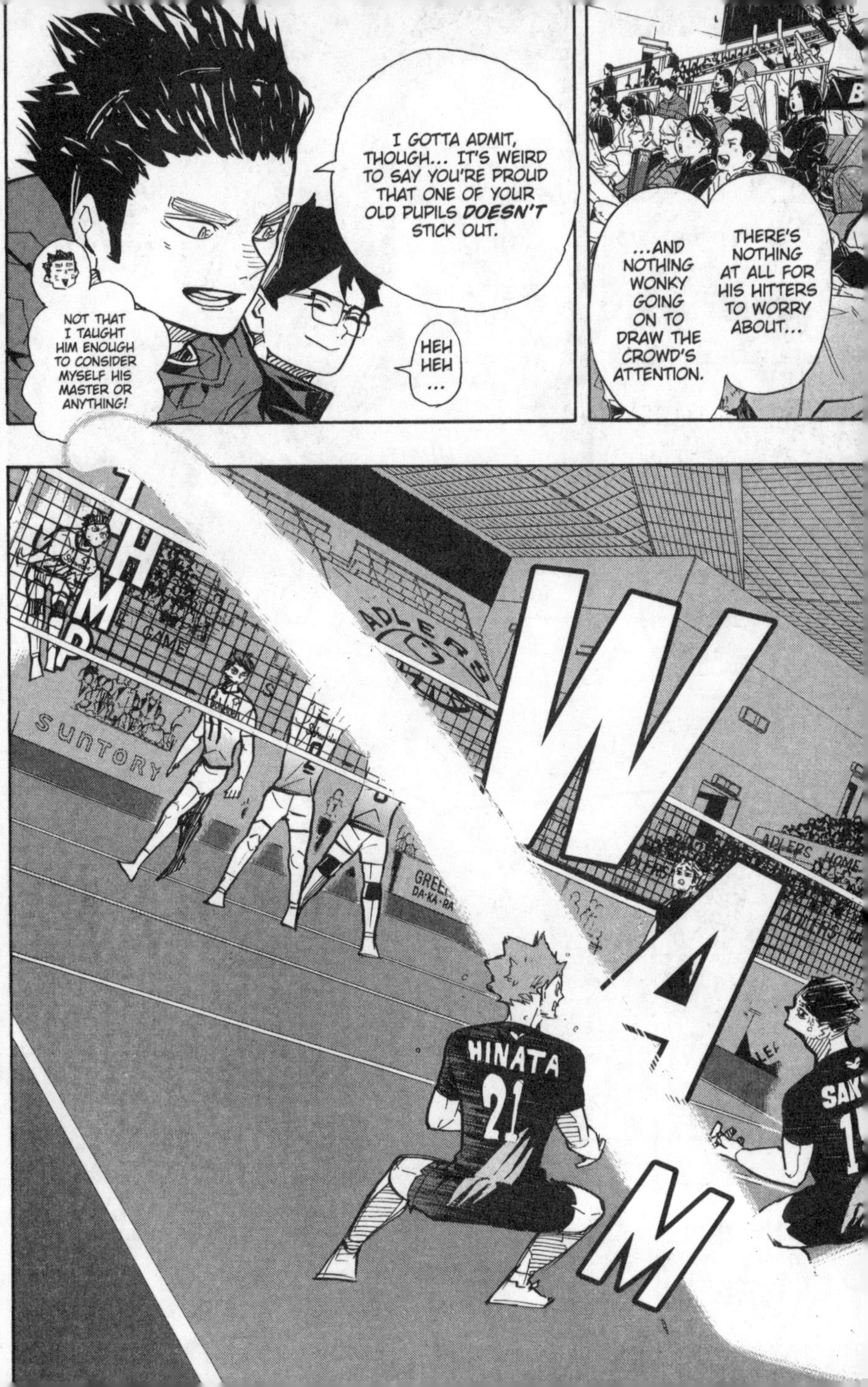
THERE'S NOTHING AT ALL FOR HIS HITTERS TO WORRY ABOUT...
...AND NOTHING WONKY GOING ON TO DRAW THE CROWD'S ATTENTION.
I GOTTA ADMIT, THOUGH... IT'S WEIRD TO SAY YOU'RE PROUD THAT ONE OF YOUR OLD PUPILS DOESN'T STICK OUT.
HEH HEH ...
NOT THAT I TAUGHT HIM ENOUGH TO CONSIDER MYSELF HIS MASTER OR ANYTHING!
THUMP
WHAM
ADLERS
SUNTORY
GREEN DA-KA-RA
HINATA
21

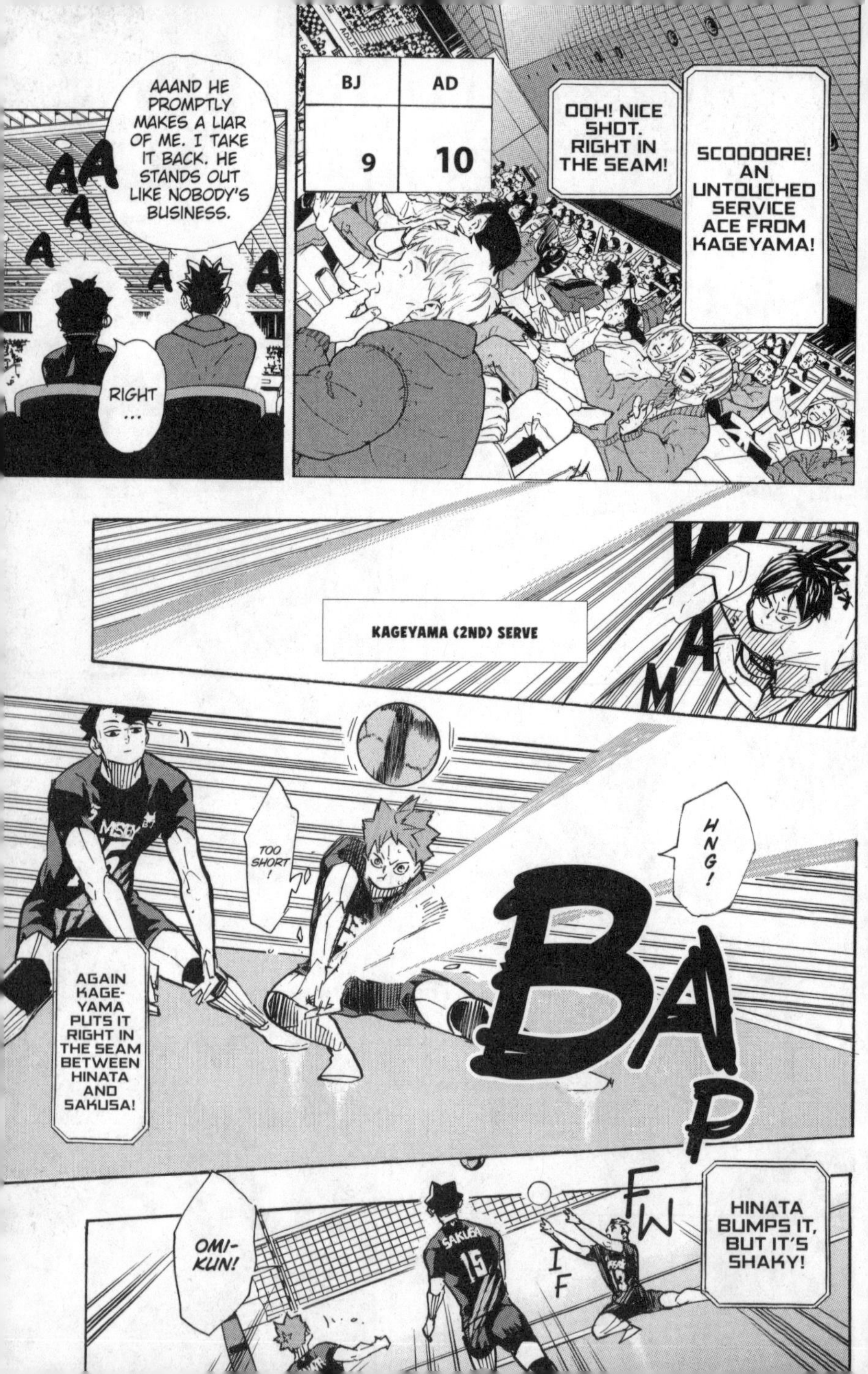
BJ 9
AD 10
SCOOOORE! AN UNTOUCHED SERVICE ACE FROM KAGEYAMA!
OOH! NICE SHOT. RIGHT IN THE SEAM!
AAAND HE PROMPTLY MAKES A LIAR OF ME. I TAKE IT BACK. HE STANDS OUT LIKE NOBODY'S BUSINESS.
AAAAAAA
RIGHT...
WHAM
KAGEYAMA (2ND) SERVE
HNG!
TOO SHORT!
AGAIN KAGEYAMA PUTS IT RIGHT IN THE SEAM BETWEEN HINATA AND SAKUSA!
BAP
HINATA BUMPS IT, BUT IT'S SHAKY!
FWIF
OMI-KUN!

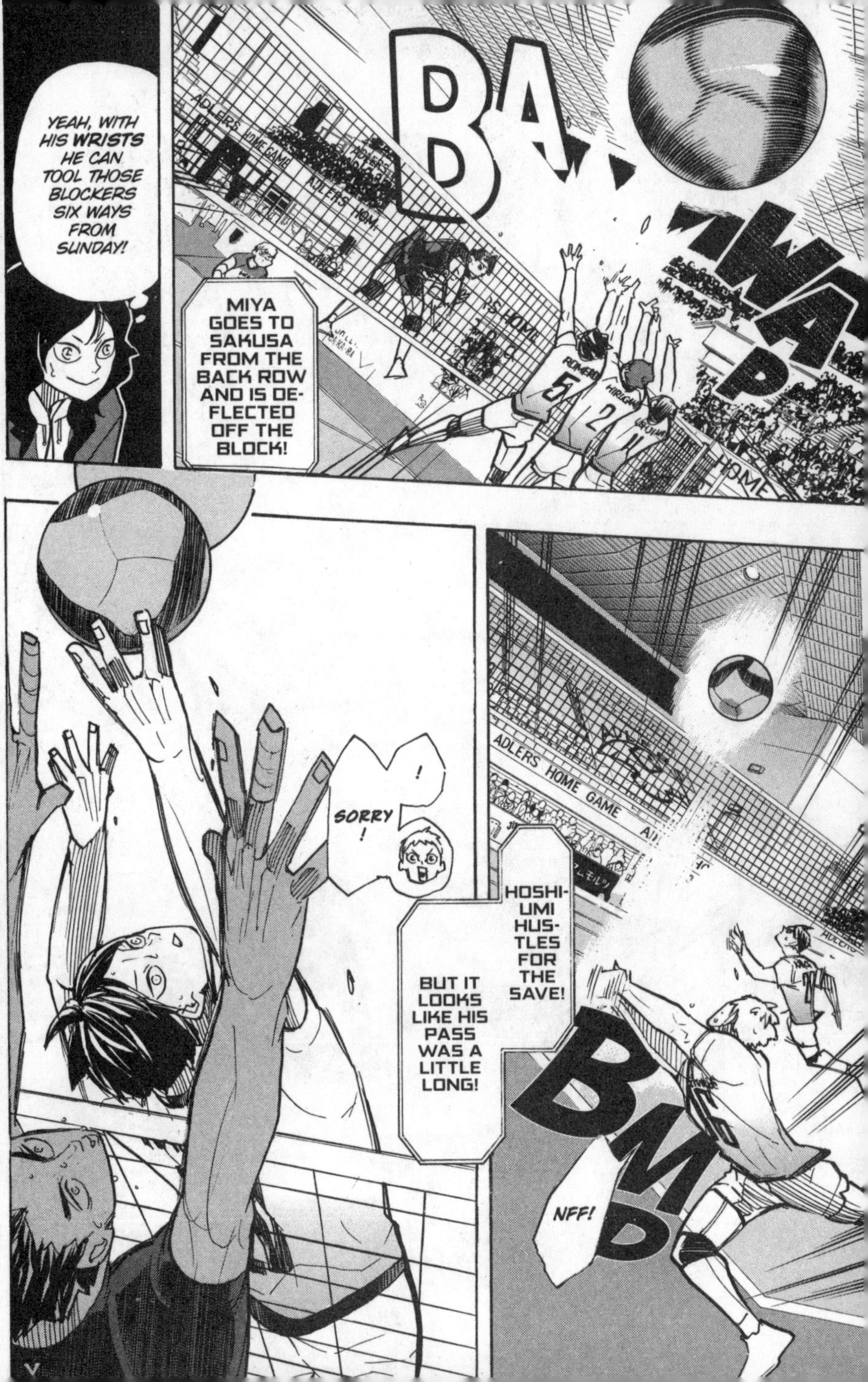
BA-WHAP
MIYA GOES TO SAKUSA FROM THE BACK ROW AND IS DE-FLECTED OFF THE BLOCK!
YEAH, WITH HIS WRISTS HE CAN TOOL THOSE BLOCKERS SIX WAYS FROM SUNDAY!
HOSHI-UMI HUS-TLES FOR THE SAVE!
BUT IT LOOKS LIKE HIS PASS WAS A LITTLE LONG!
BMP
NFF!
!
SORRY!

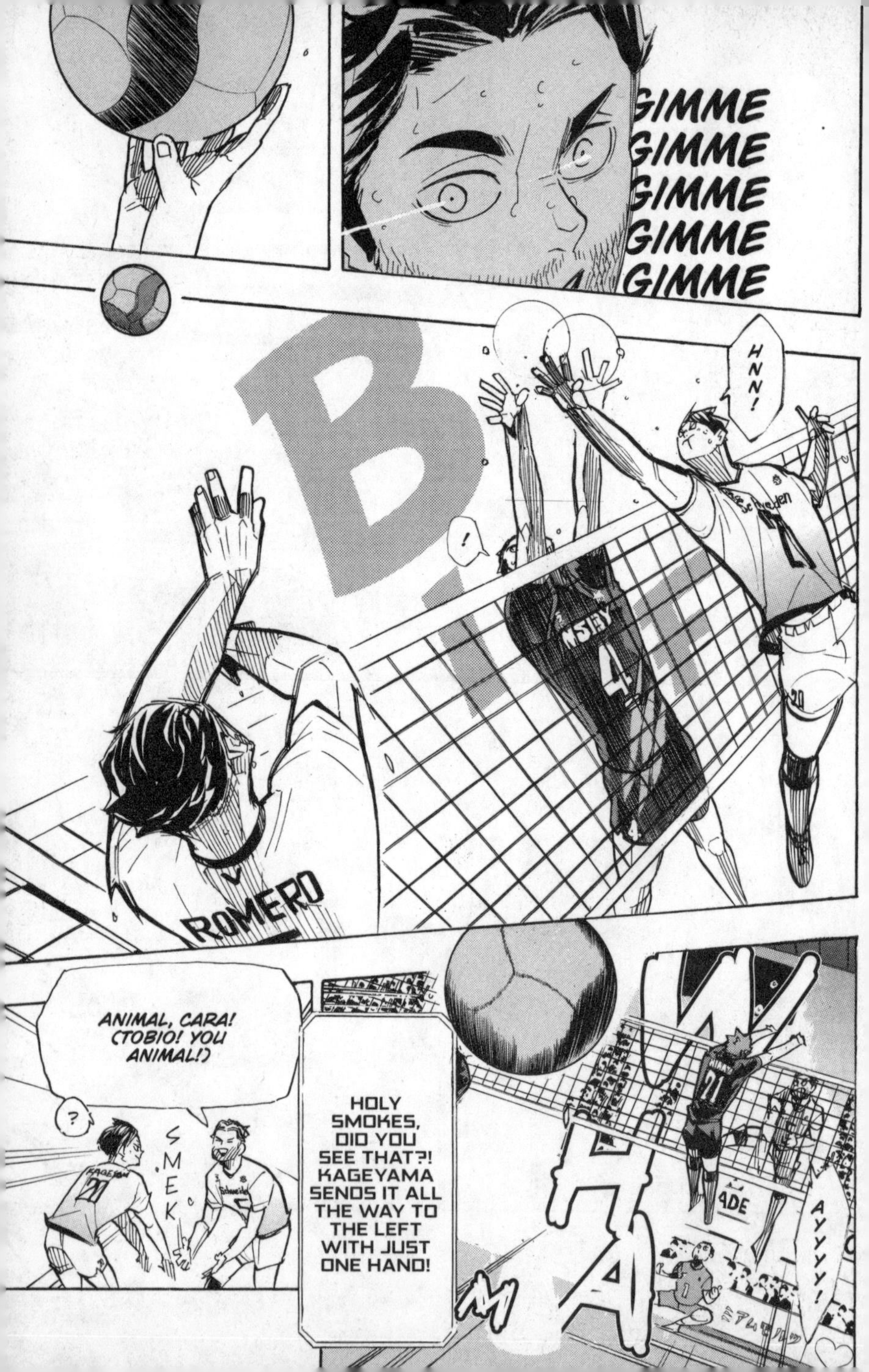
GIMME
GIMME
GIMME
GIMME
GIMME
HNN!
!
ROMERO
AYYY!
HOLY SMOKES, DID YOU SEE THAT?! KAGEYAMA SENDS IT ALL THE WAY TO THE LEFT WITH JUST ONE HAND!
ANIMAL, CARA! (TOBIO! YOU ANIMAL!)
?
SMEK

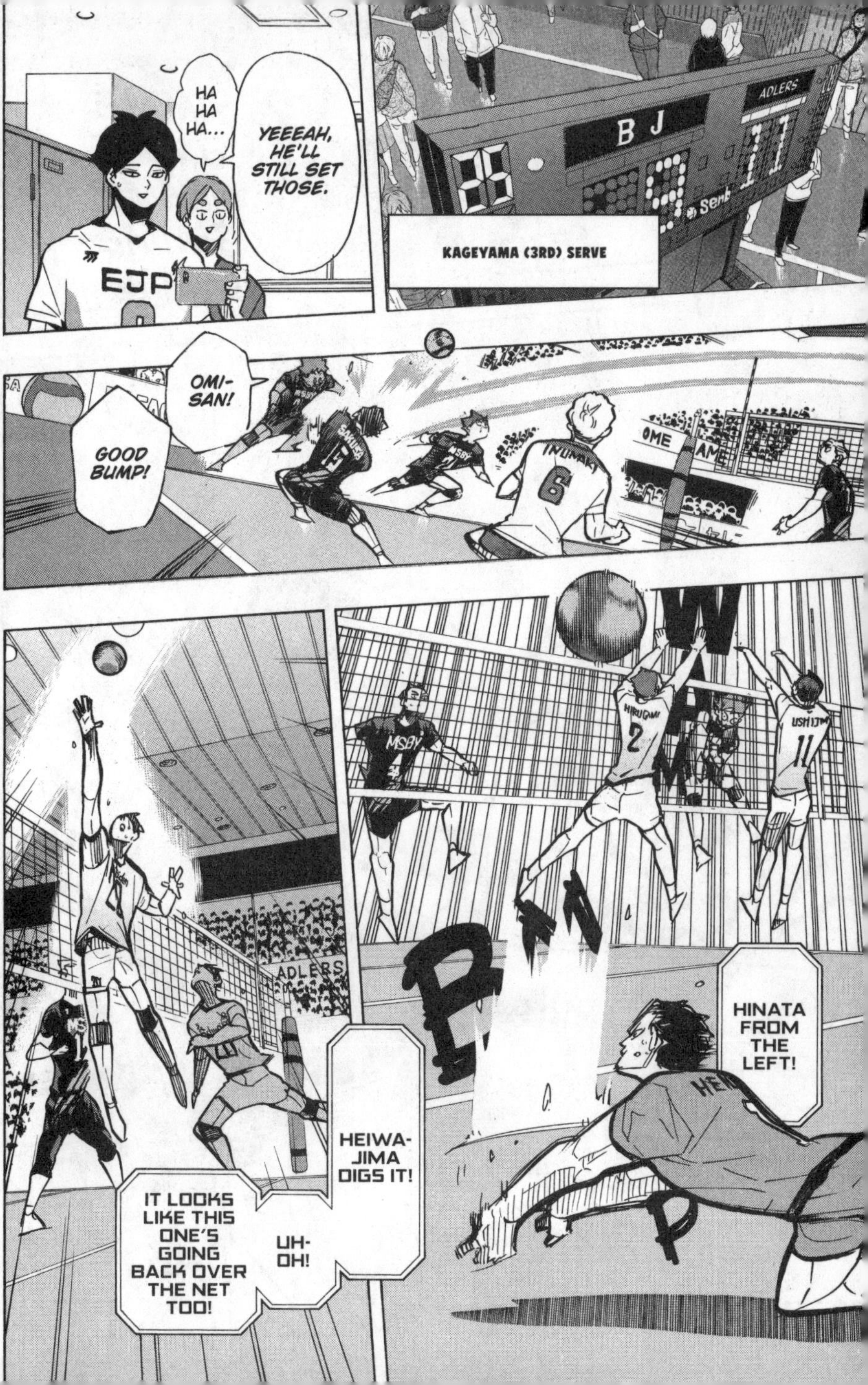
ADLERS
B J
KAGEYAMA (3RD) SERVE
YEEEAH, HE'LL STILL SET THOSE.
HA HA HA...
EJP
OMI-SAN!
GOOD BUMP!
HINATA FROM THE LEFT!
HEIWA-JIMA DIGS IT!
UH-OH!
IT LOOKS LIKE THIS ONE'S GOING BACK OVER THE NET TOO!
ADLERS

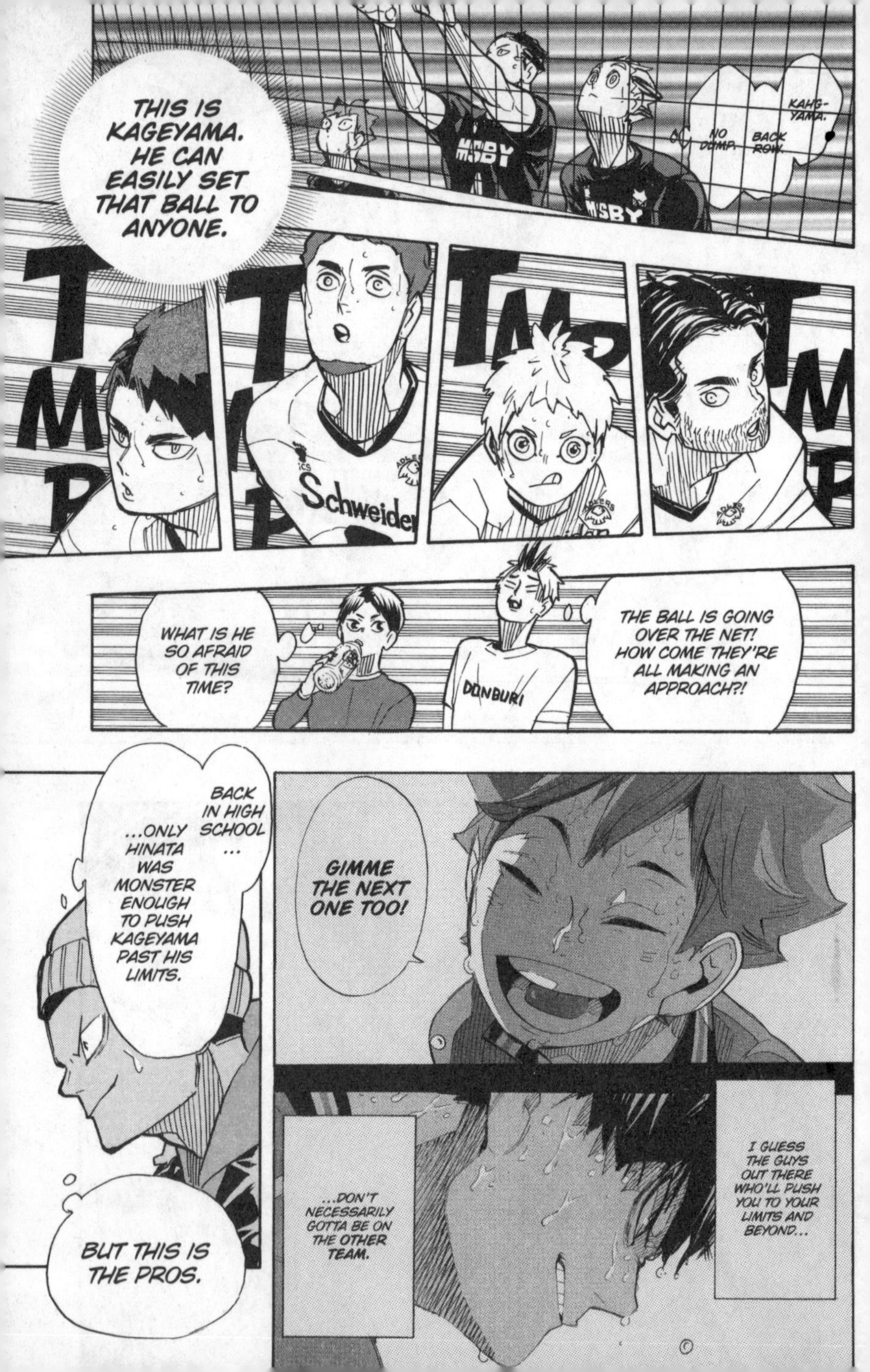
KAHG-YAMA.
BACK ROW.
NO DUMP.
THIS IS KAGEYAMA. HE CAN EASILY SET THAT BALL TO ANYONE.
TMP
TMP
TMP
TMP
THE BALL IS GOING OVER THE NET! HOW COME THEY'RE ALL MAKING AN APPROACH?!
WHAT IS HE SO AFRAID OF THIS TIME?
GIMME THE NEXT ONE TOO!
I GUESS THE GUYS OUT THERE WHO'LL PUSH YOU TO YOUR LIMITS AND BEYOND...
...DON'T NECESSARILY GOTTA BE ON THE OTHER TEAM.
BACK IN HIGH SCHOOL...
...ONLY HINATA WAS MONSTER ENOUGH TO PUSH KAGEYAMA PAST HIS LIMITS.
BUT THIS IS THE PROS.

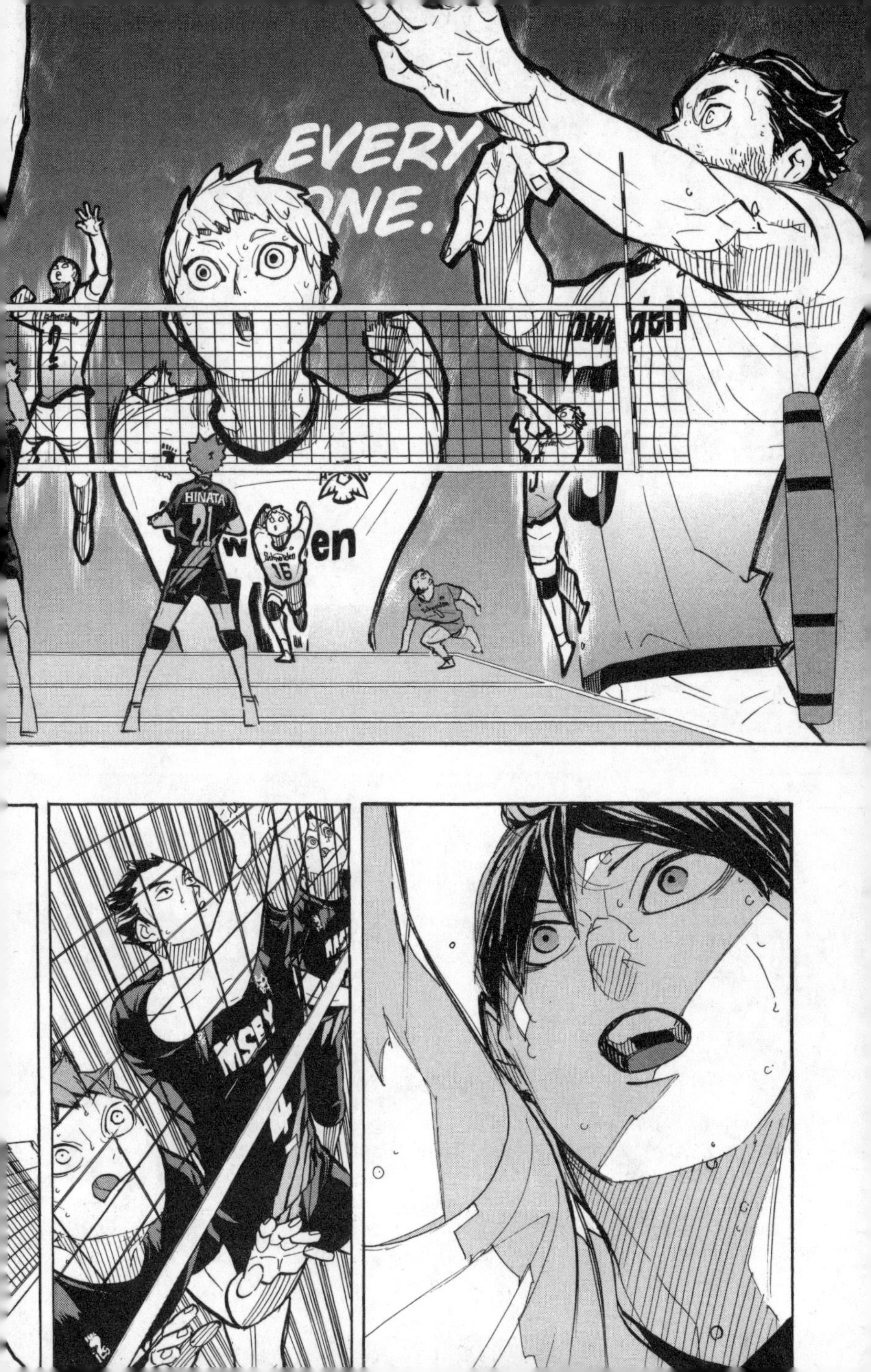
EVERY ONE.
HINATA
21
16
MSBY

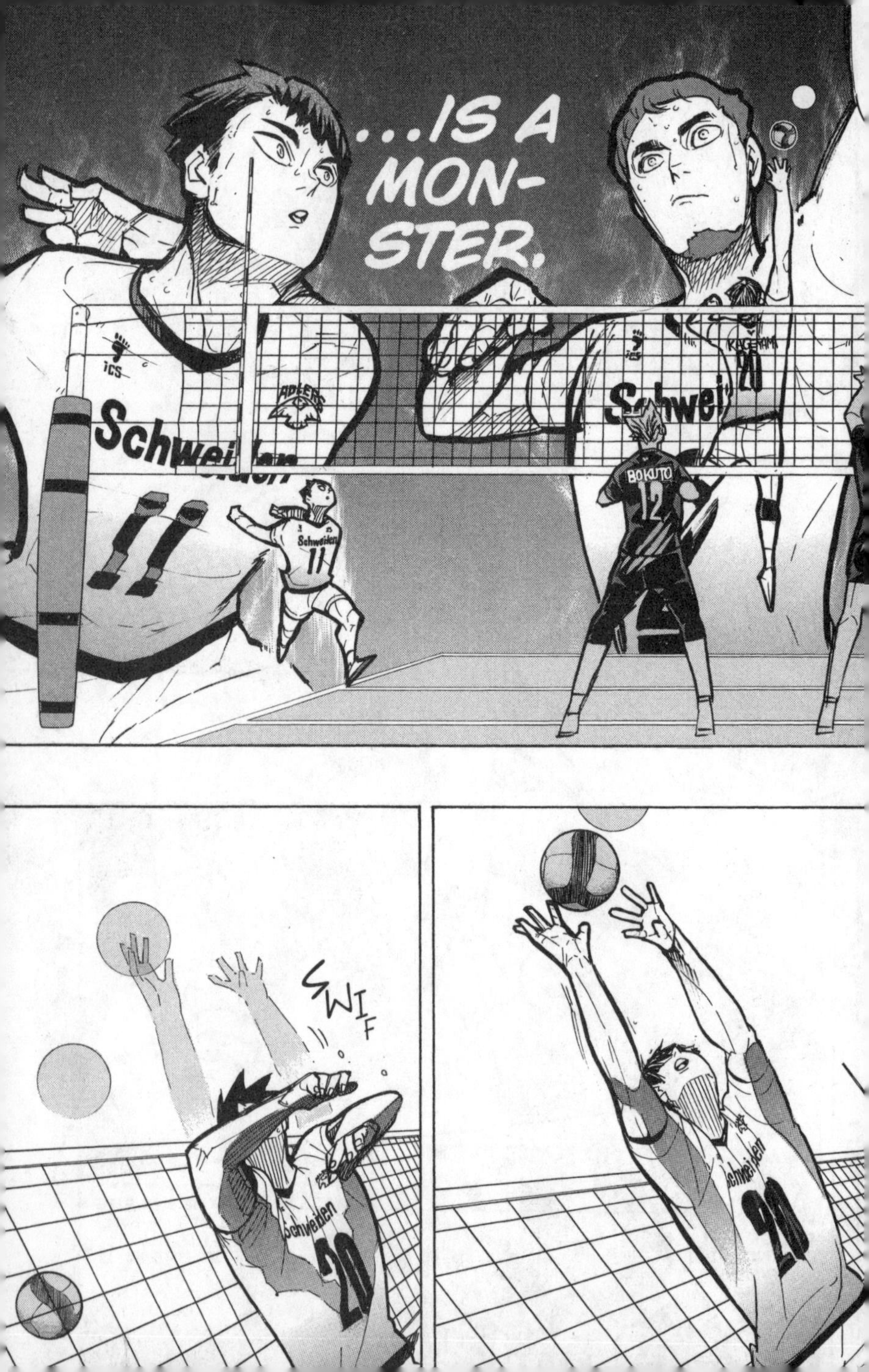
...IS A MONSTER.
SWIF

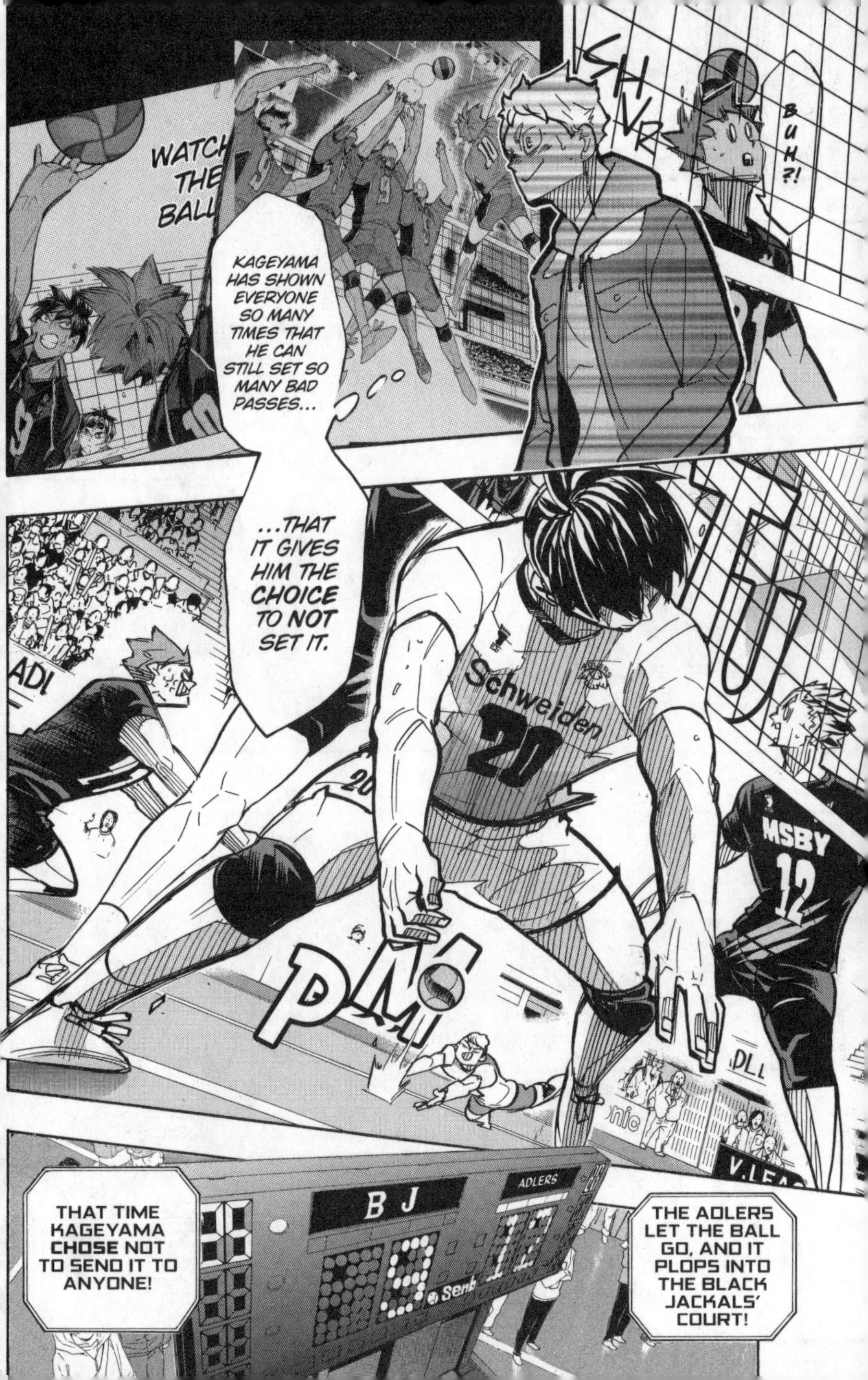

SHVR
BUH?!
KAGEYAMA HAS SHOWN EVERYONE SO MANY TIMES THAT HE CAN STILL SET SO MANY BAD PASSES...
WATCH THE BALL
...THAT IT GIVES HIM THE CHOICE TO NOT SET IT.
Schweiden 20
MSBY 12
THE ADLERS LET THE BALL GO, AND IT PLOPS INTO THE BLACK JACKALS' COURT!
ADLERS
B J
THAT TIME KAGEYAMA CHOSE NOT TO SEND IT TO ANYONE!

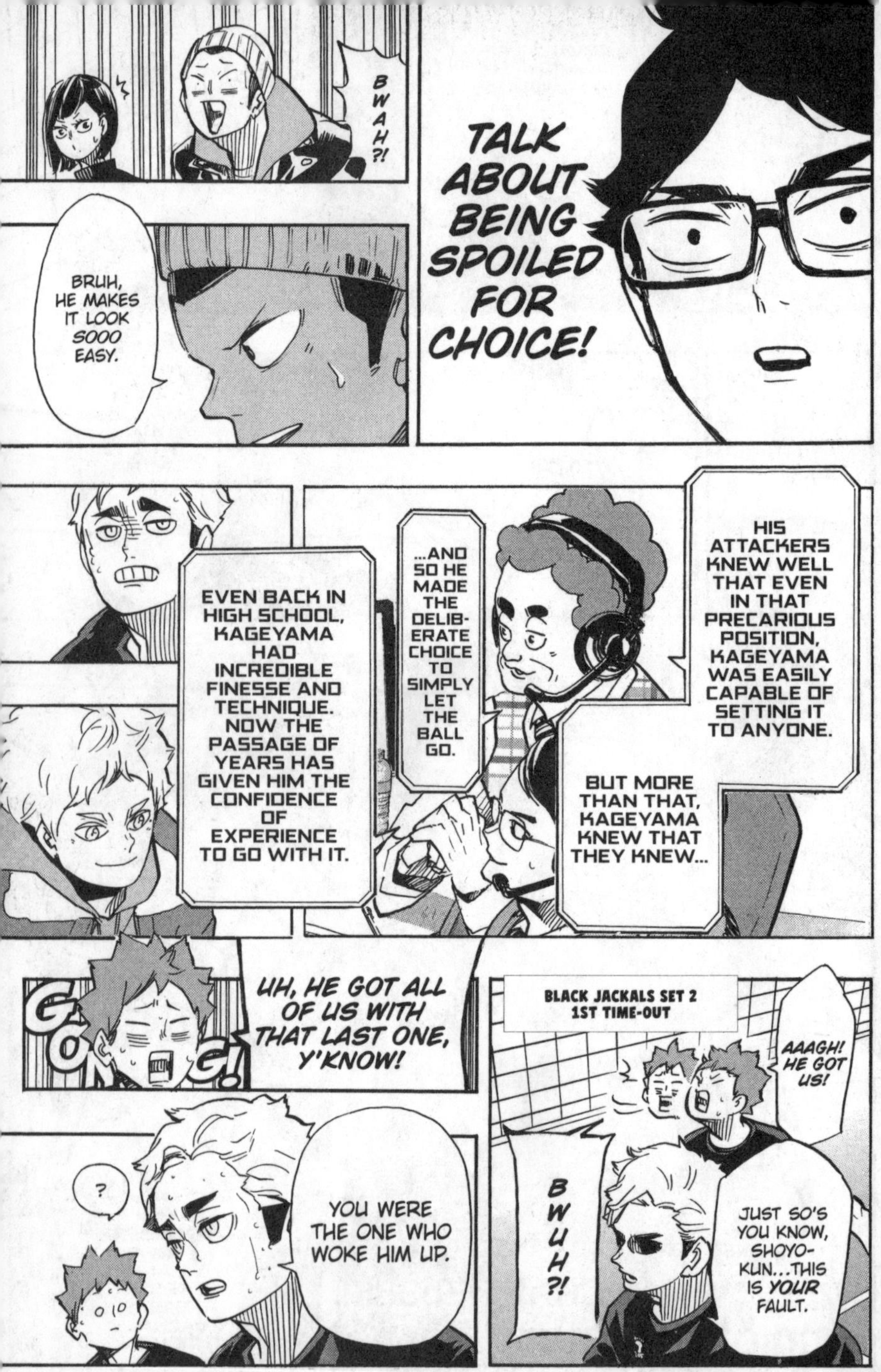
TALK ABOUT BEING SPOILED FOR CHOICE!
BWAH?!
BRUH, HE MAKES IT LOOK SOOO EASY.
HIS ATTACKERS KNEW WELL THAT EVEN IN THAT PRECARIOUS POSITION, KAGEYAMA WAS EASILY CAPABLE OF SETTING IT TO ANYONE.
BUT MORE THAN THAT, KAGEYAMA KNEW THAT THEY KNEW...
...AND SO HE MADE THE DELIBERATE CHOICE TO SIMPLY LET THE BALL GO.
EVEN BACK IN HIGH SCHOOL, KAGEYAMA HAD INCREDIBLE FINESSE AND TECHNIQUE. NOW THE PASSAGE OF YEARS HAS GIVEN HIM THE CONFIDENCE OF EXPERIENCE TO GO WITH IT.
BLACK JACKALS SET 2 1ST TIME-OUT
AAAGH! HE GOT US!
JUST SO'S YOU KNOW, SHOYO-KUN...THIS IS YOUR FAULT.
BWUH?!
UH, HE GOT ALL OF US WITH THAT LAST ONE, Y'KNOW!
GONG!
?
YOU WERE THE ONE WHO WOKE HIM UP.

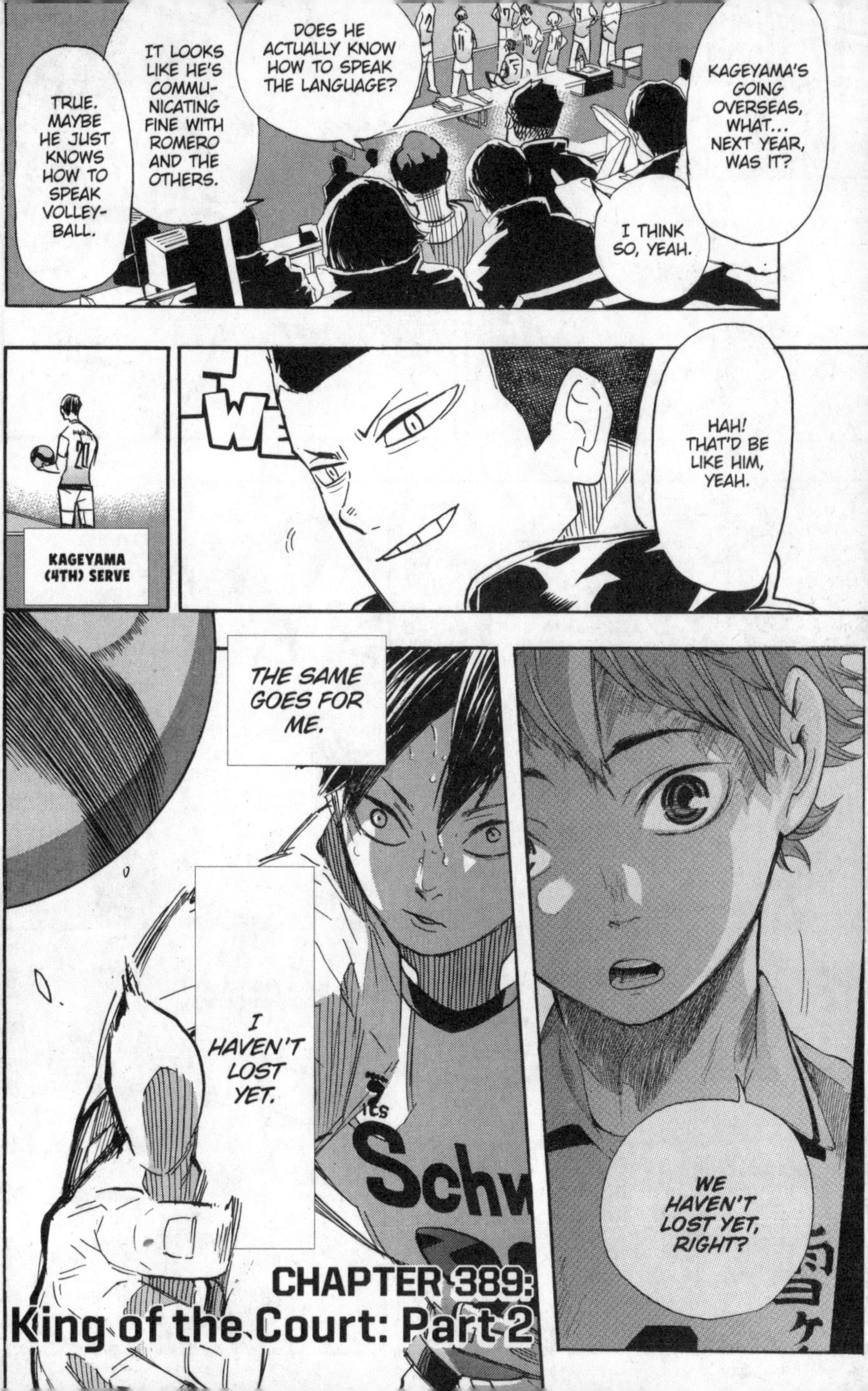
KAGEYAMA'S GOING OVERSEAS, WHAT... NEXT YEAR, WAS IT?
I THINK SO, YEAH.
DOES HE ACTUALLY KNOW HOW TO SPEAK THE LANGUAGE?
IT LOOKS LIKE HE'S COMMUNICATING FINE WITH ROMERO AND THE OTHERS.
TRUE. MAYBE HE JUST KNOWS HOW TO SPEAK VOLLEYBALL.
HAH! THAT'D BE LIKE HIM, YEAH.
KAGEYAMA (4TH) SERVE
WE HAVEN'T LOST YET, RIGHT?
THE SAME GOES FOR ME.
I HAVEN'T LOST YET.
CHAPTER 389:
King of the Court: Part 2

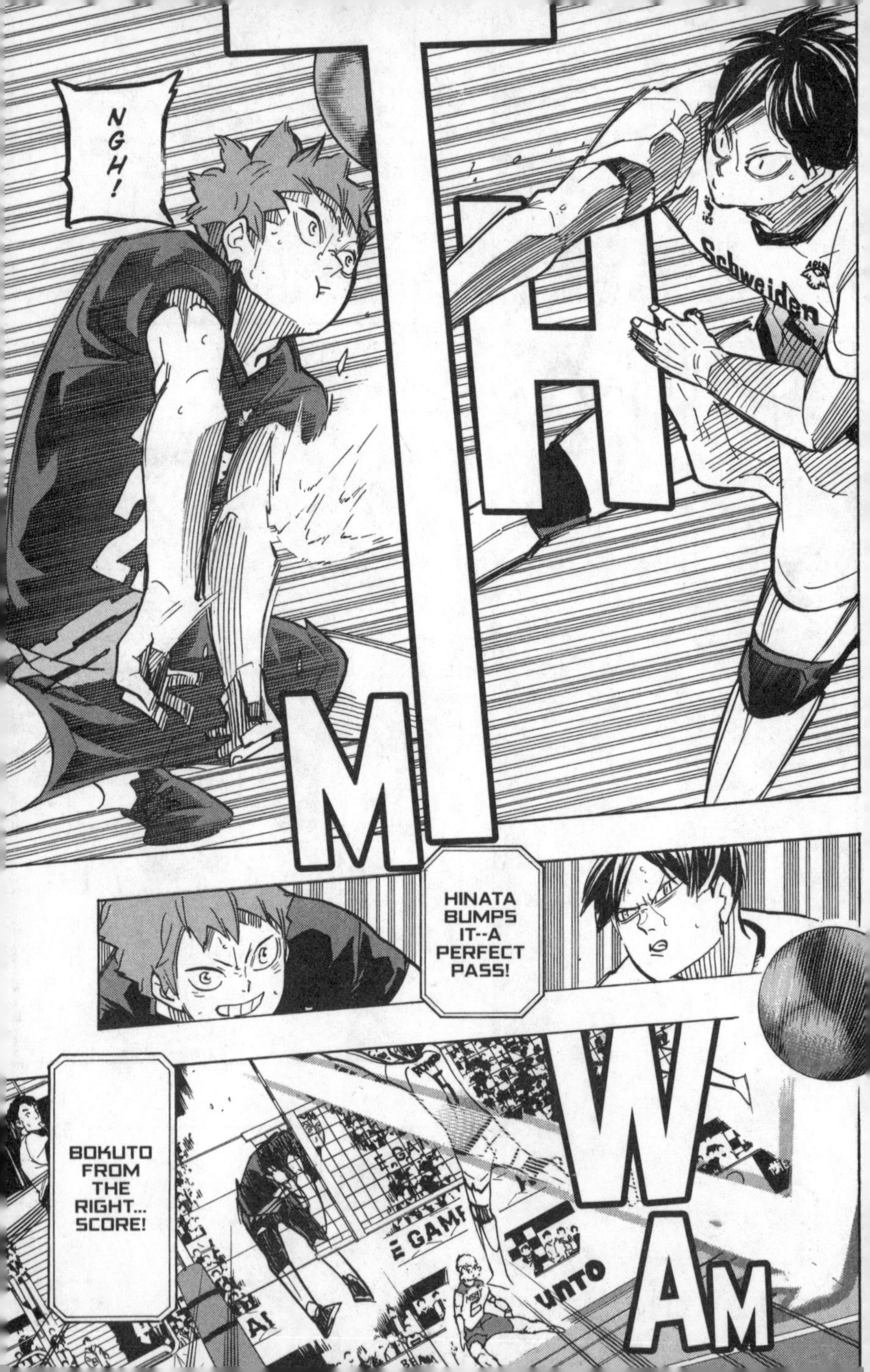
NGH!
HINATA BUMPS IT--A PERFECT PASS!
BOKUTO FROM THE RIGHT... SCORE!

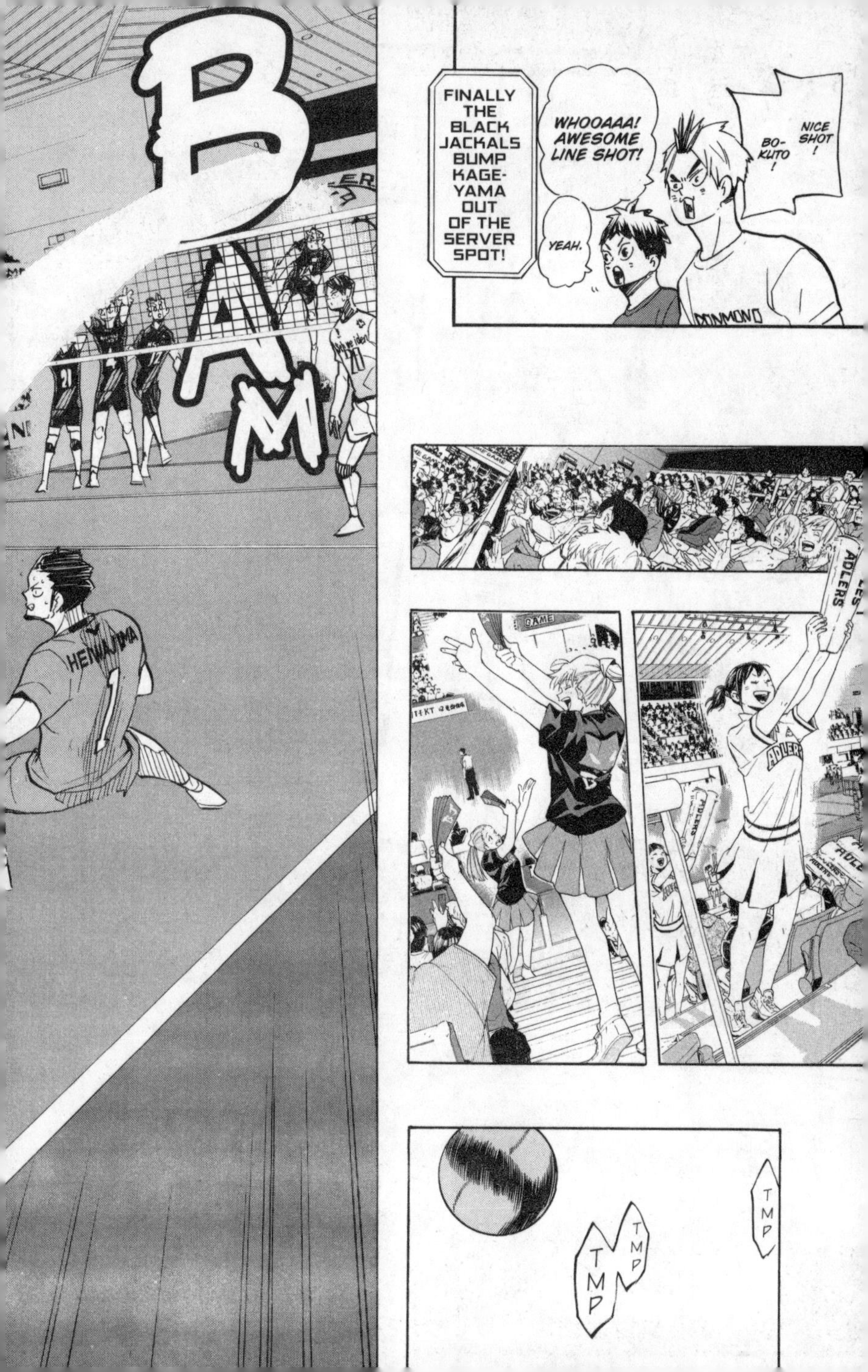

BO-KUTO! NICE SHOT!
WHOOAAA! AWESOME LINE SHOT!
YEAH.
FINALLY THE BLACK JACKALS BUMP KAGE-YAMA OUT OF THE SERVER SPOT!
ADLERS
TMP
TMP
TMP
BAM

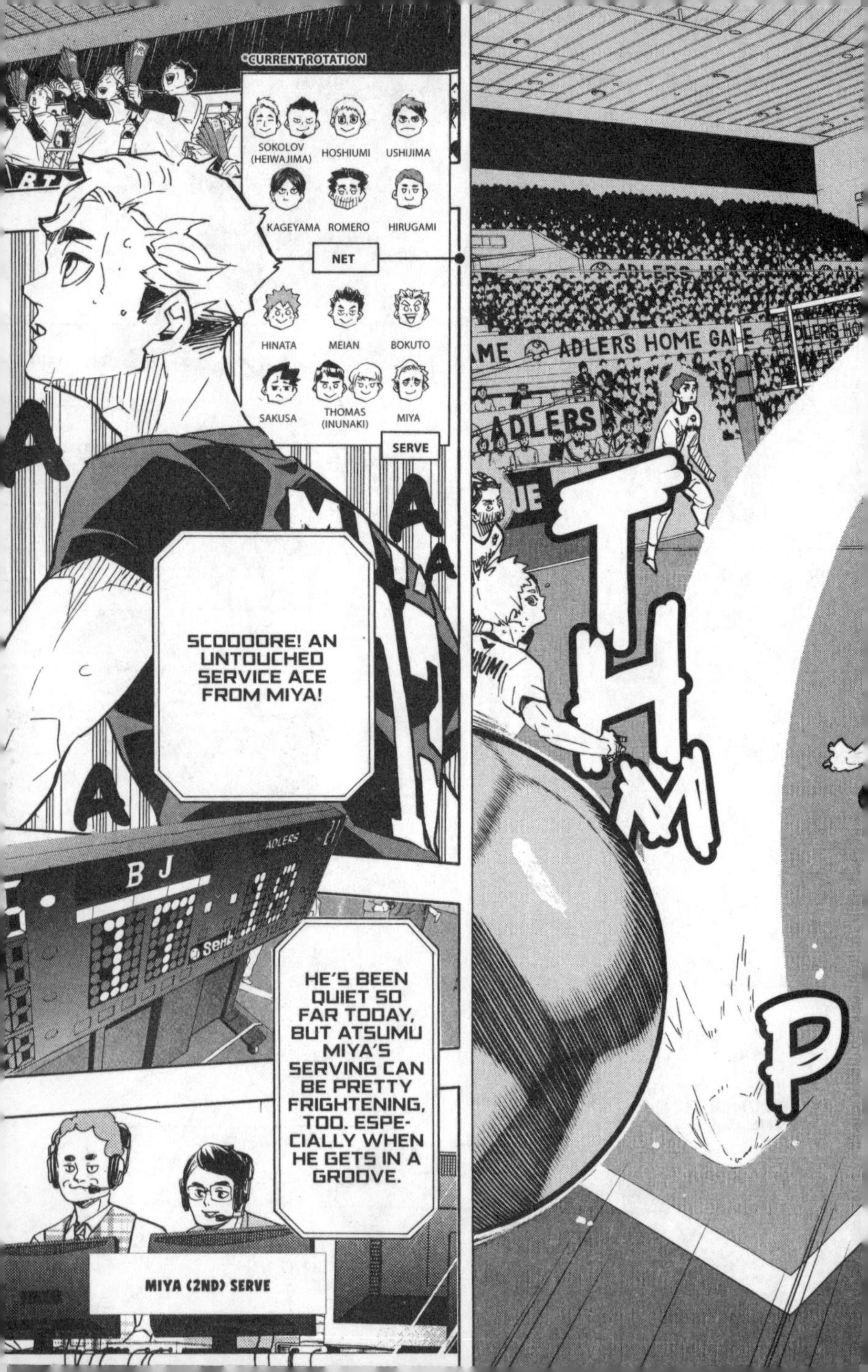

THUMP
ADLERS HOME GAME
ADLERS
*CURRENT ROTATION
SOKOLOV (HEIWAJIMA)
HOSHIUMI
USHIJIMA
KAGEYAMA
ROMERO
HIRUGAMI
NET
HINATA
MEIAN
BOKUTO
SAKUSA
THOMAS (INUNAKI)
MIYA
SERVE
SCOOOORE! AN UNTOUCHED SERVICE ACE FROM MIYA!
BJ
ADLERS
HE'S BEEN QUIET SO FAR TODAY, BUT ATSUMU MIYA'S SERVING CAN BE PRETTY FRIGHTENING, TOO. ESPECIALLY WHEN HE GETS IN A GROOVE.
MIYA (2ND) SERVE

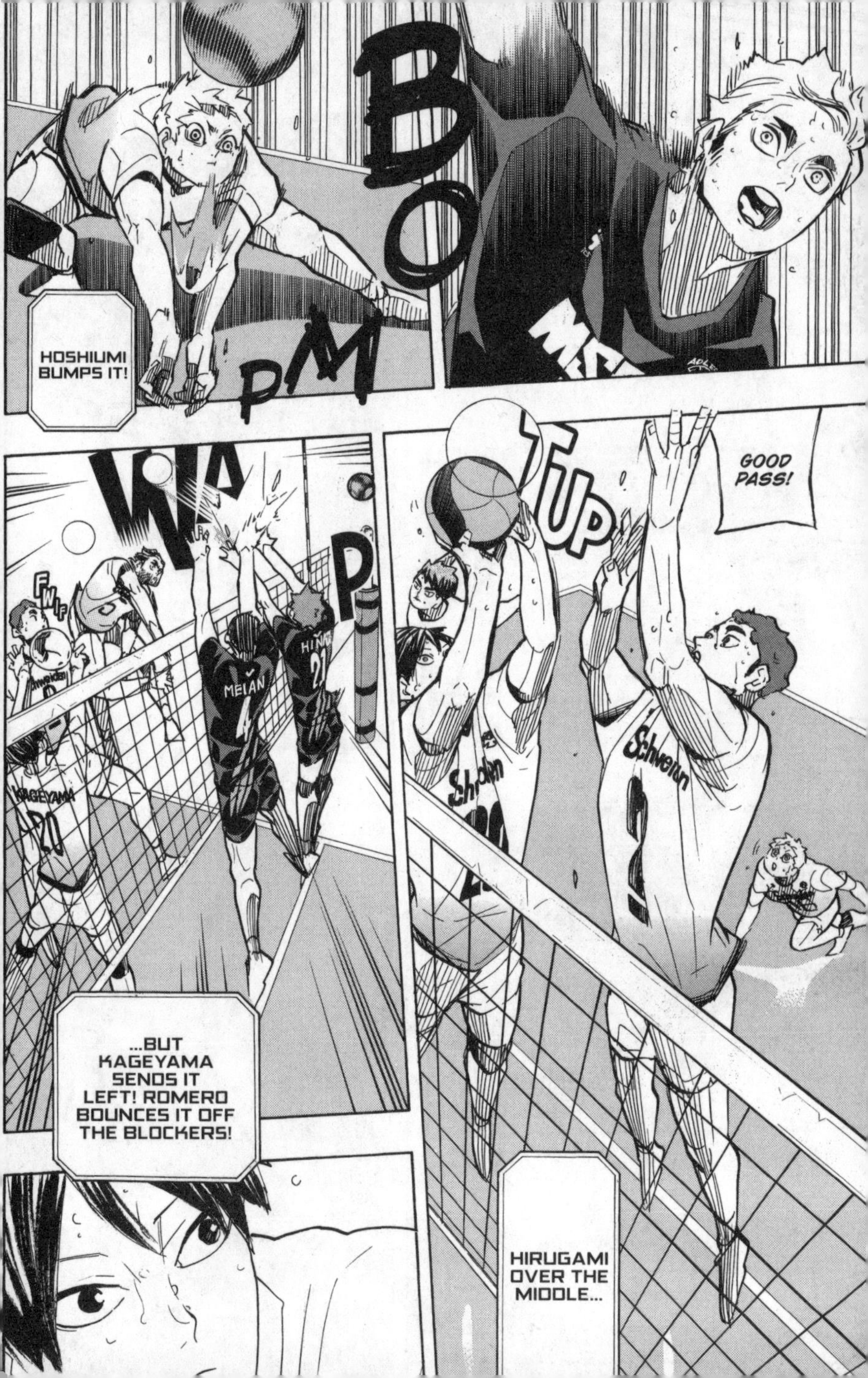
BOOM
HOSHIUMI BUMPS IT!
TUP
GOOD PASS!
HIRUGAMI OVER THE MIDDLE...
WHAP
...BUT KAGEYAMA SENDS IT LEFT! ROMERO BOUNCES IT OFF THE BLOCKERS!

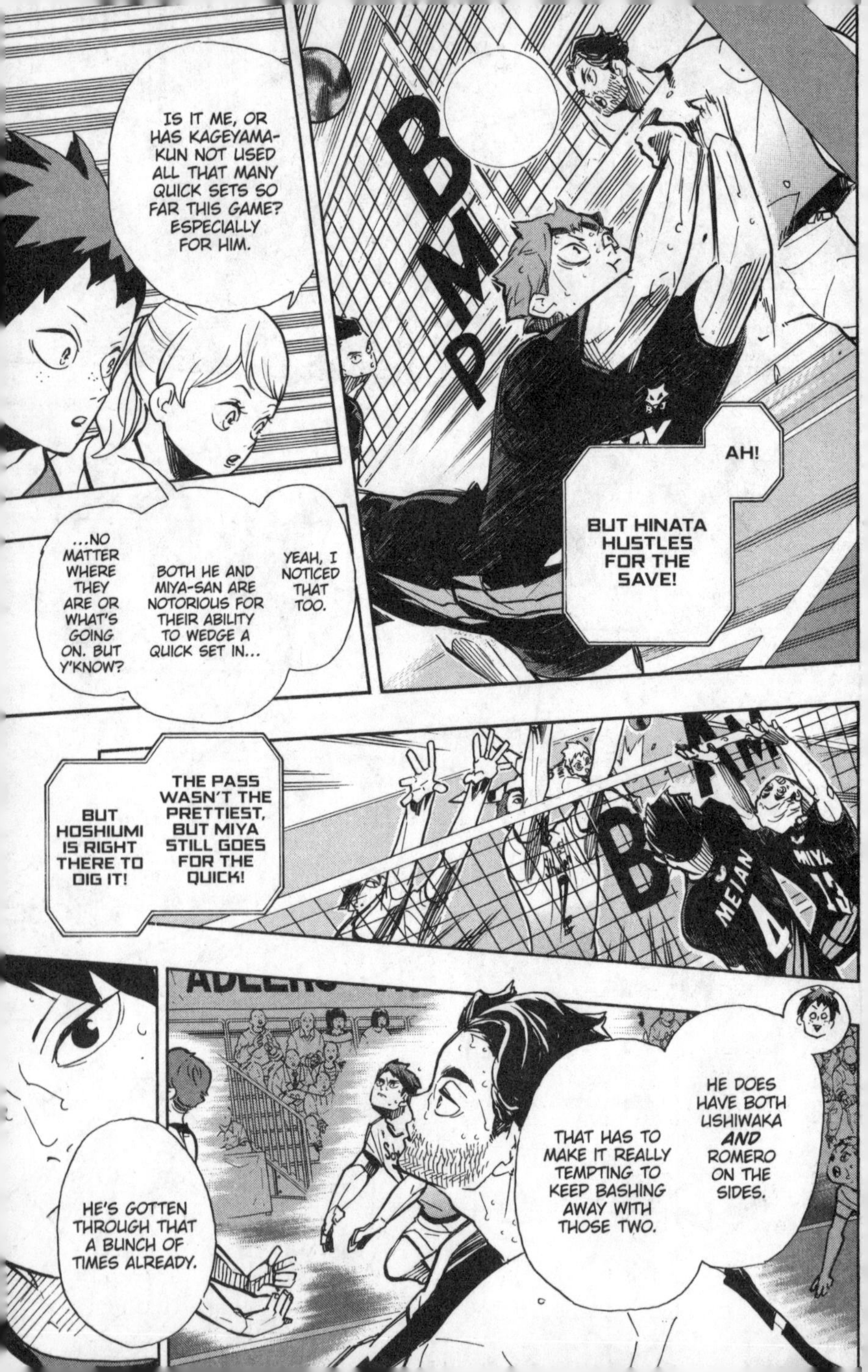
BMP
AH!
BUT HINATA HUSTLES FOR THE SAVE!
IS IT ME, OR HAS KAGEYAMA-KUN NOT USED ALL THAT MANY QUICK SETS SO FAR THIS GAME? ESPECIALLY FOR HIM.
YEAH, I NOTICED THAT TOO.
BOTH HE AND MIYA-SAN ARE NOTORIOUS FOR THEIR ABILITY TO WEDGE A QUICK SET IN...
...NO MATTER WHERE THEY ARE OR WHAT'S GOING ON. BUT Y'KNOW?
BAM
MEIAN
MIYA
THE PASS WASN'T THE PRETTIEST, BUT MIYA STILL GOES FOR THE QUICK!
BUT HOSHIUMI IS RIGHT THERE TO DIG IT!
HE DOES HAVE BOTH USHIWAKA *AND* ROMERO ON THE SIDES.
THAT HAS TO MAKE IT REALLY TEMPTING TO KEEP BASHING AWAY WITH THOSE TWO.
HE'S GOTTEN THROUGH THAT A BUNCH OF TIMES ALREADY.

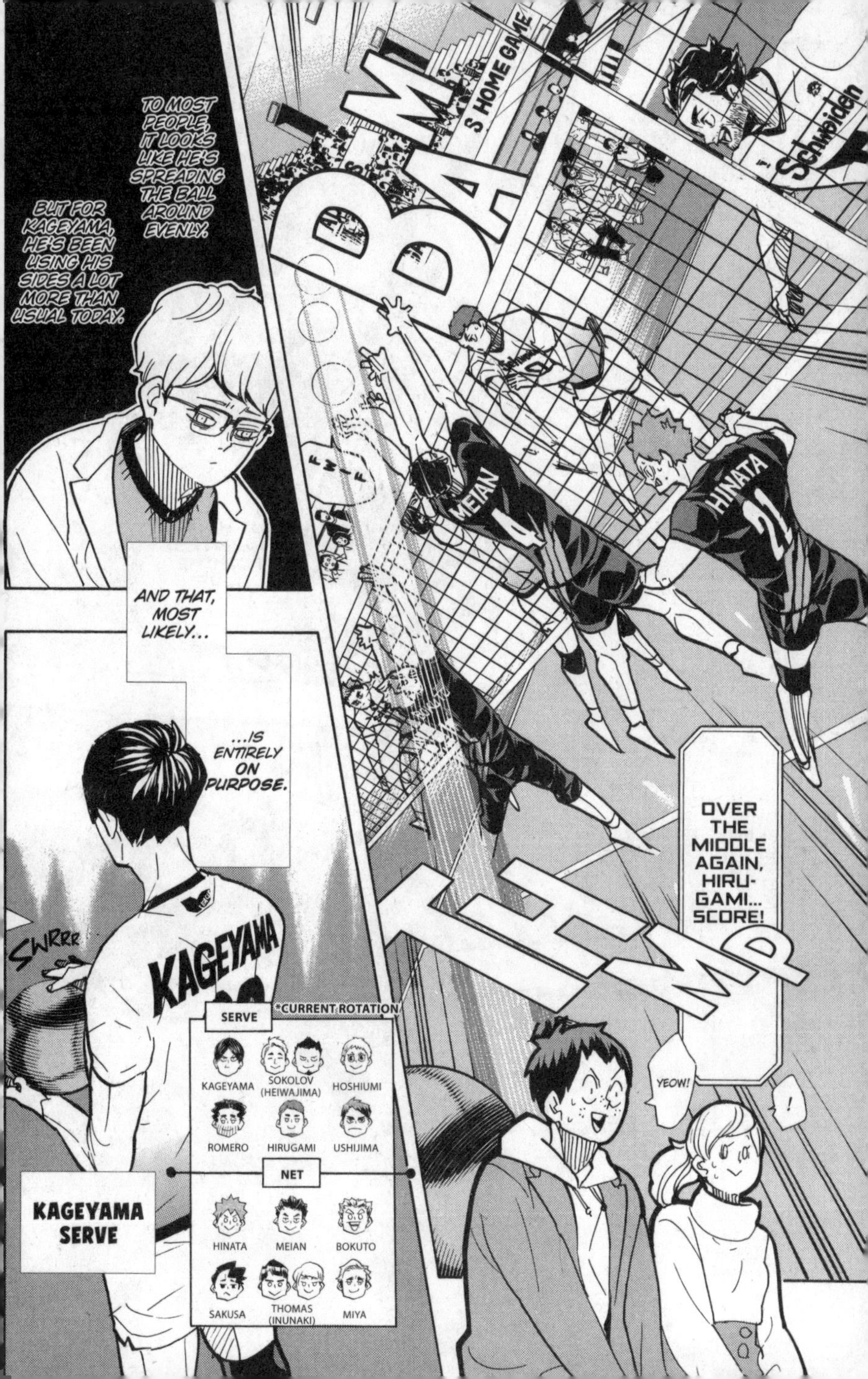
BAM
S HOME GAME
Schweiden
MEIAN
HINATA
THMP
OVER THE MIDDLE AGAIN, HIRUGAMI... SCORE!
YEOW!
!
TO MOST PEOPLE, IT LOOKS LIKE HE'S SPREADING THE BALL AROUND EVENLY.
BUT FOR KAGEYAMA, HE'S BEEN USING HIS SIDES A LOT MORE THAN USUAL TODAY.
AND THAT, MOST LIKELY...
...IS ENTIRELY ON PURPOSE.
SWRRR
KAGEYAMA
KAGEYAMA SERVE
SERVE
*CURRENT ROTATION
KAGEYAMA
SOKOLOV (HEIWAJIMA)
HOSHIUMI
ROMERO
HIRUGAMI
USHIJIMA
NET
HINATA
MEIAN
BOKUTO
SAKUSA
THOMAS (INUNAKI)
MIYA

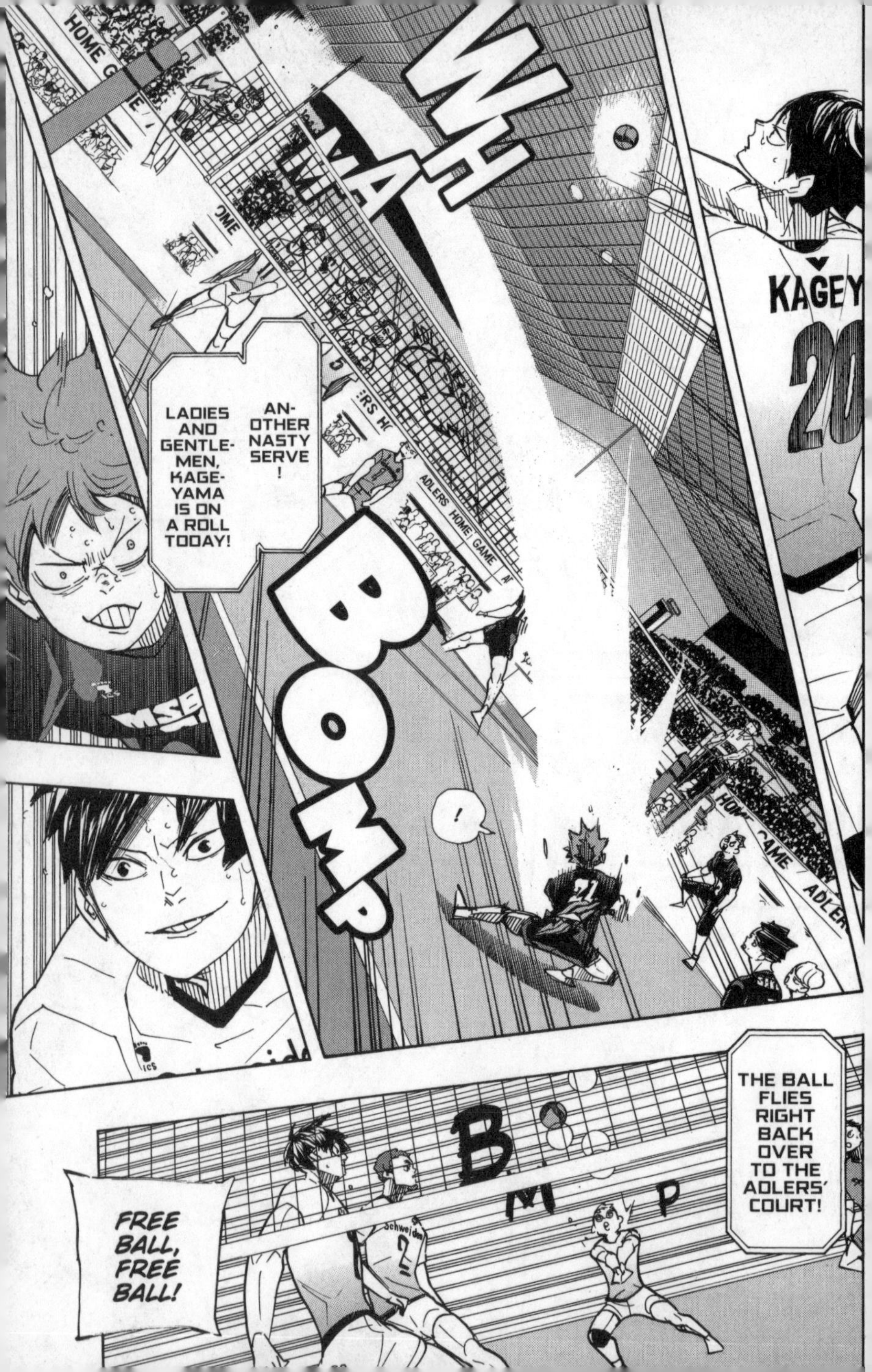

KAGEY
20
WHAM
ANOTHER NASTY SERVE!
LADIES AND GENTLEMEN, KAGEYAMA IS ON A ROLL TODAY!
ADLERS HOME GAME
BOMP
!
THE BALL FLIES RIGHT BACK OVER TO THE ADLERS' COURT!
BMP
FREE BALL, FREE BALL!

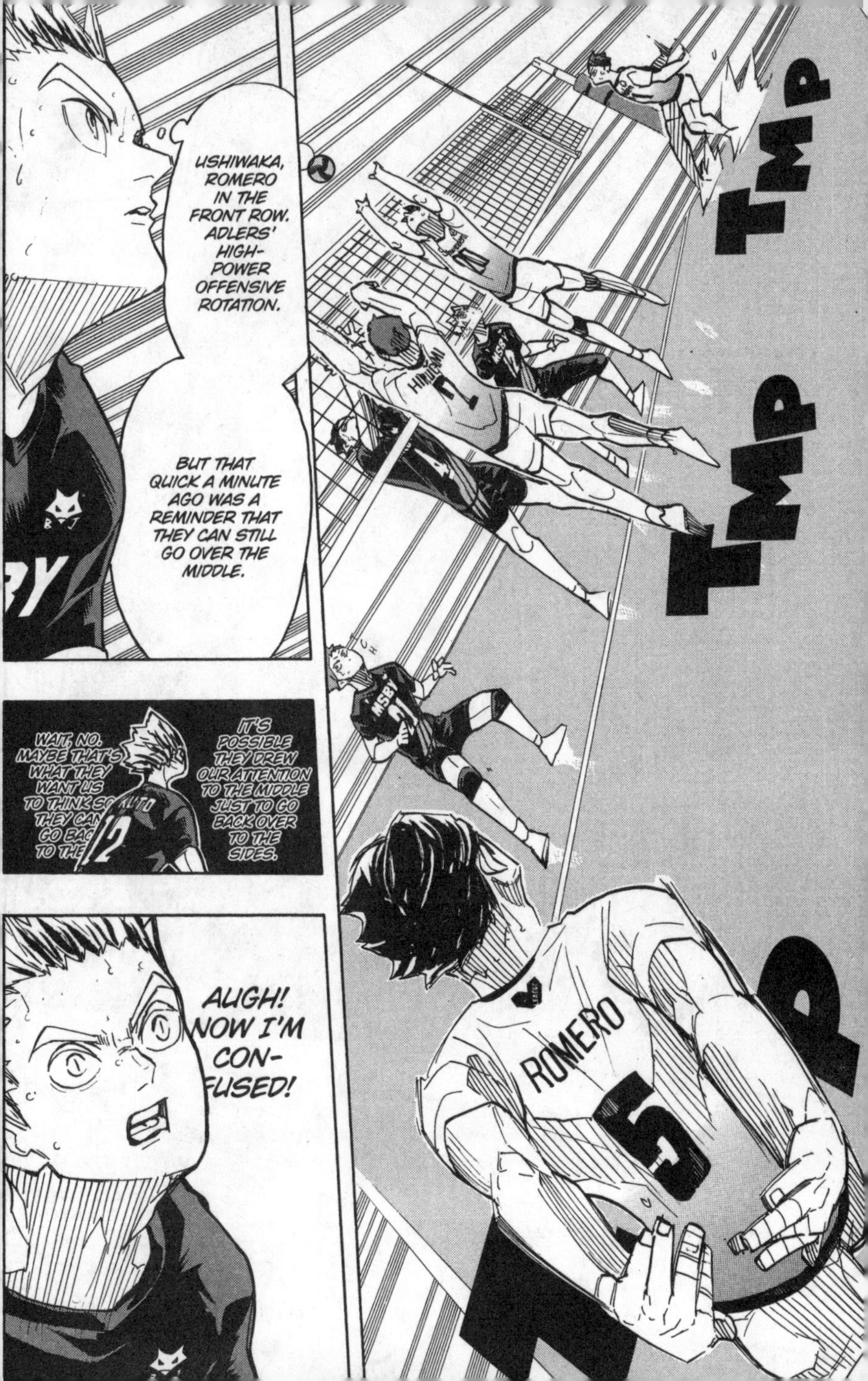
TMP
TMP
TMP
USHIWAKA, ROMERO IN THE FRONT ROW. ADLERS' HIGH-POWER OFFENSIVE ROTATION.
BUT THAT QUICK A MINUTE AGO WAS A REMINDER THAT THEY CAN STILL GO OVER THE MIDDLE.
IT'S POSSIBLE THEY DREW OUR ATTENTION TO THE MIDDLE JUST TO GO BACK OVER TO THE SIDES.
WAIT, NO. MAYBE THAT'S WHAT THEY WANT US TO THINK SO THEY CAN GO BAC TO THE
AUGH! NOW I'M CON-FUSED!

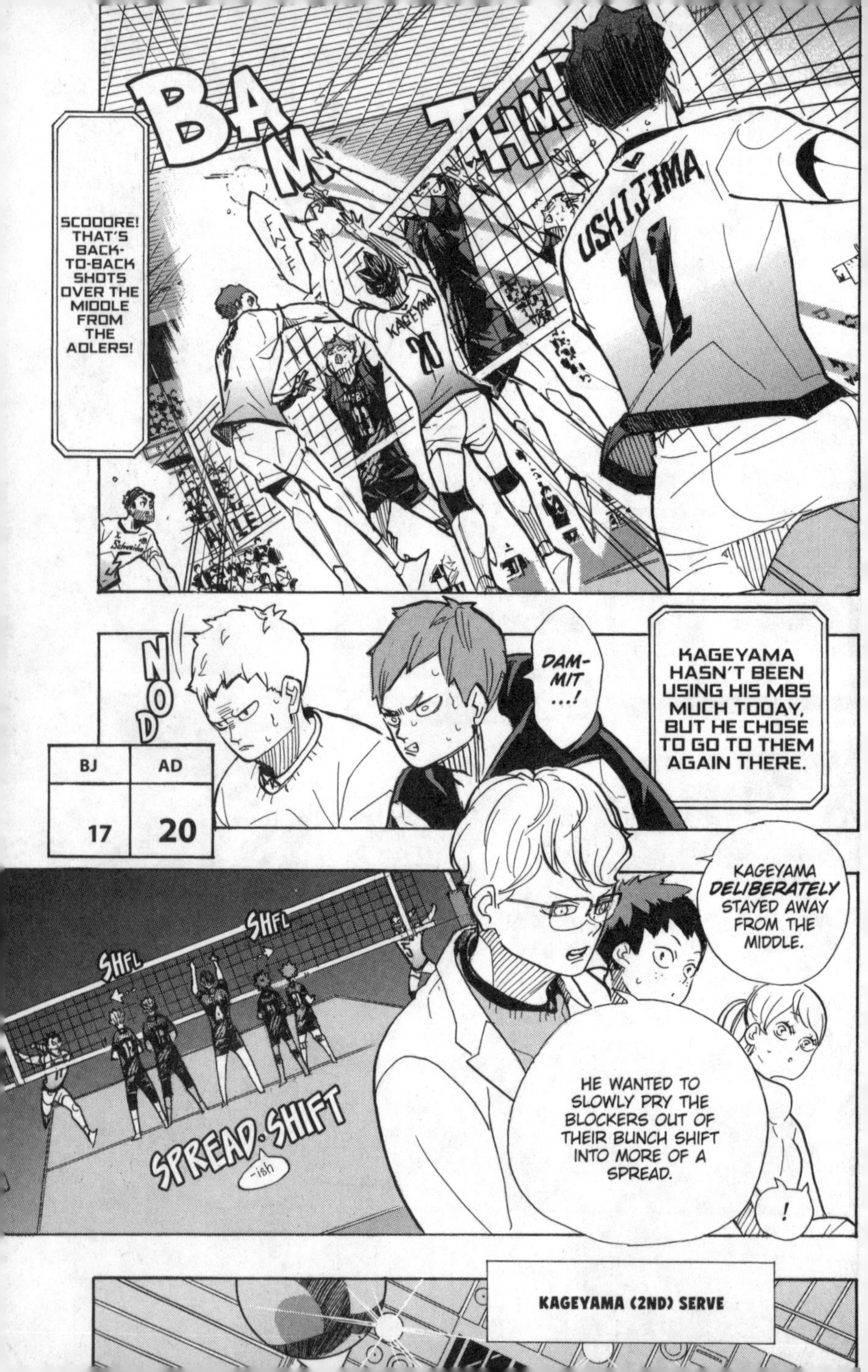
THMP
BAM
FWIF
SCOOORE! THAT'S BACK-TO-BACK SHOTS OVER THE MIDDLE FROM THE ADLERS!
KAGEYAMA HASN'T BEEN USING HIS MBS MUCH TODAY, BUT HE CHOSE TO GO TO THEM AGAIN THERE.
DAM-MIT ...!
NOD
BJ
AD
17
20
KAGEYAMA *DELIBERATELY* STAYED AWAY FROM THE MIDDLE.
HE WANTED TO SLOWLY PRY THE BLOCKERS OUT OF THEIR BUNCH SHIFT INTO MORE OF A SPREAD.
!
SHFL
SHFL
SPREAD SHIFT
-ish
KAGEYAMA (2ND) SERVE

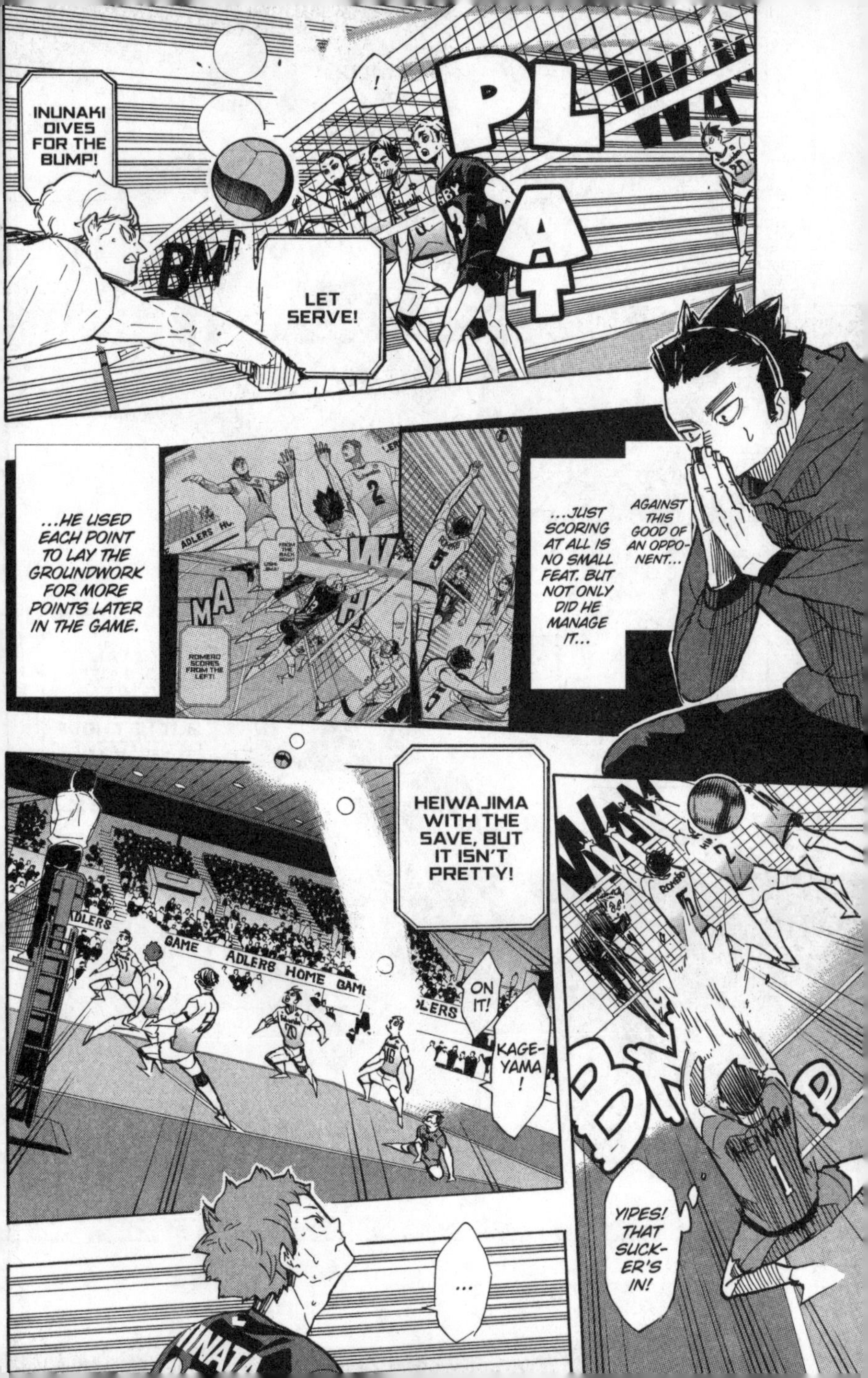
!
INUNAKI DIVES FOR THE BUMP!
LET SERVE!
AGAINST THIS GOOD OF AN OPPONENT...
...JUST SCORING AT ALL IS NO SMALL FEAT. BUT NOT ONLY DID HE MANAGE IT...
...HE USED EACH POINT TO LAY THE GROUNDWORK FOR MORE POINTS LATER IN THE GAME.
YIPES! THAT SUCKER'S IN!
HEIWAJIMA WITH THE SAVE, BUT IT ISN'T PRETTY!
ON IT!
KAGE-YAMA!
...

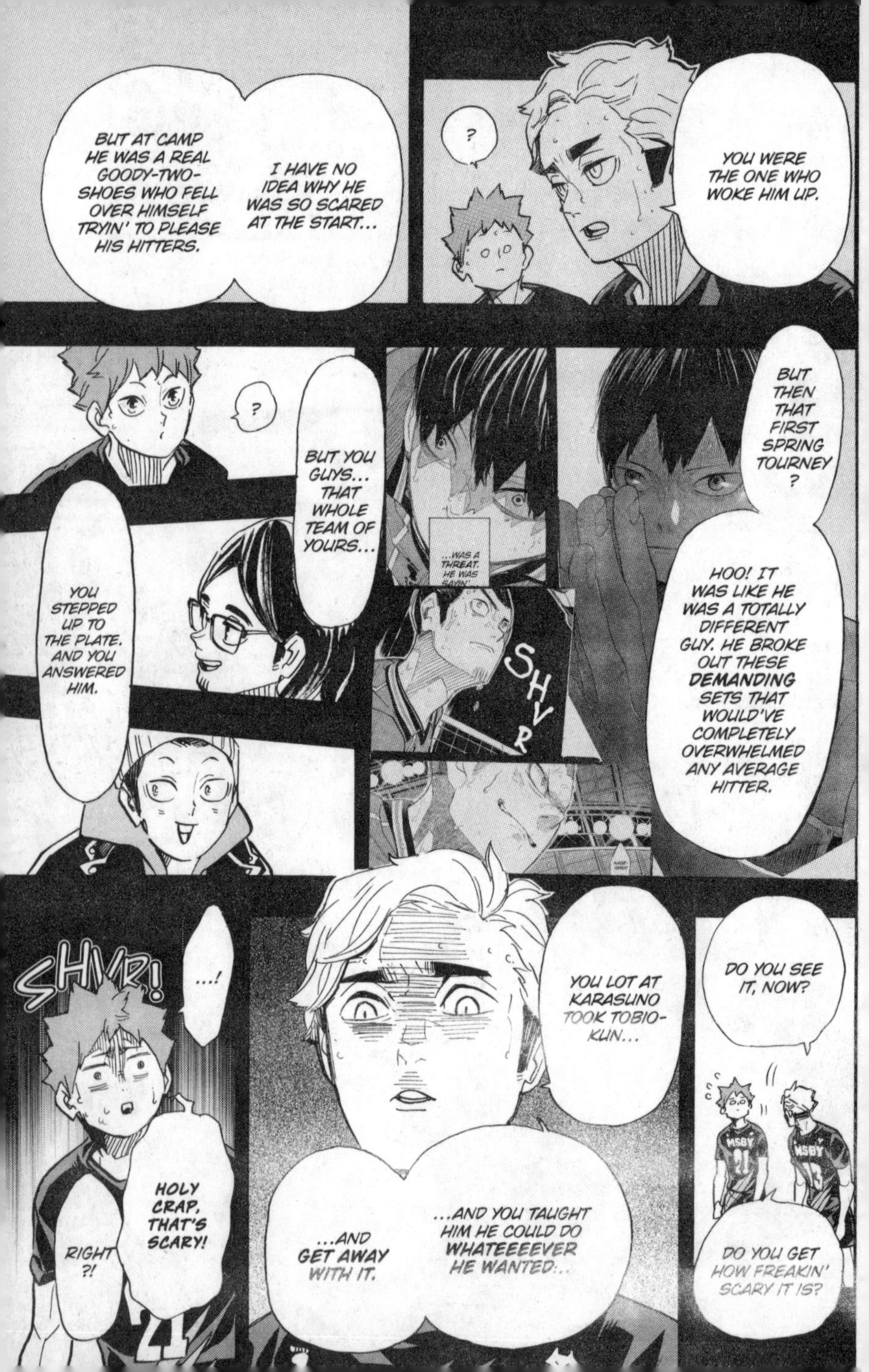
?
YOU WERE THE ONE WHO WOKE HIM UP.
I HAVE NO IDEA WHY HE WAS SO SCARED AT THE START...
BUT AT CAMP HE WAS A REAL GOODY-TWO-SHOES WHO FELL OVER HIMSELF TRYIN' TO PLEASE HIS HITTERS.
BUT THEN THAT FIRST SPRING TOURNEY?
HOO! IT WAS LIKE HE WAS A TOTALLY DIFFERENT GUY. HE BROKE OUT THESE DEMANDING SETS THAT WOULD'VE COMPLETELY OVERWHELMED ANY AVERAGE HITTER.
...WAS A THREAT. HE WAS SAYIN'
SHVR
?
BUT YOU GUYS... THAT WHOLE TEAM OF YOURS...
YOU STEPPED UP TO THE PLATE. AND YOU ANSWERED HIM.
DO YOU SEE IT, NOW?
DO YOU GET HOW FREAKIN' SCARY IT IS?
YOU LOT AT KARASUNO TOOK TOBIO-KUN...
...AND YOU TAUGHT HIM HE COULD DO WHATEEEEVER HE WANTED...
...AND GET AWAY WITH IT.
...!
SHVR!
HOLY CRAP, THAT'S SCARY!
RIGHT?!

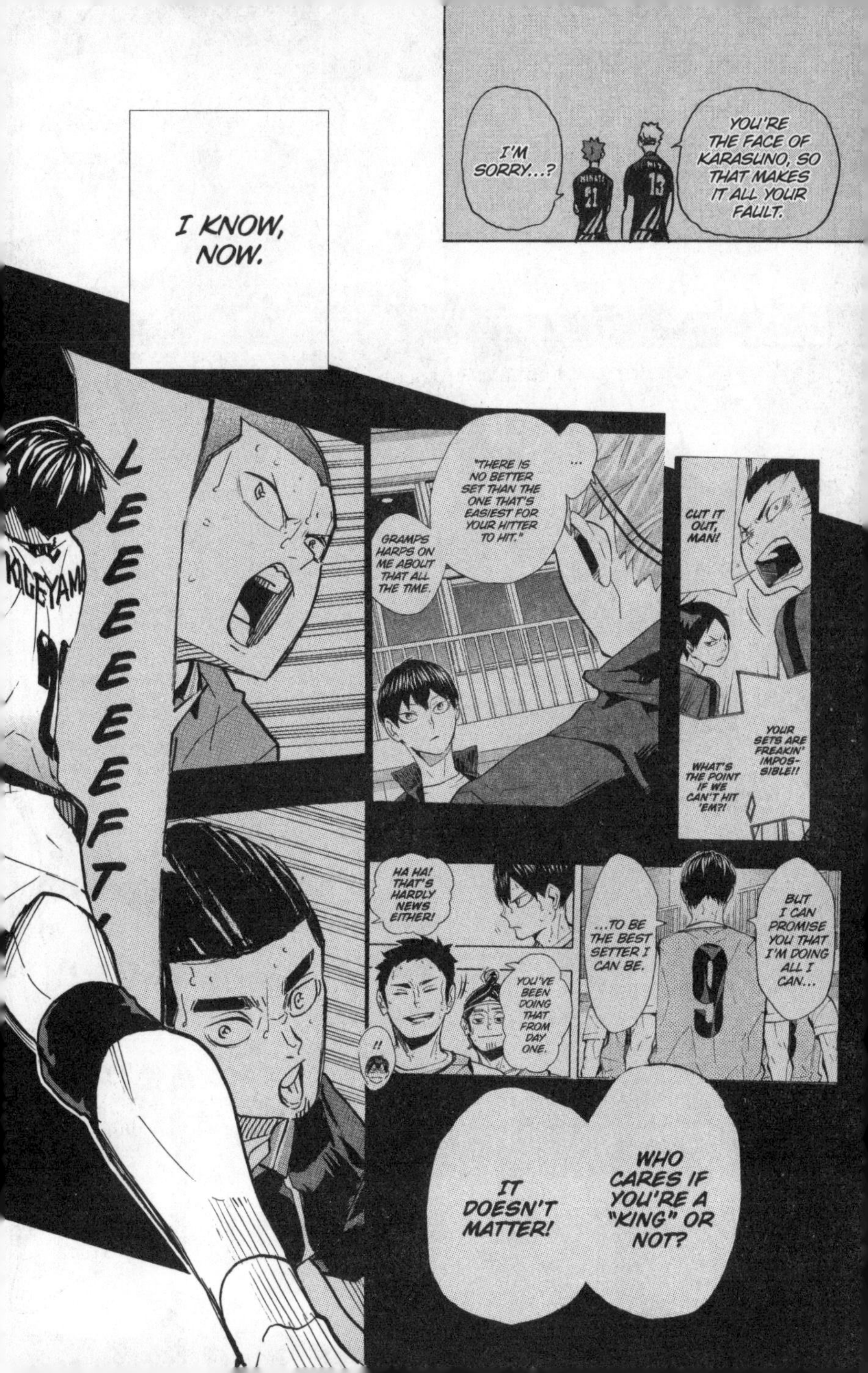
YOU'RE THE FACE OF KARASUNO, SO THAT MAKES IT ALL YOUR FAULT.
I'M SORRY...?
I KNOW, NOW.
CUT IT OUT, MAN!
YOUR SETS ARE FREAKIN' IMPOSSIBLE!!
WHAT'S THE POINT IF WE CAN'T HIT 'EM?!
...
"THERE IS NO BETTER SET THAN THE ONE THAT'S EASIEST FOR YOUR HITTER TO HIT."
GRAMPS HARPS ON ME ABOUT THAT ALL THE TIME.
LEEEEEEEFT!
BUT I CAN PROMISE YOU THAT I'M DOING ALL I CAN...
...TO BE THE BEST SETTER I CAN BE.
HA HA! THAT'S HARDLY NEWS EITHER!
YOU'VE BEEN DOING THAT FROM DAY ONE.
!!
WHO CARES IF YOU'RE A "KING" OR NOT?
IT DOESN'T MATTER!

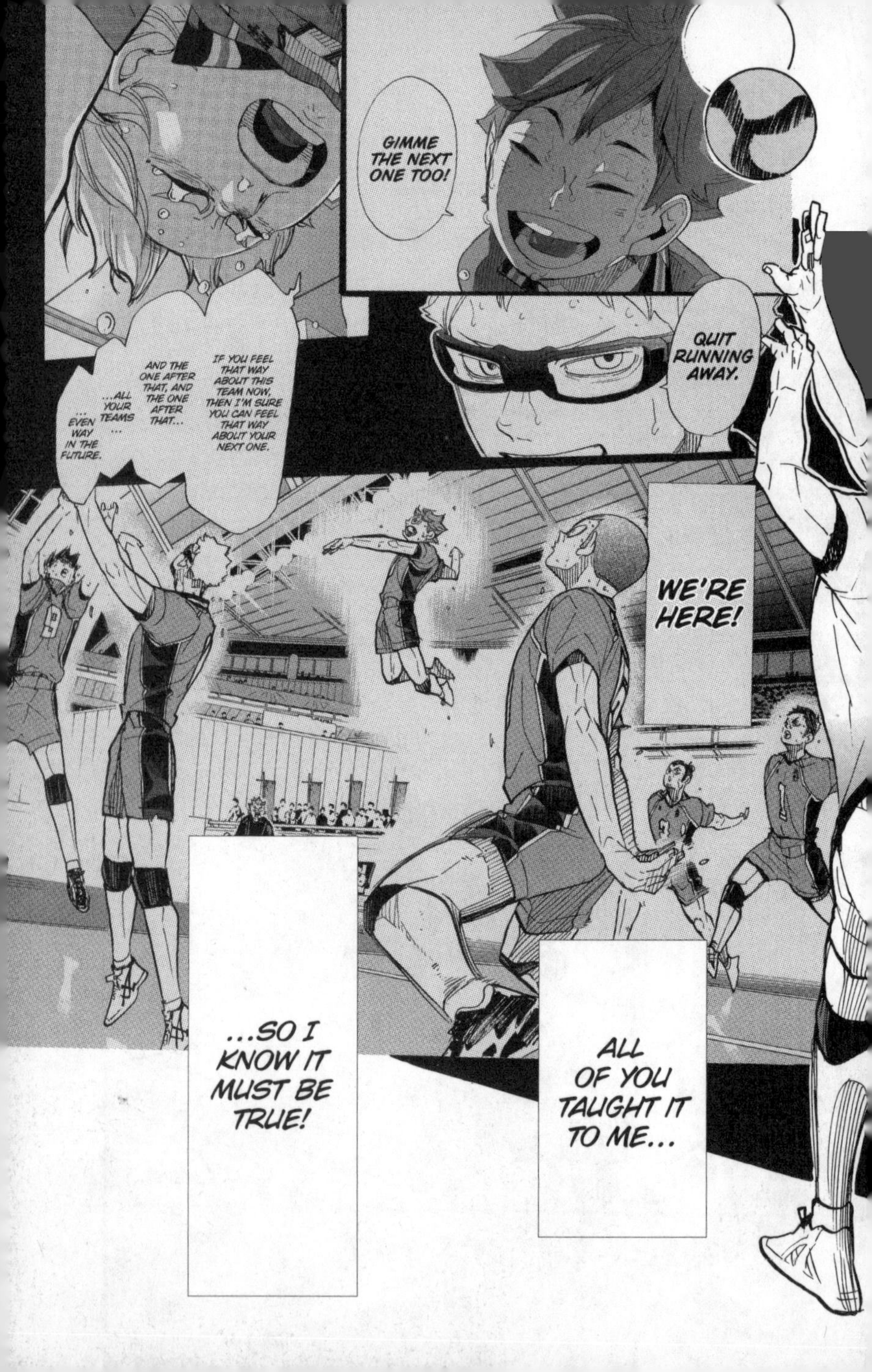
GIMME THE NEXT ONE TOO!
QUIT RUNNING AWAY.
IF YOU FEEL THAT WAY ABOUT THIS TEAM NOW, THEN I'M SURE YOU CAN FEEL THAT WAY ABOUT YOUR NEXT ONE.
AND THE ONE AFTER THAT, AND THE ONE AFTER THAT...
...ALL YOUR TEAMS...
...EVEN WAY IN THE FUTURE.
WE'RE HERE!
ALL OF YOU TAUGHT IT TO ME...
...SO I KNOW IT MUST BE TRUE!

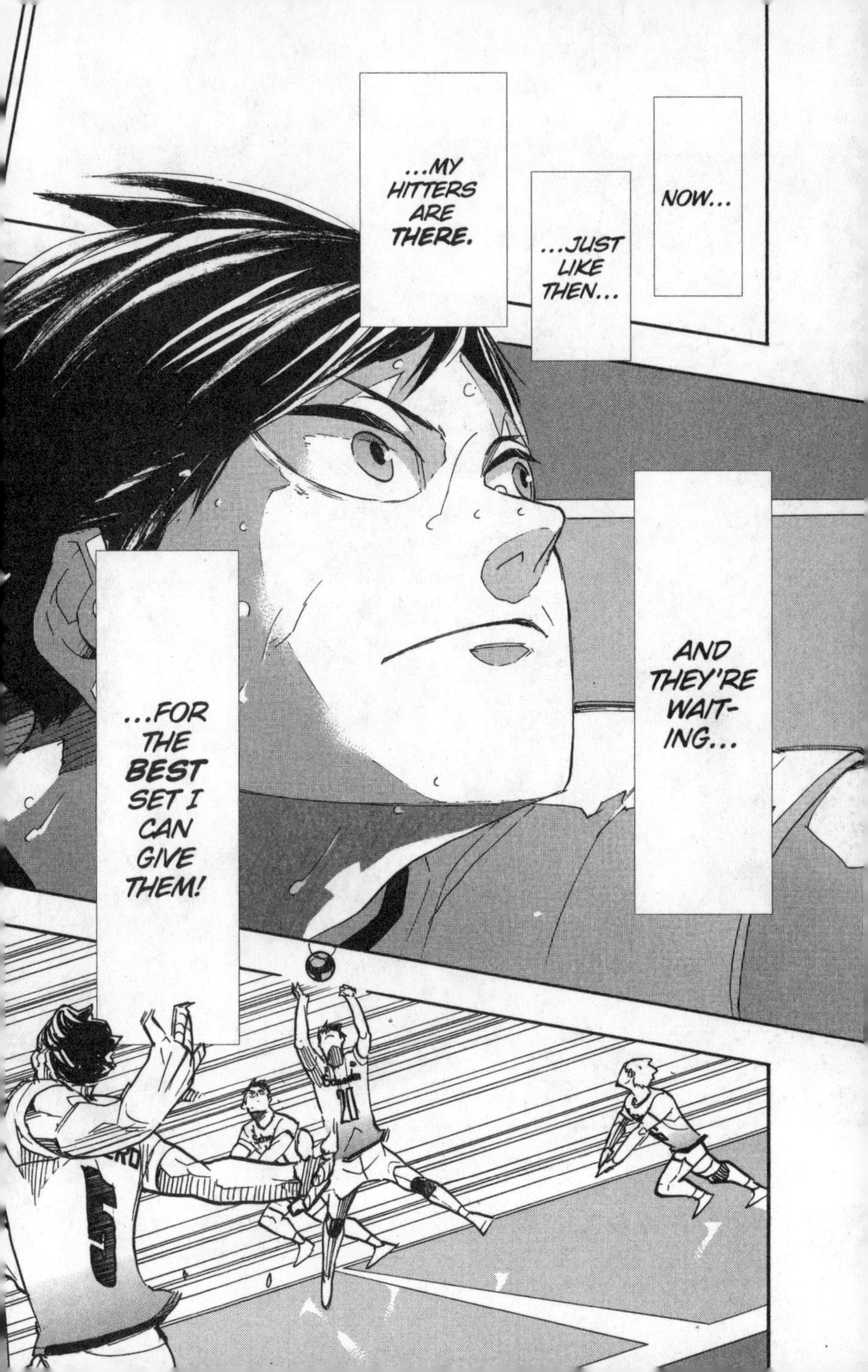
NOW...
...JUST LIKE THEN...
...MY HITTERS ARE THERE.
AND THEY'RE WAIT-ING...
...FOR THE BEST SET I CAN GIVE THEM!

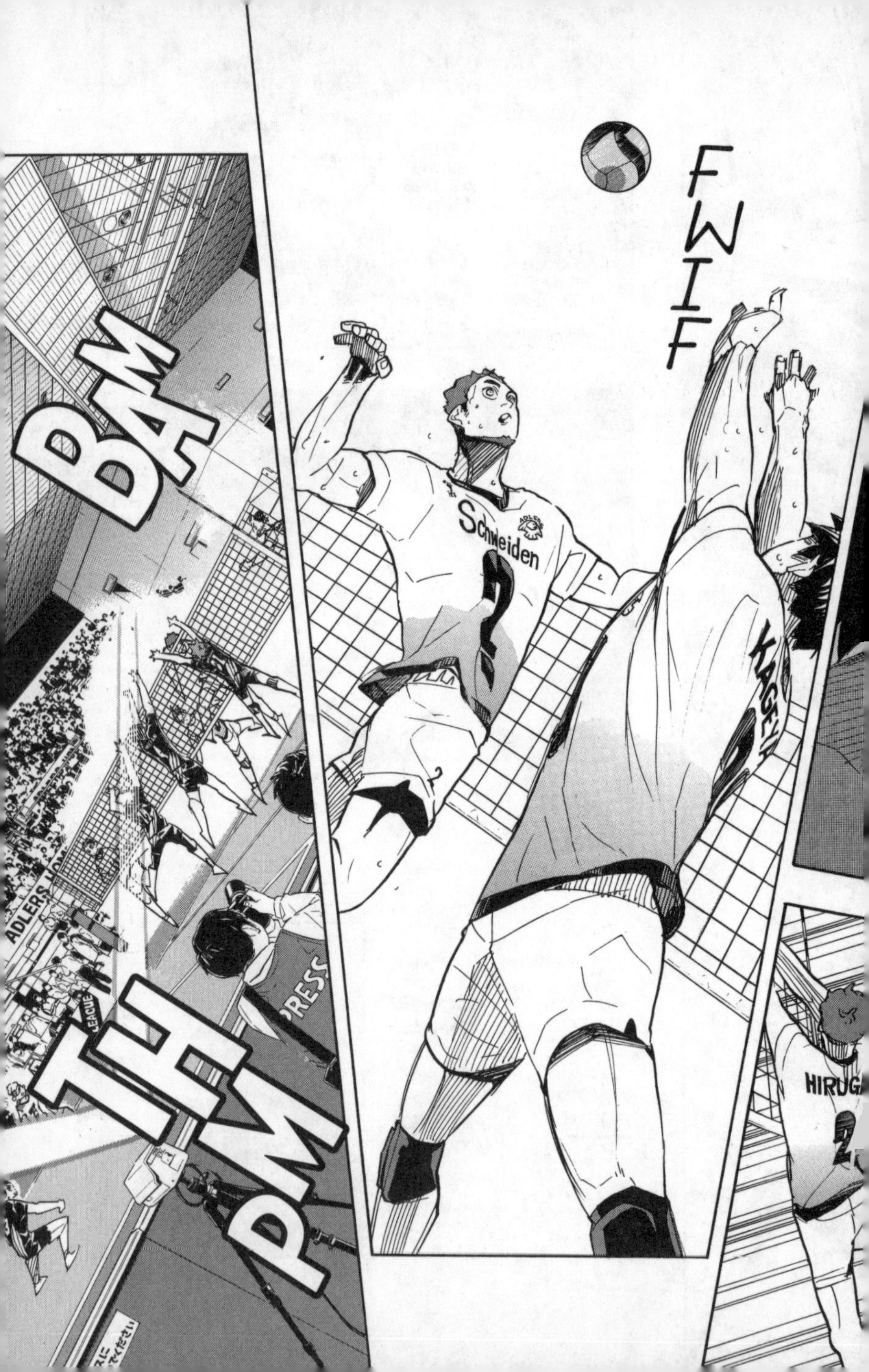

HIRUGA
FWIFF
Schweiden
KAGEYA
BAM
ADLERS HOM
LEAGUE
PRESS
THUMP

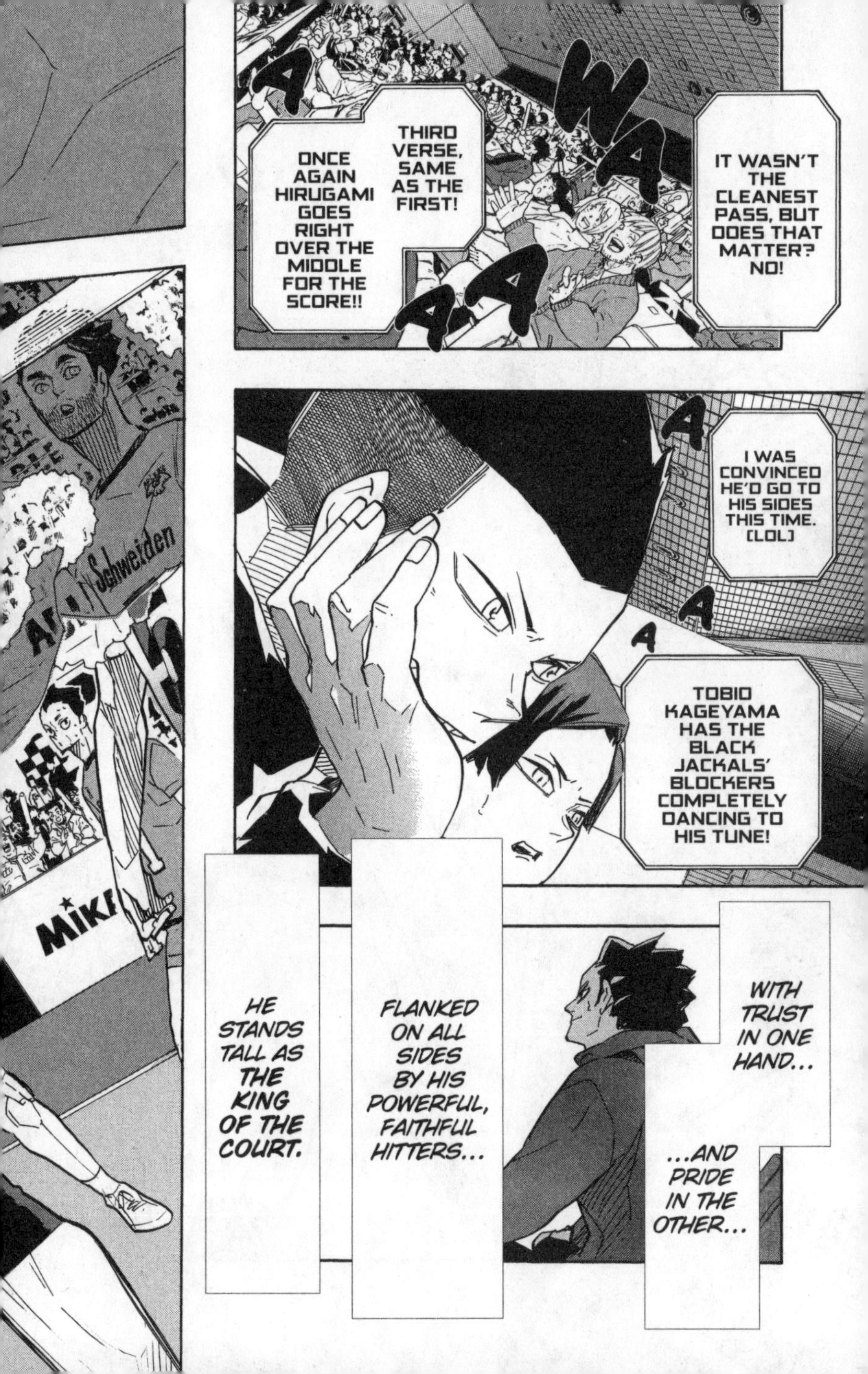
IT WASN'T THE CLEANEST PASS, BUT DOES THAT MATTER? NO!
WA
A
THIRD VERSE, SAME AS THE FIRST!
ONCE AGAIN HIRUGAMI GOES RIGHT OVER THE MIDDLE FOR THE SCORE!!
A
A
A
I WAS CONVINCED HE'D GO TO HIS SIDES THIS TIME. [LOL]
A
A
TOBIO KAGEYAMA HAS THE BLACK JACKALS' BLOCKERS COMPLETELY DANCING TO HIS TUNE!
WITH TRUST IN ONE HAND...
...AND PRIDE IN THE OTHER...
FLANKED ON ALL SIDES BY HIS POWERFUL, FAITHFUL HITTERS...
HE STANDS TALL AS THE KING OF THE COURT.
Schweiden

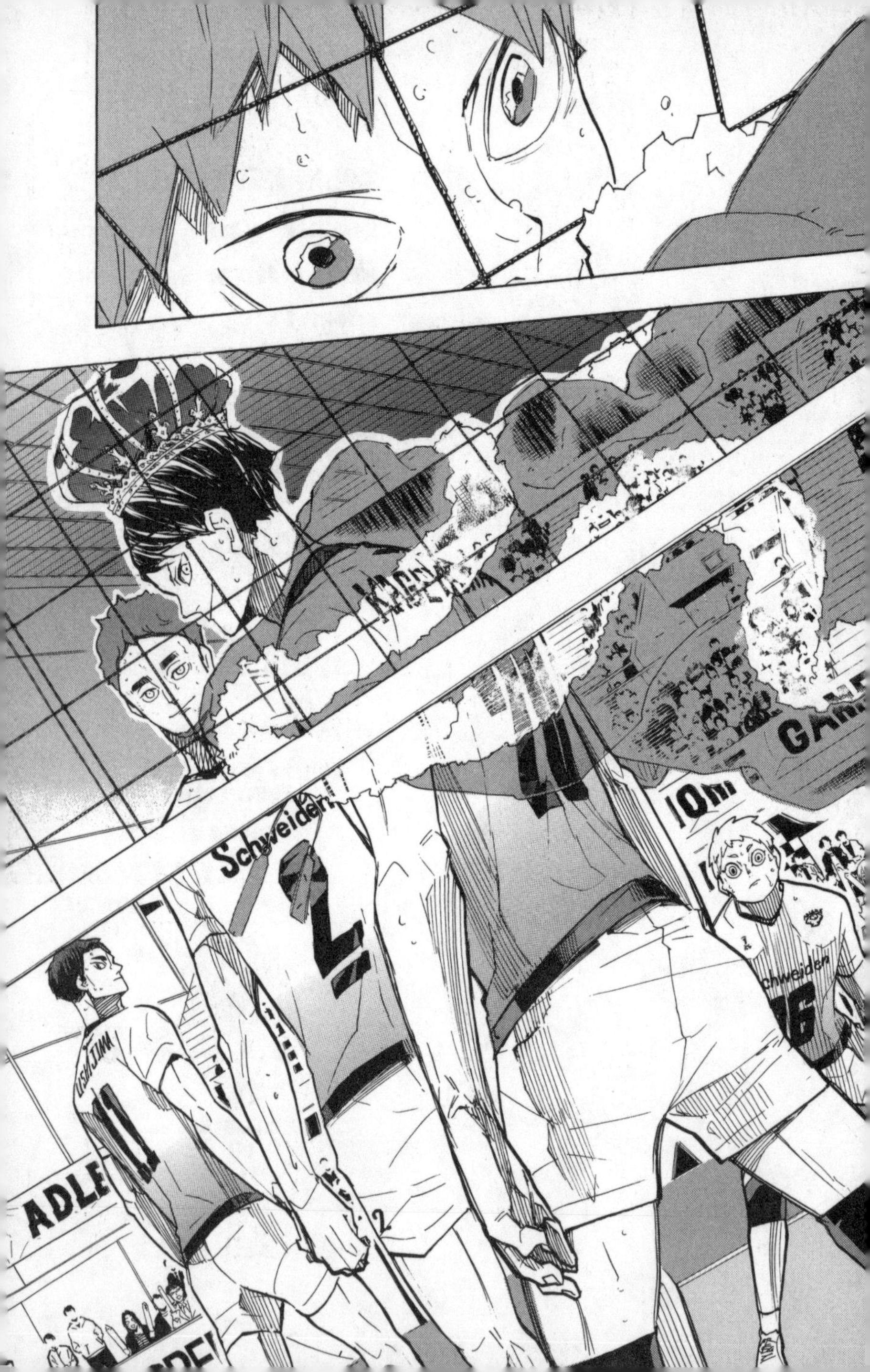
Schweiden
ADLE

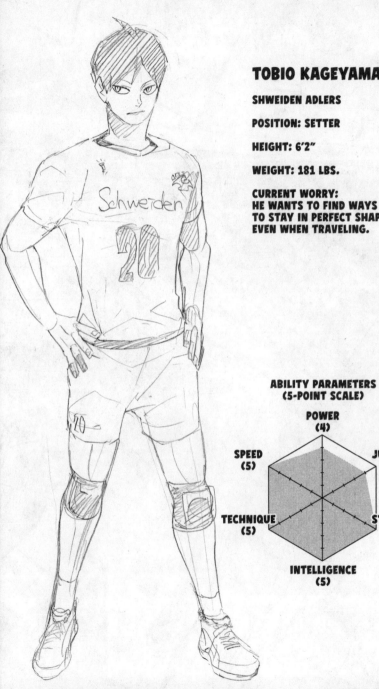

TOBIO KAGEYAMA (21)

SHWEIDEN ADLERS

POSITION: SETTER

HEIGHT: 6'2"

WEIGHT: 181 LBS.

CURRENT WORRY:
HE WANTS TO FIND WAYS
TO STAY IN PERFECT SHAPE
EVEN WHEN TRAVELING.

ABILITY PARAMETERS
(5-POINT SCALE)

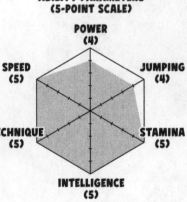

POWER (4)
JUMPING (4)
STAMINA (5)
INTELLIGENCE (5)
TECHNIQUE (5)
SPEED (5)

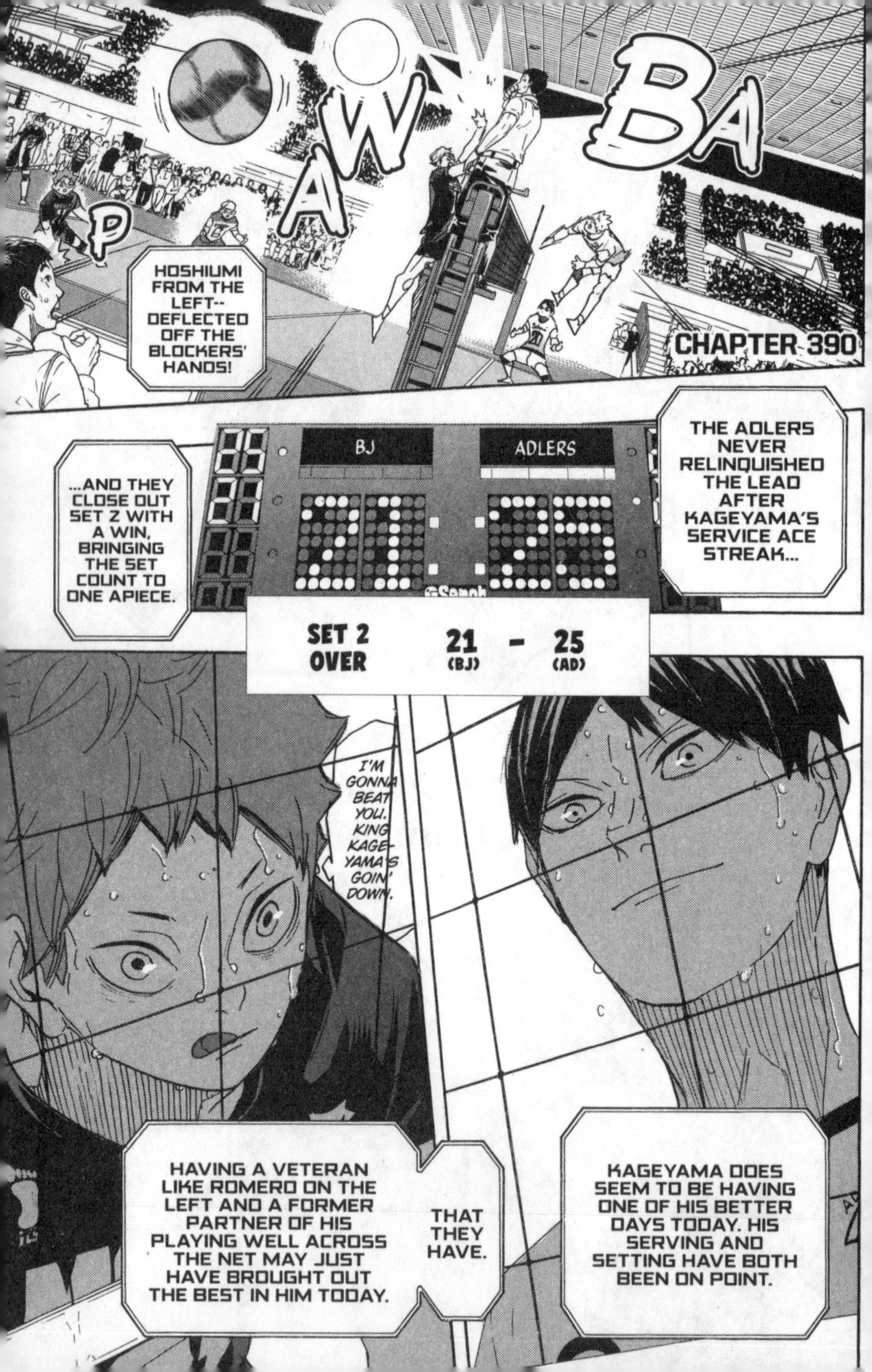
CHAPTER 390
BA W A P
HOSHIUMI FROM THE LEFT-- DEFLECTED OFF THE BLOCKERS' HANDS!
THE ADLERS NEVER RELINQUISHED THE LEAD AFTER KAGEYAMA'S SERVICE ACE STREAK...
BJ
ADLERS
21 : 25
...AND THEY CLOSE OUT SET 2 WITH A WIN, BRINGING THE SET COUNT TO ONE APIECE.
SET 2 OVER 21 (BJ) - 25 (AD)
I'M GONNA BEAT YOU. KING KAGEYAMA'S GOIN' DOWN.
KAGEYAMA DOES SEEM TO BE HAVING ONE OF HIS BETTER DAYS TODAY. HIS SERVING AND SETTING HAVE BOTH BEEN ON POINT.
THAT THEY HAVE.
HAVING A VETERAN LIKE ROMERO ON THE LEFT AND A FORMER PARTNER OF HIS PLAYING WELL ACROSS THE NET MAY JUST HAVE BROUGHT OUT THE BEST IN HIM TODAY.

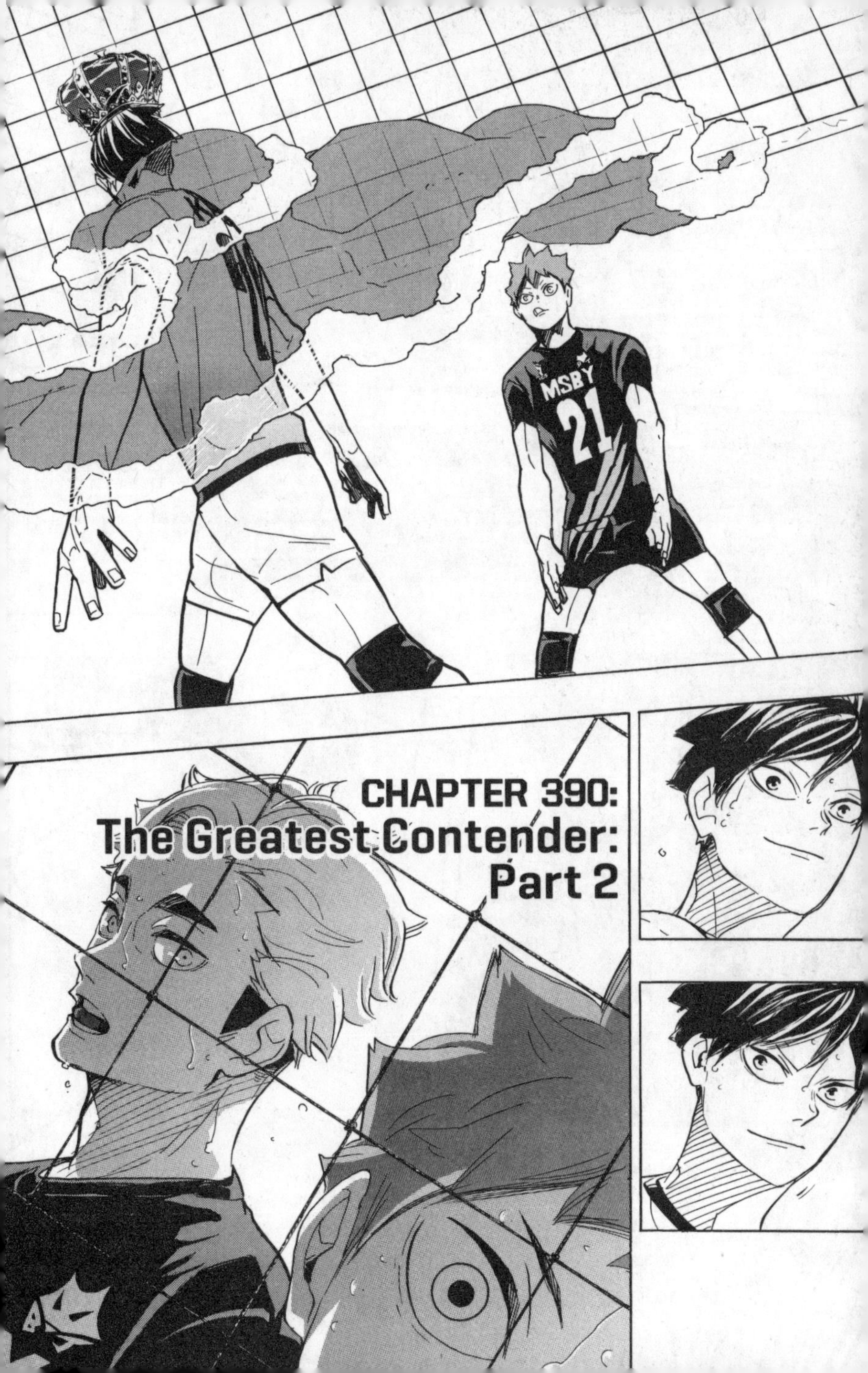
MSBY
21
CHAPTER 390:
The Greatest Contender:
Part 2

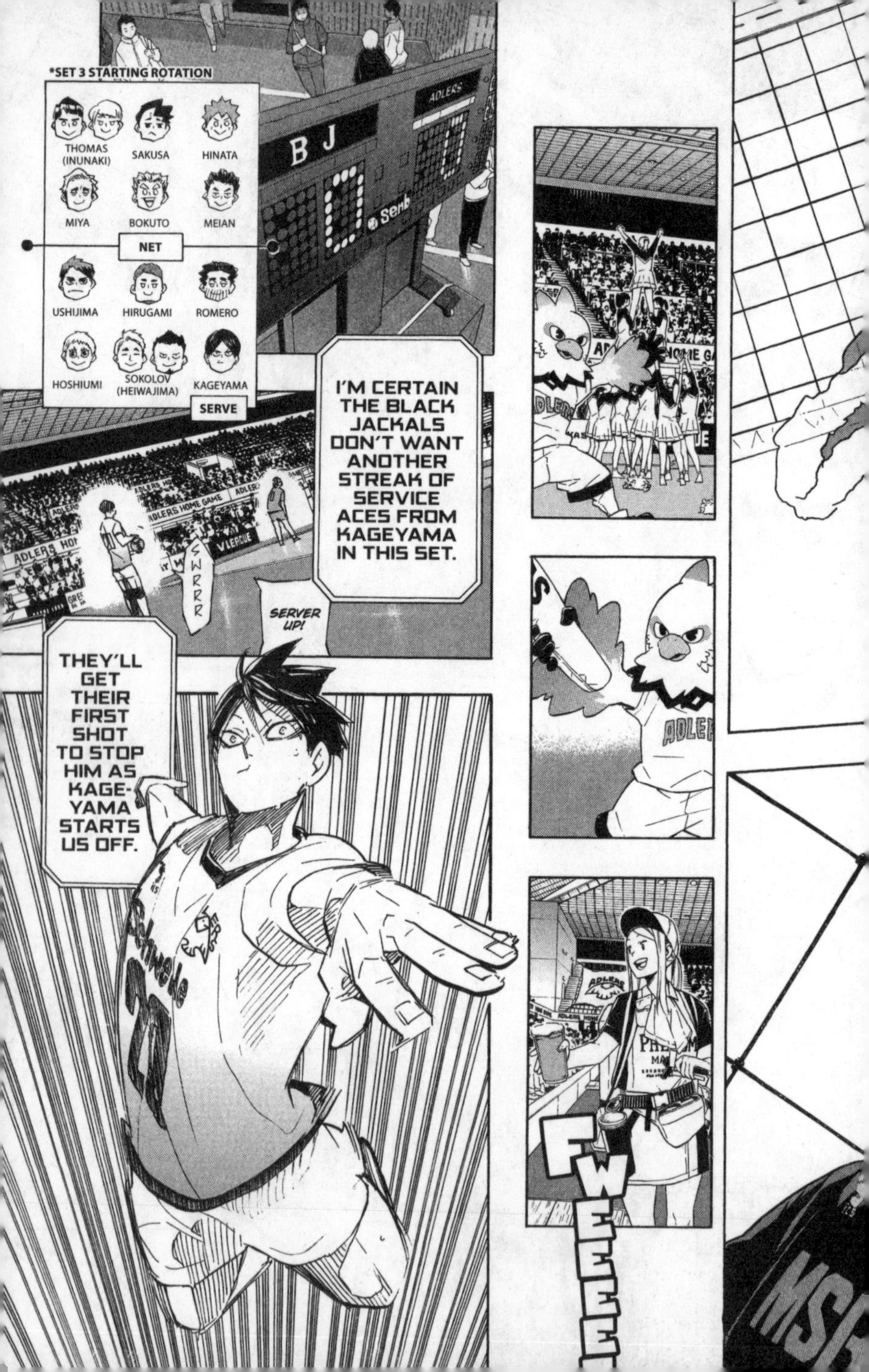
FWEEEE
*SET 3 STARTING ROTATION
THOMAS (INUNAKI)
SAKUSA
HINATA
MIYA
BOKUTO
MEIAN
NET
USHIJIMA
HIRUGAMI
ROMERO
HOSHIUMI
SOKOLOV (HEIWAJIMA)
KAGEYAMA
SERVE
I'M CERTAIN THE BLACK JACKALS DON'T WANT ANOTHER STREAK OF SERVICE ACES FROM KAGEYAMA IN THIS SET.
SWRRR
SERVER UP!
THEY'LL GET THEIR FIRST SHOT TO STOP HIM AS KAGE-YAMA STARTS US OFF.

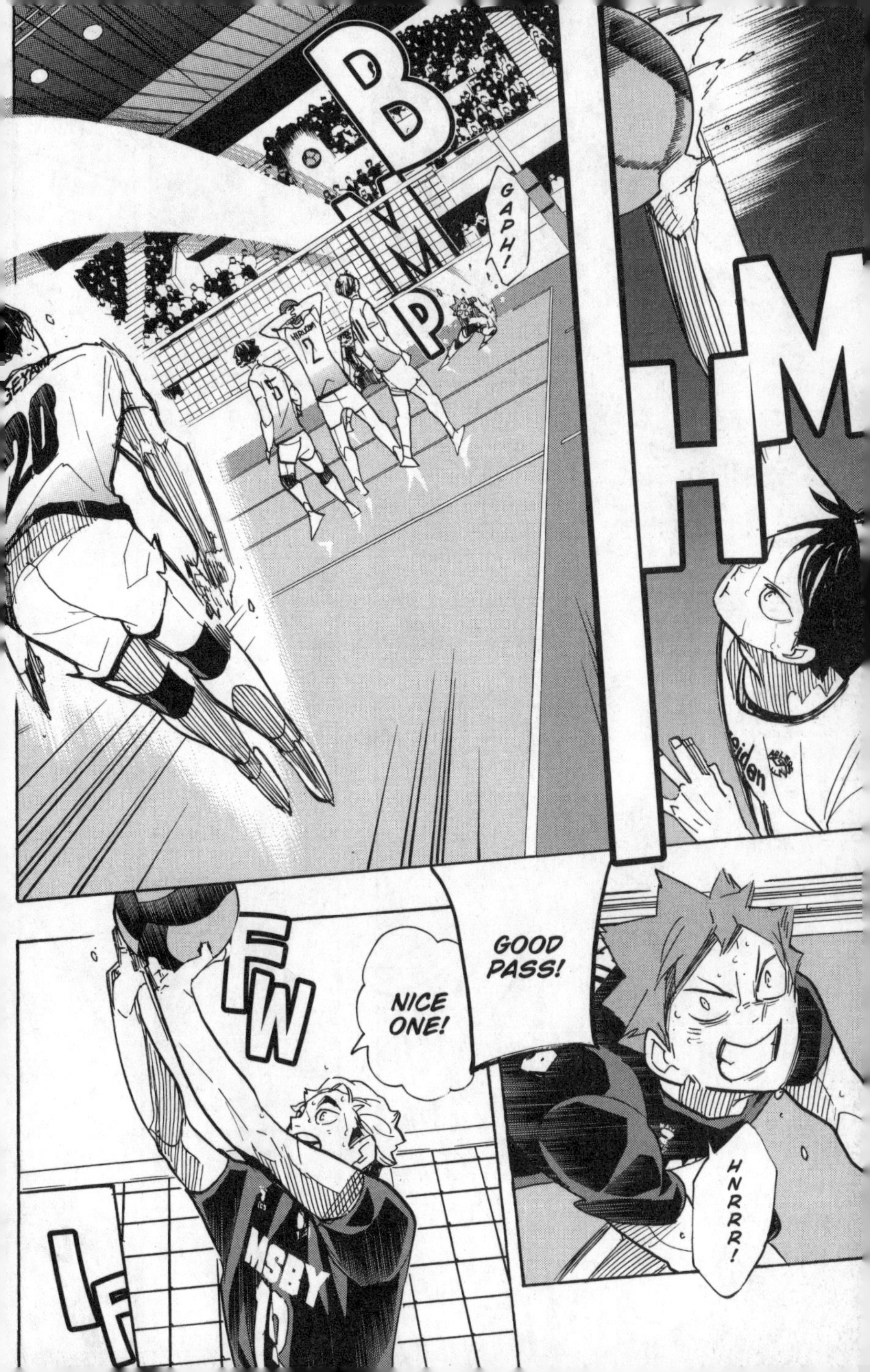
HMM
BUMP
GAPH!
GOOD PASS!
HNRRR!
NICE ONE!

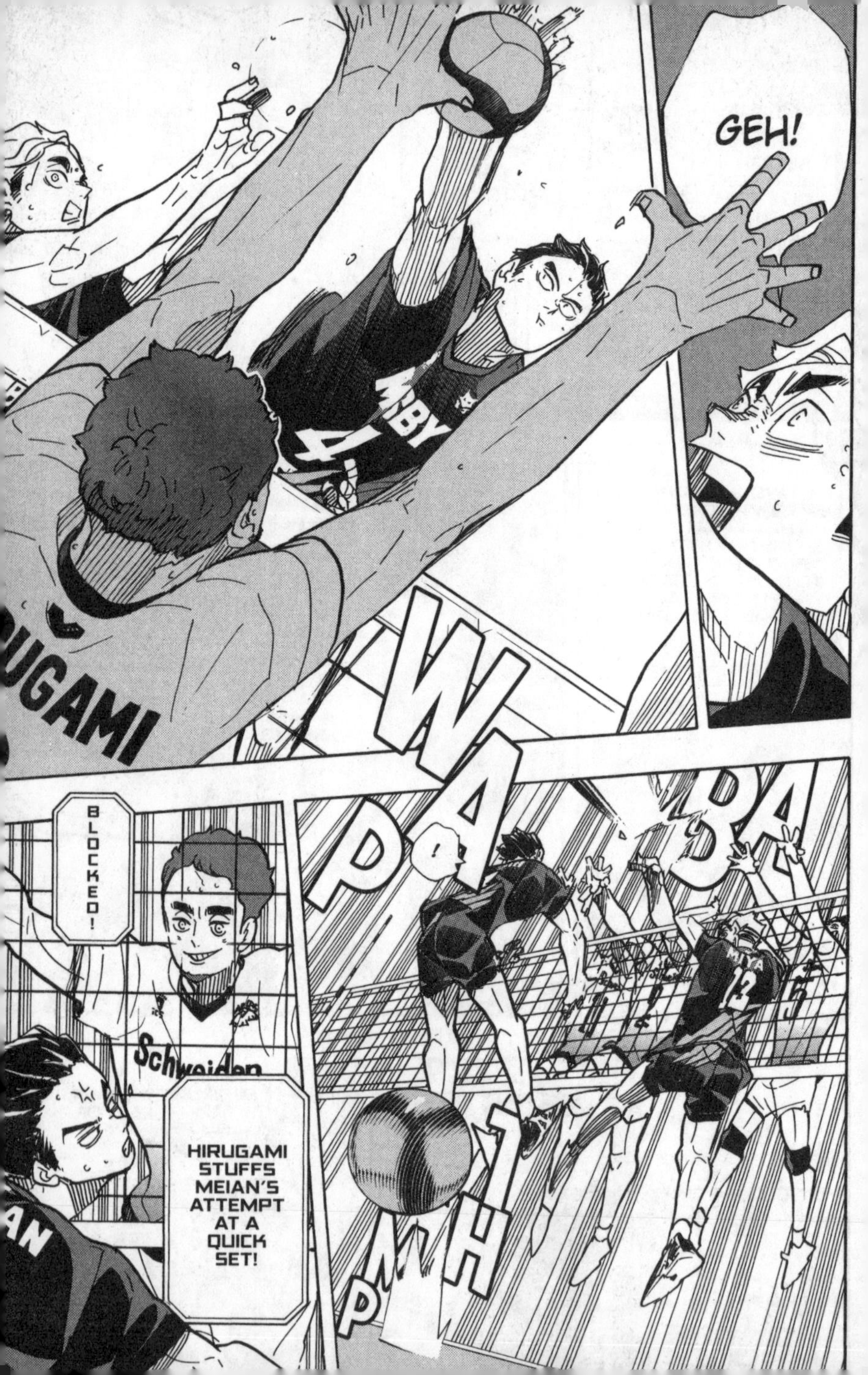
GEH!
BLOCKED!
HIRUGAMI STUFFS MEIAN'S ATTEMPT AT A QUICK SET!

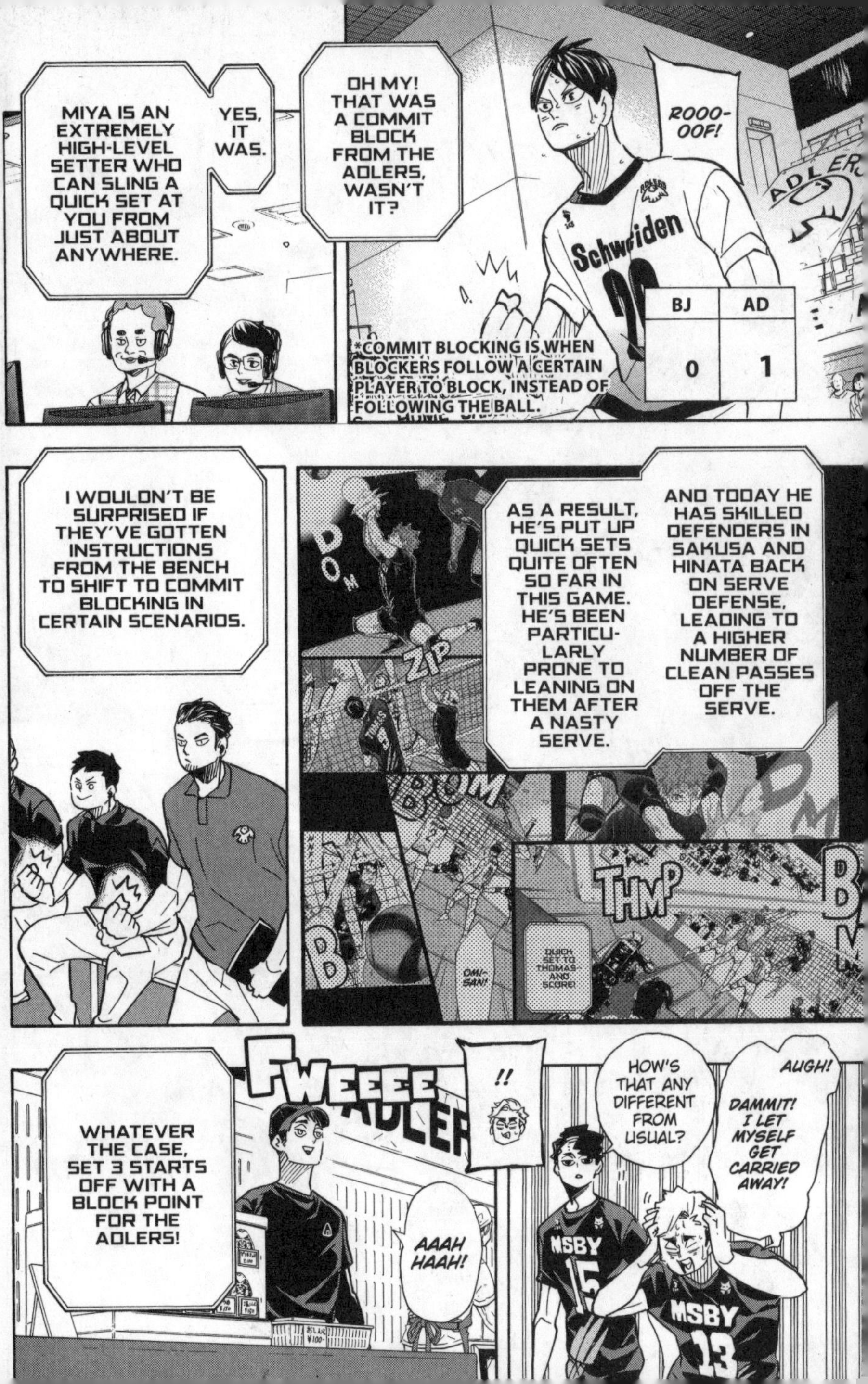
ROOOOOF!
OH MY! THAT WAS A COMMIT BLOCK FROM THE ADLERS, WASN'T IT?
*COMMIT BLOCKING IS WHEN BLOCKERS FOLLOW A CERTAIN PLAYER TO BLOCK, INSTEAD OF FOLLOWING THE BALL.
BJ AD
0 1
YES, IT WAS.
MIYA IS AN EXTREMELY HIGH-LEVEL SETTER WHO CAN SLING A QUICK SET AT YOU FROM JUST ABOUT ANYWHERE.
AND TODAY HE HAS SKILLED DEFENDERS IN SAKUSA AND HINATA BACK ON SERVE DEFENSE, LEADING TO A HIGHER NUMBER OF CLEAN PASSES OFF THE SERVE.
AS A RESULT, HE'S PUT UP QUICK SETS QUITE OFTEN SO FAR IN THIS GAME. HE'S BEEN PARTICU-LARLY PRONE TO LEANING ON THEM AFTER A NASTY SERVE.
BOOM
ZIP
BOOM
THMP
QUICK SET TO THOMAS AND SCORE!
OMI-SAN!
I WOULDN'T BE SURPRISED IF THEY'VE GOTTEN INSTRUCTIONS FROM THE BENCH TO SHIFT TO COMMIT BLOCKING IN CERTAIN SCENARIOS.
AUGH!
DAMMIT! I LET MYSELF GET CARRIED AWAY!
HOW'S THAT ANY DIFFERENT FROM USUAL?
!!
FWEEEE
AAAH HAAH!
WHATEVER THE CASE, SET 3 STARTS OFF WITH A BLOCK POINT FOR THE ADLERS!

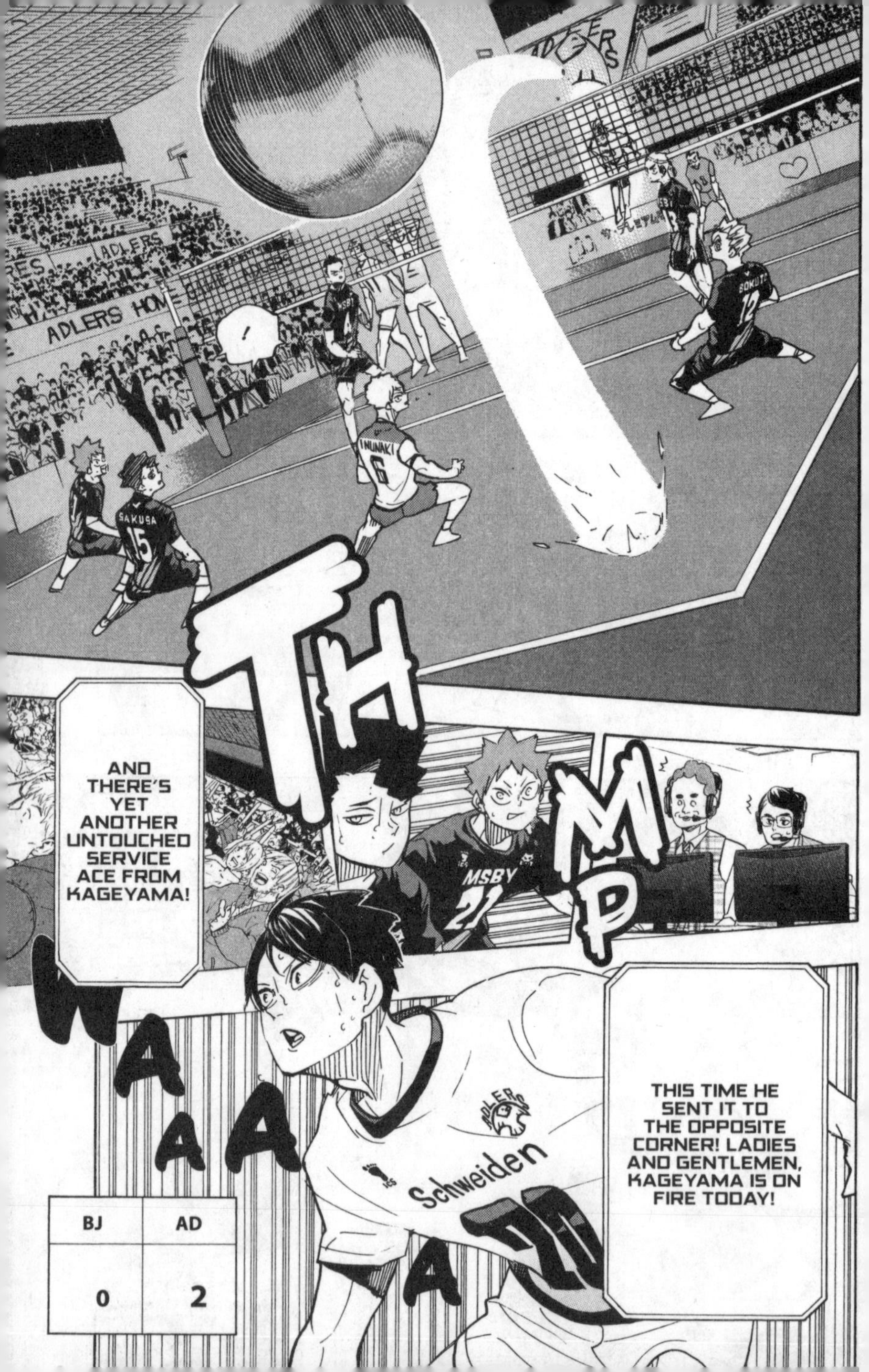
!
THUMP
AND THERE'S YET ANOTHER UNTOUCHED SERVICE ACE FROM KAGEYAMA!
THIS TIME HE SENT IT TO THE OPPOSITE CORNER! LADIES AND GENTLEMEN, KAGEYAMA IS ON FIRE TODAY!
WAAAA
BJ AD
0 2

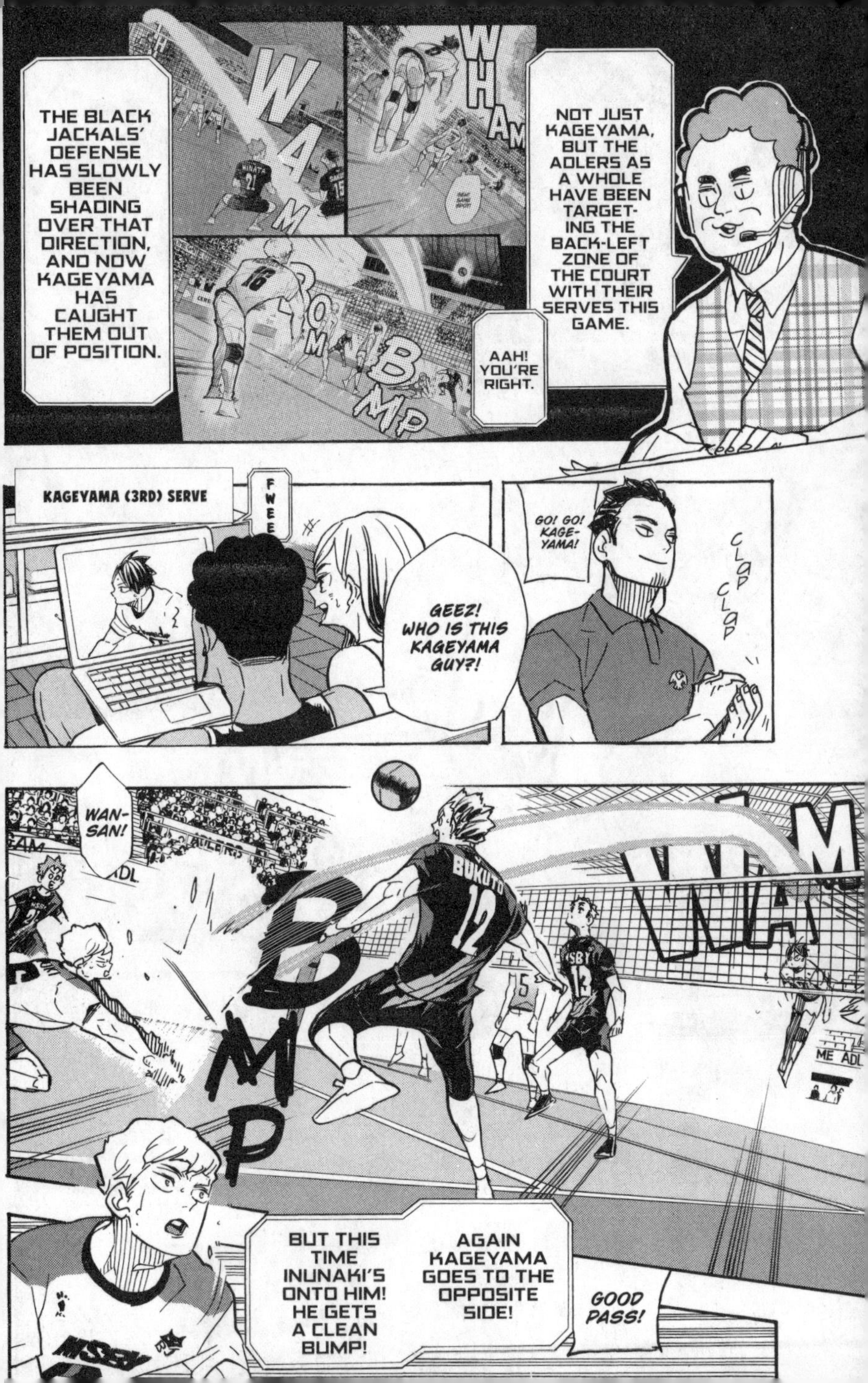
NOT JUST KAGEYAMA, BUT THE ADLERS AS A WHOLE HAVE BEEN TARGET-ING THE BACK-LEFT ZONE OF THE COURT WITH THEIR SERVES THIS GAME.
AAH! YOU'RE RIGHT.
WHAM
WHAM
BOMP
BUMP
THE BLACK JACKALS' DEFENSE HAS SLOWLY BEEN SHADING OVER THAT DIRECTION, AND NOW KAGEYAMA HAS CAUGHT THEM OUT OF POSITION.
GO! GO! KAGEYAMA!
CLAP CLAP
KAGEYAMA (3RD) SERVE
FWEE
GEEZ! WHO IS THIS KAGEYAMA GUY?!
WAM
BUKUTO
12
BUMP
WAN-SAN!
GOOD PASS!
AGAIN KAGEYAMA GOES TO THE OPPOSITE SIDE!
BUT THIS TIME INUNAKI'S ONTO HIM! HE GETS A CLEAN BUMP!

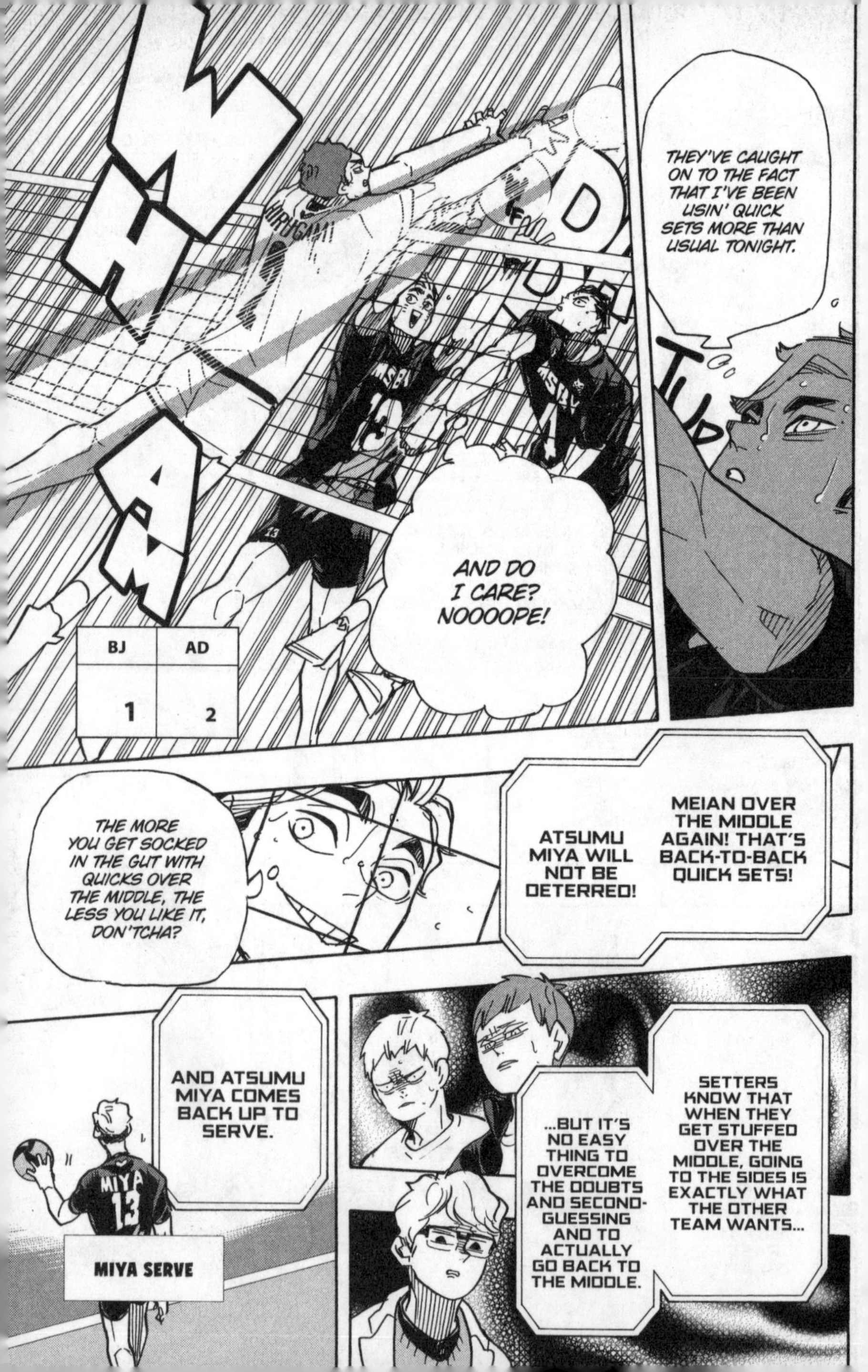
THEY'VE CAUGHT ON TO THE FACT THAT I'VE BEEN USIN' QUICK SETS MORE THAN USUAL TONIGHT.
WHAM
AND DO I CARE? NOOOOPE!
BJ AD
1 2
MEIAN OVER THE MIDDLE AGAIN! THAT'S BACK-TO-BACK QUICK SETS!
ATSUMU MIYA WILL NOT BE DETERRED!
THE MORE YOU GET SOCKED IN THE GUT WITH QUICKS OVER THE MIDDLE, THE LESS YOU LIKE IT, DON'TCHA?
SETTERS KNOW THAT WHEN THEY GET STUFFED OVER THE MIDDLE, GOING TO THE SIDES IS EXACTLY WHAT THE OTHER TEAM WANTS...
...BUT IT'S NO EASY THING TO OVERCOME THE DOUBTS AND SECOND-GUESSING AND TO ACTUALLY GO BACK TO THE MIDDLE.
AND ATSUMU MIYA COMES BACK UP TO SERVE.
MIYA SERVE

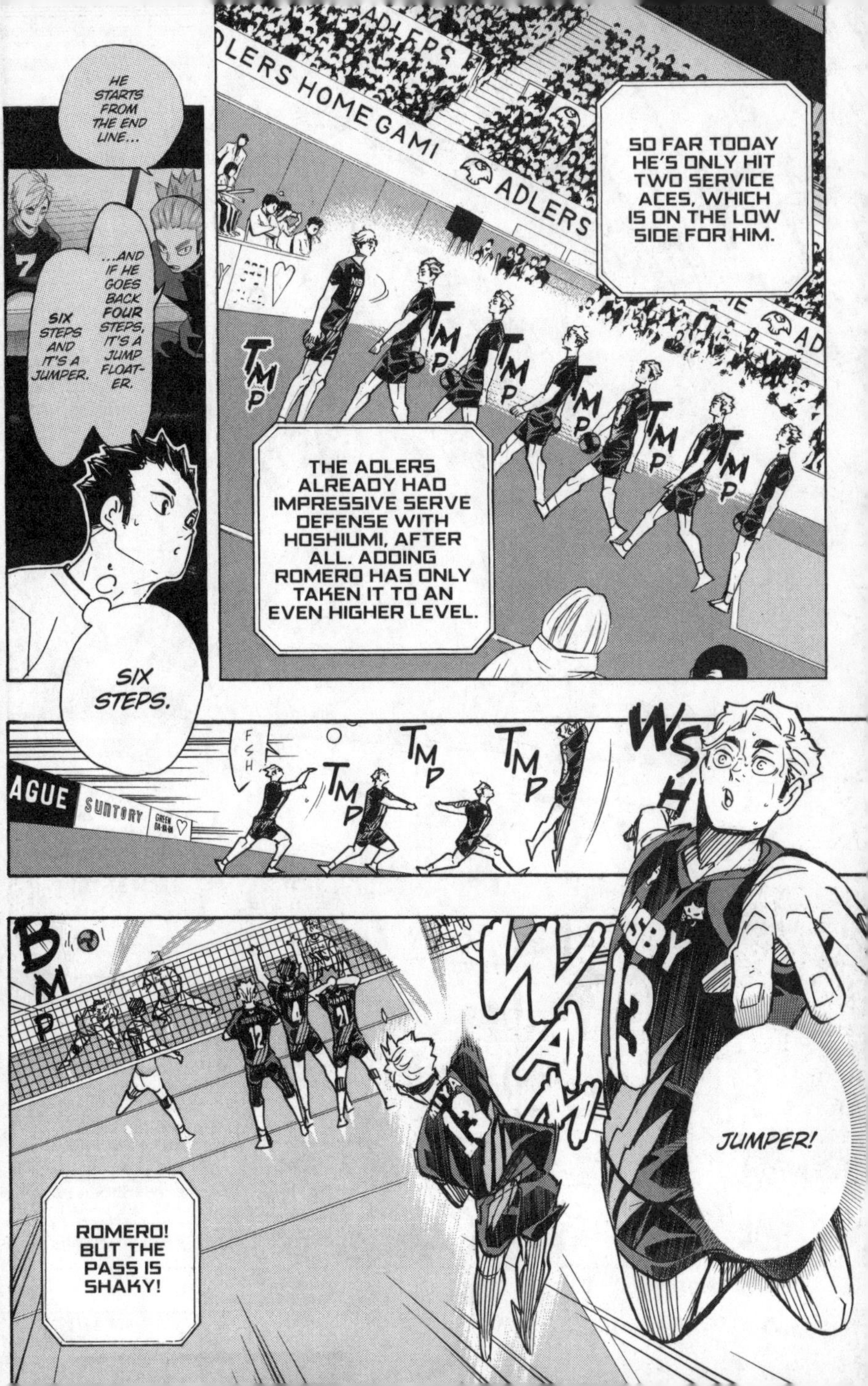
ADLERS
ADLERS HOME GAMI
ADLERS
SO FAR TODAY HE'S ONLY HIT TWO SERVICE ACES, WHICH IS ON THE LOW SIDE FOR HIM.
TMP TMP TMP TMP TMP TMP
THE ADLERS ALREADY HAD IMPRESSIVE SERVE DEFENSE WITH HOSHIUMI, AFTER ALL. ADDING ROMERO HAS ONLY TAKEN IT TO AN EVEN HIGHER LEVEL.
HE STARTS FROM THE END LINE...
...AND IF HE GOES BACK FOUR STEPS, IT'S A JUMP FLOATER.
SIX STEPS AND IT'S A JUMPER.
SIX STEPS.
WSH
TMP TMP TMP
FSH
AGUE
SUNTORY
WAM
JUMPER!
BMP
ROMERO! BUT THE PASS IS SHAKY!

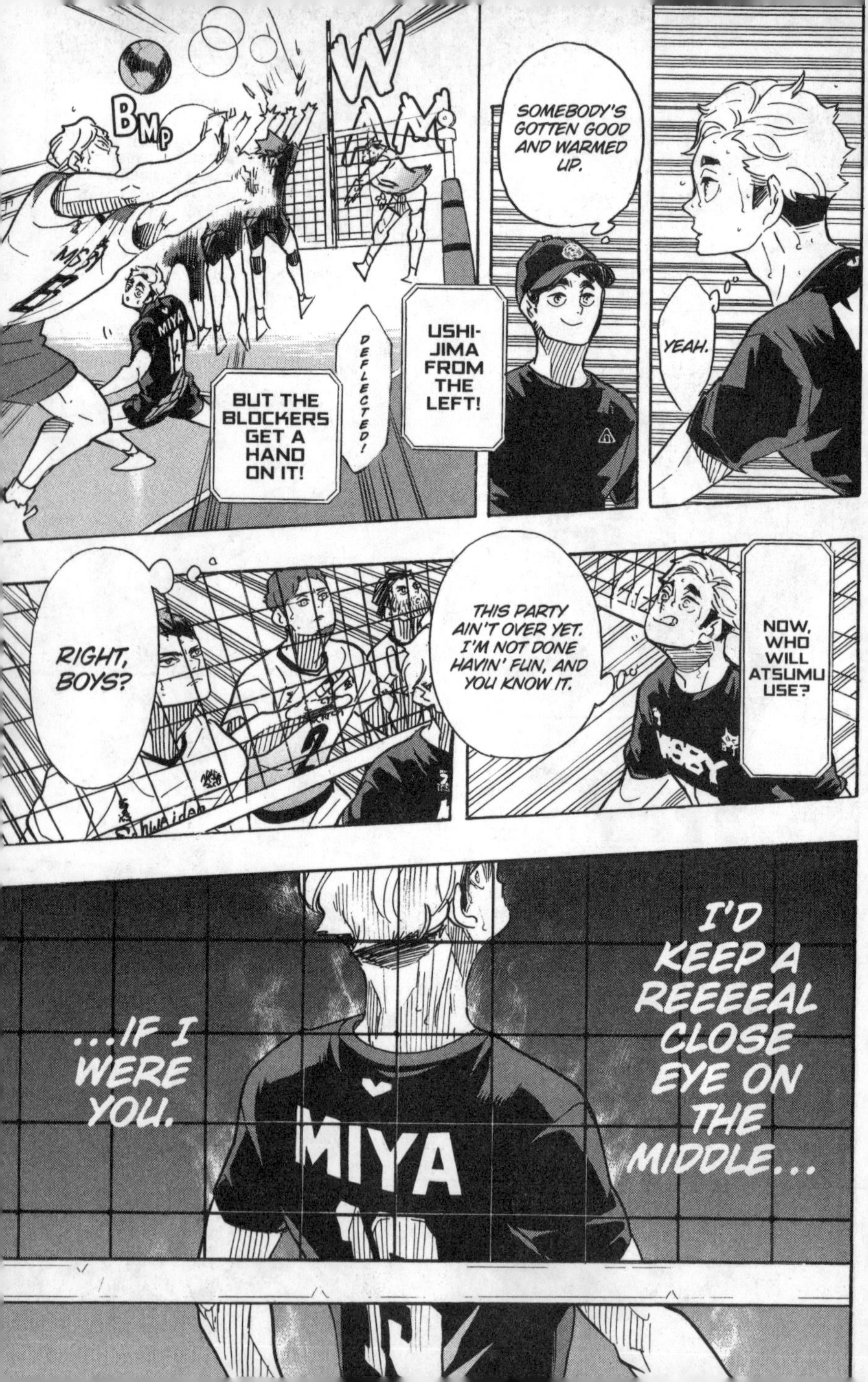
SOMEBODY'S GOTTEN GOOD AND WARMED UP.
YEAH.
USHI-JIMA FROM THE LEFT!
WAM
DEFLECTED!
BUT THE BLOCKERS GET A HAND ON IT!
BMP
NOW, WHO WILL ATSUMU USE?
THIS PARTY AIN'T OVER YET. I'M NOT DONE HAVIN' FUN, AND YOU KNOW IT.
RIGHT, BOYS?
I'D KEEP A REEEEAL CLOSE EYE ON THE MIDDLE...
...IF I WERE YOU.

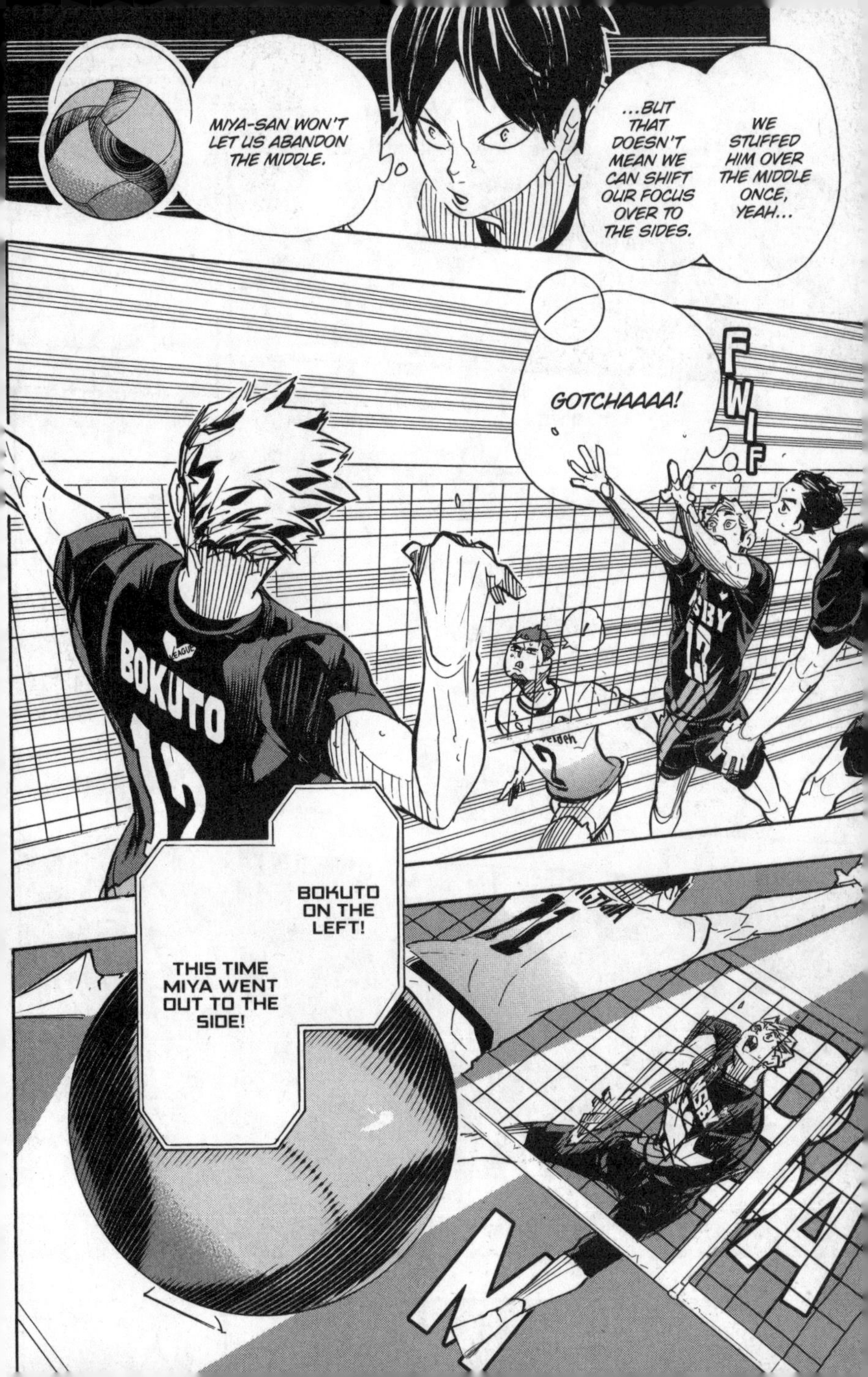
WE STUFFED HIM OVER THE MIDDLE ONCE, YEAH...
...BUT THAT DOESN'T MEAN WE CAN SHIFT OUR FOCUS OVER TO THE SIDES.
MIYA-SAN WON'T LET US ABANDON THE MIDDLE.
FWIF
GOTCHAAAA!
BOKUTO ON THE LEFT!
THIS TIME MIYA WENT OUT TO THE SIDE!

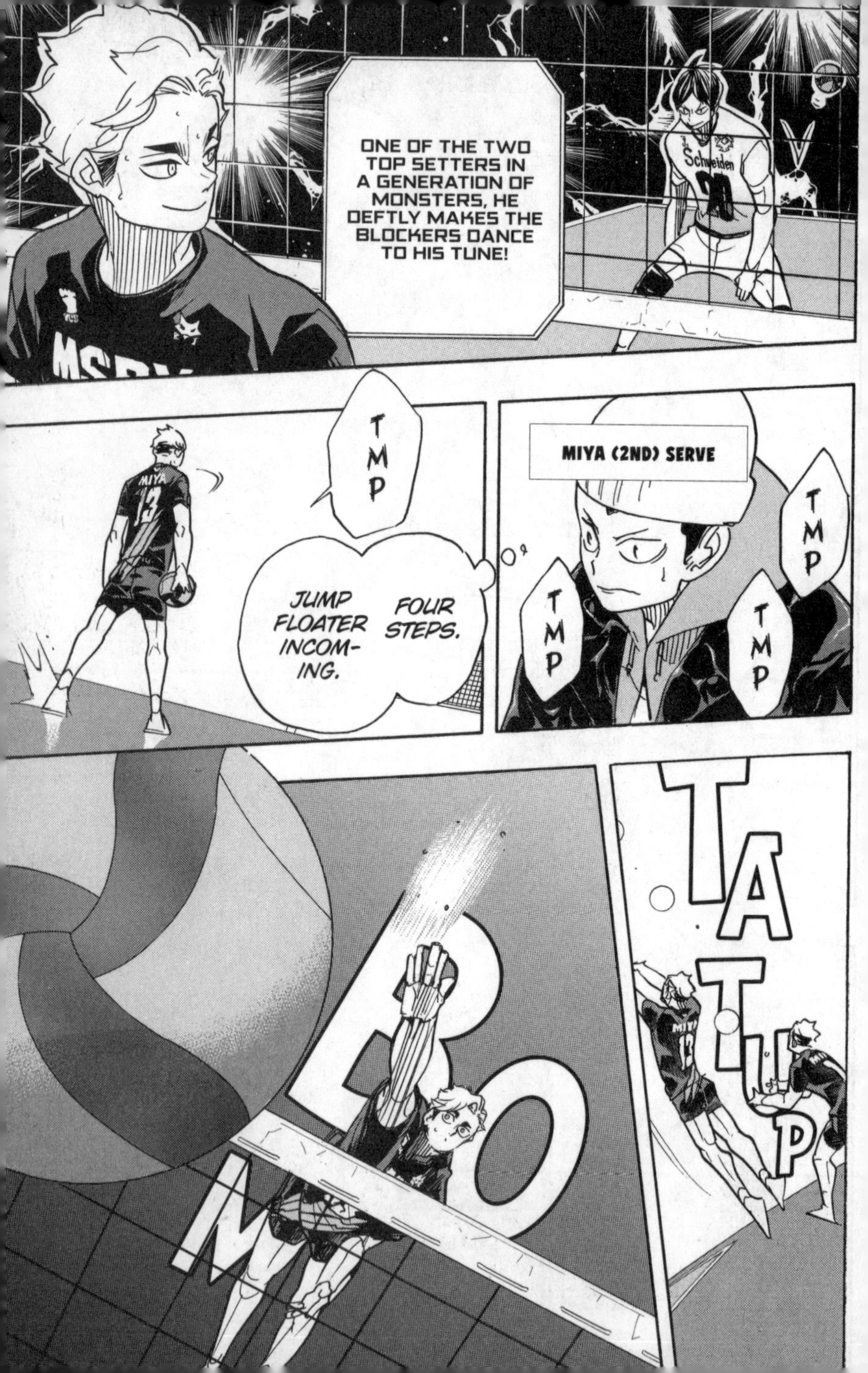
ONE OF THE TWO TOP SETTERS IN A GENERATION OF MONSTERS, HE DEFTLY MAKES THE BLOCKERS DANCE TO HIS TUNE!
MIYA (2ND) SERVE
TMP
TMP
TMP
TMP
JUMP FLOATER INCOMING.
FOUR STEPS.
TATUP
BOM

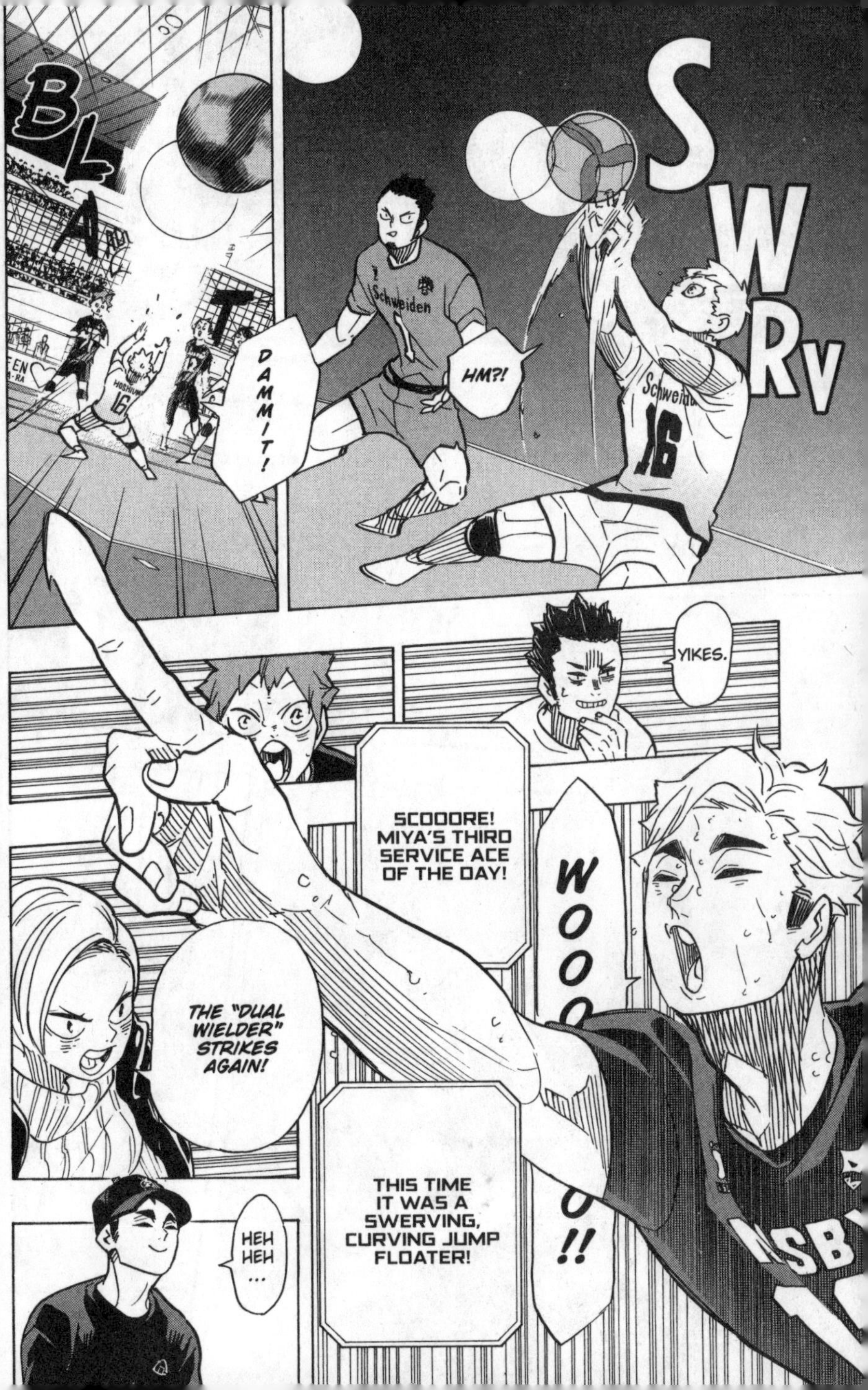
SWRV
HM?!
DAMMIT!
BLAST
YIKES.
SCOOORE! MIYA'S THIRD SERVICE ACE OF THE DAY!
WOOOO!!
THE "DUAL WIELDER" STRIKES AGAIN!
THIS TIME IT WAS A SWERVING, CURVING JUMP FLOATER!
HEH HEH ...

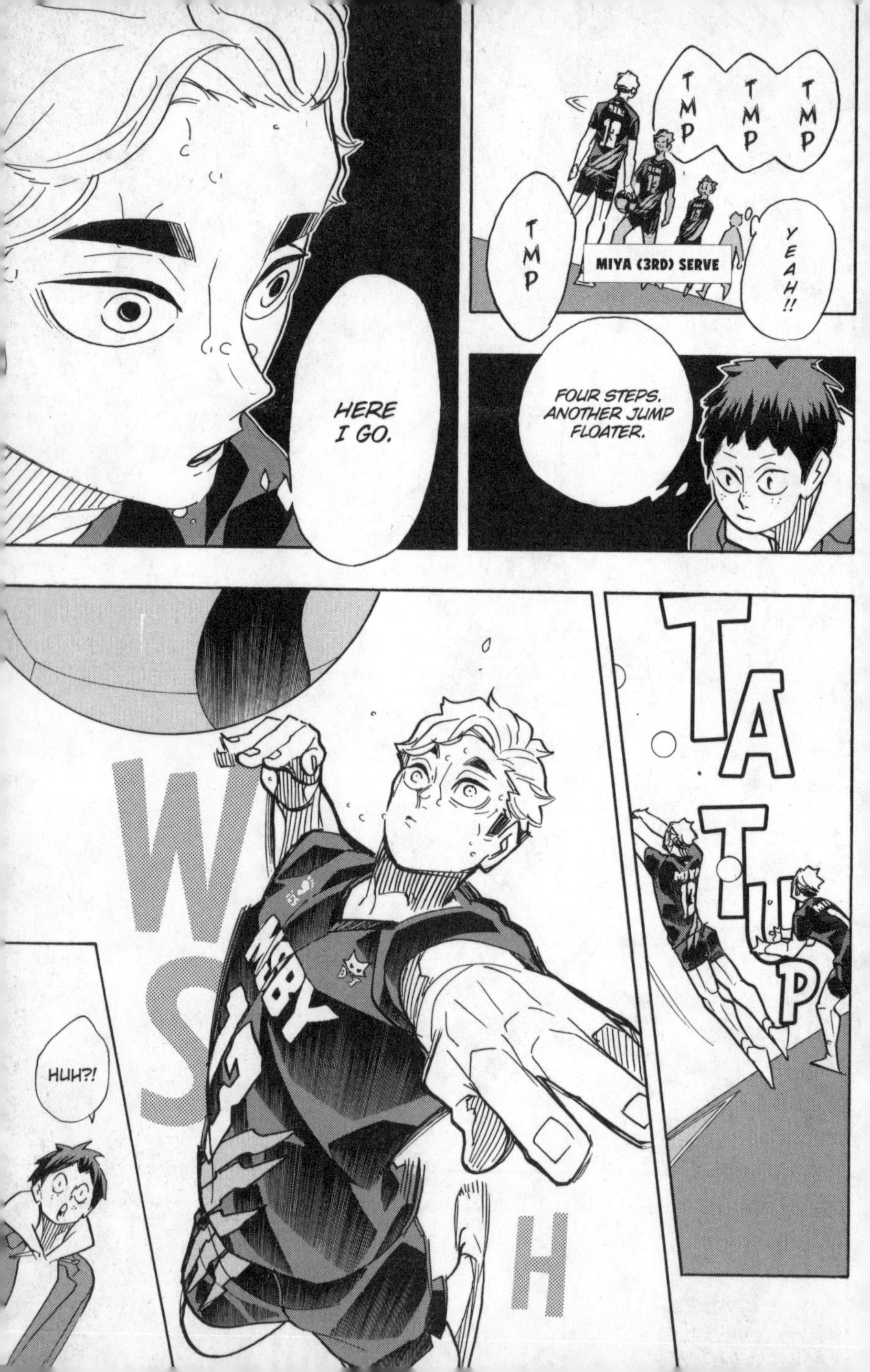

TMP TMP TMP
YEAH!!
MIYA (3RD) SERVE
TMP
FOUR STEPS. ANOTHER JUMP FLOATER.
HERE I GO.
TATUP
WSH
HUH?!

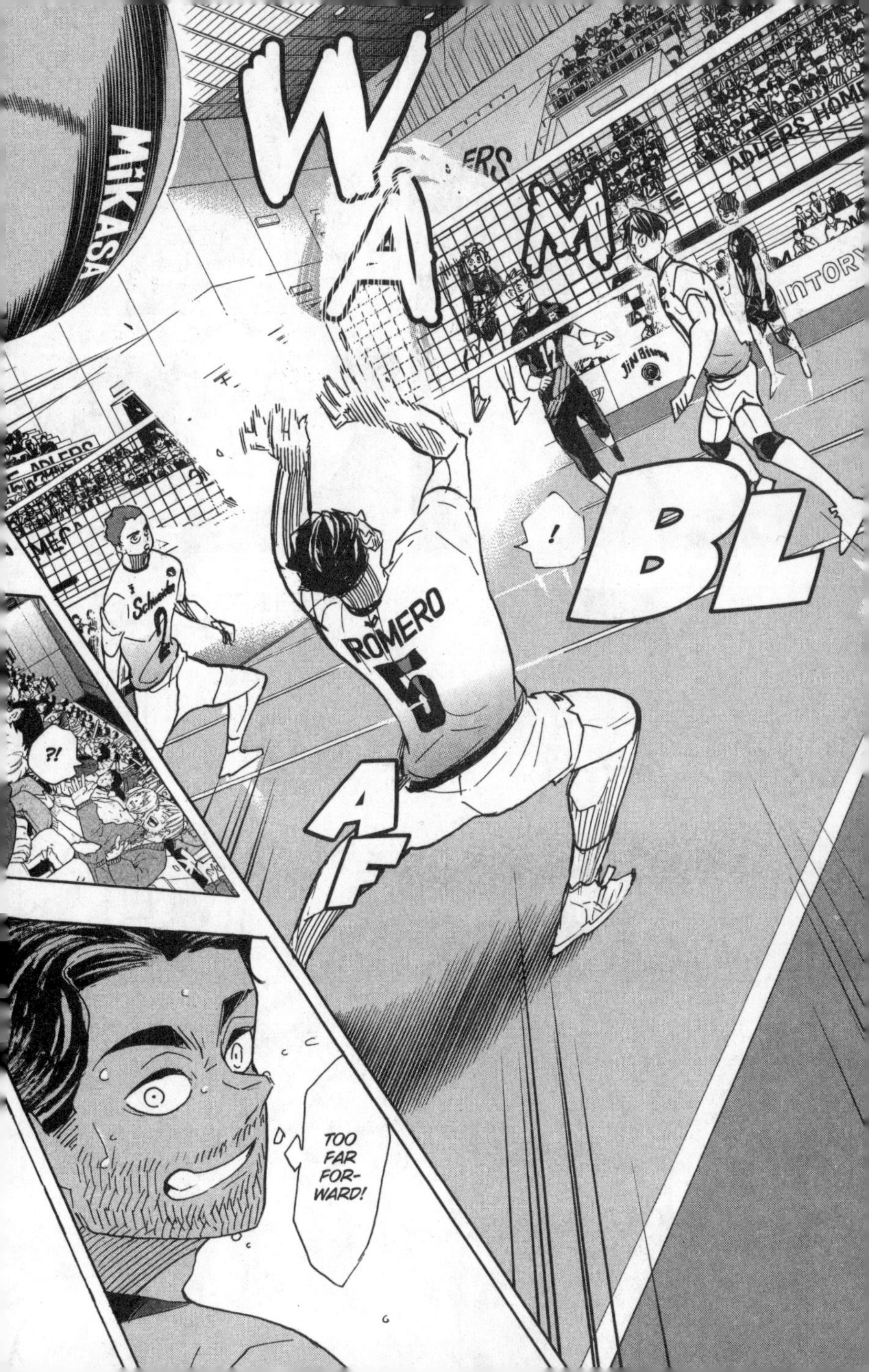

MIKASA
WAM
ADLERS HOME
BLAF
!
ROMERO
5
?!
TOO FAR FORWARD!

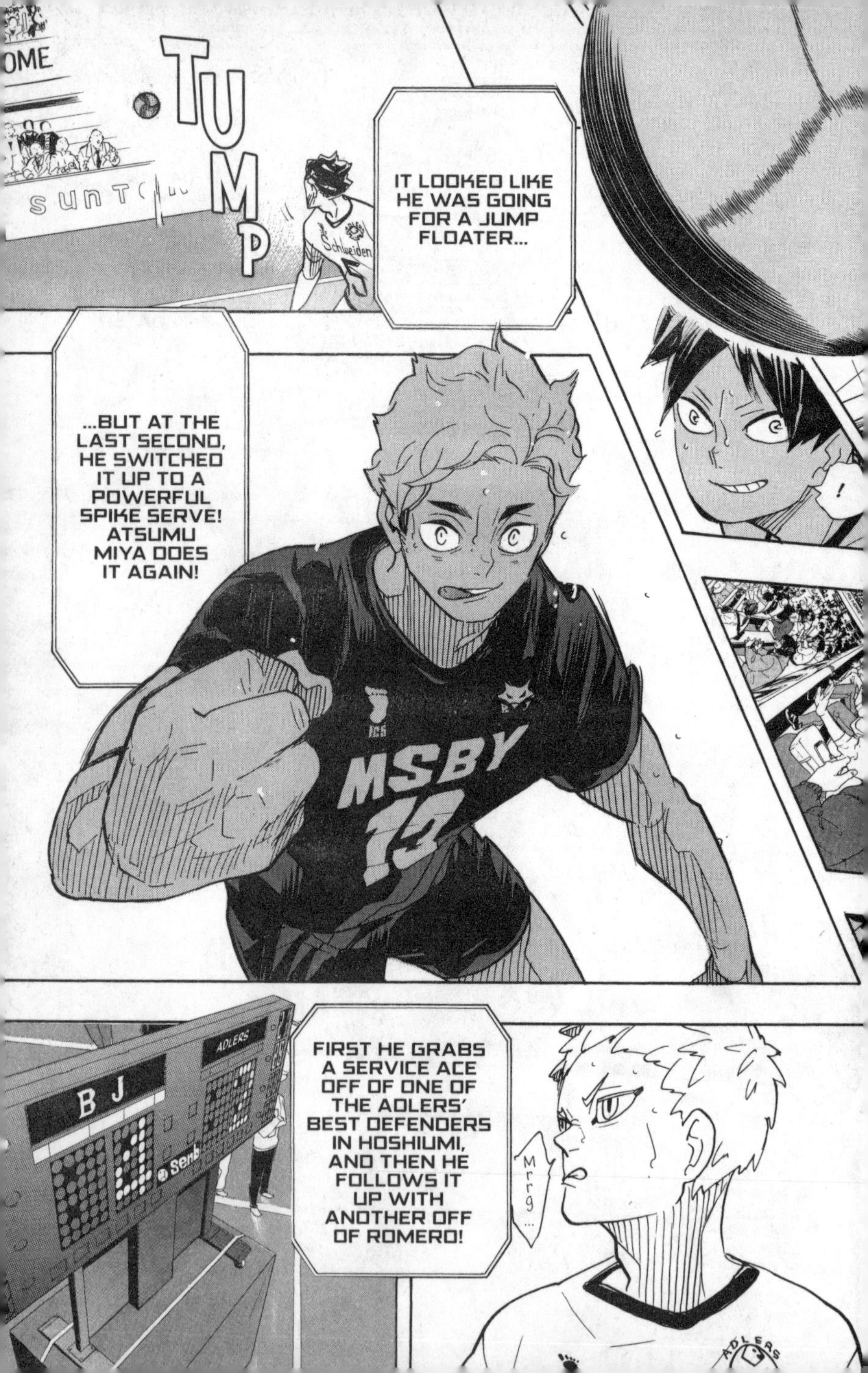
TUMP
Schweiden
IT LOOKED LIKE HE WAS GOING FOR A JUMP FLOATER...
...BUT AT THE LAST SECOND, HE SWITCHED IT UP TO A POWERFUL SPIKE SERVE! ATSUMU MIYA DOES IT AGAIN!
!
MSBY 13
FIRST HE GRABS A SERVICE ACE OFF OF ONE OF THE ADLERS' BEST DEFENDERS IN HOSHIUMI, AND THEN HE FOLLOWS IT UP WITH ANOTHER OFF OF ROMERO!
Mrrg...
ADLERS
B J
ADLERS

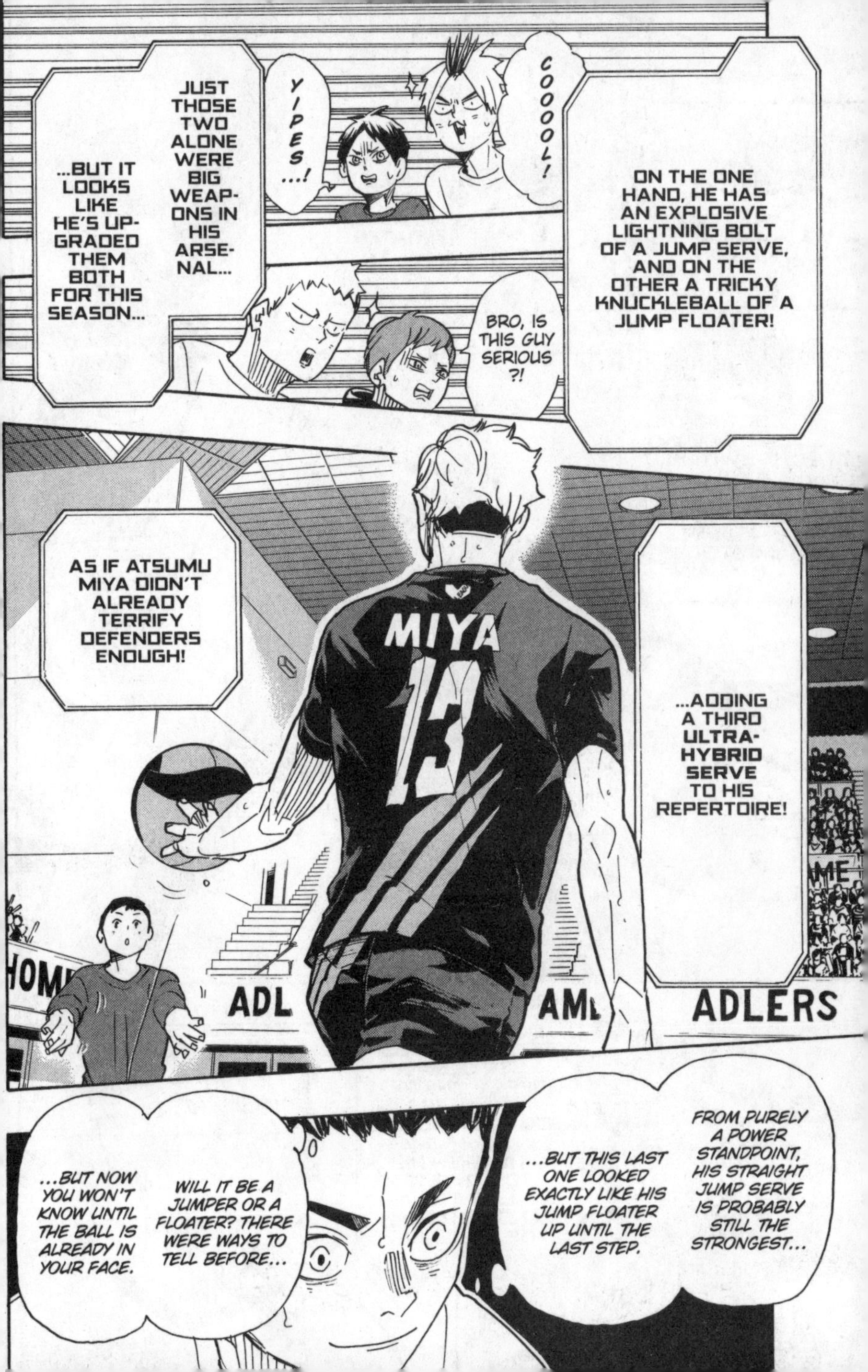
ON THE ONE HAND, HE HAS AN EXPLOSIVE LIGHTNING BOLT OF A JUMP SERVE, AND ON THE OTHER A TRICKY KNUCKLEBALL OF A JUMP FLOATER!
COOOOOL!
YIPES...!
BRO, IS THIS GUY SERIOUS?!
JUST THOSE TWO ALONE WERE BIG WEAPONS IN HIS ARSENAL...
...BUT IT LOOKS LIKE HE'S UPGRADED THEM BOTH FOR THIS SEASON...
...ADDING A THIRD ULTRA-HYBRID SERVE TO HIS REPERTOIRE!
AS IF ATSUMU MIYA DIDN'T ALREADY TERRIFY DEFENDERS ENOUGH!
MIYA
ADLERS
FROM PURELY A POWER STANDPOINT, HIS STRAIGHT JUMP SERVE IS PROBABLY STILL THE STRONGEST...
...BUT THIS LAST ONE LOOKED EXACTLY LIKE HIS JUMP FLOATER UP UNTIL THE LAST STEP.
WILL IT BE A JUMPER OR A FLOATER? THERE WERE WAYS TO TELL BEFORE...
...BUT NOW YOU WON'T KNOW UNTIL THE BALL IS ALREADY IN YOUR FACE.

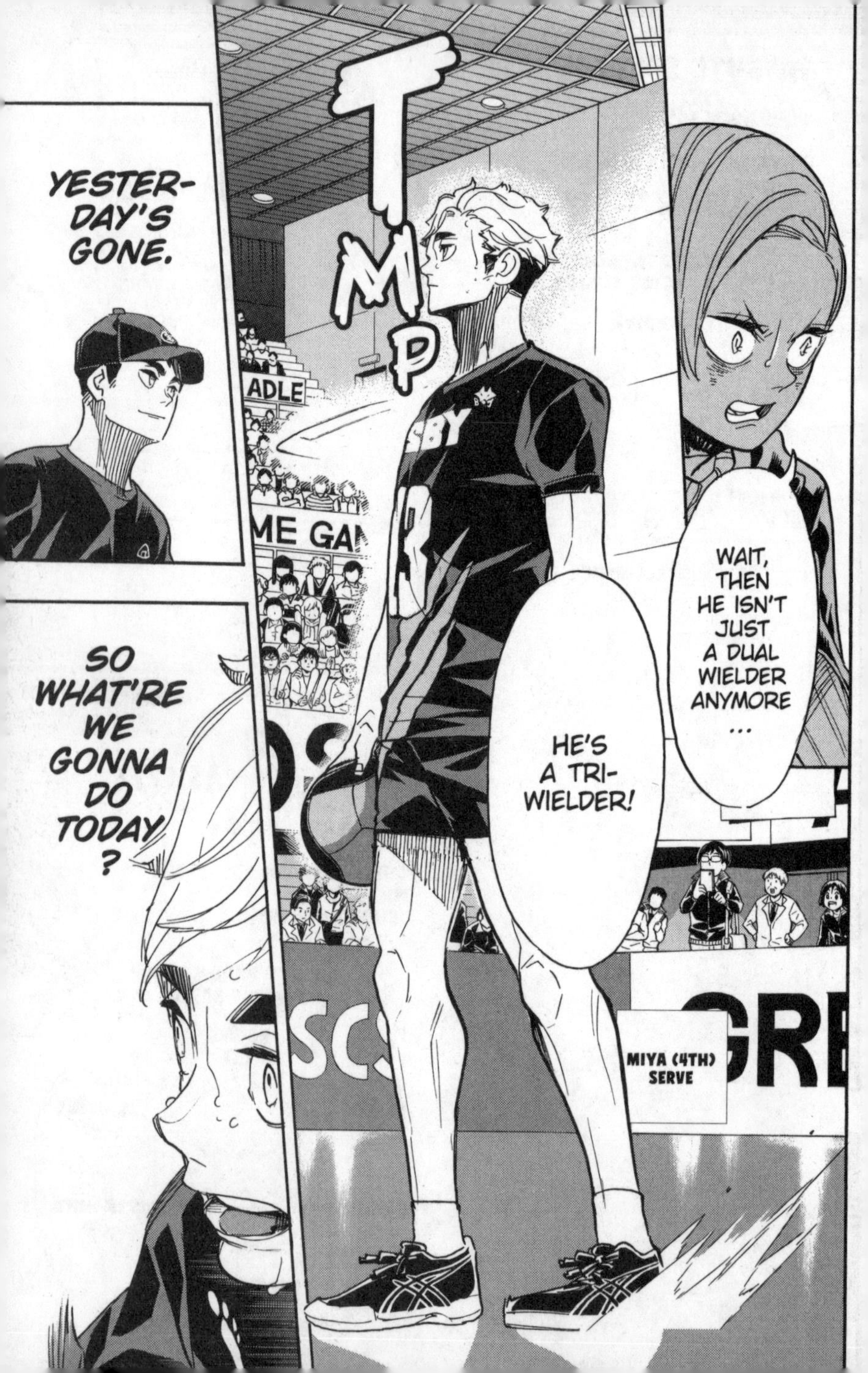
WAIT, THEN HE ISN'T JUST A DUAL WIELDER ANYMORE ...
HE'S A TRI-WIELDER!
TMP
MIYA (4TH) SERVE
YESTER-DAY'S GONE.
SO WHAT'RE WE GONNA DO TODAY?

TATSUTO SOKOLOV (25)

SCHWEIDEN ADLERS

POSITION: MIDDLE BLOCKER
HEIGHT: 6'7"
WEIGHT: 217 LBS.

ABILITY PARAMETERS
(5-POINT SCALE)

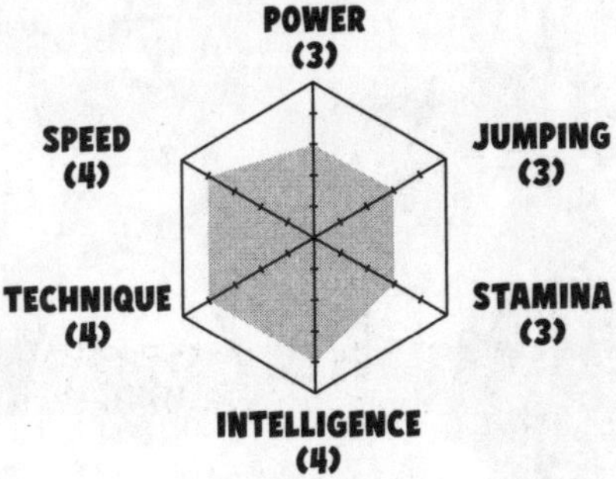
POWER (3)
JUMPING (3)
STAMINA (3)
INTELLIGENCE (4)
TECHNIQUE (4)
SPEED (4)

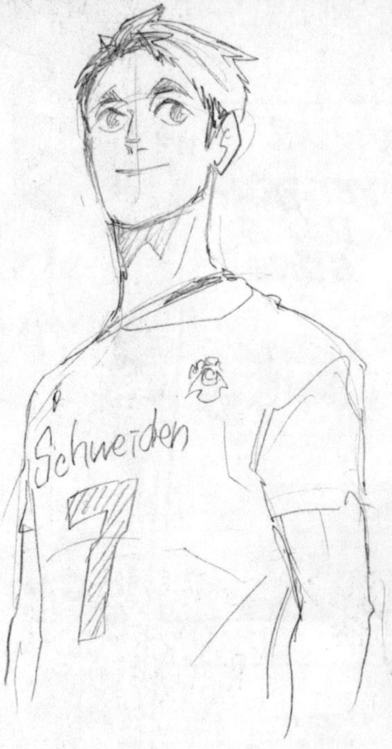
Schweiden
7

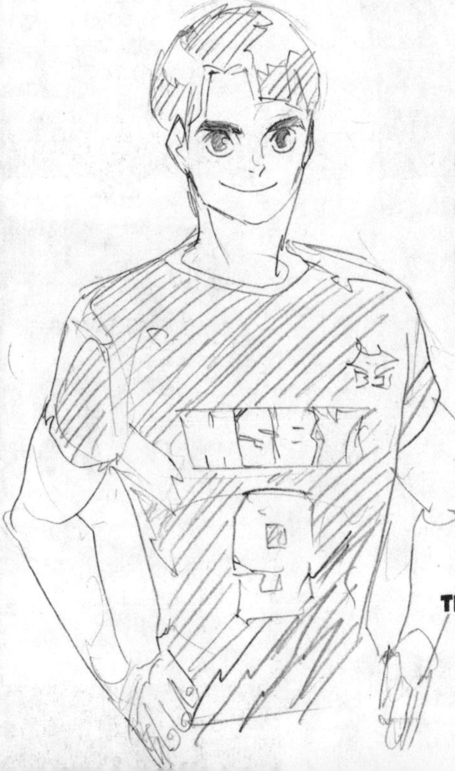

ADRIAH THOMAS (27)

MSBY BLACK JACKALS

POSITION: MIDDLE BLOCKER
HEIGHT: 6'7"
WEIGHT: 211 LBS.

ABILITY PARAMETERS
(5-POINT SCALE)

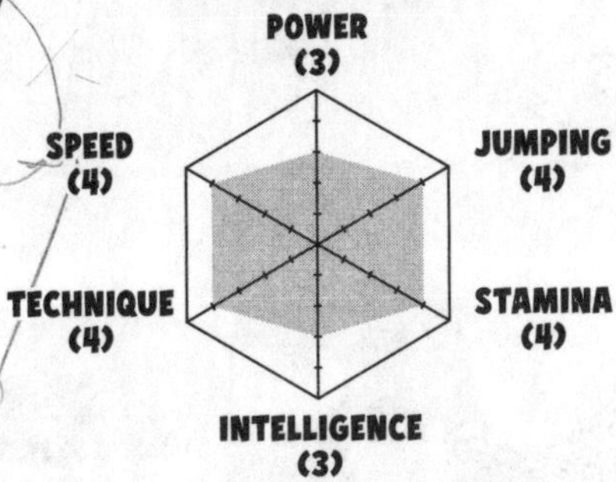
POWER (3)
JUMPING (4)
STAMINA (4)
INTELLIGENCE (3)
TECHNIQUE (4)
SPEED (4)

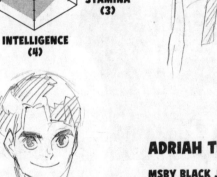

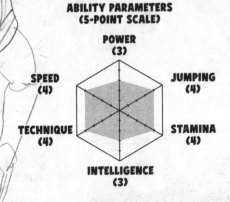

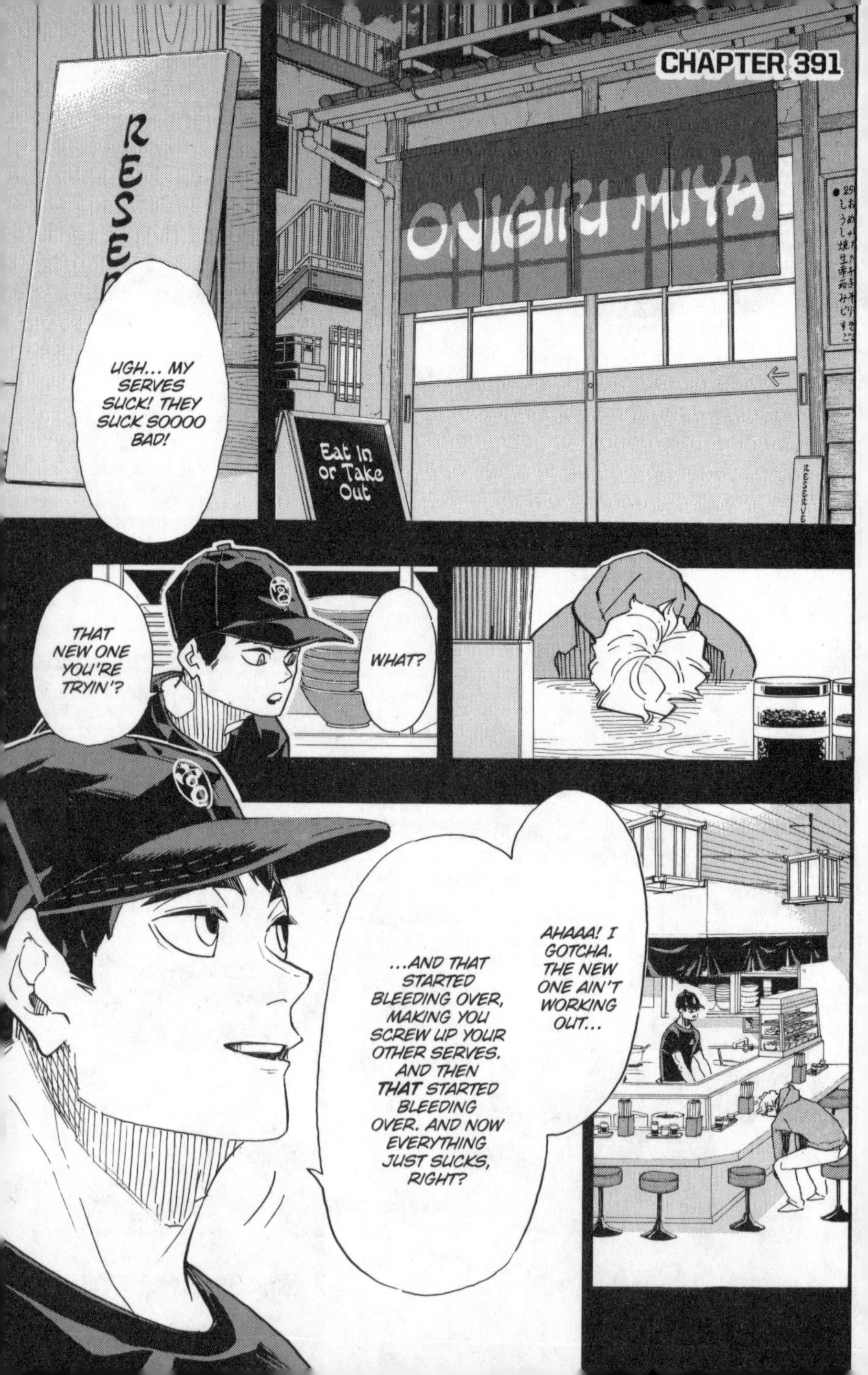
CHAPTER 391
ONIGIRI MIYA
Eat In or Take Out
UGH… MY SERVES SUCK! THEY SUCK SOOOO BAD!
WHAT?
THAT NEW ONE YOU'RE TRYIN'?
AHAAA! I GOTCHA. THE NEW ONE AIN'T WORKING OUT…
…AND THAT STARTED BLEEDING OVER, MAKING YOU SCREW UP YOUR OTHER SERVES. AND THEN THAT STARTED BLEEDING OVER. AND NOW EVERYTHING JUST SUCKS, RIGHT?

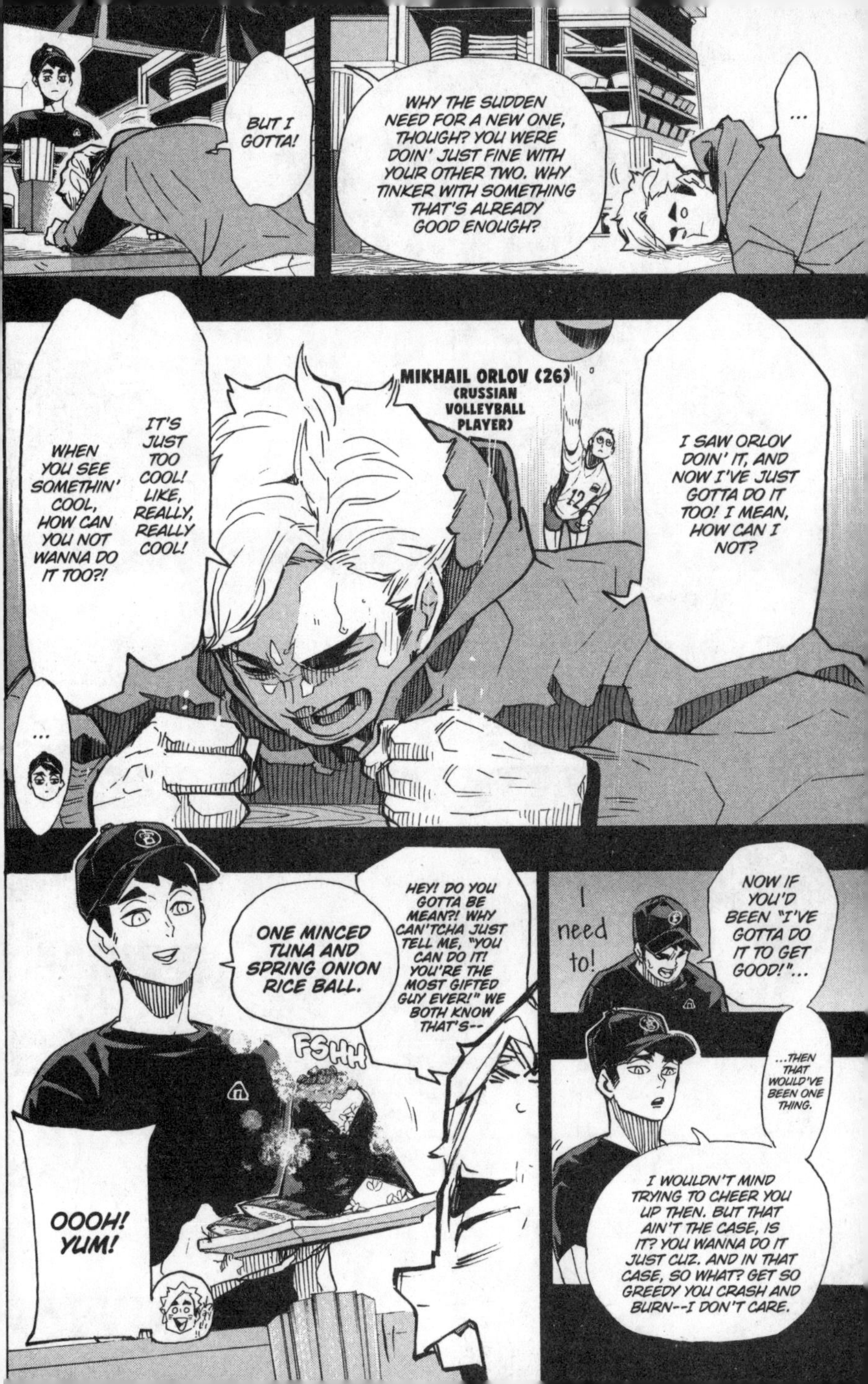
...
WHY THE SUDDEN NEED FOR A NEW ONE, THOUGH? YOU WERE DOIN' JUST FINE WITH YOUR OTHER TWO. WHY TINKER WITH SOMETHING THAT'S ALREADY GOOD ENOUGH?
BUT I GOTTA!
I SAW ORLOV DOIN' IT, AND NOW I'VE JUST GOTTA DO IT TOO! I MEAN, HOW CAN I NOT?
MIKHAIL ORLOV (26) (RUSSIAN VOLLEYBALL PLAYER)
IT'S JUST TOO COOL! LIKE, REALLY, REALLY COOL!
WHEN YOU SEE SOMETHIN' COOL, HOW CAN YOU NOT WANNA DO IT TOO?!
...
NOW IF YOU'D BEEN "I'VE GOTTA DO IT TO GET GOOD!"...
I need to!
...THEN THAT WOULD'VE BEEN ONE THING.
I WOULDN'T MIND TRYING TO CHEER YOU UP THEN. BUT THAT AIN'T THE CASE, IS IT? YOU WANNA DO IT JUST CUZ. AND IN THAT CASE, SO WHAT? GET SO GREEDY YOU CRASH AND BURN--I DON'T CARE.
HEY! DO YOU GOTTA BE MEAN?! WHY CAN'TCHA JUST TELL ME, "YOU CAN DO IT! YOU'RE THE MOST GIFTED GUY EVER!" WE BOTH KNOW THAT'S--
ONE MINCED TUNA AND SPRING ONION RICE BALL.
FSHH
OOOH! YUM!

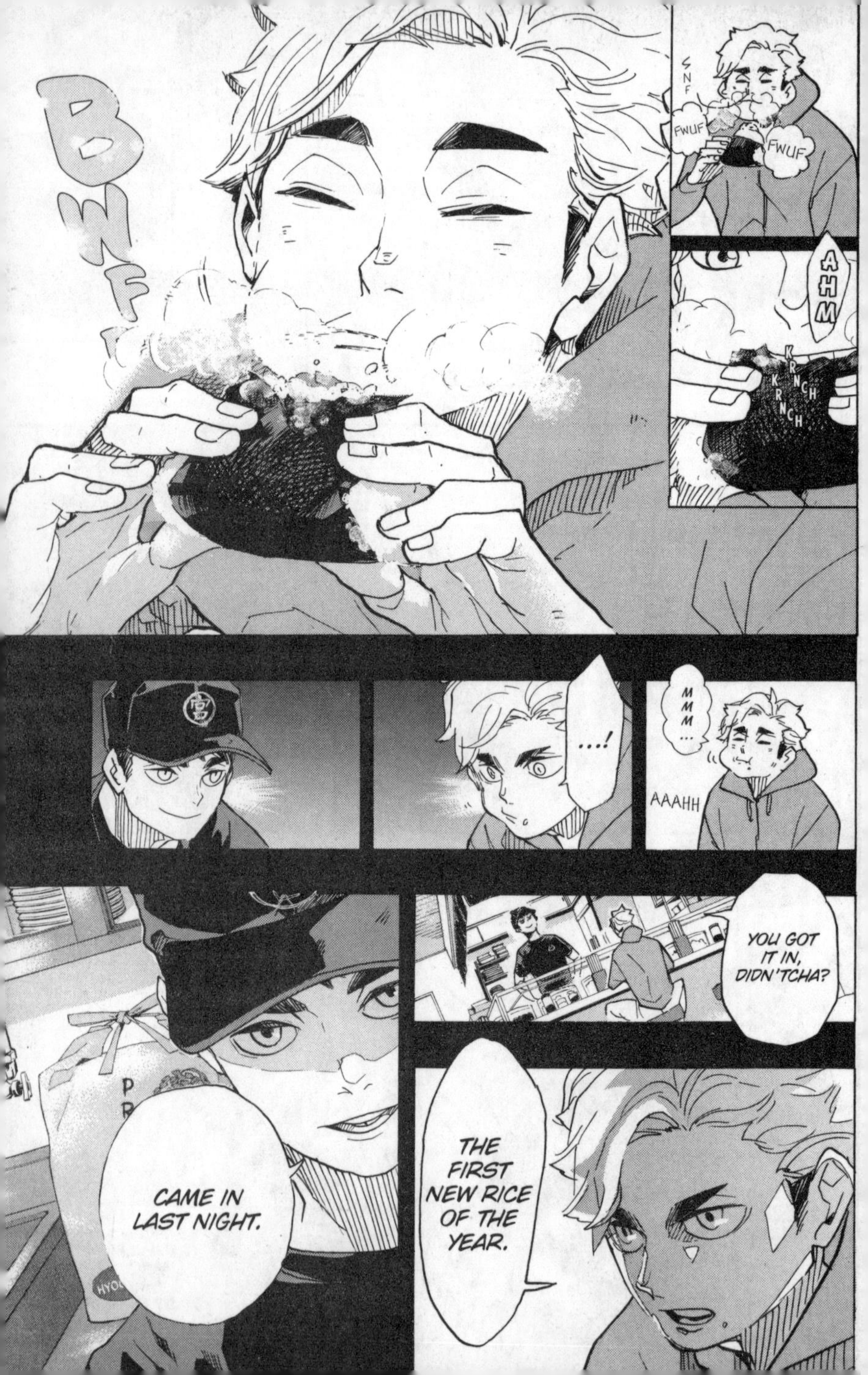
SNF
FWUF
FWUF
AHM
KRNCH
KRNCH
BWNF
MMM...
AAAHH
...!
YOU GOT IT IN, DIDN'TCHA?
THE FIRST NEW RICE OF THE YEAR.
CAME IN LAST NIGHT.

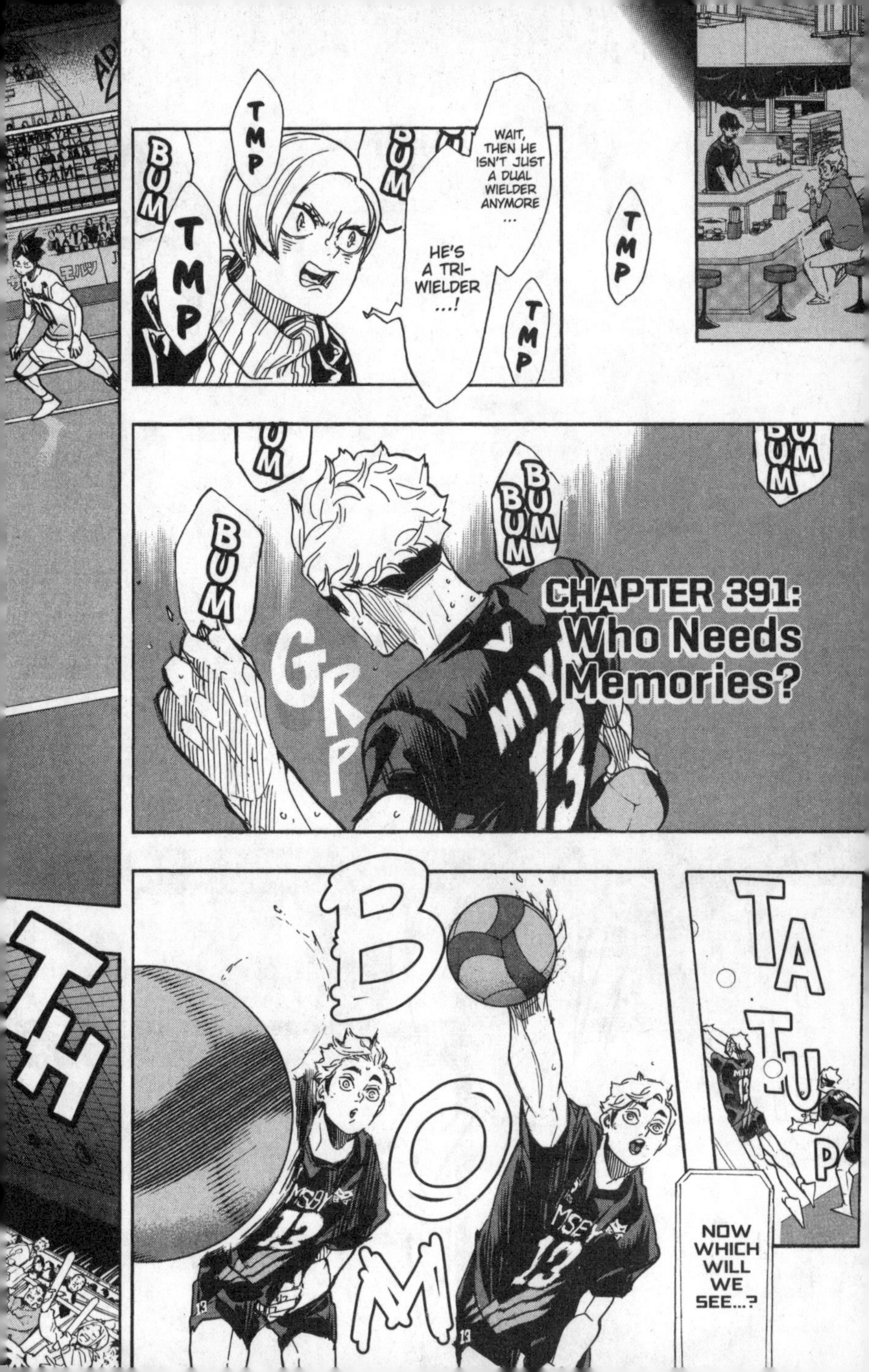
TMP
WAIT, THEN HE ISN'T JUST A DUAL WIELDER ANYMORE ...
HE'S A TRI-WIELDER ...!
BUM
BUM
TMP
TMP
TMP
BUM
BUM
BUM
BUM BUM BUM
CHAPTER 391: Who Needs Memories?
BUM
GRP
TATUP
NOW WHICH WILL WE SEE...?
BOOM
TH

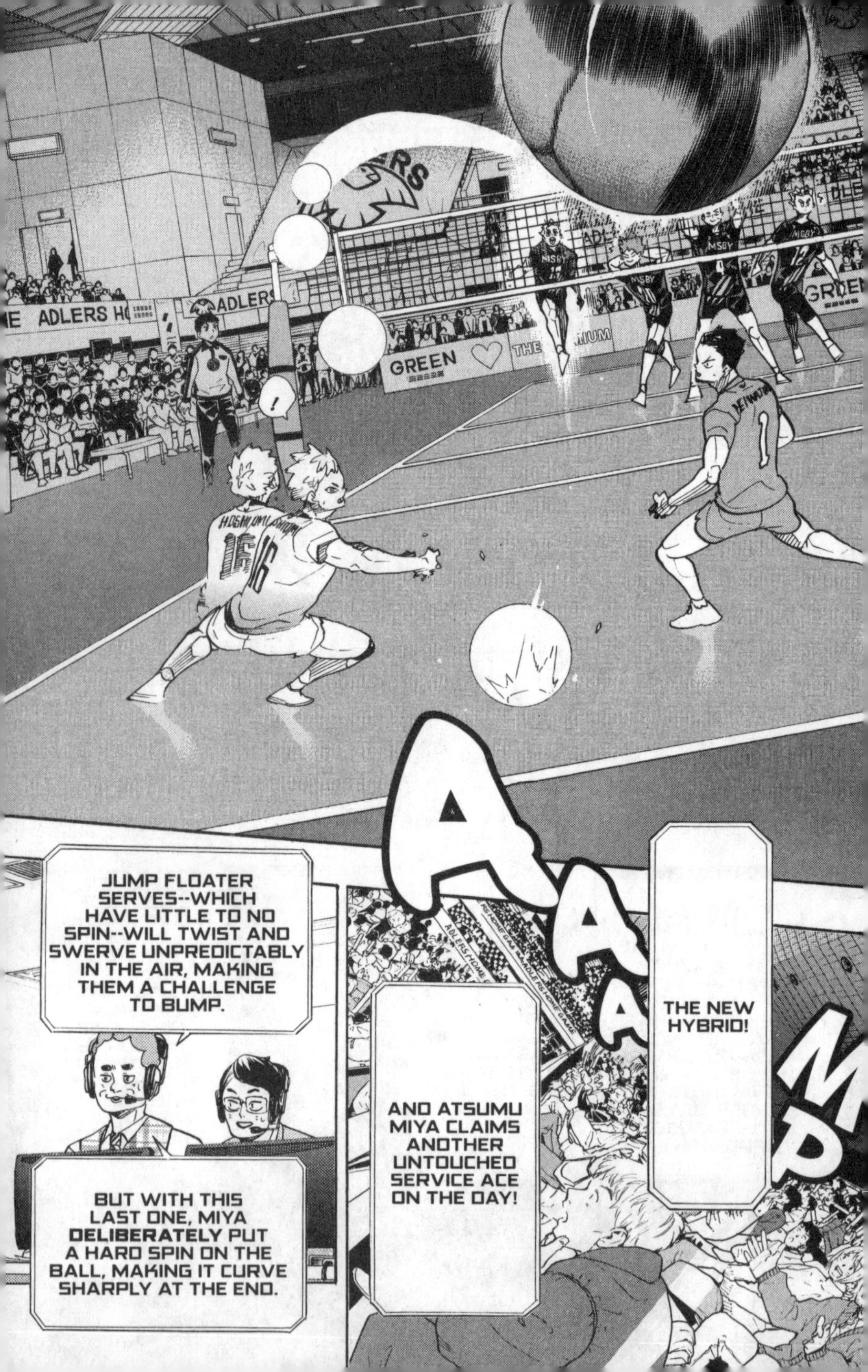

!
THE NEW HYBRID!
AND ATSUMU MIYA CLAIMS ANOTHER UNTOUCHED SERVICE ACE ON THE DAY!
JUMP FLOATER SERVES--WHICH HAVE LITTLE TO NO SPIN--WILL TWIST AND SWERVE UNPREDICTABLY IN THE AIR, MAKING THEM A CHALLENGE TO BUMP.
BUT WITH THIS LAST ONE, MIYA DELIBERATELY PUT A HARD SPIN ON THE BALL, MAKING IT CURVE SHARPLY AT THE END.

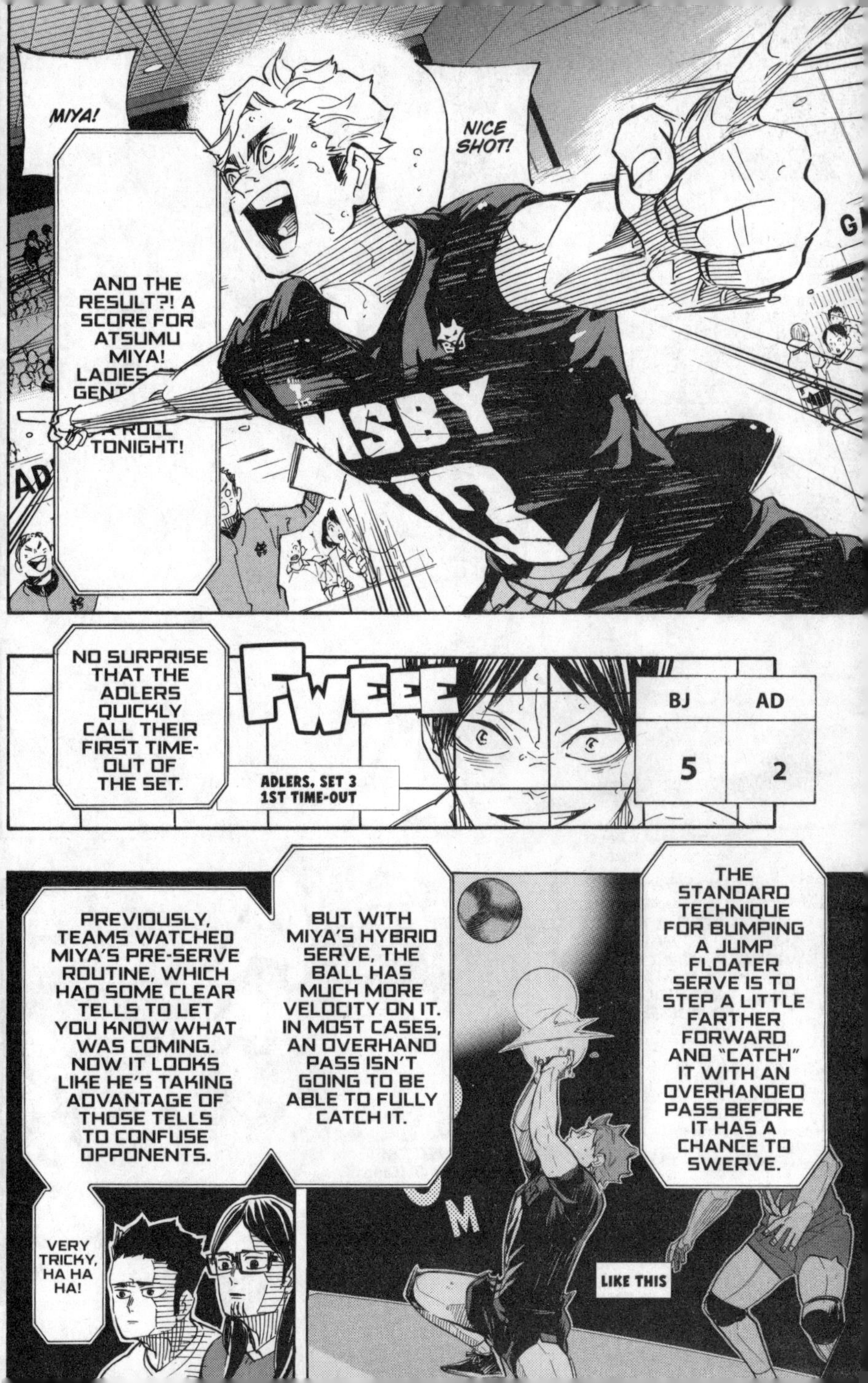
NICE SHOT!
MIYA!
AND THE RESULT?! A SCORE FOR ATSUMU MIYA! LADIES
TONIGHT!
BJ AD
5 2
FWEEE
ADLERS, SET 3 1ST TIME-OUT
NO SURPRISE THAT THE ADLERS QUICKLY CALL THEIR FIRST TIME-OUT OF THE SET.
THE STANDARD TECHNIQUE FOR BUMPING A JUMP FLOATER SERVE IS TO STEP A LITTLE FARTHER FORWARD AND "CATCH" IT WITH AN OVERHANDED PASS BEFORE IT HAS A CHANCE TO SWERVE.
LIKE THIS
PREVIOUSLY, TEAMS WATCHED MIYA'S PRE-SERVE ROUTINE, WHICH HAD SOME CLEAR TELLS TO LET YOU KNOW WHAT WAS COMING. NOW IT LOOKS LIKE HE'S TAKING ADVANTAGE OF THOSE TELLS TO CONFUSE OPPONENTS.
BUT WITH MIYA'S HYBRID SERVE, THE BALL HAS MUCH MORE VELOCITY ON IT. IN MOST CASES, AN OVERHAND PASS ISN'T GOING TO BE ABLE TO FULLY CATCH IT.
VERY TRICKY, HA HA HA!

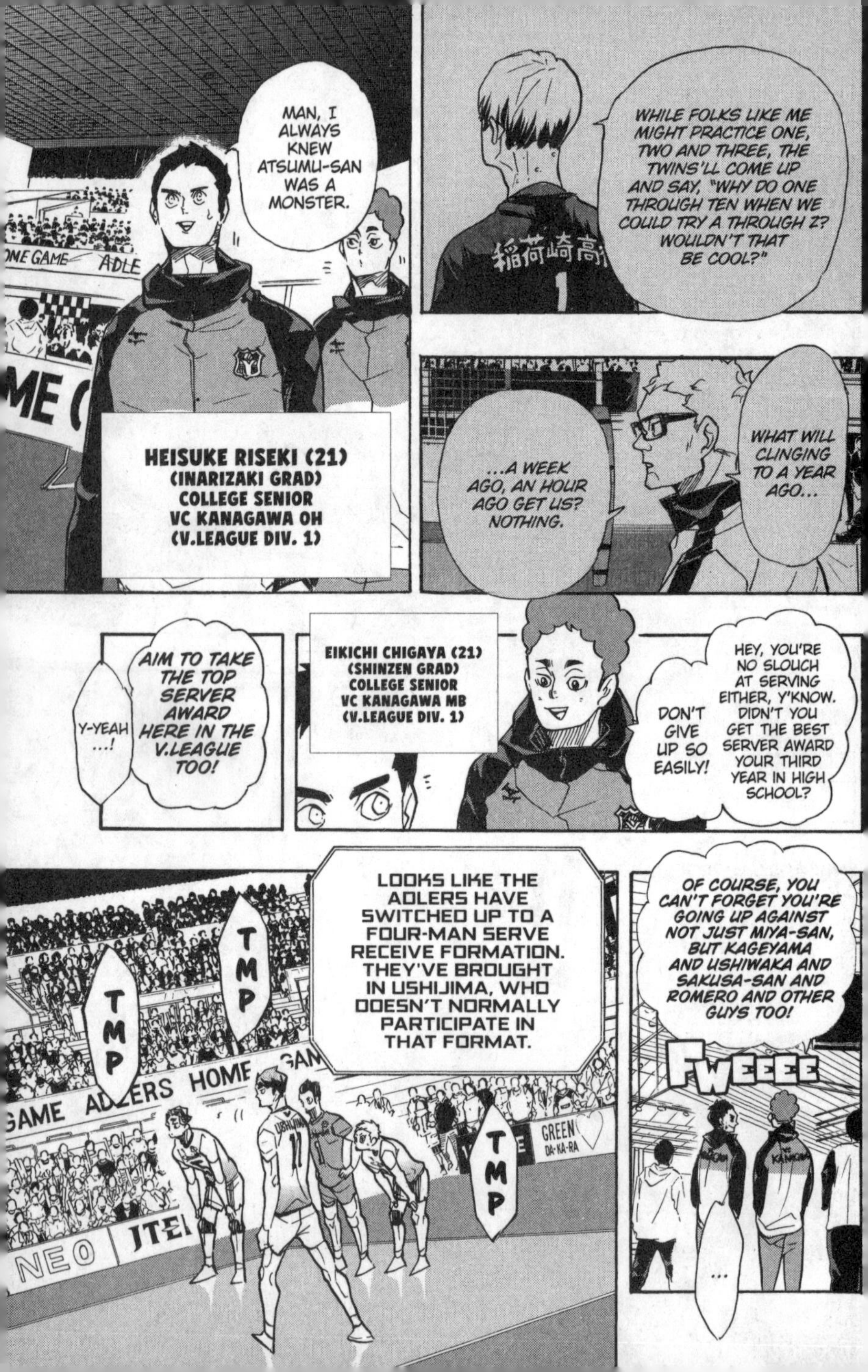

WHILE FOLKS LIKE ME MIGHT PRACTICE ONE, TWO AND THREE, THE TWINS'LL COME UP AND SAY, "WHY DO ONE THROUGH TEN WHEN WE COULD TRY A THROUGH Z? WOULDN'T THAT BE COOL?"
稲荷崎高
WHAT WILL CLINGING TO A YEAR AGO...
...A WEEK AGO, AN HOUR AGO GET US? NOTHING.
MAN, I ALWAYS KNEW ATSUMU-SAN WAS A MONSTER.
ONE GAME ADLE
HEISUKE RISEKI (21) (INARIZAKI GRAD) COLLEGE SENIOR VC KANAGAWA OH (V.LEAGUE DIV. 1)
HEY, YOU'RE NO SLOUCH AT SERVING EITHER, Y'KNOW. DIDN'T YOU GET THE BEST SERVER AWARD YOUR THIRD YEAR IN HIGH SCHOOL?
DON'T GIVE UP SO EASILY!
EIKICHI CHIGAYA (21) (SHINZEN GRAD) COLLEGE SENIOR VC KANAGAWA MB (V.LEAGUE DIV. 1)
AIM TO TAKE THE TOP SERVER AWARD HERE IN THE V.LEAGUE TOO!
Y-YEAH ...!
OF COURSE, YOU CAN'T FORGET YOU'RE GOING UP AGAINST NOT JUST MIYA-SAN, BUT KAGEYAMA AND USHIWAKA AND SAKUSA-SAN AND ROMERO AND OTHER GUYS TOO!
FWEEEE
...
LOOKS LIKE THE ADLERS HAVE SWITCHED UP TO A FOUR-MAN SERVE RECEIVE FORMATION. THEY'VE BROUGHT IN USHIJIMA, WHO DOESN'T NORMALLY PARTICIPATE IN THAT FORMAT.
TMP
TMP
TMP
TMP
GAME ADLERS HOME GAM
GREEN DA-KA-RA
NEO
JTE

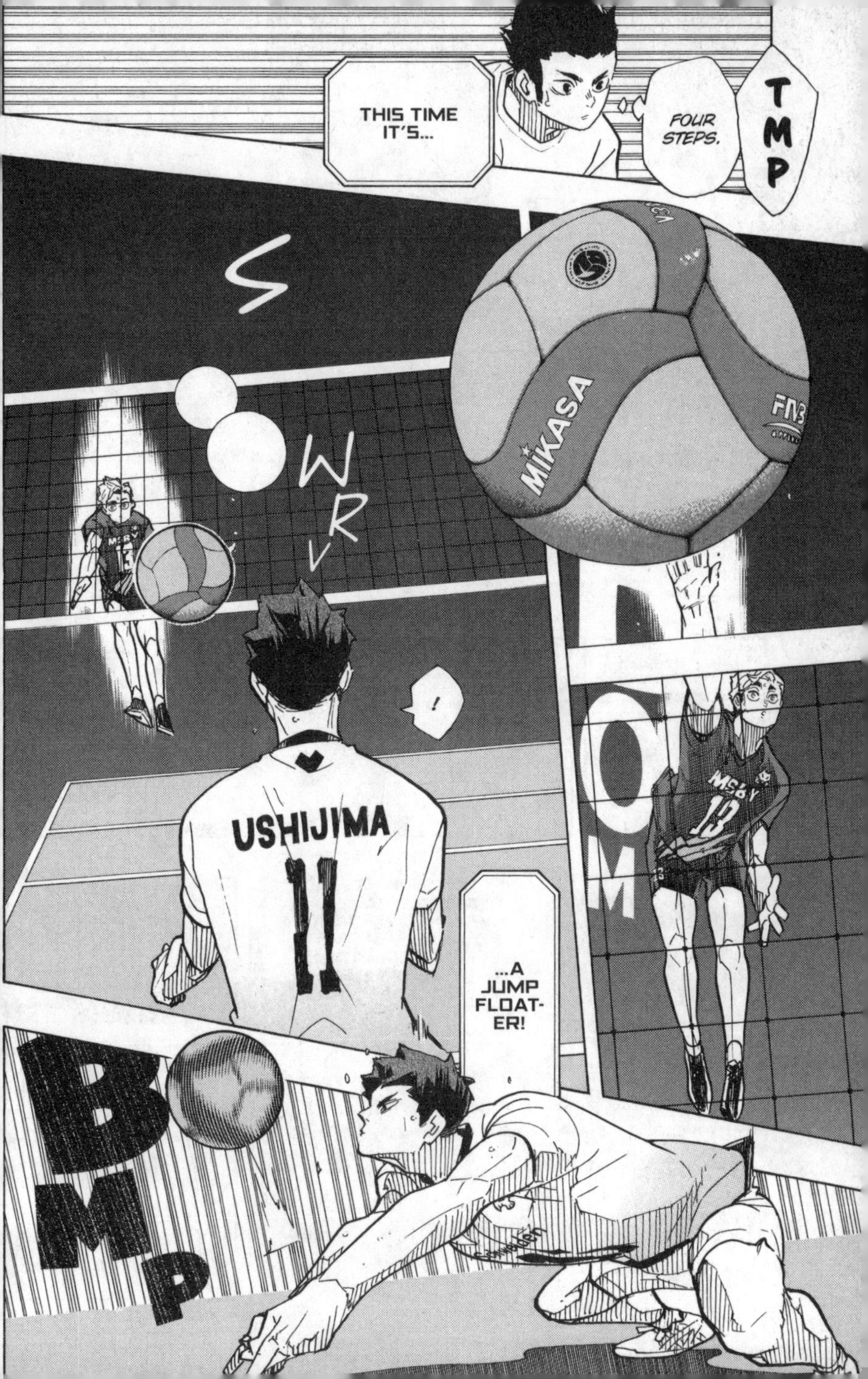
TMP
FOUR STEPS.
THIS TIME IT'S...
S
WRRV
MIKASA
!
USHIJIMA
11
...A JUMP FLOAT-ER!
BUMP

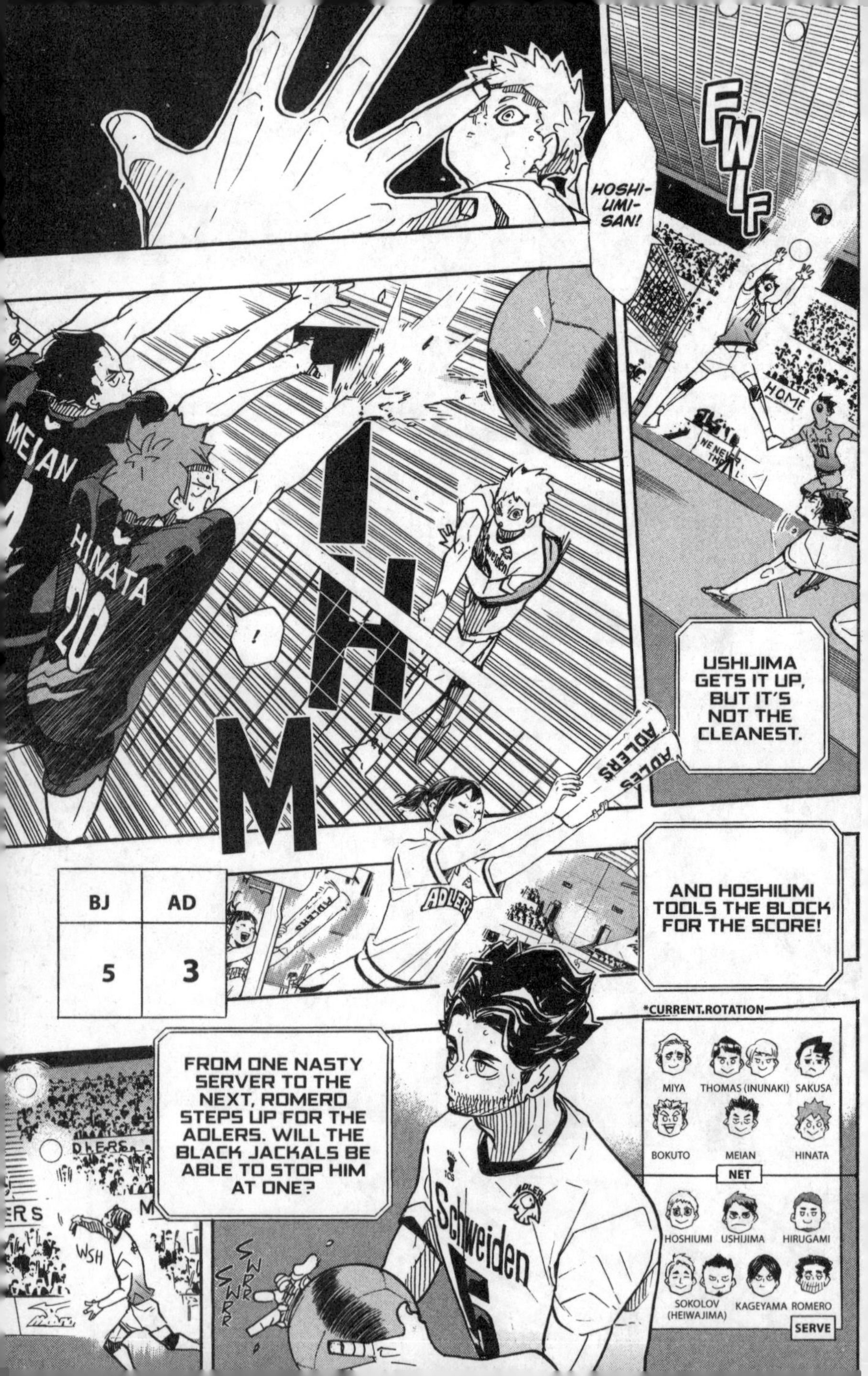

FWIF
USHIJIMA GETS IT UP, BUT IT'S NOT THE CLEANEST.
HOSHI-UMI-SAN!
!
THMM
MEIAN
HINATA 20
AND HOSHIUMI TOOLS THE BLOCK FOR THE SCORE!
ADLERS
BJ AD
5 3
*CURRENT.ROTATION
MIYA THOMAS (INUNAKI) SAKUSA
BOKUTO MEIAN HINATA
NET
HOSHIUMI USHIJIMA HIRUGAMI
SOKOLOV (HEIWAJIMA) KAGEYAMA ROMERO
SERVE
FROM ONE NASTY SERVER TO THE NEXT, ROMERO STEPS UP FOR THE ADLERS. WILL THE BLACK JACKALS BE ABLE TO STOP HIM AT ONE?
SWRR SWRR
Schweiden
WSH

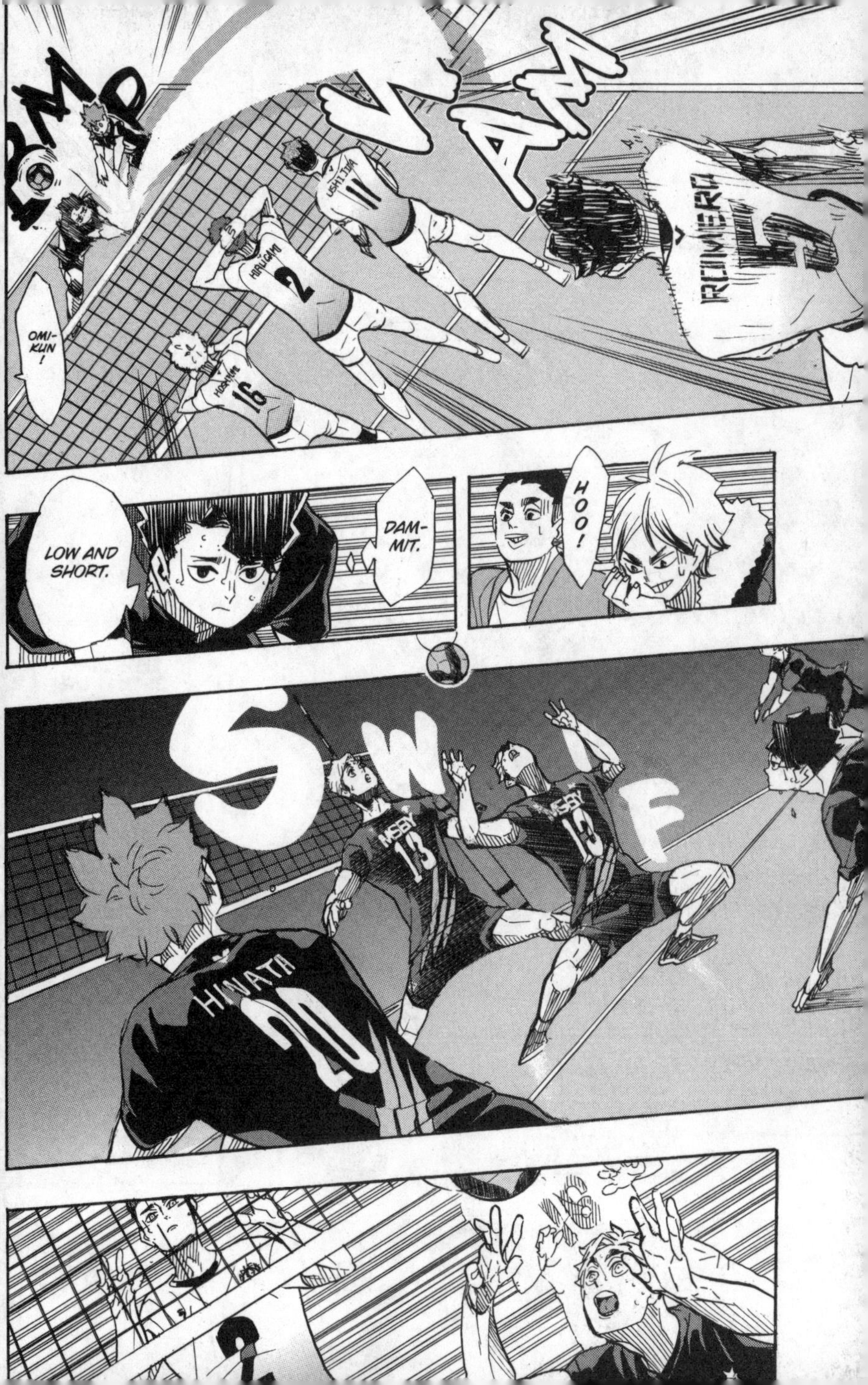
OMI-KUN!
HOO!
DAM-MIT.
LOW AND SHORT.
SWIF

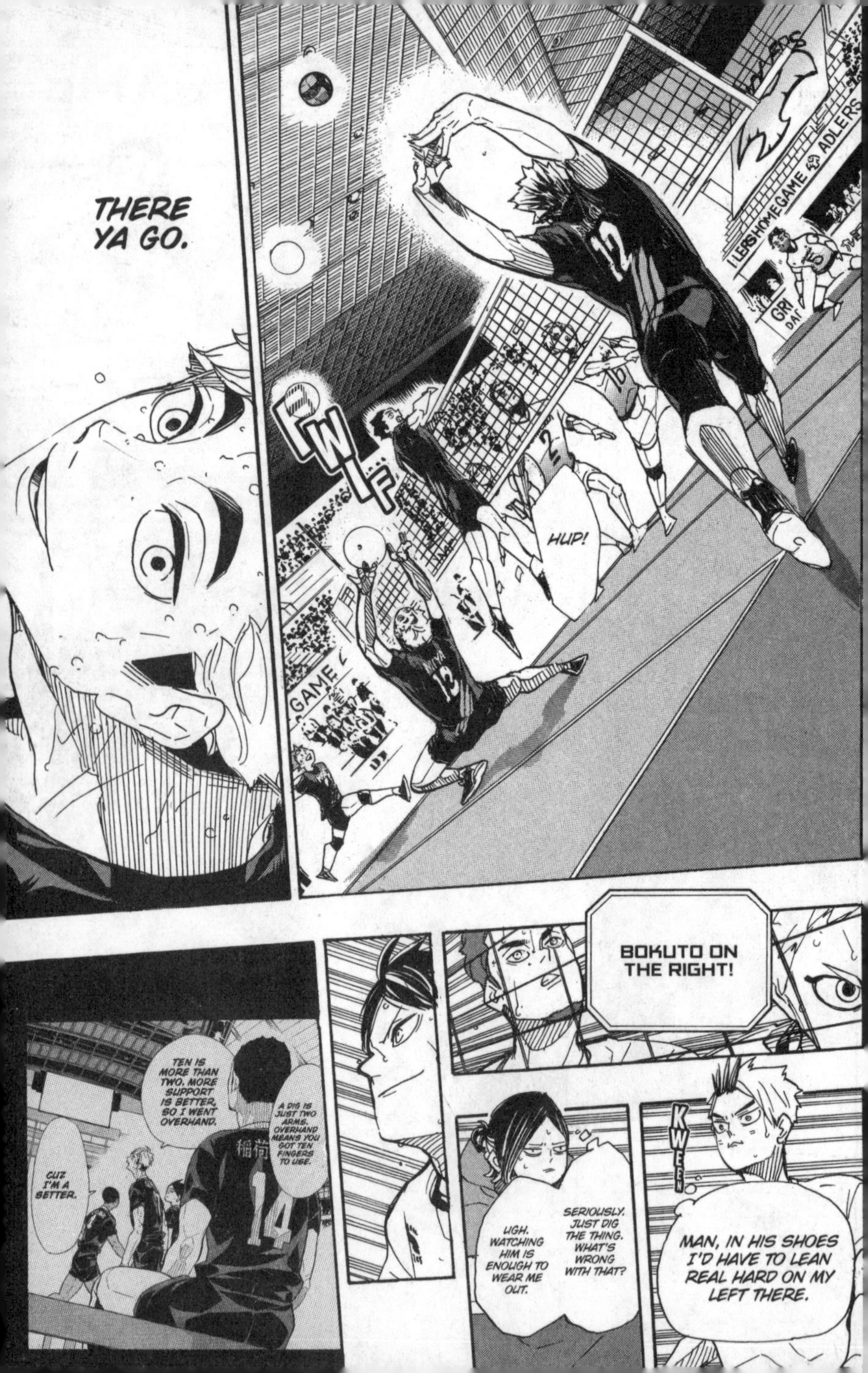
ADLERS
PWIF
HUP!
THERE YA GO.
BOKUTO ON THE RIGHT!
KWEEN
MAN, IN HIS SHOES I'D HAVE TO LEAN REAL HARD ON MY LEFT THERE.
SERIOUSLY. JUST DIG THE THING. WHAT'S WRONG WITH THAT?
UGH. WATCHING HIM IS ENOUGH TO WEAR ME OUT.
A DIG IS JUST TWO ARMS. OVERHAND MEANS YOU GOT TEN FINGERS TO USE.
TEN IS MORE THAN TWO. MORE SUPPORT IS BETTER, SO I WENT OVERHAND.
稲荷
CUZ I'M A SETTER.

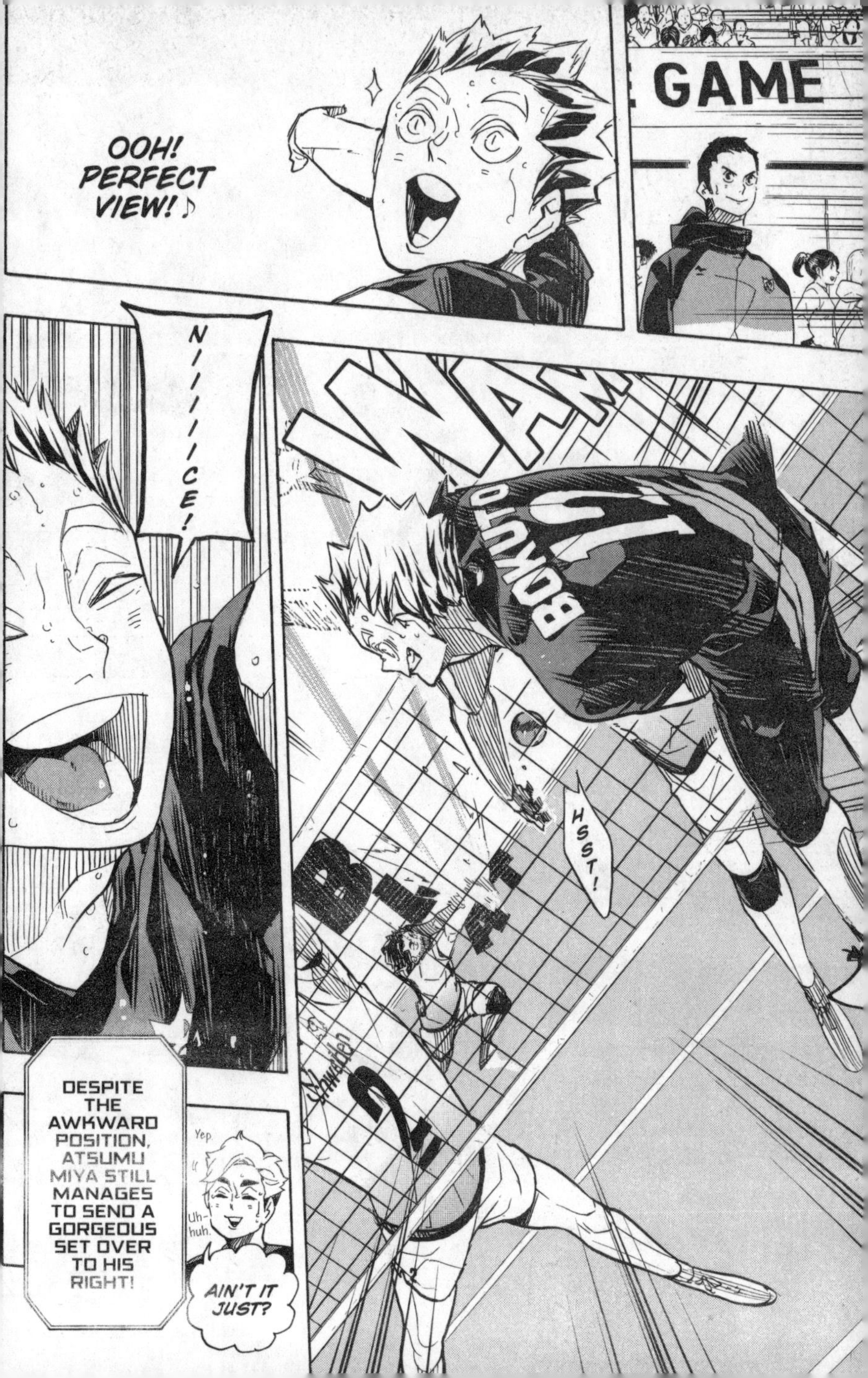

GAME
OOH! PERFECT VIEW!♪
BOKUTO
1
HSST!
2
N//////CE!
DESPITE THE AWKWARD POSITION, ATSUMU MIYA STILL MANAGES TO SEND A GORGEOUS SET OVER TO HIS RIGHT!
Yep.
Uh-huh.
AIN'T IT JUST?

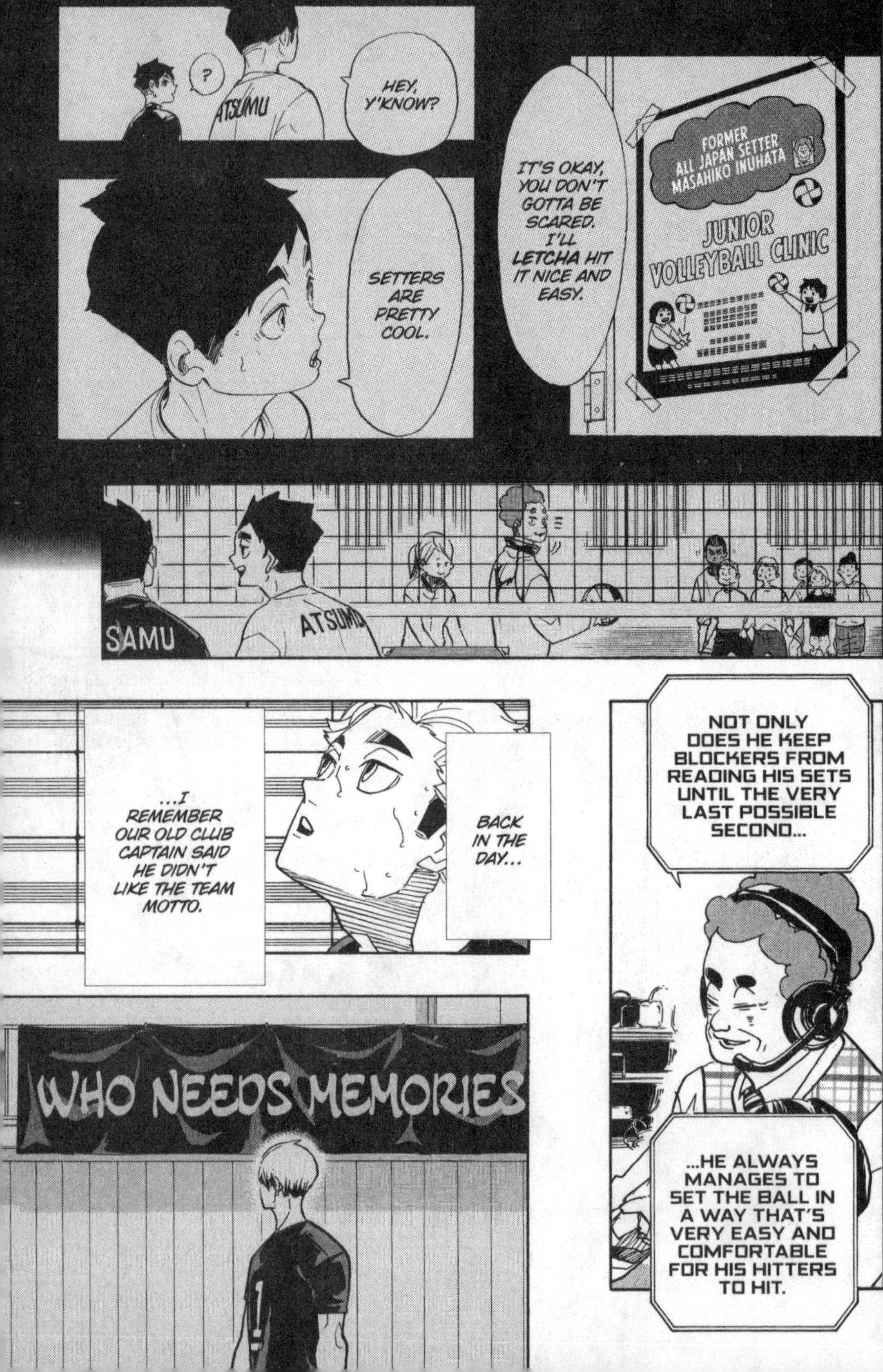
FORMER ALL JAPAN SETTER MASAHIKO INUHATA
JUNIOR VOLLEYBALL CLINIC
IT'S OKAY, YOU DON'T GOTTA BE SCARED. I'LL LETCHA HIT IT NICE AND EASY.
?
ATSUMU
HEY, Y'KNOW?
SETTERS ARE PRETTY COOL.
SAMU
ATSUMU
NOT ONLY DOES HE KEEP BLOCKERS FROM READING HIS SETS UNTIL THE VERY LAST POSSIBLE SECOND...
...HE ALWAYS MANAGES TO SET THE BALL IN A WAY THAT'S VERY EASY AND COMFORTABLE FOR HIS HITTERS TO HIT.
BACK IN THE DAY...
...I REMEMBER OUR OLD CLUB CAPTAIN SAID HE DIDN'T LIKE THE TEAM MOTTO.
WHO NEEDS MEMORIES

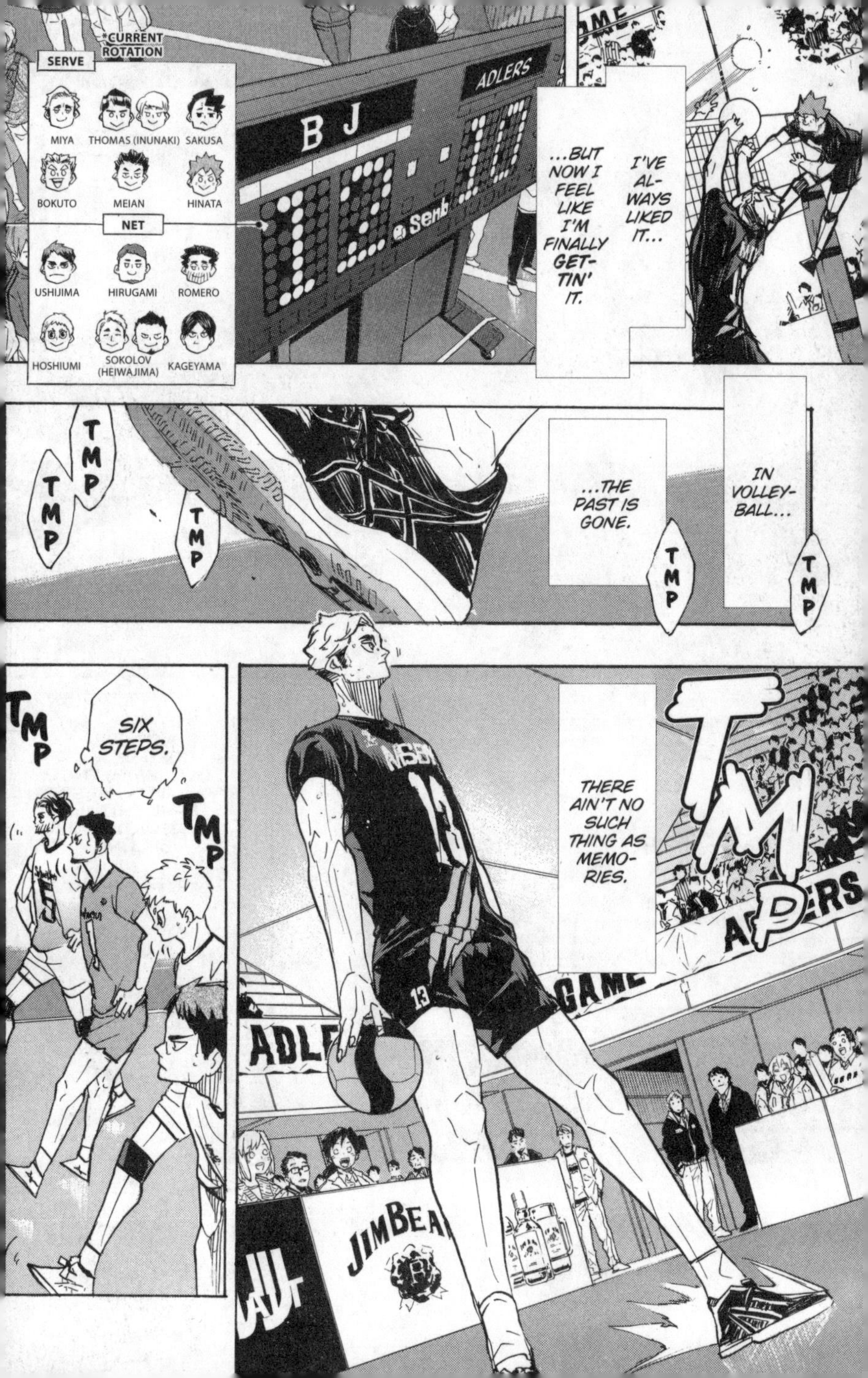

I'VE ALWAYS LIKED IT...
...BUT NOW I FEEL LIKE I'M FINALLY GETTIN' IT.
ADLERS
B J
*CURRENT ROTATION
SERVE
MIYA
THOMAS (INUNAKI)
SAKUSA
BOKUTO
MEIAN
HINATA
NET
USHIJIMA
HIRUGAMI
ROMERO
HOSHIUMI
SOKOLOV (HEIWAJIMA)
KAGEYAMA
IN VOLLEYBALL...
TMP
...THE PAST IS GONE.
TMP
TMP
TMP
TMP
TMP
THERE AIN'T NO SUCH THING AS MEMORIES.
ADLERS
GAME
ADLE
JIMBEAM
TMP
SIX STEPS.
TMP

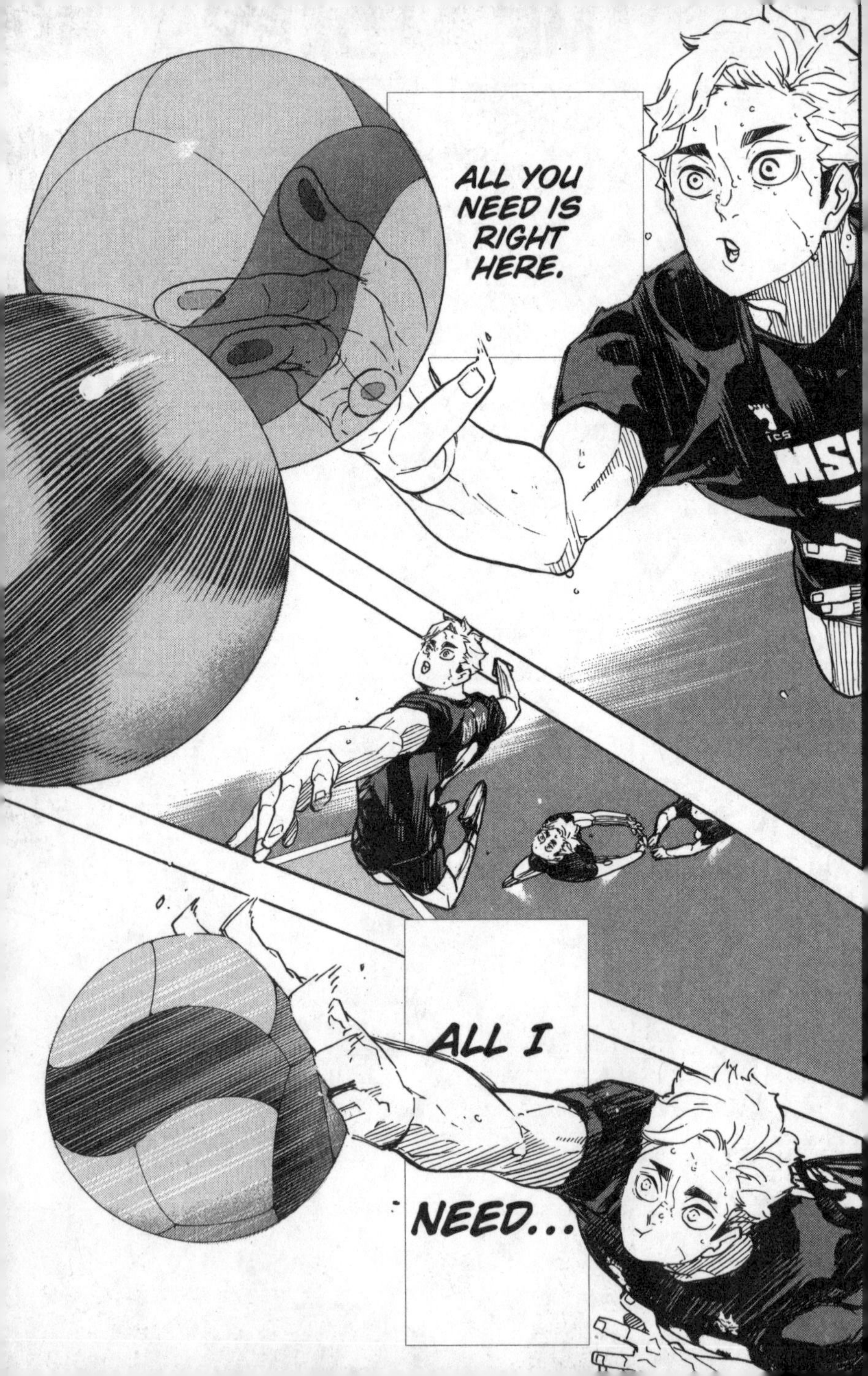
ALL YOU NEED IS RIGHT HERE.
MSB
ALL I
NEED...

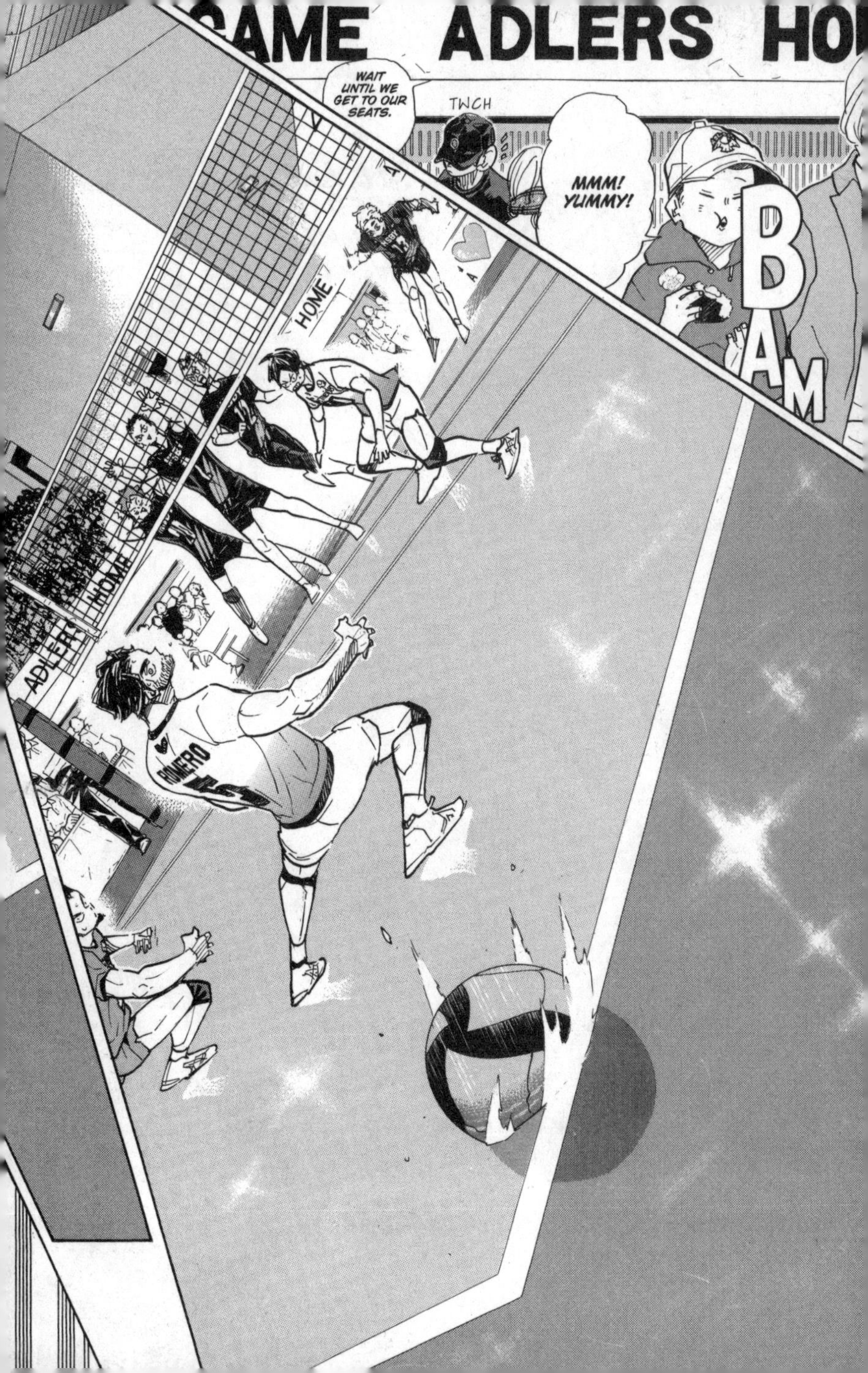
GAME ADLERS HO
BAM
MMM! YUMMY!
TWCH
WAIT UNTIL WE GET TO OUR SEATS.
HOME
HOME
ADLERS
ROMERO

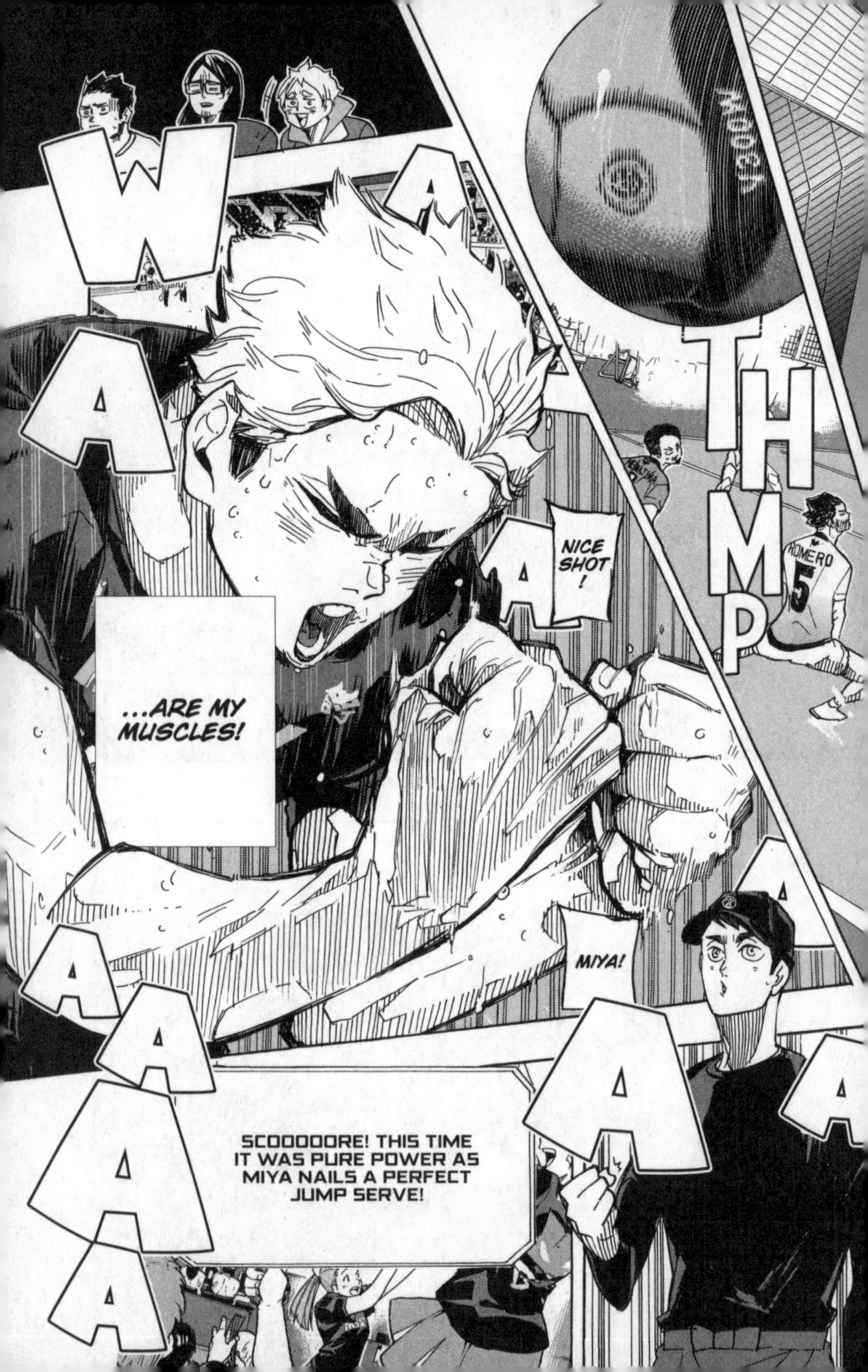
THUMP
ROMERO 5
WAAAAAAAAAAAAA
NICE SHOT!
...ARE MY MUSCLES!
MIYA!
SCOOOOORE! THIS TIME IT WAS PURE POWER AS MIYA NAILS A PERFECT JUMP SERVE!

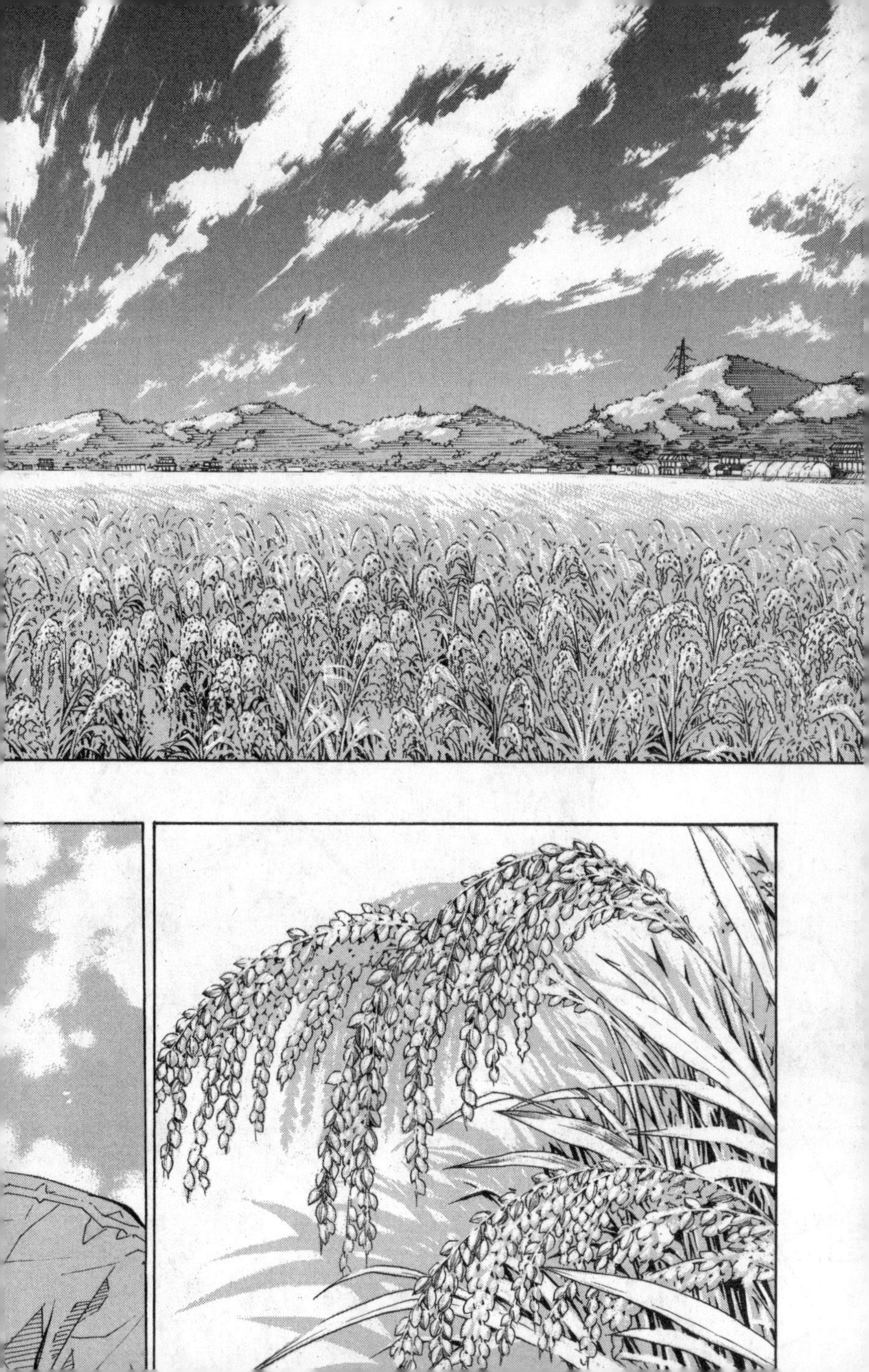

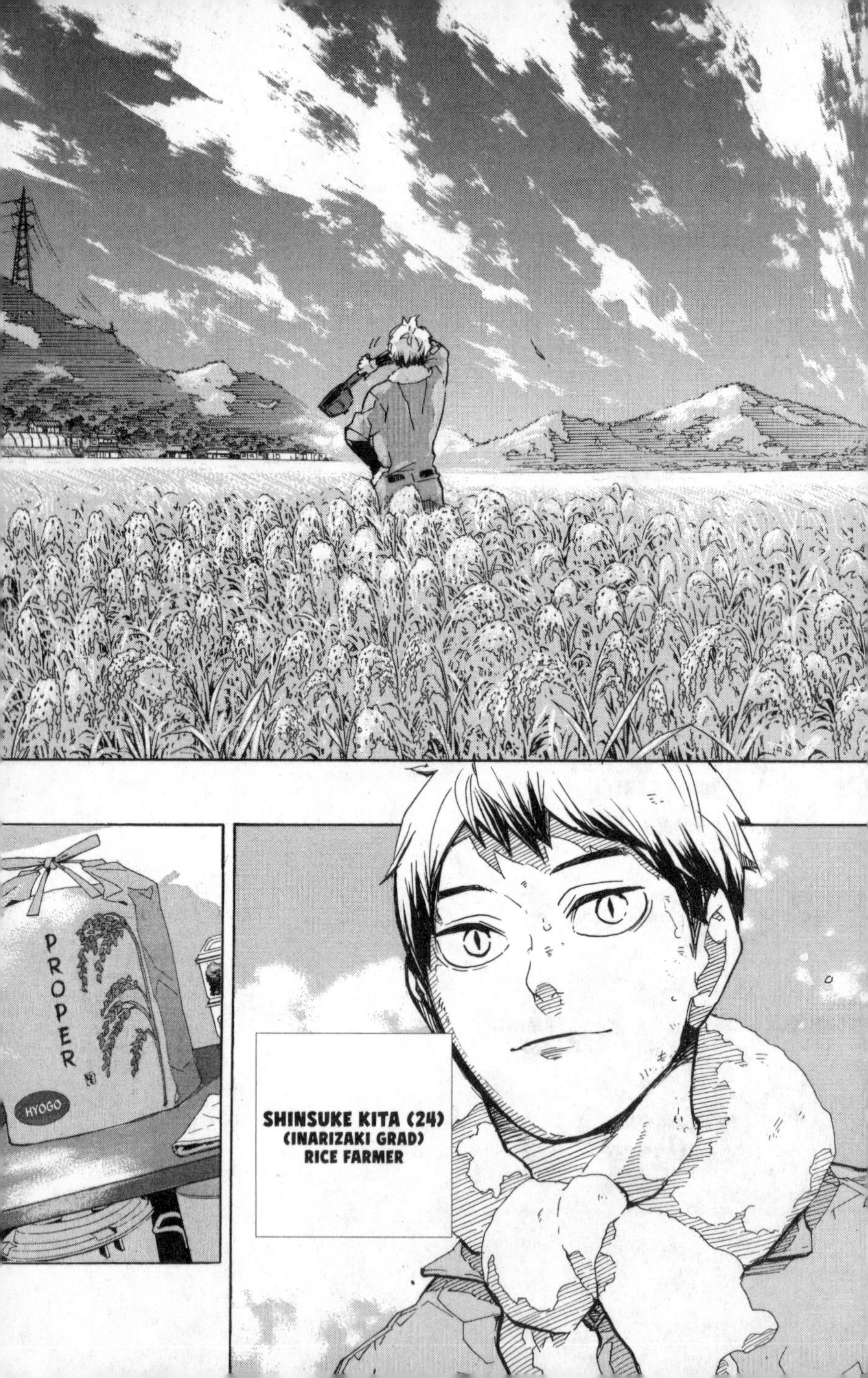
SHINSUKE KITA (24)
(INARIZAKI GRAD)
RICE FARMER
PROPER
HYOGO

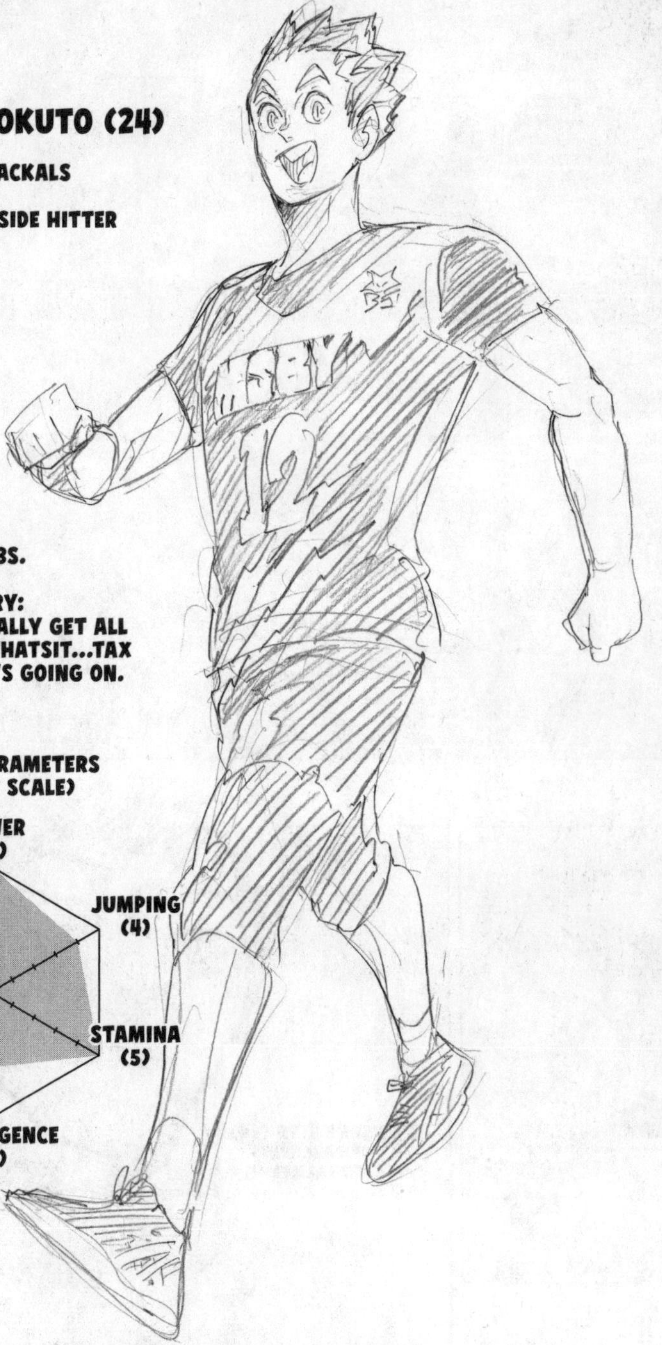

KOTARO BOKUTO (24)

MSBY BLACK JACKALS

POSITION: OUTSIDE HITTER

HEIGHT: 6'3"

WEIGHT: 193 LBS.

CURRENT WORRY:
HE DOESN'T REALLY GET ALL THAT...UHH, WHATSIT...TAX STUFF?...THAT'S GOING ON.

ABILITY PARAMETERS
(5-POINT SCALE)

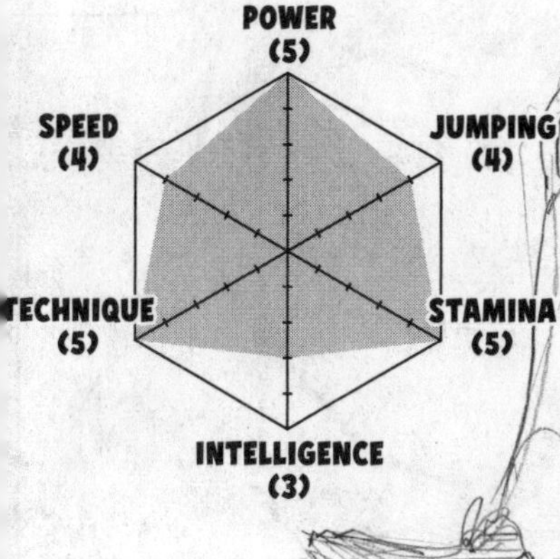
POWER (5)
JUMPING (4)
STAMINA (5)
INTELLIGENCE (3)
TECHNIQUE (5)
SPEED (4)

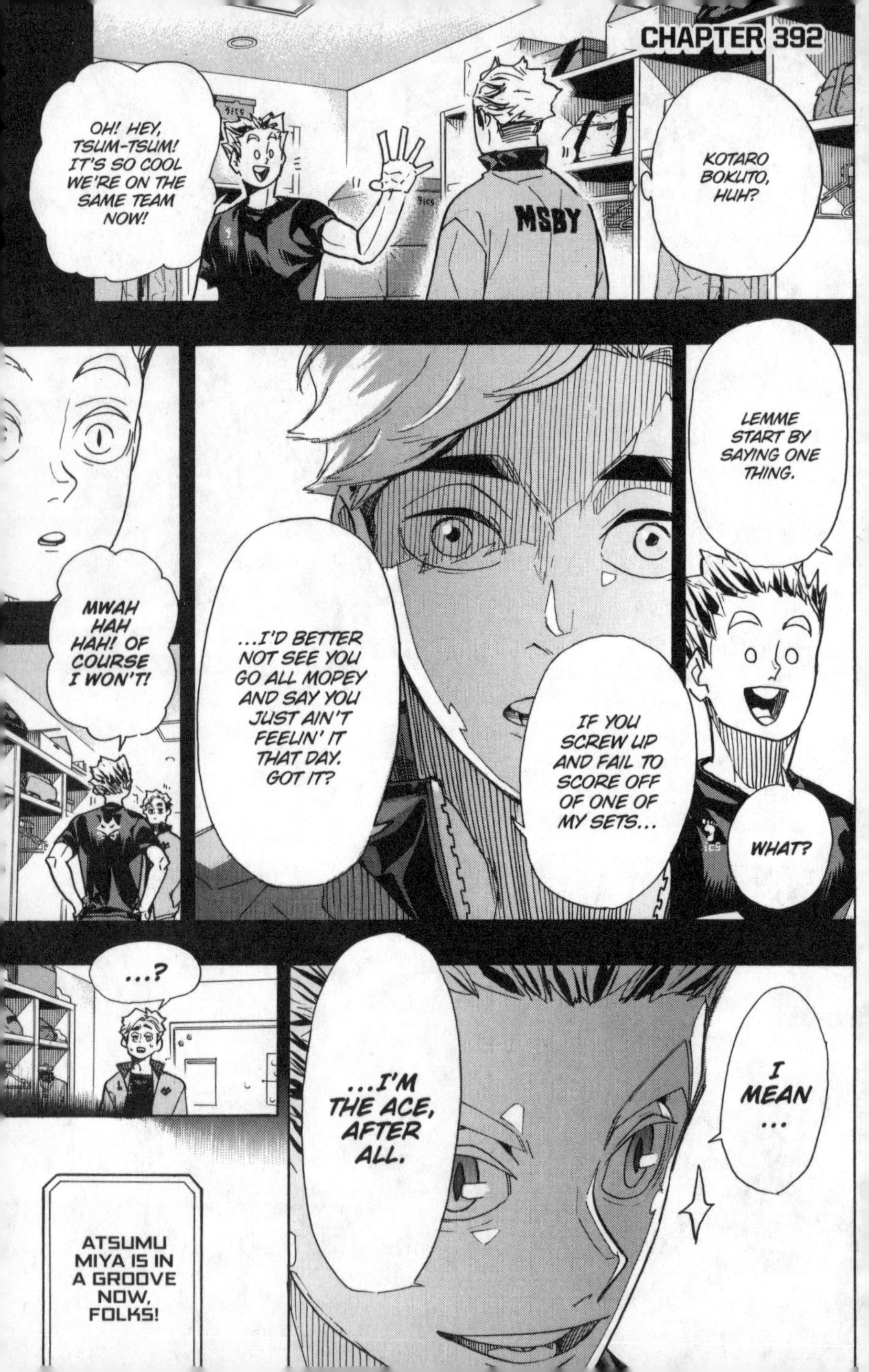
CHAPTER 392
KOTARO BOKUTO, HUH?
OH! HEY, TSUM-TSUM! IT'S SO COOL WE'RE ON THE SAME TEAM NOW!
LEMME START BY SAYING ONE THING.
WHAT?
IF YOU SCREW UP AND FAIL TO SCORE OFF OF ONE OF MY SETS...
...I'D BETTER NOT SEE YOU GO ALL MOPEY AND SAY YOU JUST AIN'T FEELIN' IT THAT DAY. GOT IT?
MWAH HAH HAH! OF COURSE I WON'T!
I MEAN...
...I'M THE ACE, AFTER ALL.
...?
ATSUMU MIYA IS IN A GROOVE NOW, FOLKS!

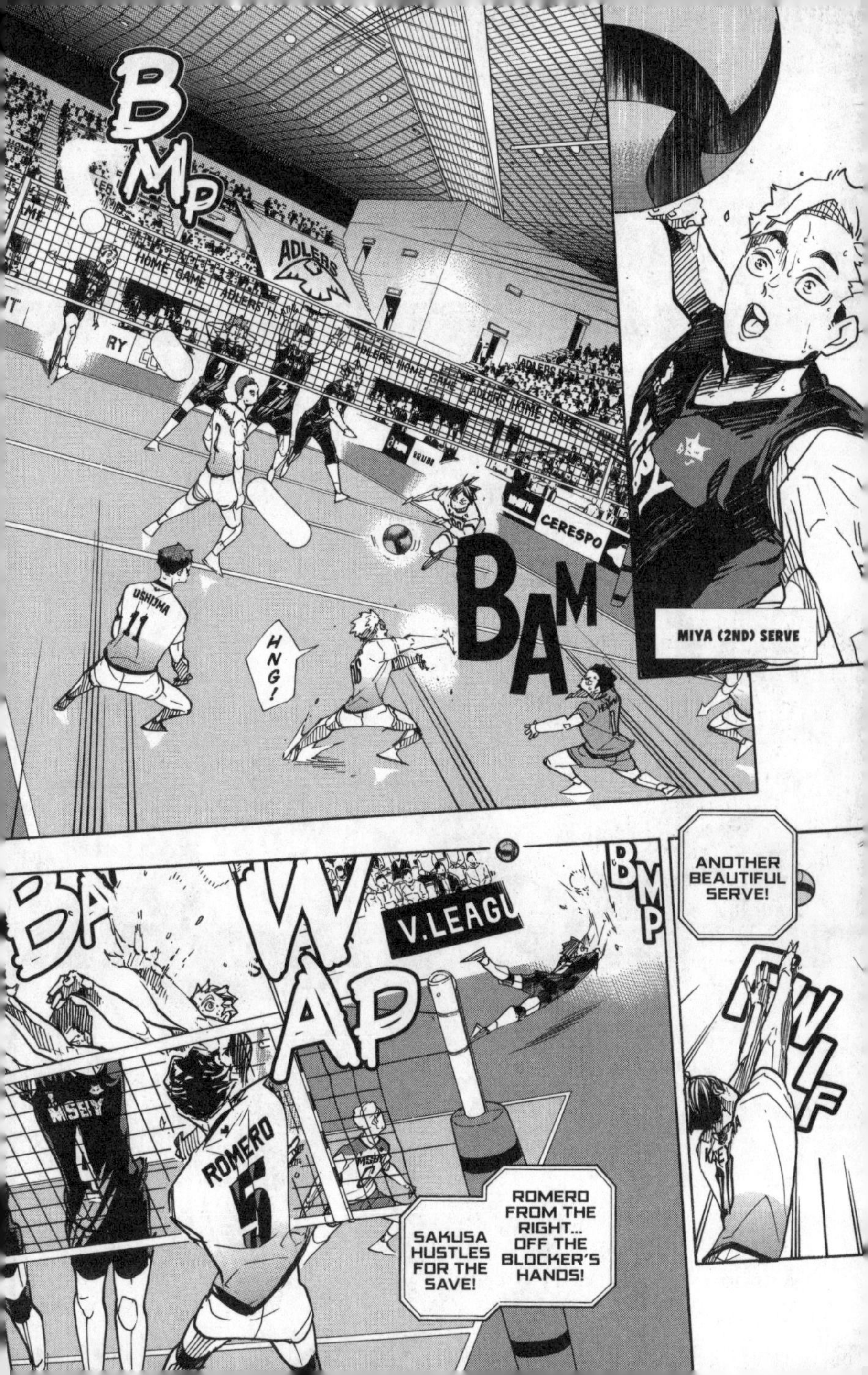
MIYA (2ND) SERVE
BMP
ADLERS
ADLERS HOME GAME
CERESPO
BAM
HNG!
ANOTHER BEAUTIFUL SERVE!
BMP
V.LEAGU
ROMERO FROM THE RIGHT... OFF THE BLOCKER'S HANDS!
SAKUSA HUSTLES FOR THE SAVE!

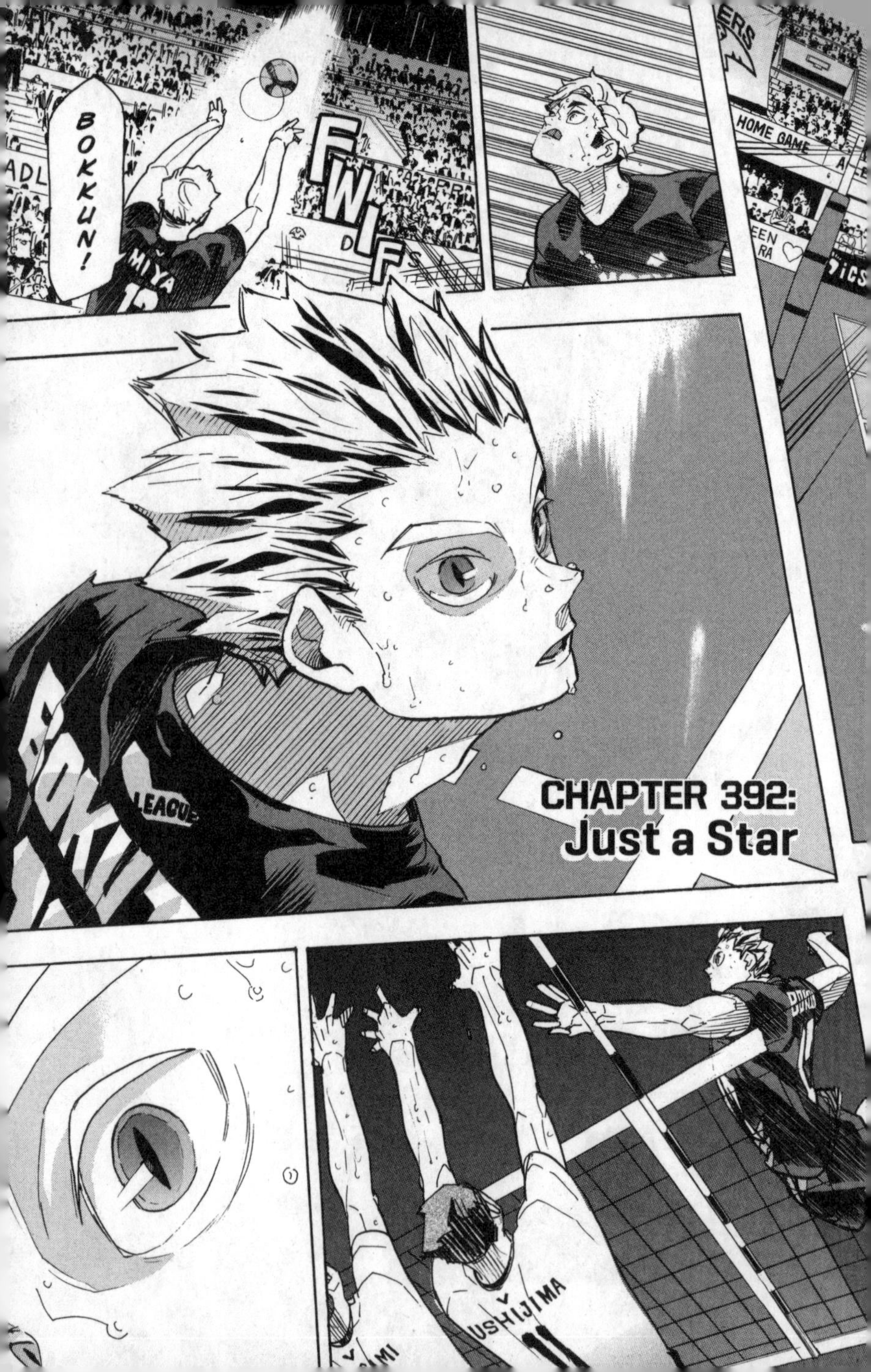
HOME GAME
BOKKUN!
FWIF
MIYA
CHAPTER 392:
Just a Star
LEAGUE
USHIJIMA

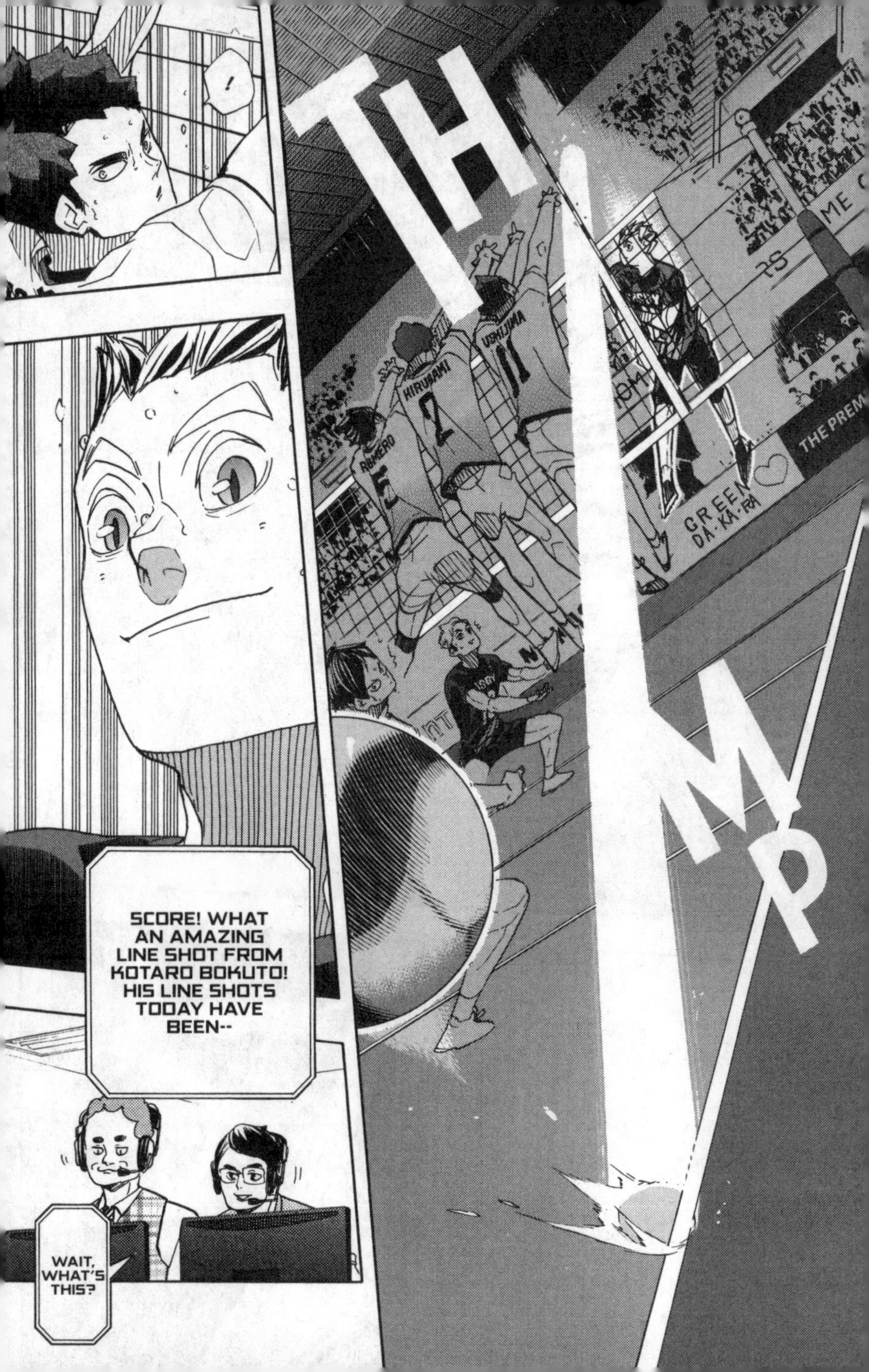
THMP
!
SCORE! WHAT AN AMAZING LINE SHOT FROM KOTARO BOKUTO! HIS LINE SHOTS TODAY HAVE BEEN--
WAIT, WHAT'S THIS?

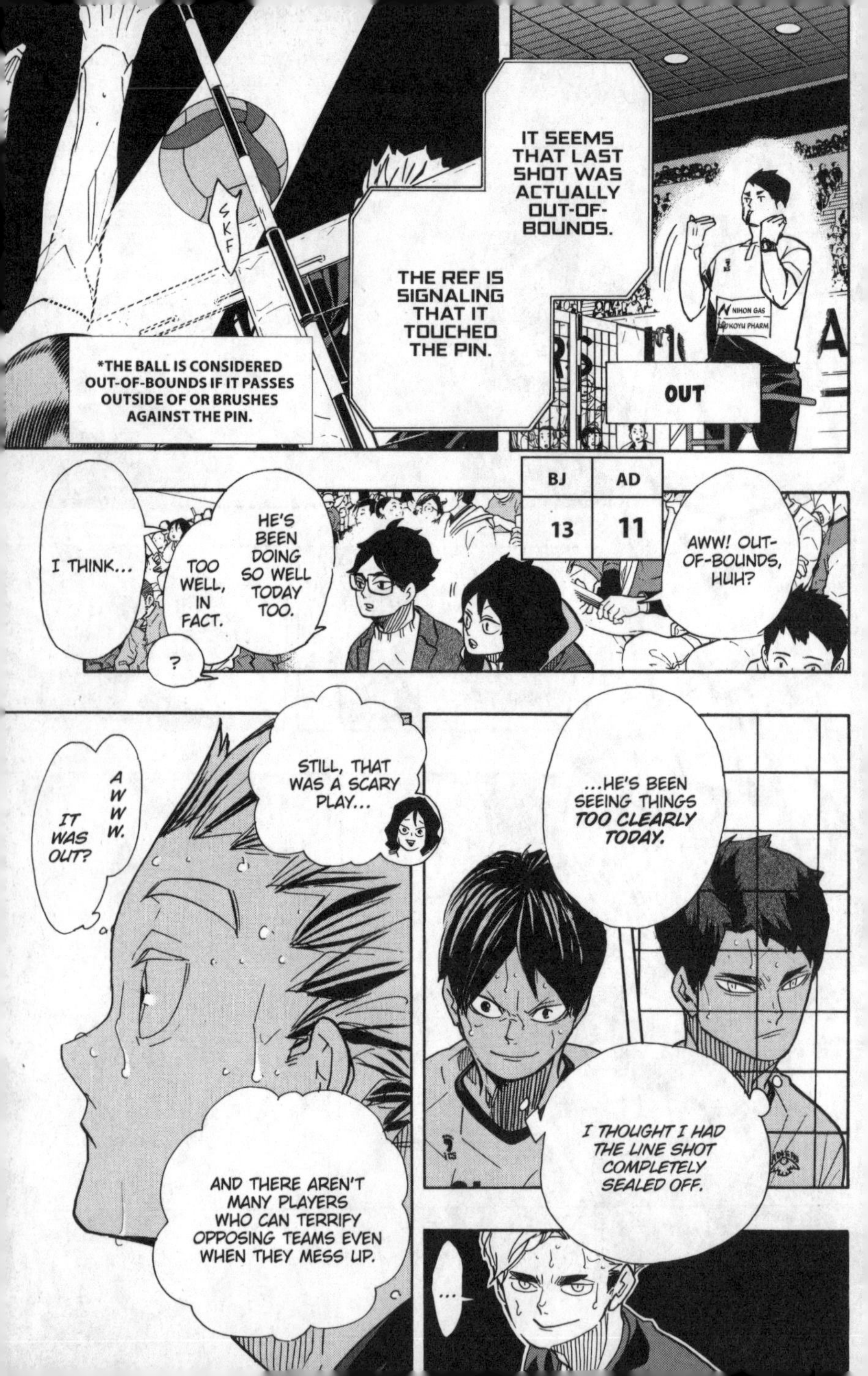
IT SEEMS THAT LAST SHOT WAS ACTUALLY OUT-OF-BOUNDS.
THE REF IS SIGNALING THAT IT TOUCHED THE PIN.
OUT
SKF
*THE BALL IS CONSIDERED OUT-OF-BOUNDS IF IT PASSES OUTSIDE OF OR BRUSHES AGAINST THE PIN.
BJ 13 AD 11
AWW! OUT-OF-BOUNDS, HUH?
HE'S BEEN DOING SO WELL TODAY TOO.
TOO WELL, IN FACT.
?
I THINK...
...HE'S BEEN SEEING THINGS *TOO CLEARLY TODAY.*
I THOUGHT I HAD THE LINE SHOT COMPLETELY SEALED OFF.
...
STILL, THAT WAS A SCARY PLAY...
AWWW.
IT WAS OUT?
AND THERE AREN'T MANY PLAYERS WHO CAN TERRIFY OPPOSING TEAMS EVEN WHEN THEY MESS UP.

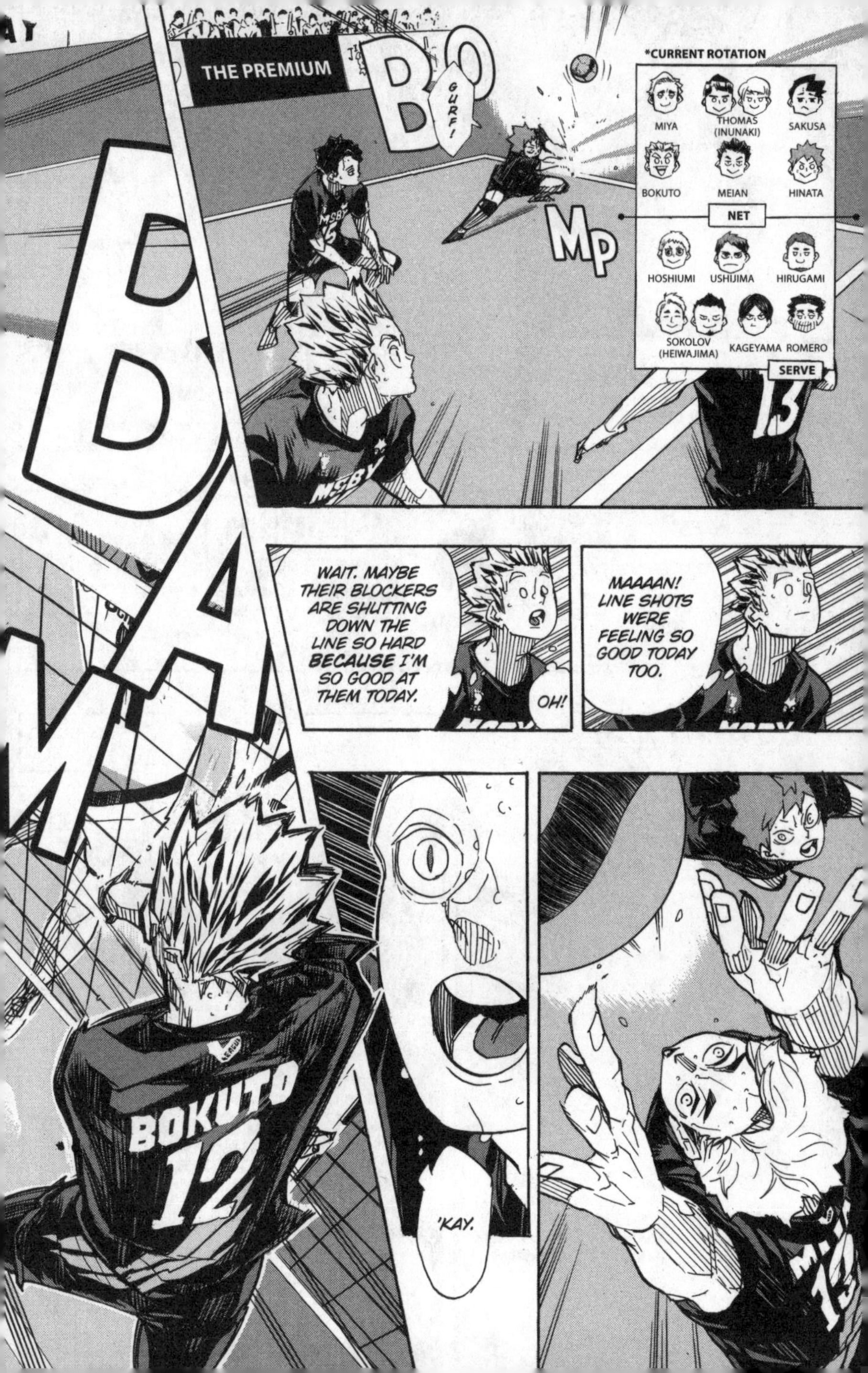
THE PREMIUM
BO
GURF!
*CURRENT ROTATION
MIYA
THOMAS (INUNAKI)
SAKUSA
BOKUTO
MEIAN
HINATA
NET
HOSHIUMI
USHIJIMA
HIRUGAMI
SOKOLOV (HEIWAJIMA)
KAGEYAMA
ROMERO
SERVE
MP
MAAAAN! LINE SHOTS WERE FEELING SO GOOD TODAY TOO.
WAIT. MAYBE THEIR BLOCKERS ARE SHUTTING DOWN THE LINE SO HARD BECAUSE I'M SO GOOD AT THEM TODAY.
OH!
'KAY.
BOKUTO 12

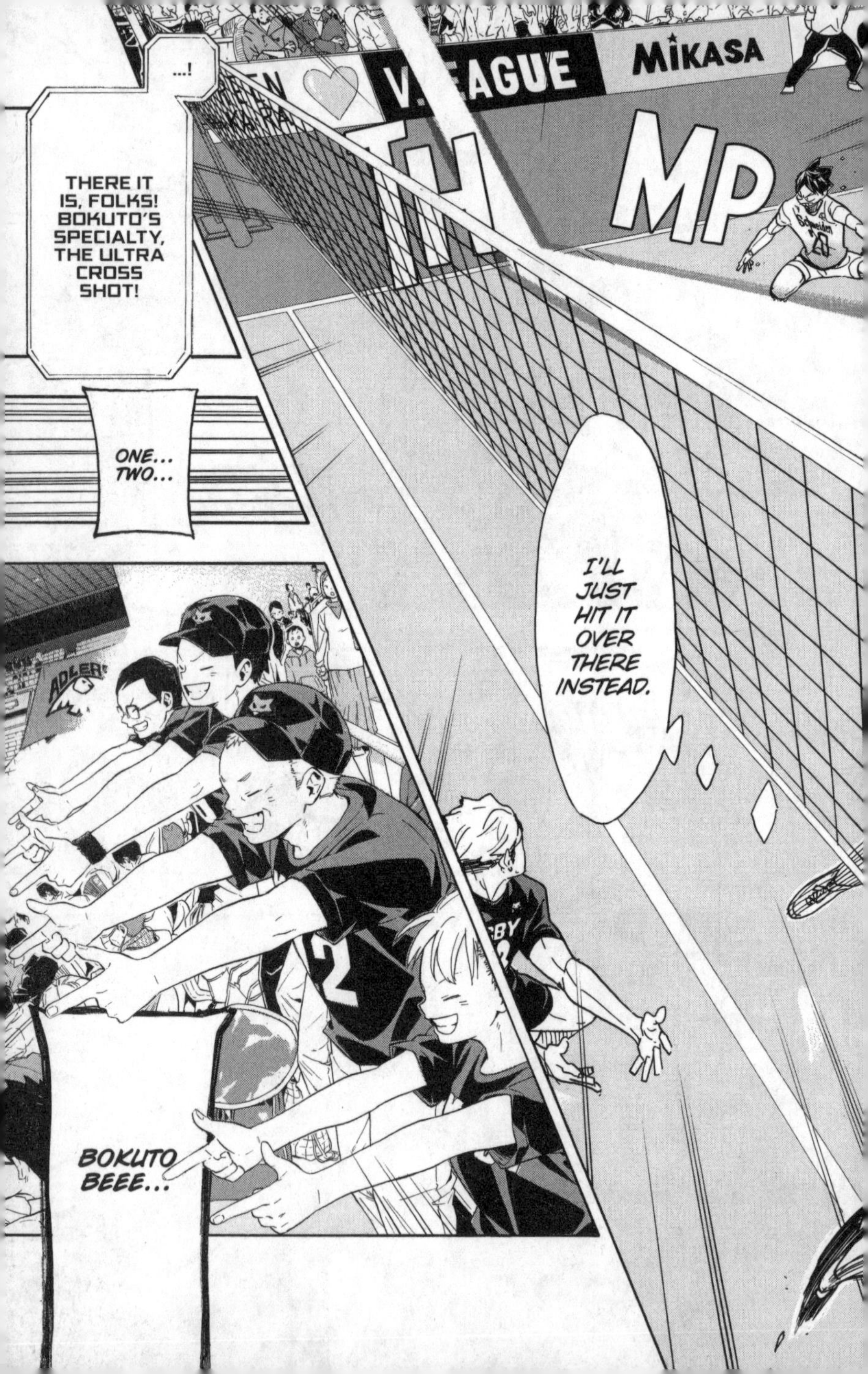

I'LL JUST HIT IT OVER THERE INSTEAD.
...!
THERE IT IS, FOLKS! BOKUTO'S SPECIALTY, THE ULTRA CROSS SHOT!
ONE... TWO...
BOKUTO BEEE...

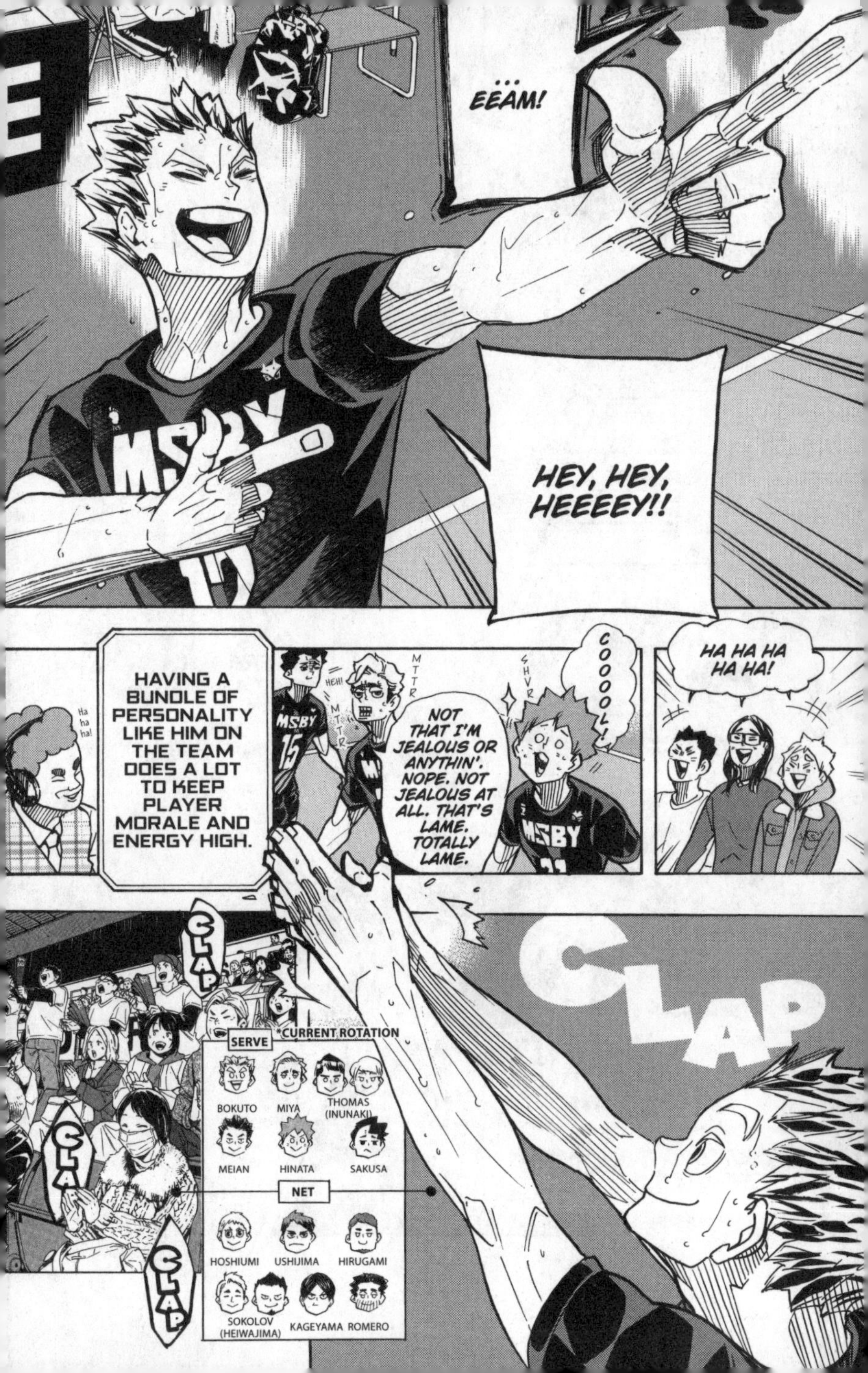
...EEAM!
HEY, HEY, HEEEEY!!
HA HA HA HA HA!
COOOOOL!
SHVR
NOT THAT I'M JEALOUS OR ANYTHIN'. NOPE. NOT JEALOUS AT ALL. THAT'S LAME. TOTALLY LAME.
MTTR
MTTR
HEH!
HAVING A BUNDLE OF PERSONALITY LIKE HIM ON THE TEAM DOES A LOT TO KEEP PLAYER MORALE AND ENERGY HIGH.
Ha ha ha!
CLAP
CLAP
*CURRENT ROTATION
SERVE
BOKUTO
MIYA
THOMAS (INUNAKI)
MEIAN
HINATA
SAKUSA
NET
HOSHIUMI
USHIJIMA
HIRUGAMI
SOKOLOV (HEIWAJIMA)
KAGEYAMA
ROMERO
CLAP
CLAP

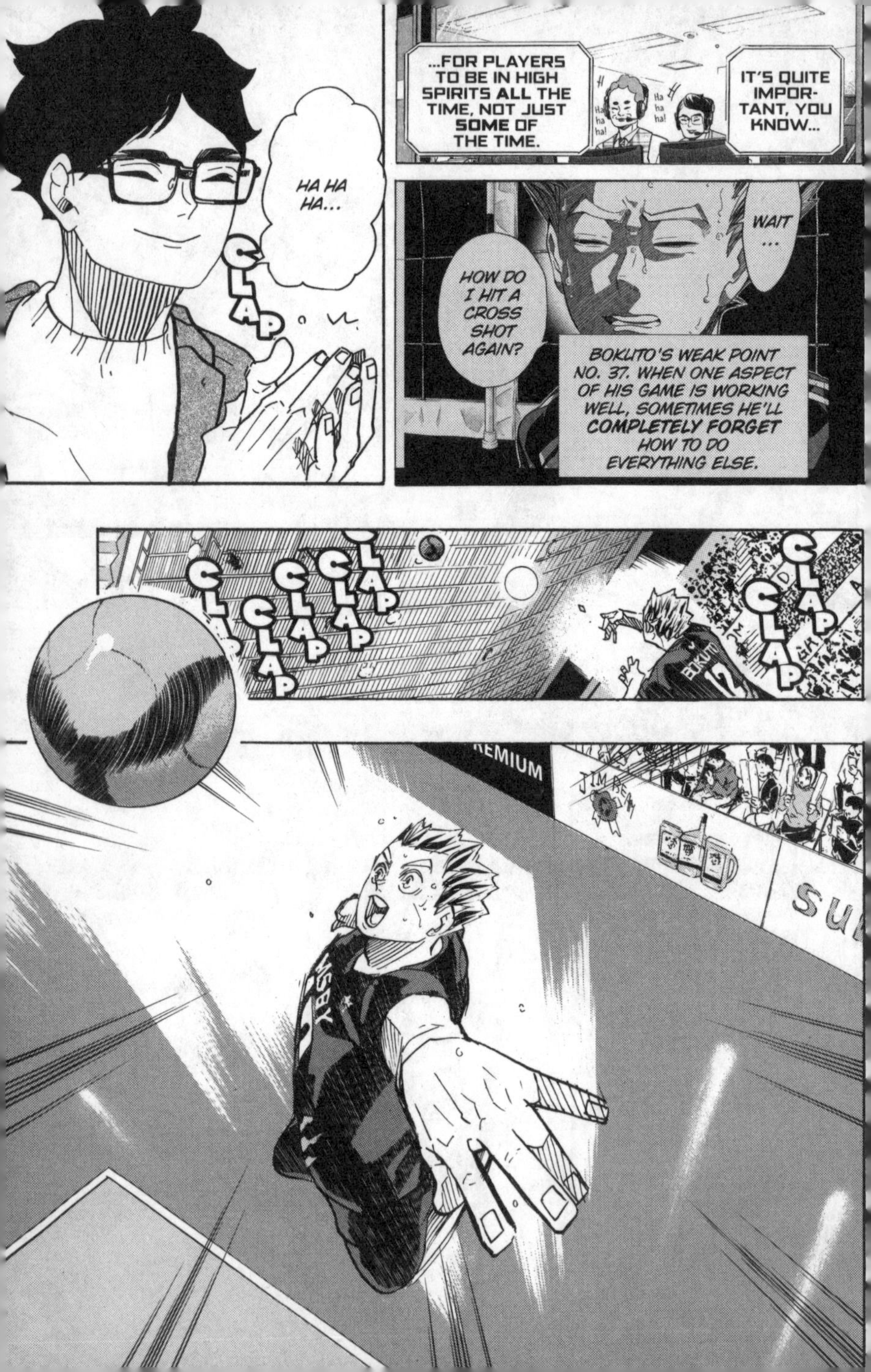

IT'S QUITE IMPORTANT, YOU KNOW...
...FOR PLAYERS TO BE IN HIGH SPIRITS ALL THE TIME, NOT JUST SOME OF THE TIME.
Ha ha ha!
Ha ha ha!
WAIT...
HOW DO I HIT A CROSS SHOT AGAIN?
BOKUTO'S WEAK POINT NO. 37. WHEN ONE ASPECT OF HIS GAME IS WORKING WELL, SOMETIMES HE'LL COMPLETELY FORGET HOW TO DO EVERYTHING ELSE.
HA HA HA...
CLAP
CLAP
CLAP
CLAP
CLAP
CLAP
CLAP
CLAP
BOKUTO
MSBY

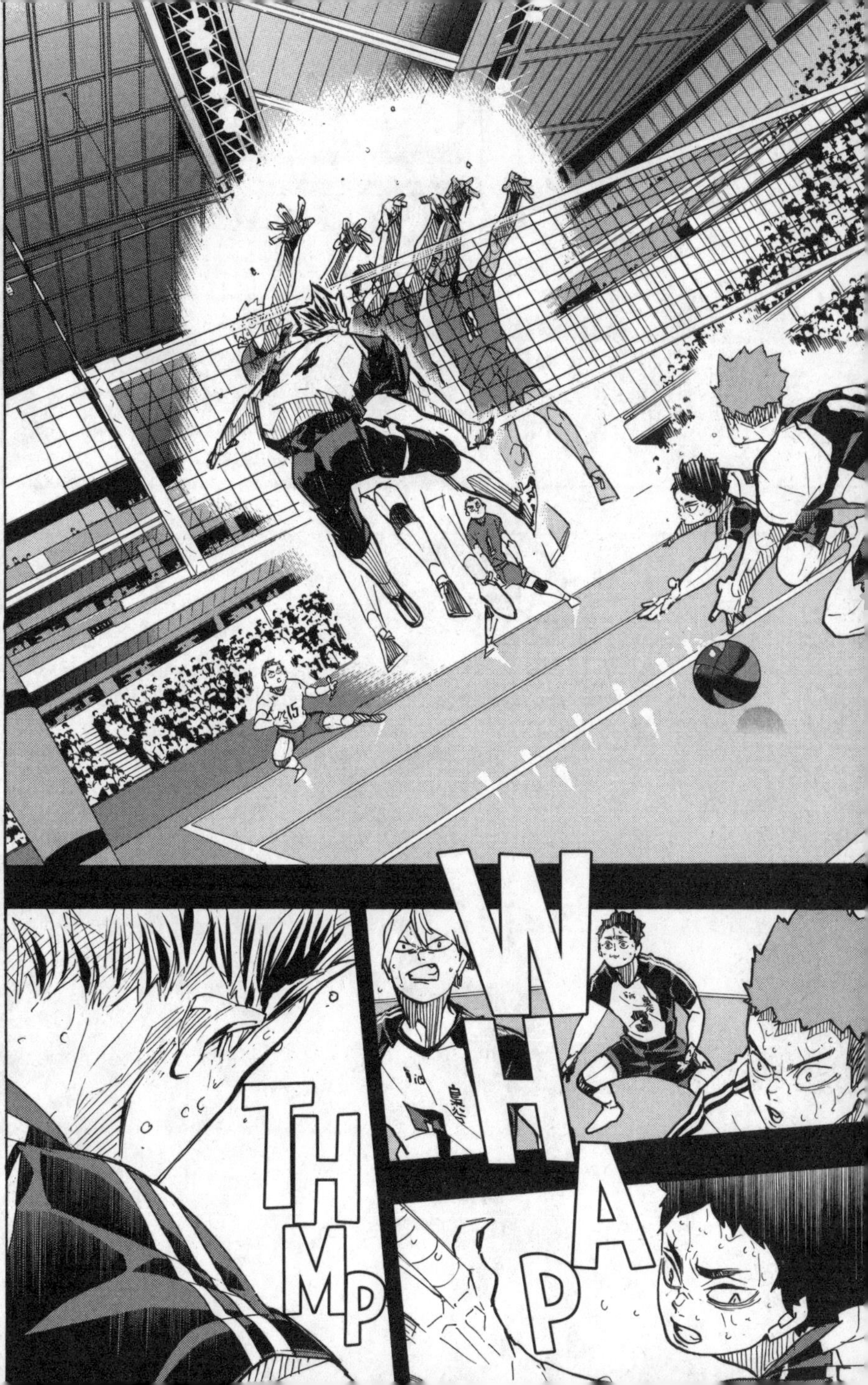
WHAP
THMP

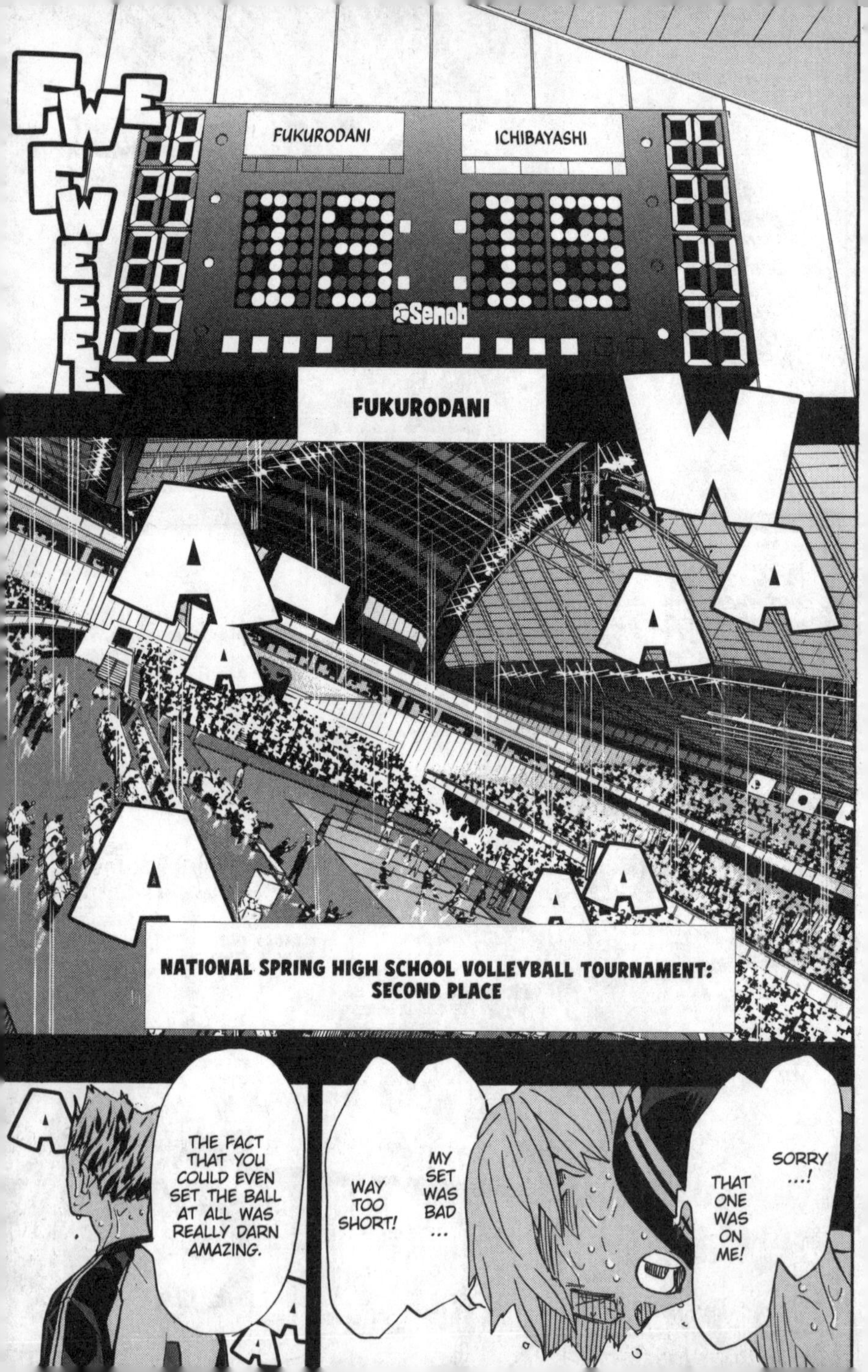
FUKURODANI
ICHIBAYASHI
Senob
FUKURODANI
NATIONAL SPRING HIGH SCHOOL VOLLEYBALL TOURNAMENT: SECOND PLACE
SORRY ...!
THAT ONE WAS ON ME!
MY SET WAS BAD ...
WAY TOO SHORT!
THE FACT THAT YOU COULD EVEN SET THE BALL AT ALL WAS REALLY DARN AMAZING.

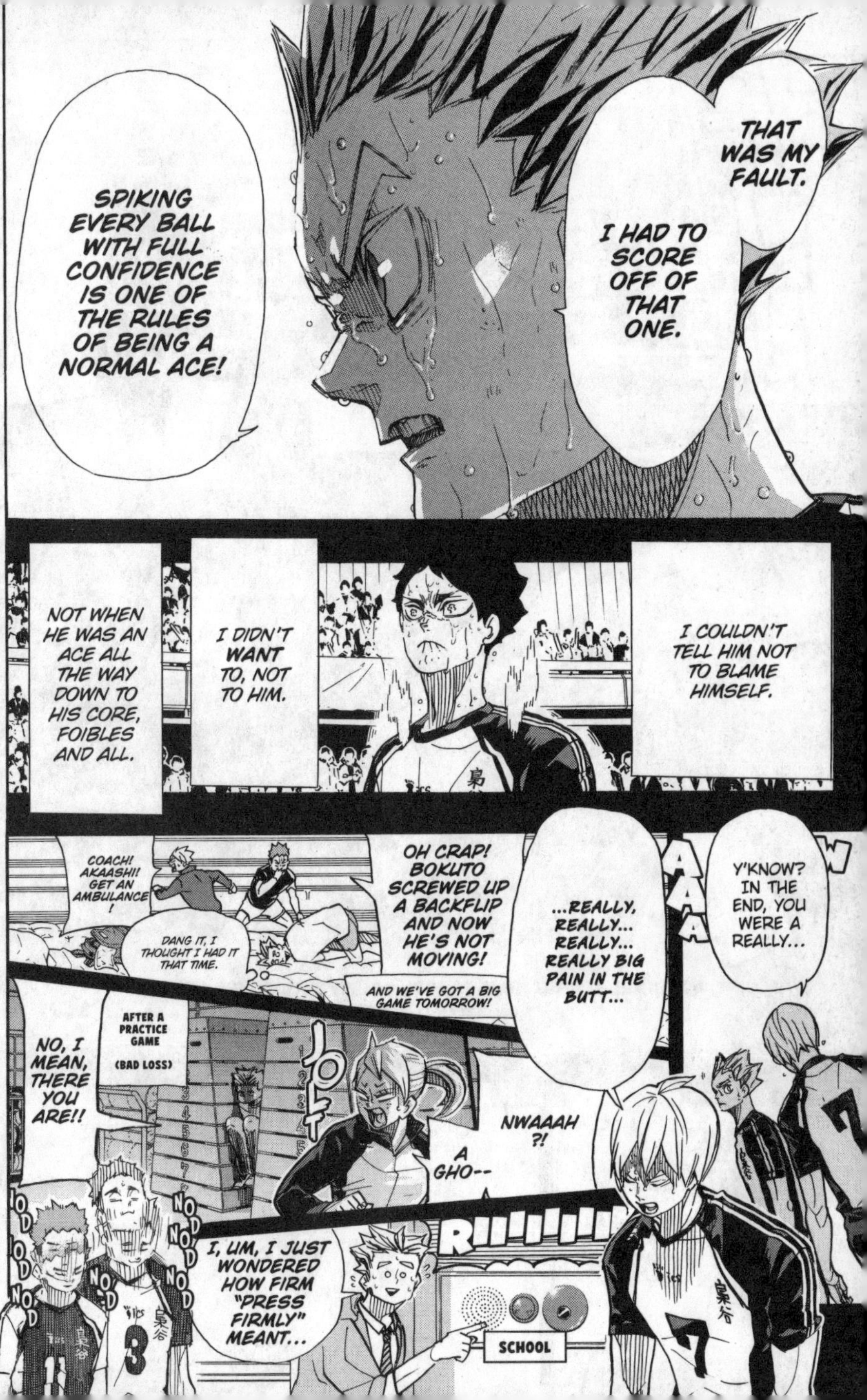
THAT WAS MY FAULT.
I HAD TO SCORE OFF OF THAT ONE.
SPIKING EVERY BALL WITH FULL CONFIDENCE IS ONE OF THE RULES OF BEING A NORMAL ACE!
I COULDN'T TELL HIM NOT TO BLAME HIMSELF.
I DIDN'T WANT TO, NOT TO HIM.
NOT WHEN HE WAS AN ACE ALL THE WAY DOWN TO HIS CORE, FOIBLES AND ALL.
Y'KNOW? IN THE END, YOU WERE A REALLY...
...REALLY, REALLY... REALLY... REALLY BIG PAIN IN THE BUTT...
OH CRAP! BOKUTO SCREWED UP A BACKFLIP AND NOW HE'S NOT MOVING!
COACH! AKAASHI! GET AN AMBULANCE!
DANG IT, I THOUGHT I HAD IT THAT TIME.
AND WE'VE GOT A BIG GAME TOMORROW!
AFTER A PRACTICE GAME
(BAD LOSS)
NWAAAH?!
A GHO--
JOLT
NO, I MEAN, THERE YOU ARE!!
RIIIIIIII
I, UM, I JUST WONDERED HOW FIRM "PRESS FIRMLY" MEANT...
SCHOOL
NOD NOD NOD
NOD NOD NOD

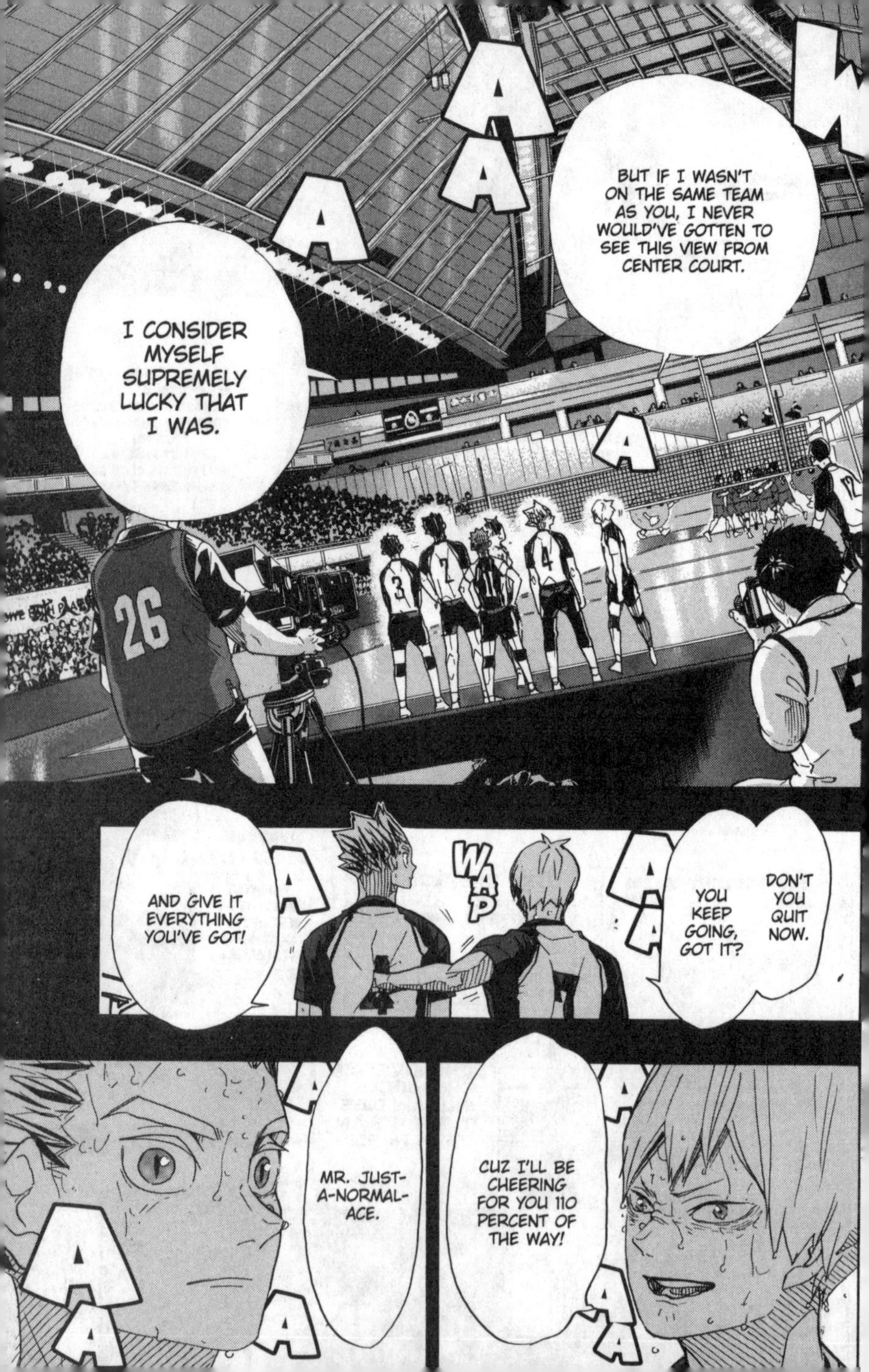
BUT IF I WASN'T ON THE SAME TEAM AS YOU, I NEVER WOULD'VE GOTTEN TO SEE THIS VIEW FROM CENTER COURT.
I CONSIDER MYSELF SUPREMELY LUCKY THAT I WAS.
DON'T YOU QUIT NOW.
YOU KEEP GOING, GOT IT?
WAP
AND GIVE IT EVERYTHING YOU'VE GOT!
CUZ I'LL BE CHEERING FOR YOU 110 PERCENT OF THE WAY!
MR. JUST-A-NORMAL-ACE.

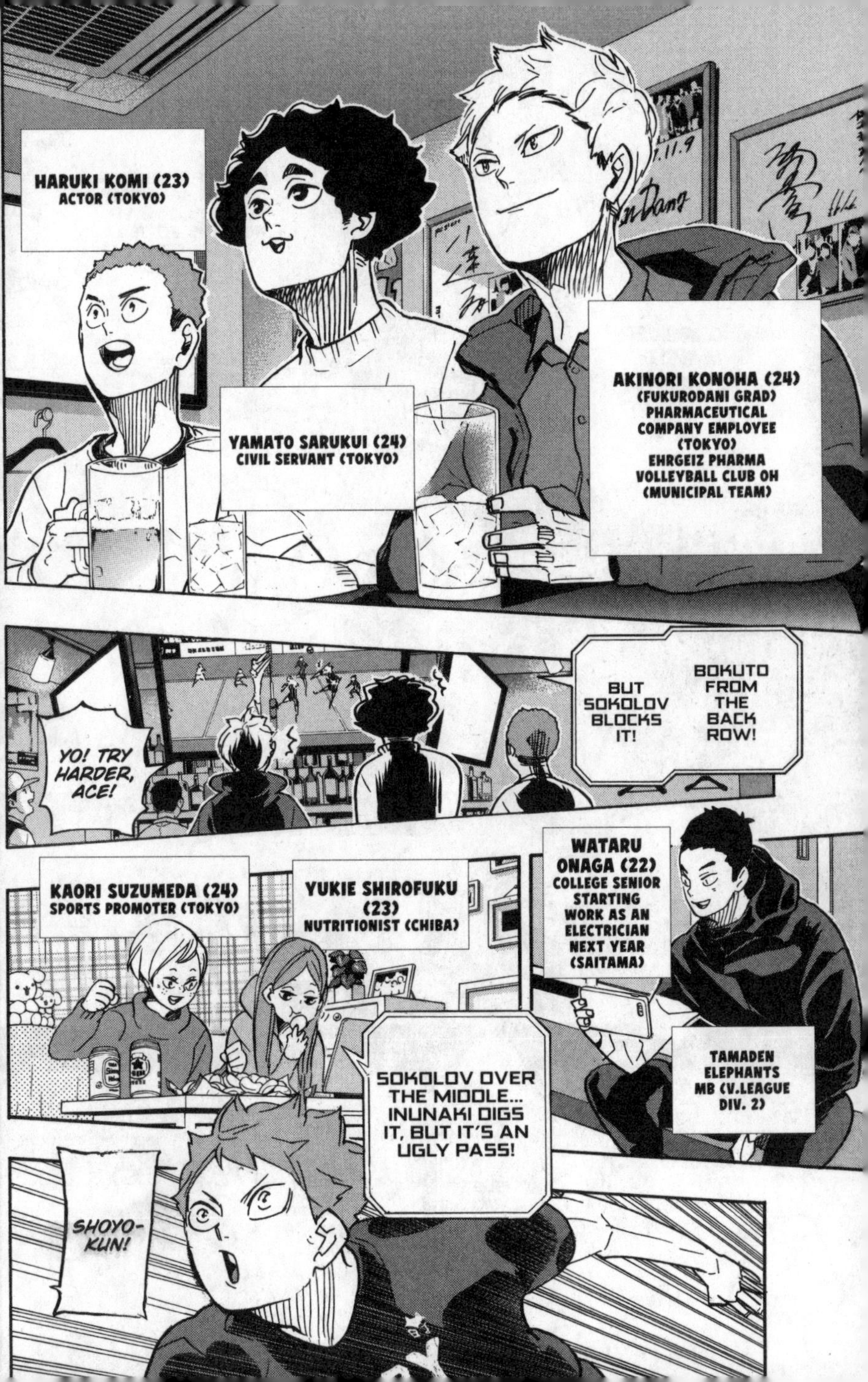
AKINORI KONOHA (24)
(FUKURODANI GRAD)
PHARMACEUTICAL
COMPANY EMPLOYEE
(TOKYO)
EHRGEIZ PHARMA
VOLLEYBALL CLUB OH
(MUNICIPAL TEAM)
YAMATO SARUKUI (24)
CIVIL SERVANT (TOKYO)
HARUKI KOMI (23)
ACTOR (TOKYO)
BOKUTO FROM THE BACK ROW!
BUT SOKOLOV BLOCKS IT!
YO! TRY HARDER, ACE!
WATARU ONAGA (22)
COLLEGE SENIOR
STARTING
WORK AS AN
ELECTRICIAN
NEXT YEAR
(SAITAMA)
TAMADEN
ELEPHANTS
MB (V.LEAGUE
DIV. 2)
YUKIE SHIROFUKU
(23)
NUTRITIONIST (CHIBA)
KAORI SUZUMEDA (24)
SPORTS PROMOTER (TOKYO)
SOKOLOV OVER THE MIDDLE... INUNAKI DIGS IT, BUT IT'S AN UGLY PASS!
SHOYO-KUN!

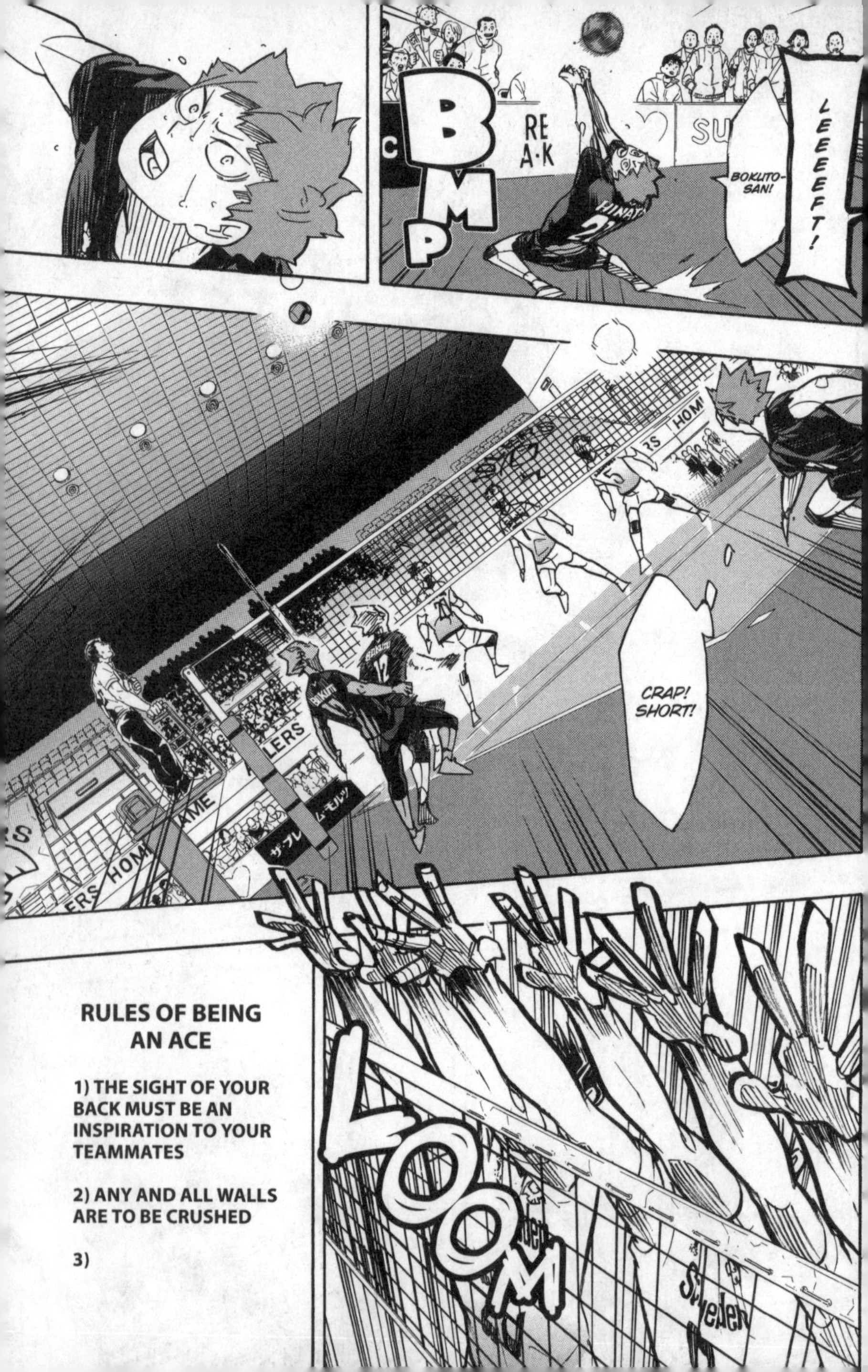
LEEEEEFT!
BOKUTO-SAN!
BMP
CRAP! SHORT!
LOOOM
RULES OF BEING AN ACE
1) THE SIGHT OF YOUR BACK MUST BE AN INSPIRATION TO YOUR TEAMMATES
2) ANY AND ALL WALLS ARE TO BE CRUSHED
3)

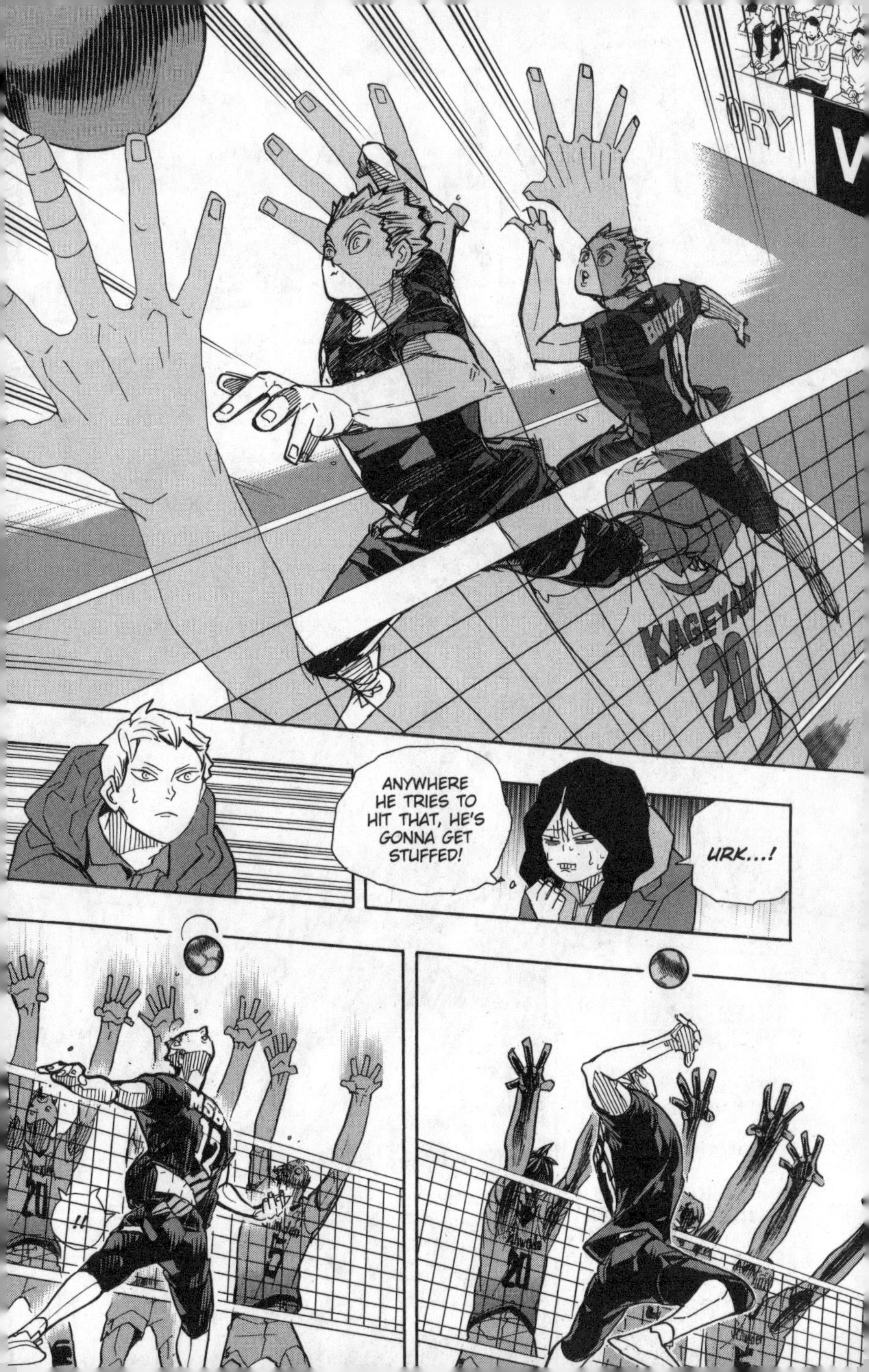
ANYWHERE HE TRIES TO HIT THAT, HE'S GONNA GET STUFFED!
URK...!
!!

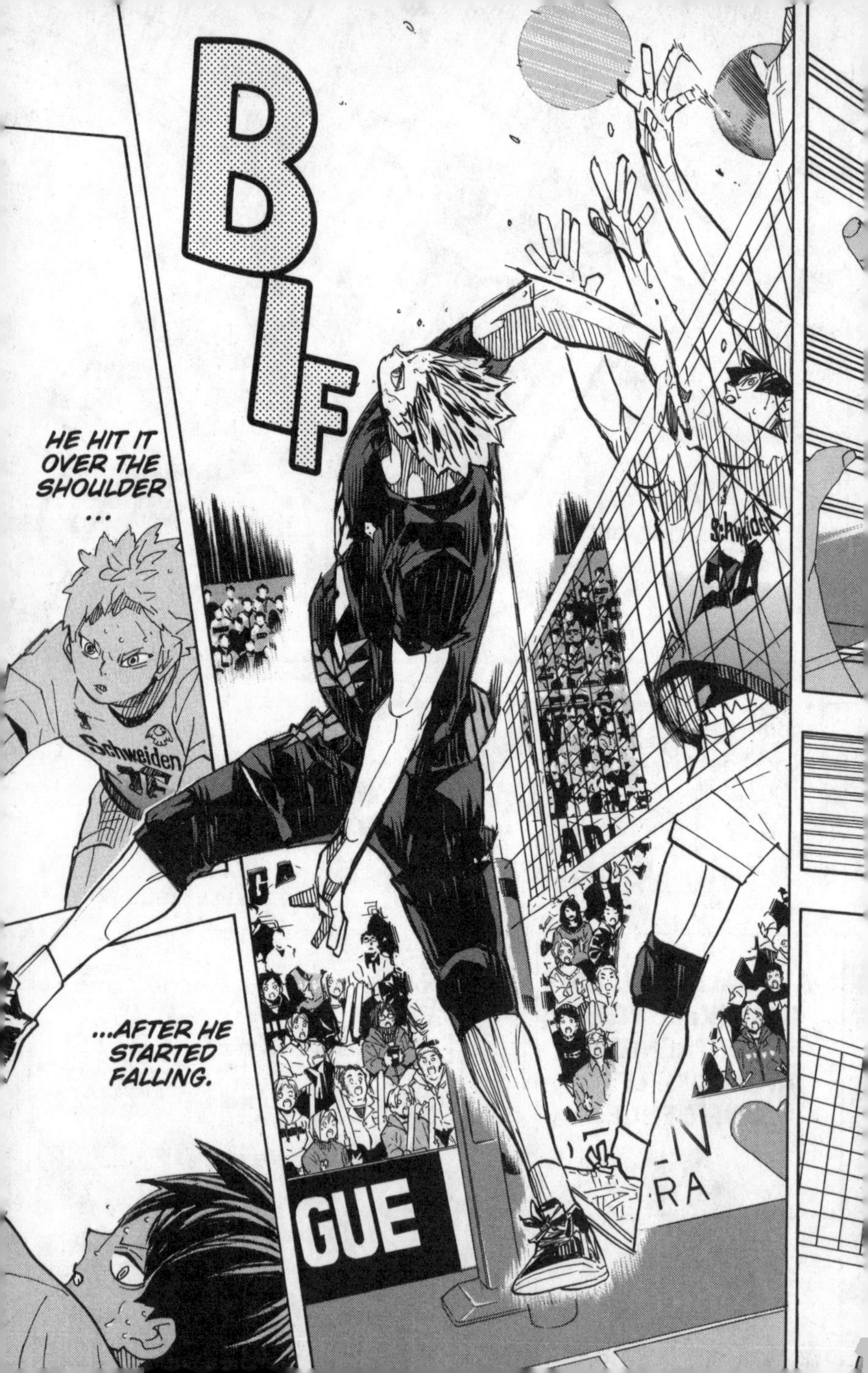
BIF
HE HIT IT OVER THE SHOULDER ...
...AFTER HE STARTED FALLING.
Schweiden
GUE

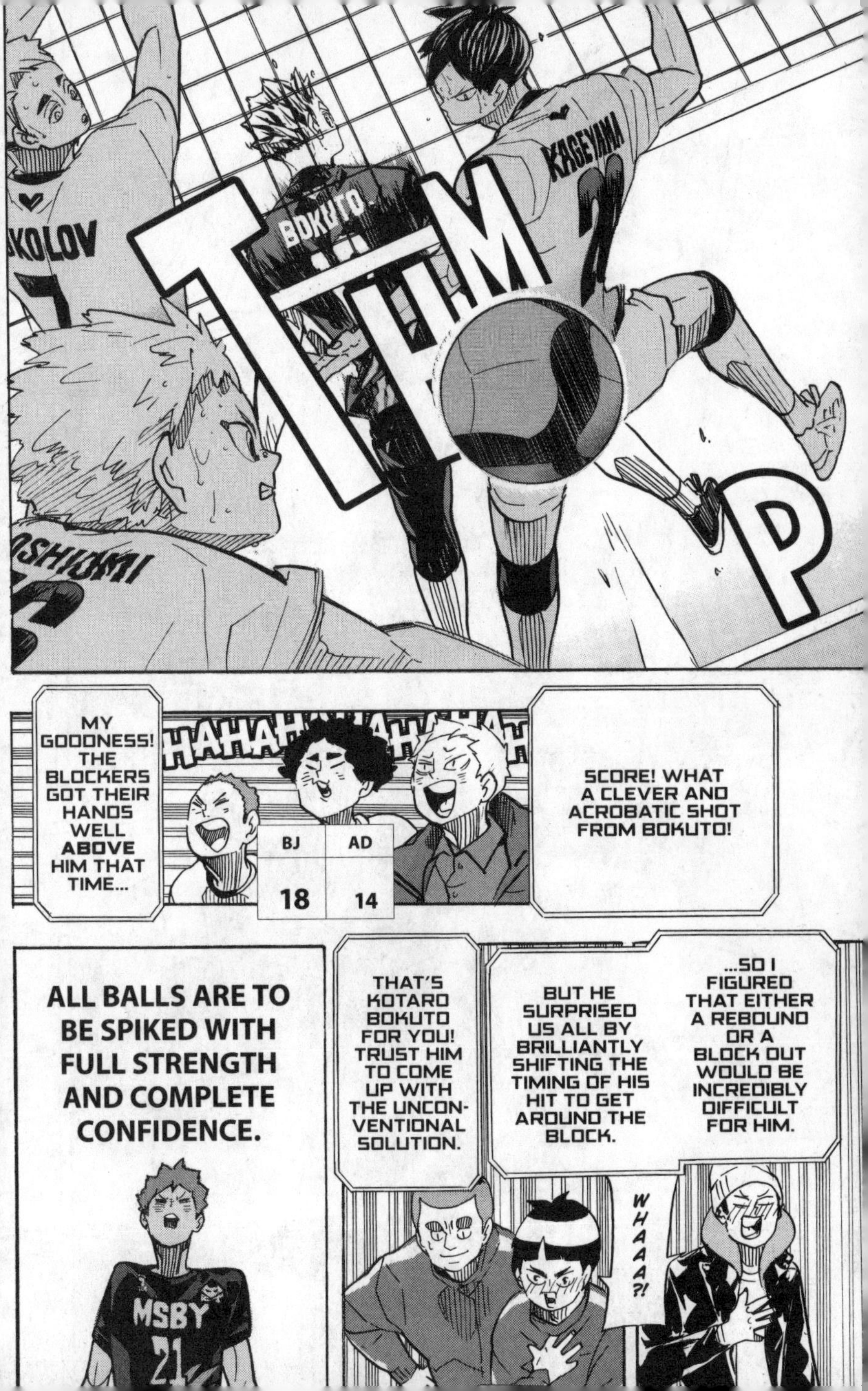
THMP
KAGEYAMA
BOKUTO
SCORE! WHAT A CLEVER AND ACROBATIC SHOT FROM BOKUTO!
HAHAHAHAHAHAH
BJ 18
AD 14
MY GOODNESS! THE BLOCKERS GOT THEIR HANDS WELL ABOVE HIM THAT TIME...
...SO I FIGURED THAT EITHER A REBOUND OR A BLOCK OUT WOULD BE INCREDIBLY DIFFICULT FOR HIM.
BUT HE SURPRISED US ALL BY BRILLIANTLY SHIFTING THE TIMING OF HIS HIT TO GET AROUND THE BLOCK.
THAT'S KOTARO BOKUTO FOR YOU! TRUST HIM TO COME UP WITH THE UNCONVENTIONAL SOLUTION.
WHAAAA?!
ALL BALLS ARE TO BE SPIKED WITH FULL STRENGTH AND COMPLETE CONFIDENCE.
MSBY 21

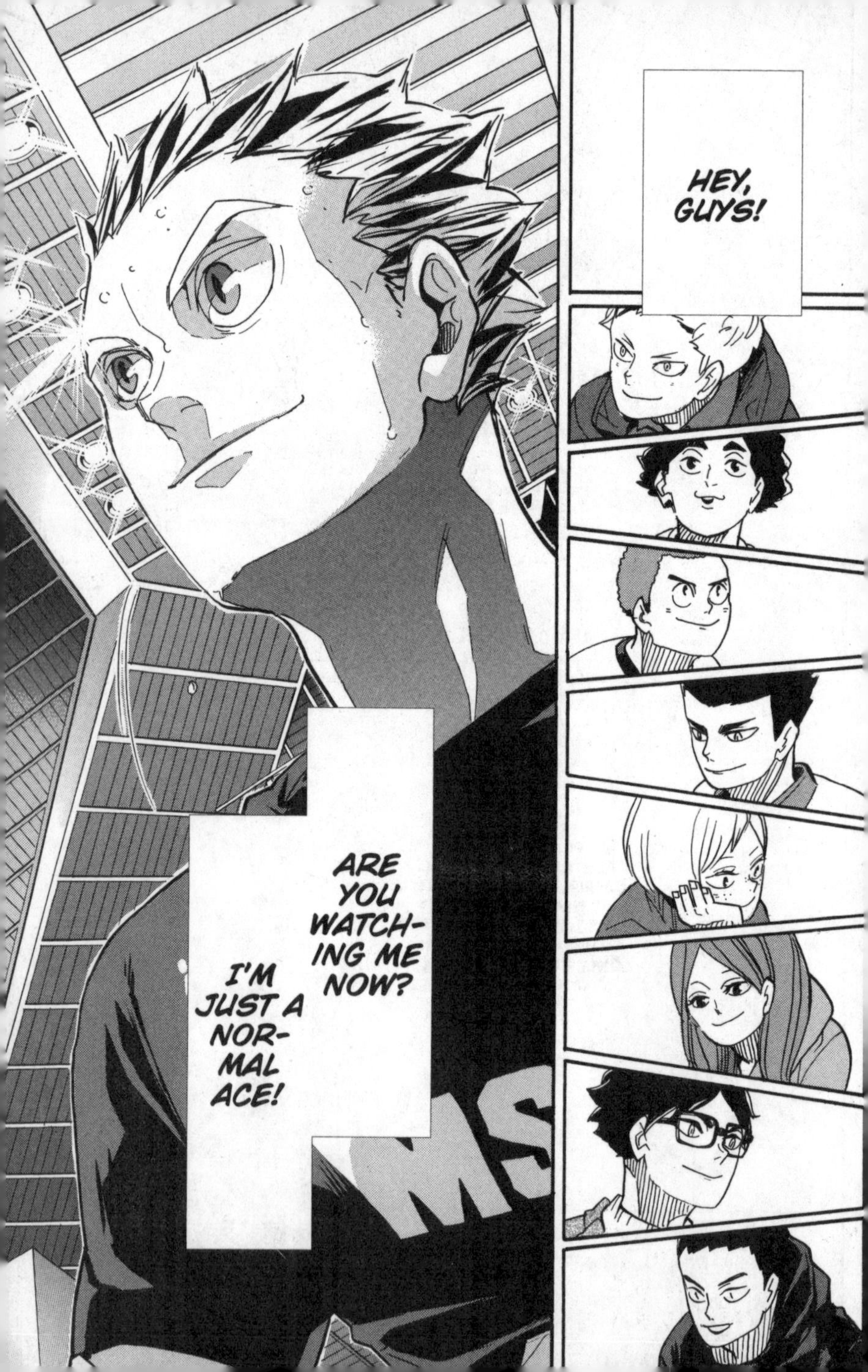
HEY, GUYS!
ARE YOU WATCH-ING ME NOW?
I'M JUST A NOR-MAL ACE!

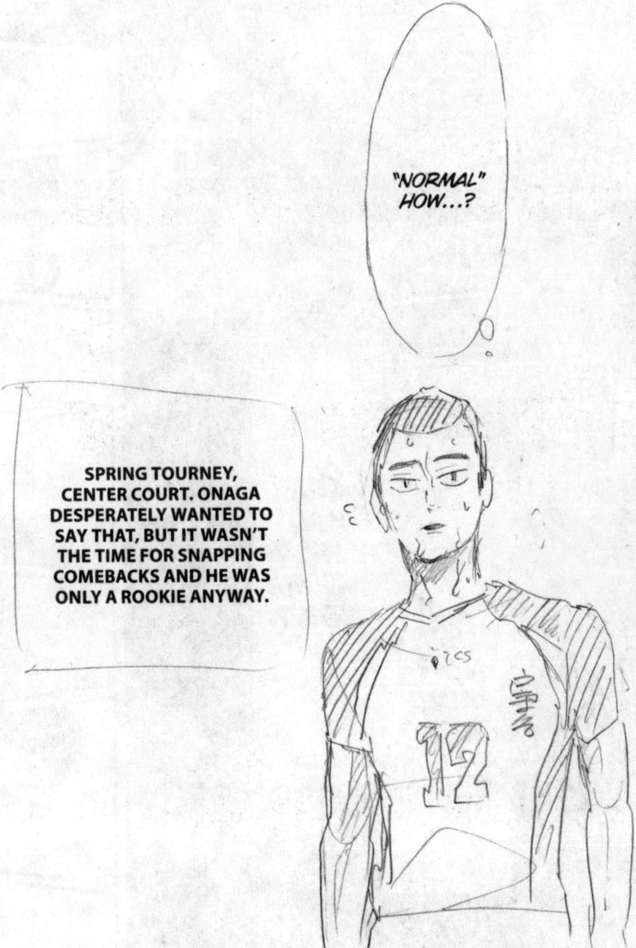
"NORMAL" HOW...?
SPRING TOURNEY, CENTER COURT. ONAGA DESPERATELY WANTED TO SAY THAT, BUT IT WASN'T THE TIME FOR SNAPPING COMEBACKS AND HE WAS ONLY A ROOKIE ANYWAY.

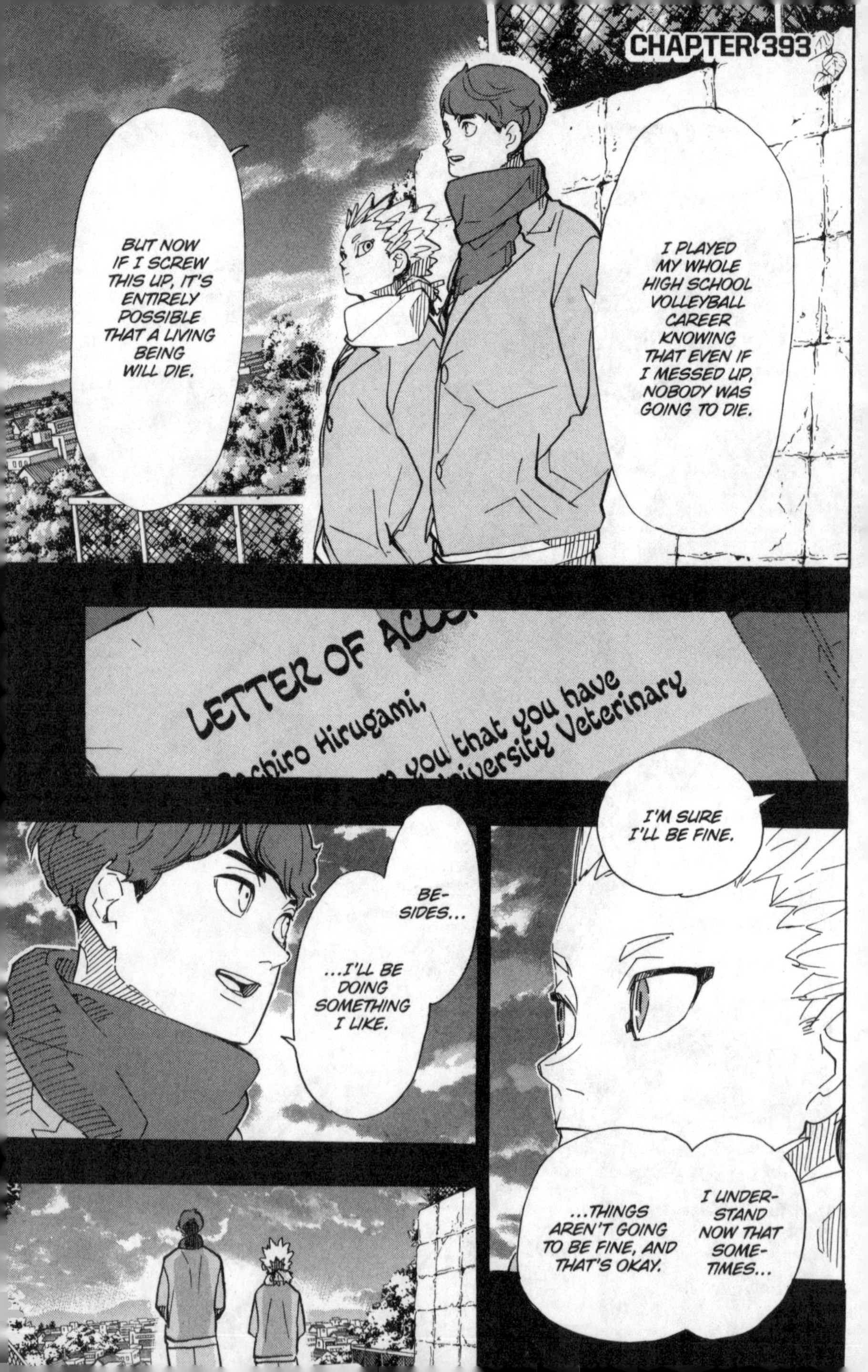
CHAPTER 393
I PLAYED MY WHOLE HIGH SCHOOL VOLLEYBALL CAREER KNOWING THAT EVEN IF I MESSED UP, NOBODY WAS GOING TO DIE.
BUT NOW IF I SCREW THIS UP, IT'S ENTIRELY POSSIBLE THAT A LIVING BEING WILL DIE.
LETTER OF ACC
Hirugami,
you that you have
Veterinary
I'M SURE I'LL BE FINE.
I UNDER-STAND NOW THAT SOME-TIMES...
...THINGS AREN'T GOING TO BE FINE, AND THAT'S OKAY.
BE-SIDES...
...I'LL BE DOING SOMETHING I LIKE.

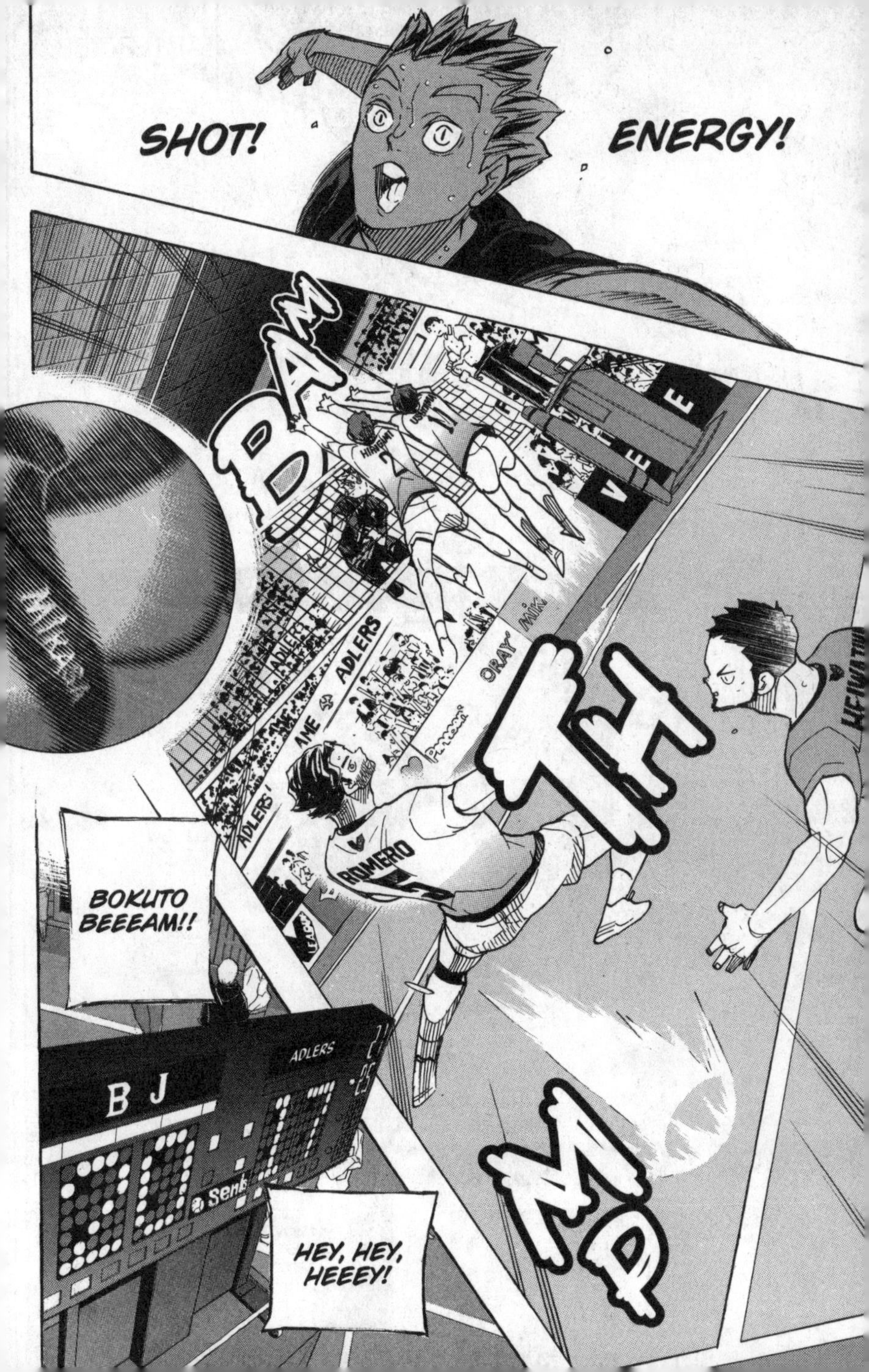
ENERGY!
SHOT!
BAM
THUMP
BOKUTO BEEEAM!!
HEY, HEY, HEEEY!

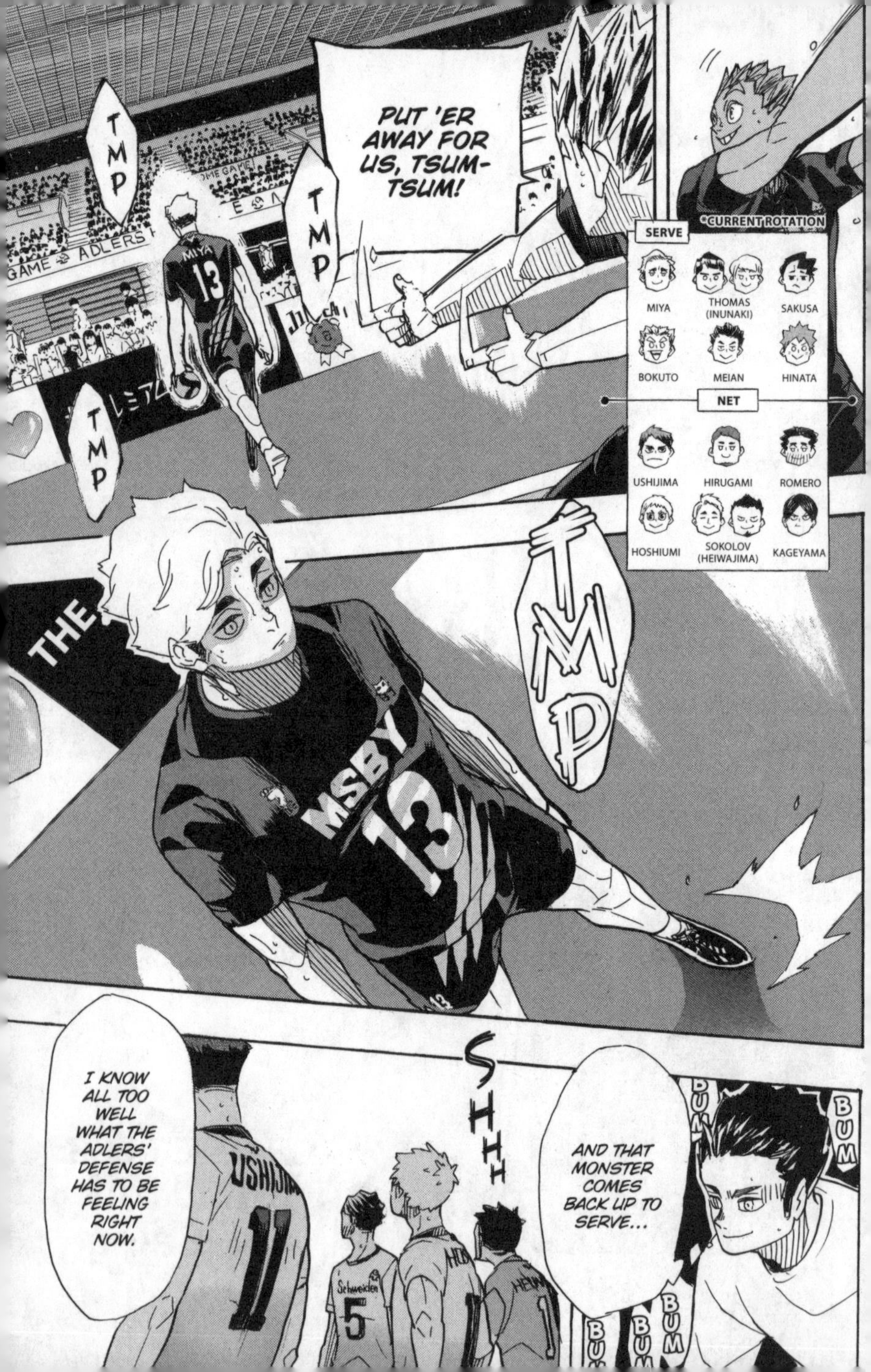

PUT 'ER AWAY FOR US, TSUM-TSUM!
TMP
TMP
TMP
*CURRENT ROTATION
SERVE
MIYA
THOMAS (INUNAKI)
SAKUSA
BOKUTO
MEIAN
HINATA
NET
USHIJIMA
HIRUGAMI
ROMERO
HOSHIUMI
SOKOLOV (HEIWAJIMA)
KAGEYAMA
TMP
AND THAT MONSTER COMES BACK UP TO SERVE...
BUM BUM
BUM BUM BUM BUM
SHHH
I KNOW ALL TOO WELL WHAT THE ADLERS' DEFENSE HAS TO BE FEELING RIGHT NOW.

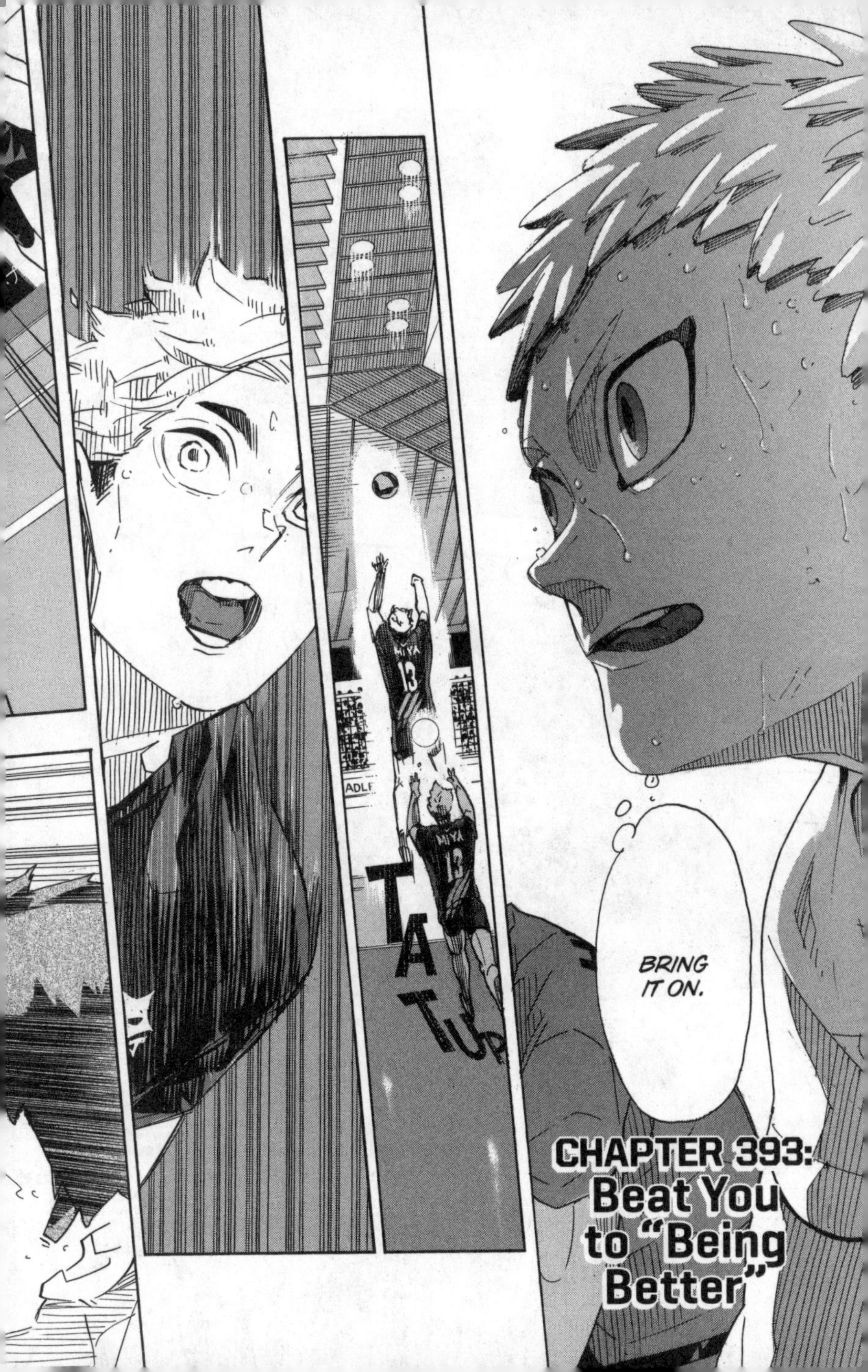
BRING IT ON.
MIYA 13
MIYA 13

CHAPTER 393: Beat You to "Being Better"

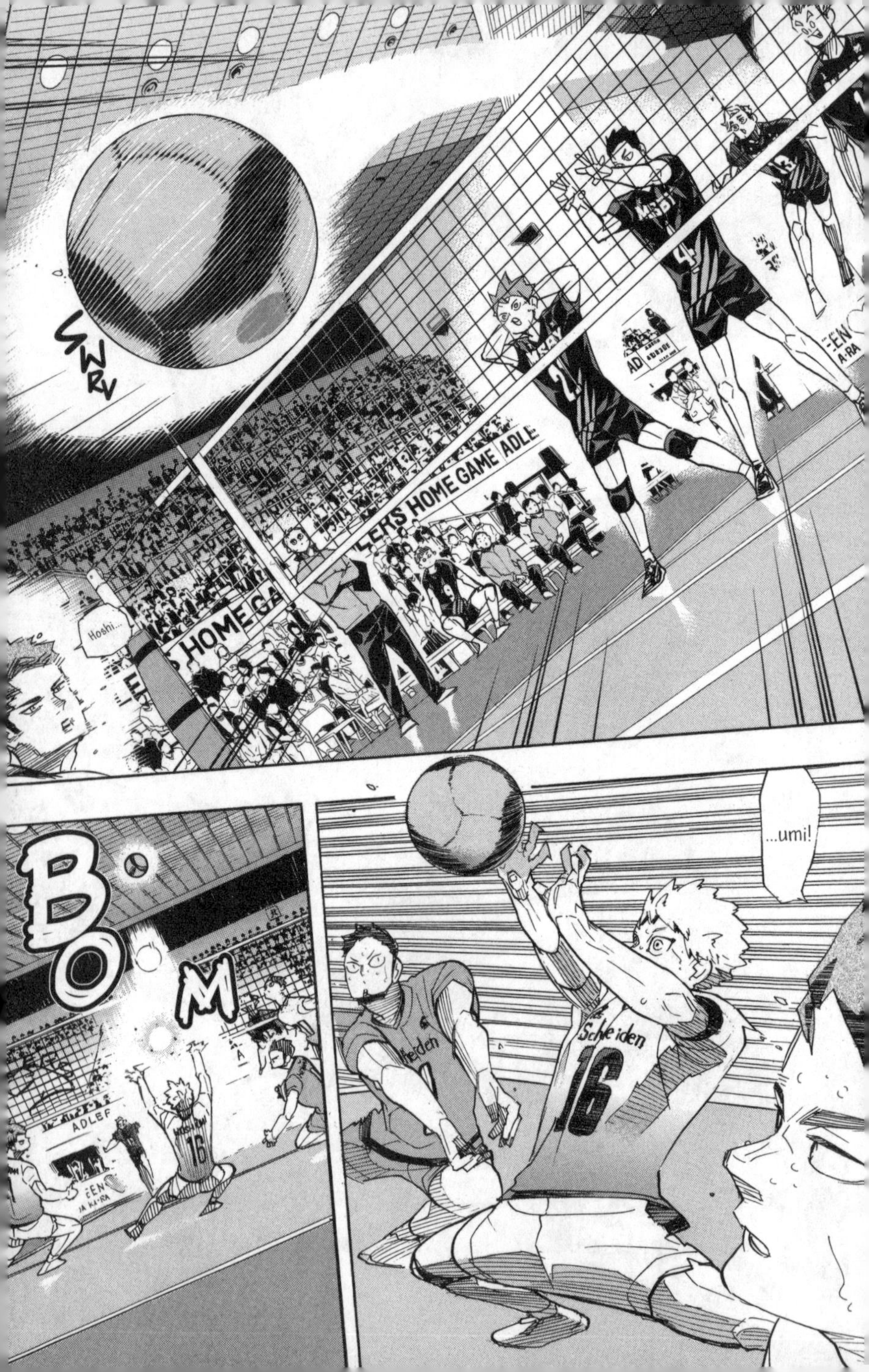
SWRV
ERS HOME GAME ADLE
Hoshi...
...umi!
BOOM

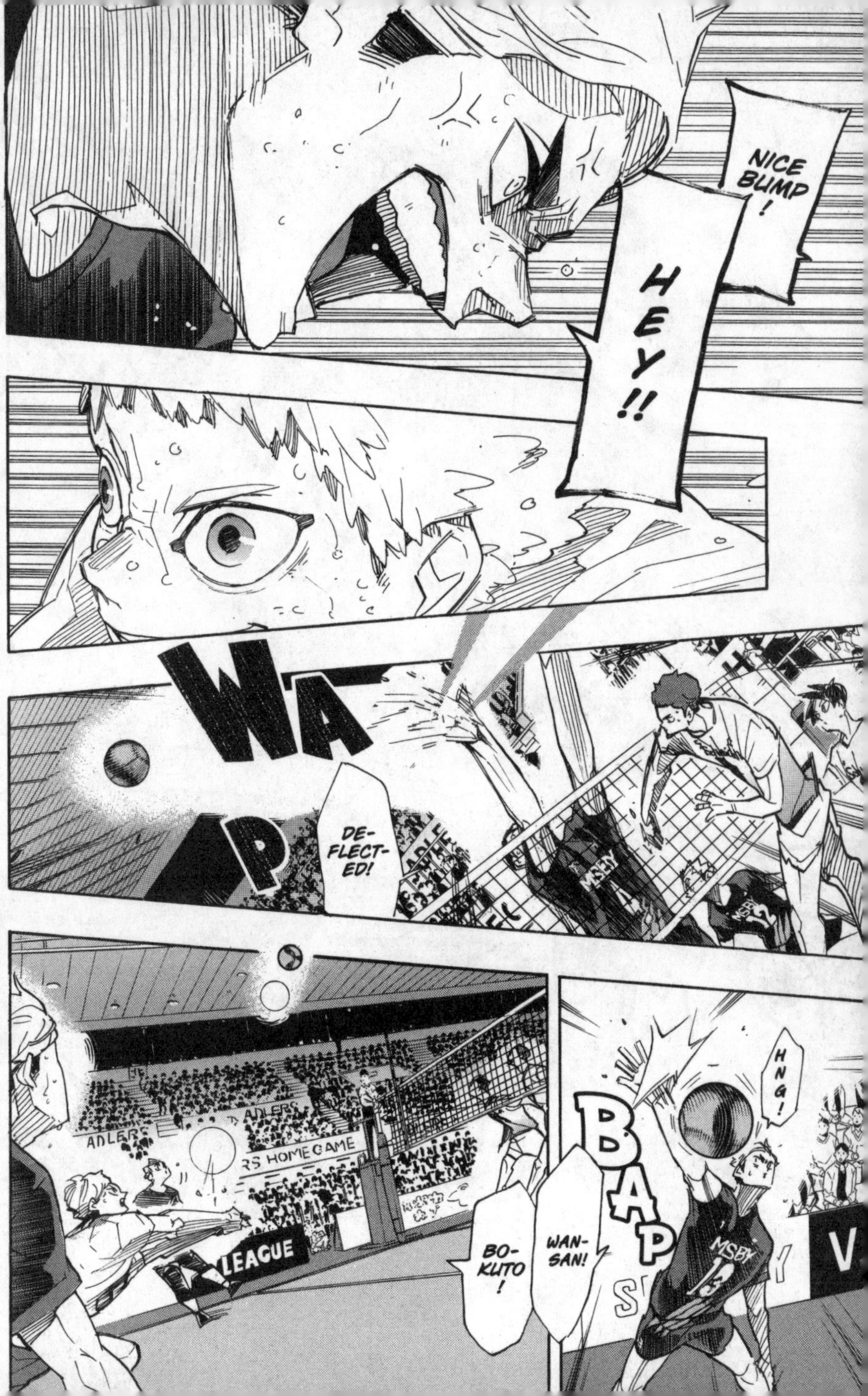
NICE BUMP!
HEY!!
WAP
DE-FLECTED!
HNG!
BAP
WAN-SAN!
BO-KUTO!
MSBY
ADLERS
RS HOME GAME
LEAGUE

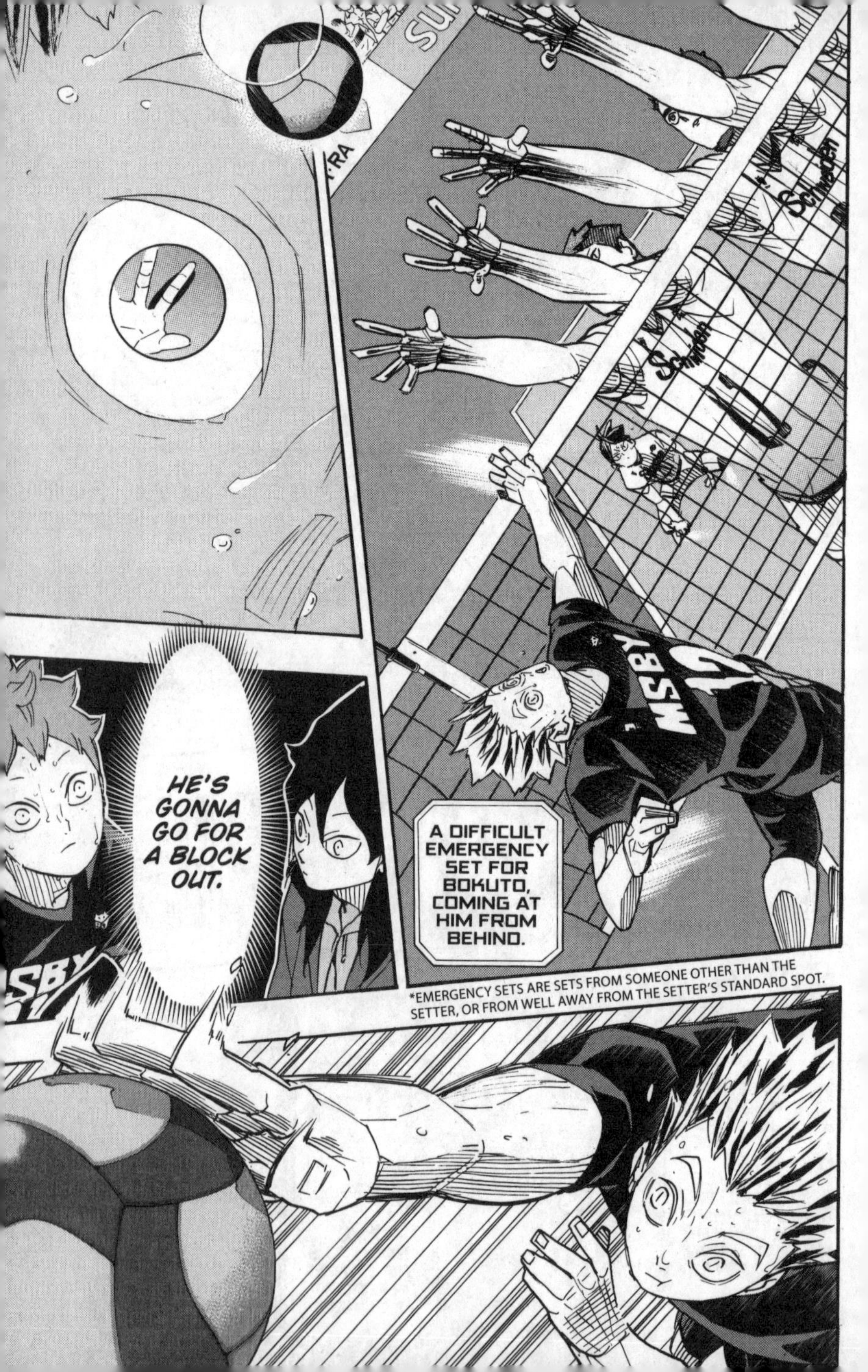
A DIFFICULT EMERGENCY SET FOR BOKUTO, COMING AT HIM FROM BEHIND.
HE'S GONNA GO FOR A BLOCK OUT.

*EMERGENCY SETS ARE SETS FROM SOMEONE OTHER THAN THE SETTER, OR FROM WELL AWAY FROM THE SETTER'S STANDARD SPOT.

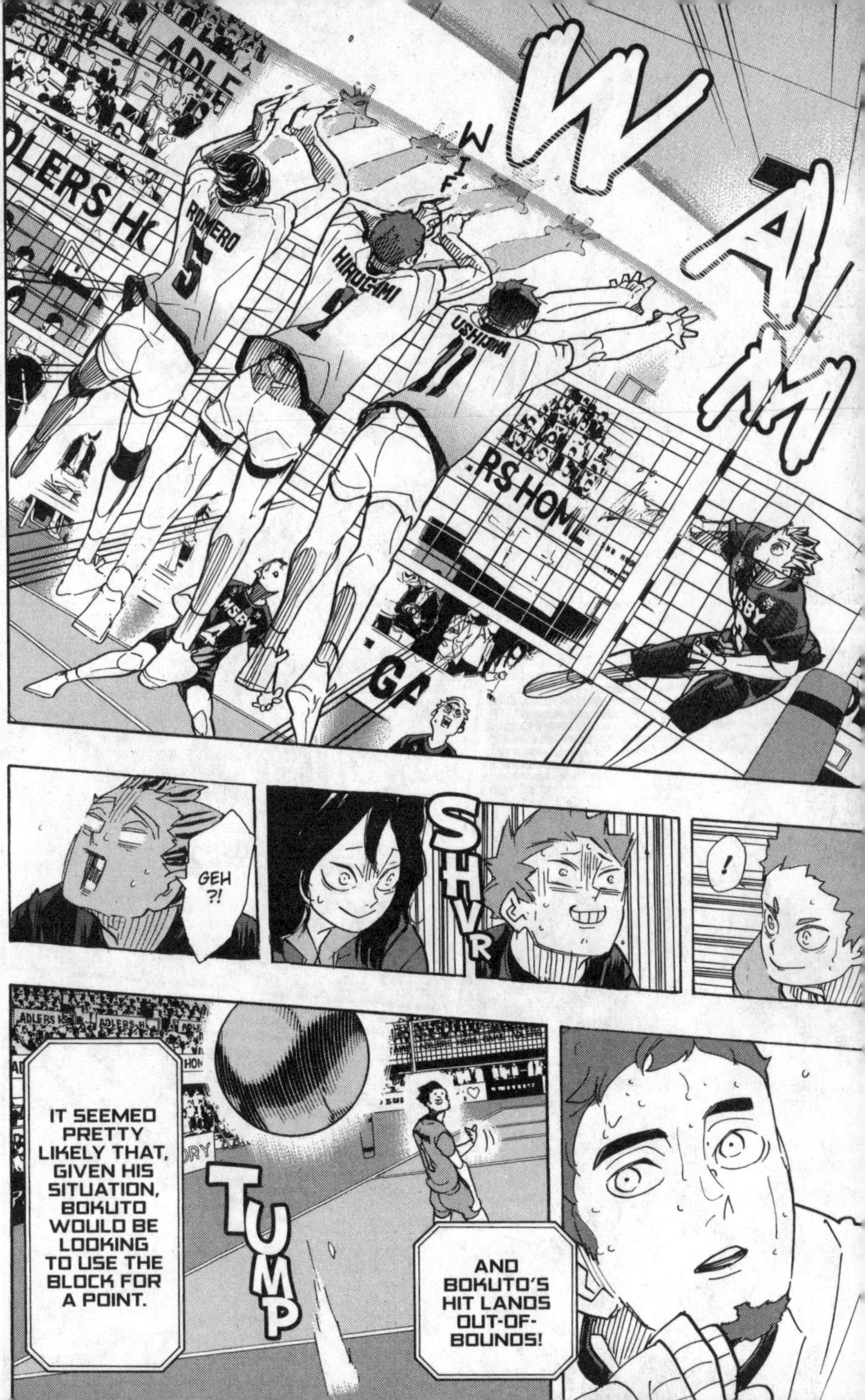
WAM
WIF
ROMERO
HIRUGAMI
USHIJIMA
MSBY
!
SHVR
GEH ?!
AND BOKUTO'S HIT LANDS OUT-OF-BOUNDS!
IT SEEMED PRETTY LIKELY THAT, GIVEN HIS SITUATION, BOKUTO WOULD BE LOOKING TO USE THE BLOCK FOR A POINT.
TUMP

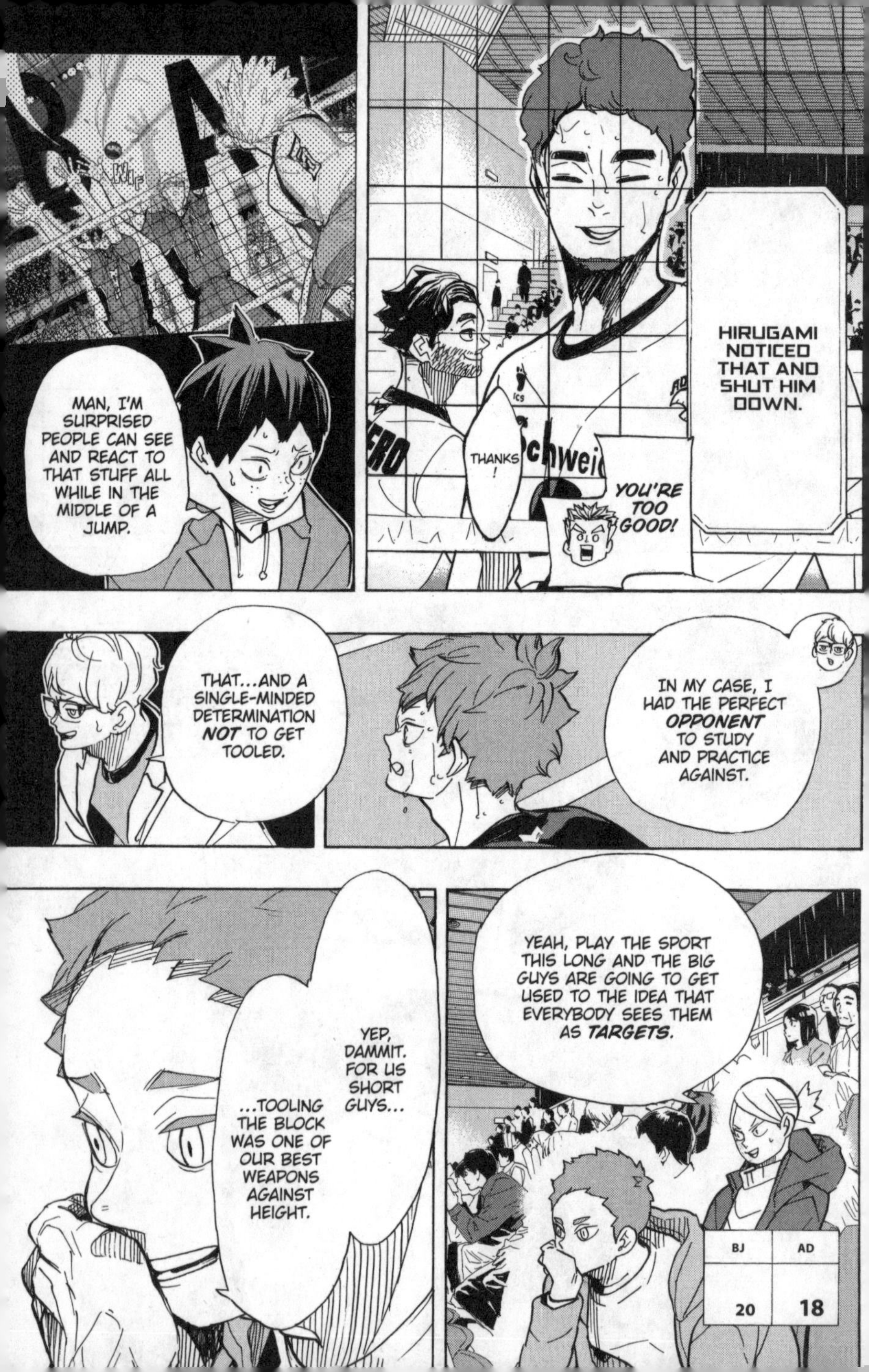
HIRUGAMI NOTICED THAT AND SHUT HIM DOWN.
YOU'RE TOO GOOD!
THANKS!
MAN, I'M SURPRISED PEOPLE CAN SEE AND REACT TO THAT STUFF ALL WHILE IN THE MIDDLE OF A JUMP.
IN MY CASE, I HAD THE PERFECT OPPONENT TO STUDY AND PRACTICE AGAINST.
THAT...AND A SINGLE-MINDED DETERMINATION NOT TO GET TOOLED.
YEAH, PLAY THE SPORT THIS LONG AND THE BIG GUYS ARE GOING TO GET USED TO THE IDEA THAT EVERYBODY SEES THEM AS TARGETS.
YEP, DAMMIT. FOR US SHORT GUYS...
...TOOLING THE BLOCK WAS ONE OF OUR BEST WEAPONS AGAINST HEIGHT.
BJ AD
20 18

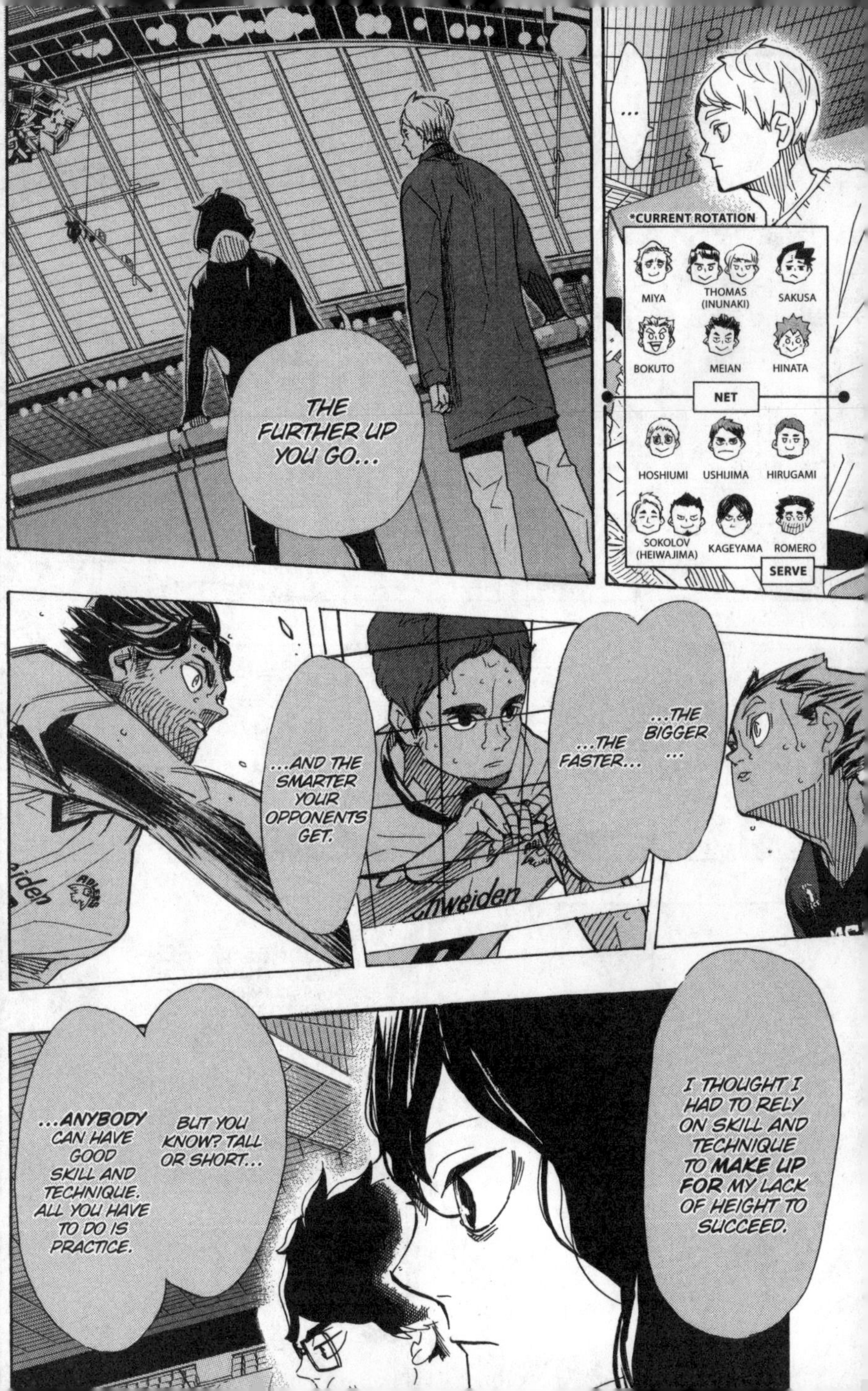
...
*CURRENT ROTATION
MIYA
THOMAS (INUNAKI)
SAKUSA
BOKUTO
MEIAN
HINATA
NET
HOSHIUMI
USHIJIMA
HIRUGAMI
SOKOLOV (HEIWAJIMA)
KAGEYAMA
ROMERO
SERVE
THE FURTHER UP YOU GO...
...THE BIGGER ...
...THE FASTER...
...AND THE SMARTER YOUR OPPONENTS GET.
I THOUGHT I HAD TO RELY ON SKILL AND TECHNIQUE TO MAKE UP FOR MY LACK OF HEIGHT TO SUCCEED.
BUT YOU KNOW? TALL OR SHORT...
...ANYBODY CAN HAVE GOOD SKILL AND TECHNIQUE. ALL YOU HAVE TO DO IS PRACTICE.

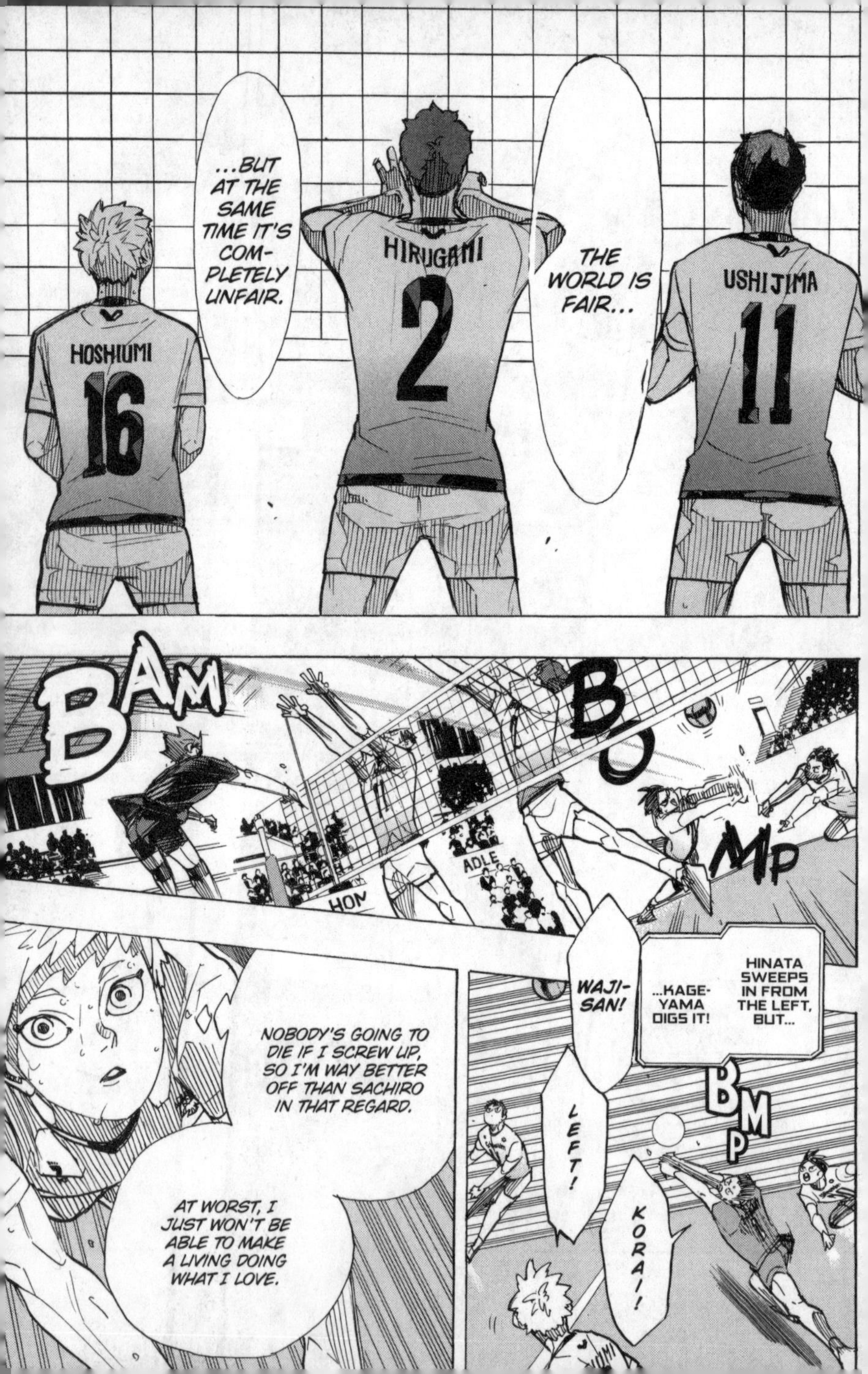
USHIJIMA
11
THE WORLD IS FAIR...
HIRUGAMI
2
...BUT AT THE SAME TIME IT'S COMPLETELY UNFAIR.
HOSHIUMI
16
BOOMP
BAM
HINATA SWEEPS IN FROM THE LEFT, BUT...
...KAGEYAMA DIGS IT!
WAJI-SAN!
BMP
KORAI!
LEFT!
NOBODY'S GOING TO DIE IF I SCREW UP, SO I'M WAY BETTER OFF THAN SACHIRO IN THAT REGARD.
AT WORST, I JUST WON'T BE ABLE TO MAKE A LIVING DOING WHAT I LOVE.

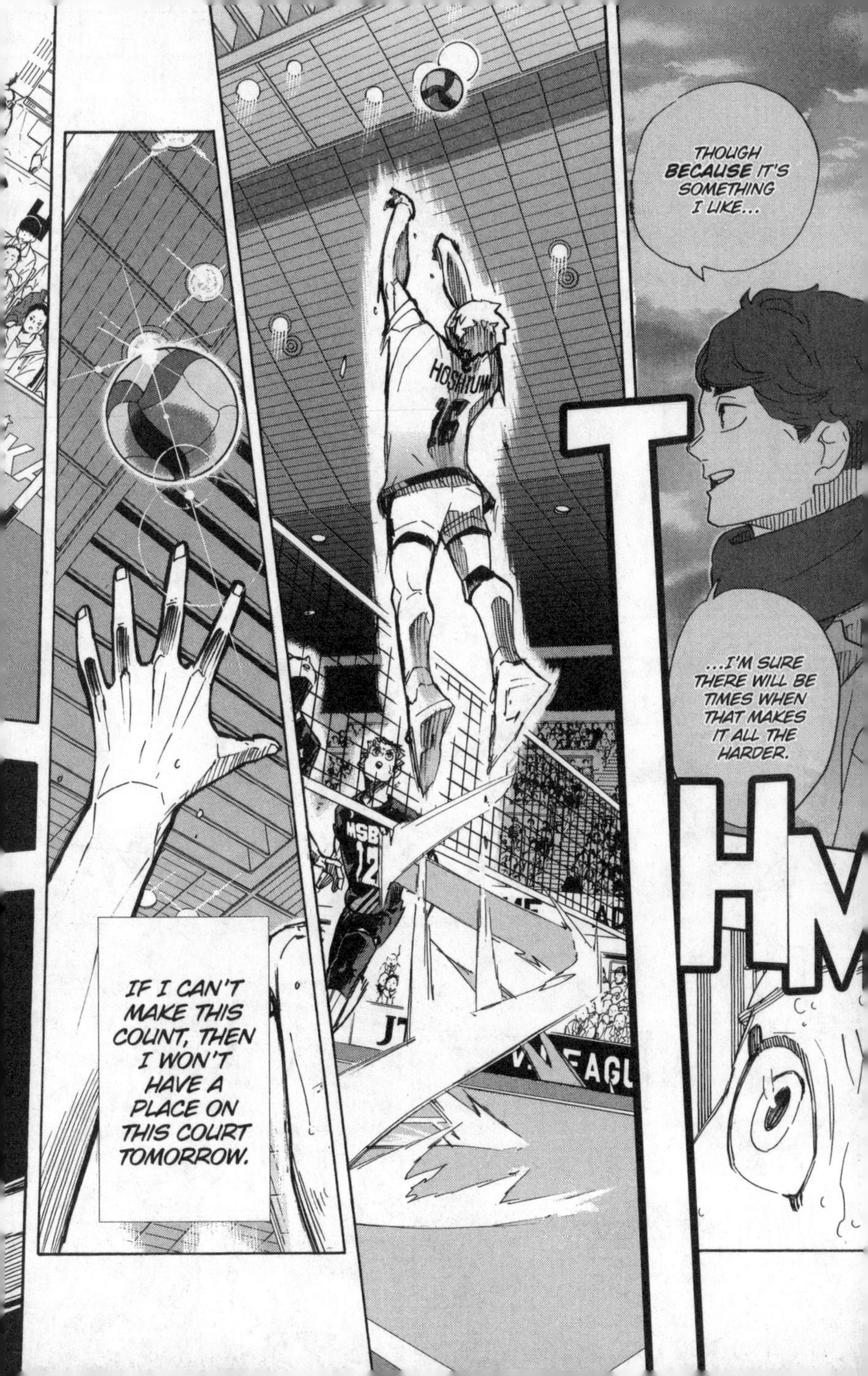
THOUGH BECAUSE IT'S SOMETHING I LIKE...
...I'M SURE THERE WILL BE TIMES WHEN THAT MAKES IT ALL THE HARDER.
THM
IF I CAN'T MAKE THIS COUNT, THEN I WON'T HAVE A PLACE ON THIS COURT TOMORROW.

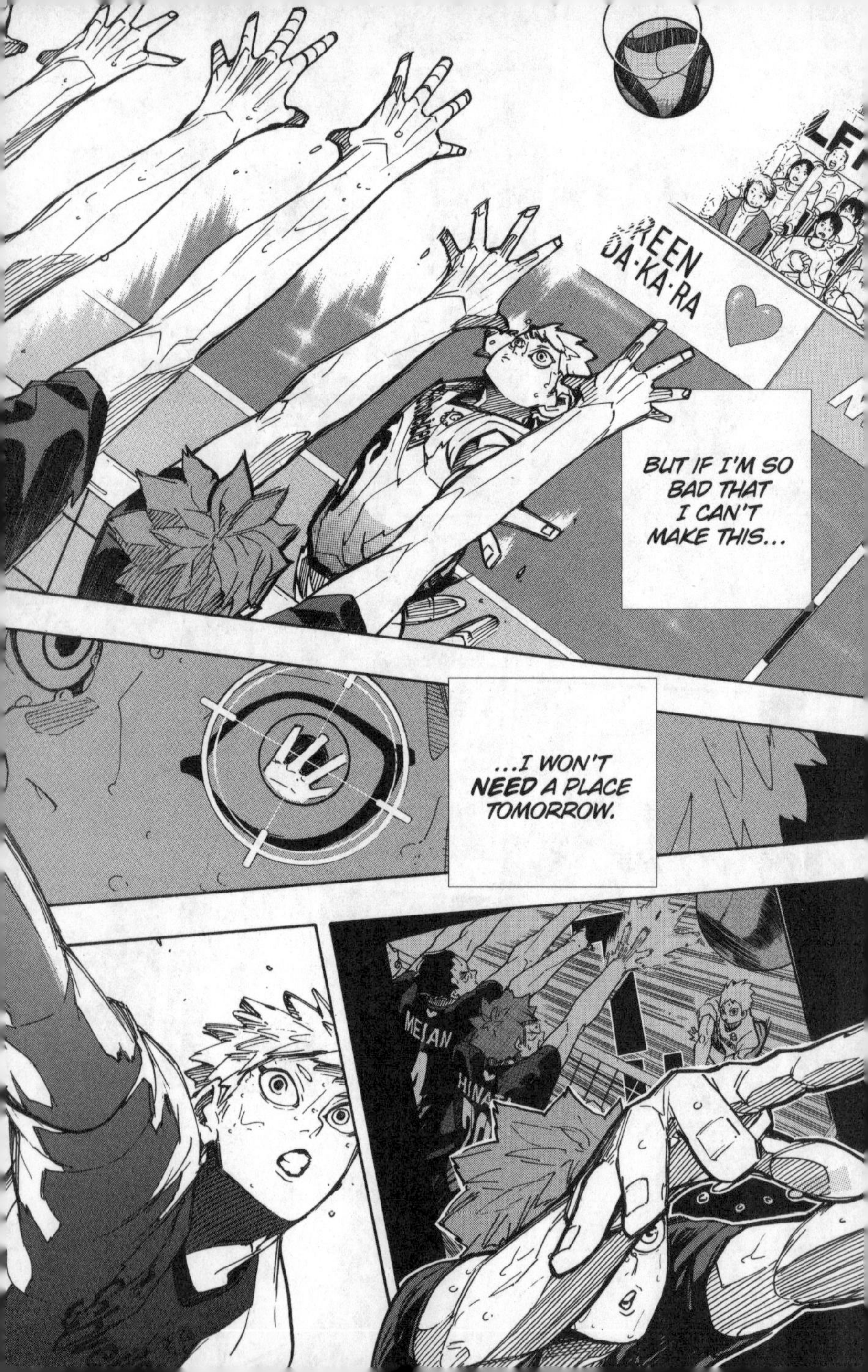
DA·KA·RA
BUT IF I'M SO BAD THAT I CAN'T MAKE THIS...
...I WON'T NEED A PLACE TOMORROW.
MEIAN

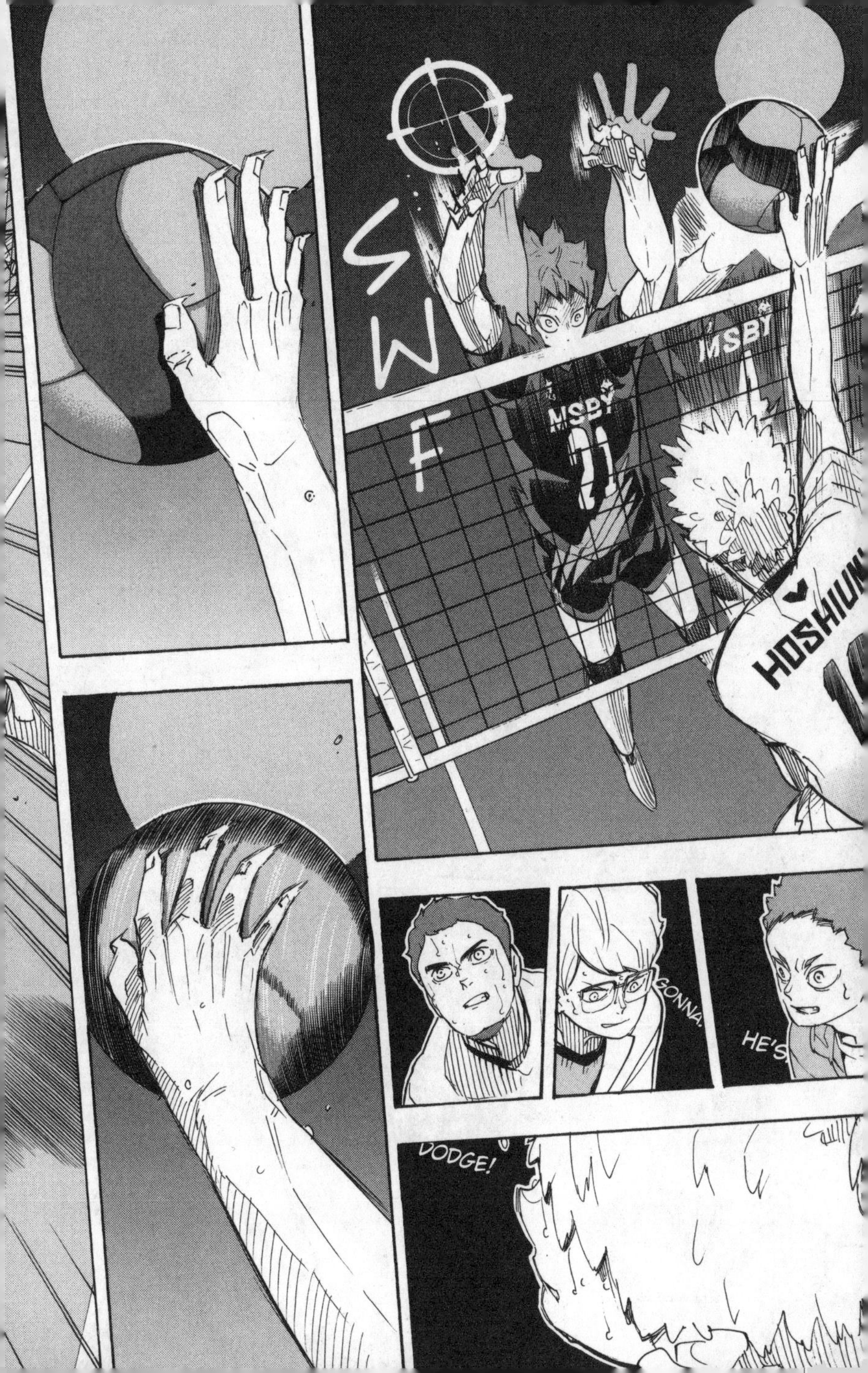
SWF
HE'S
GONNA.
DODGE!

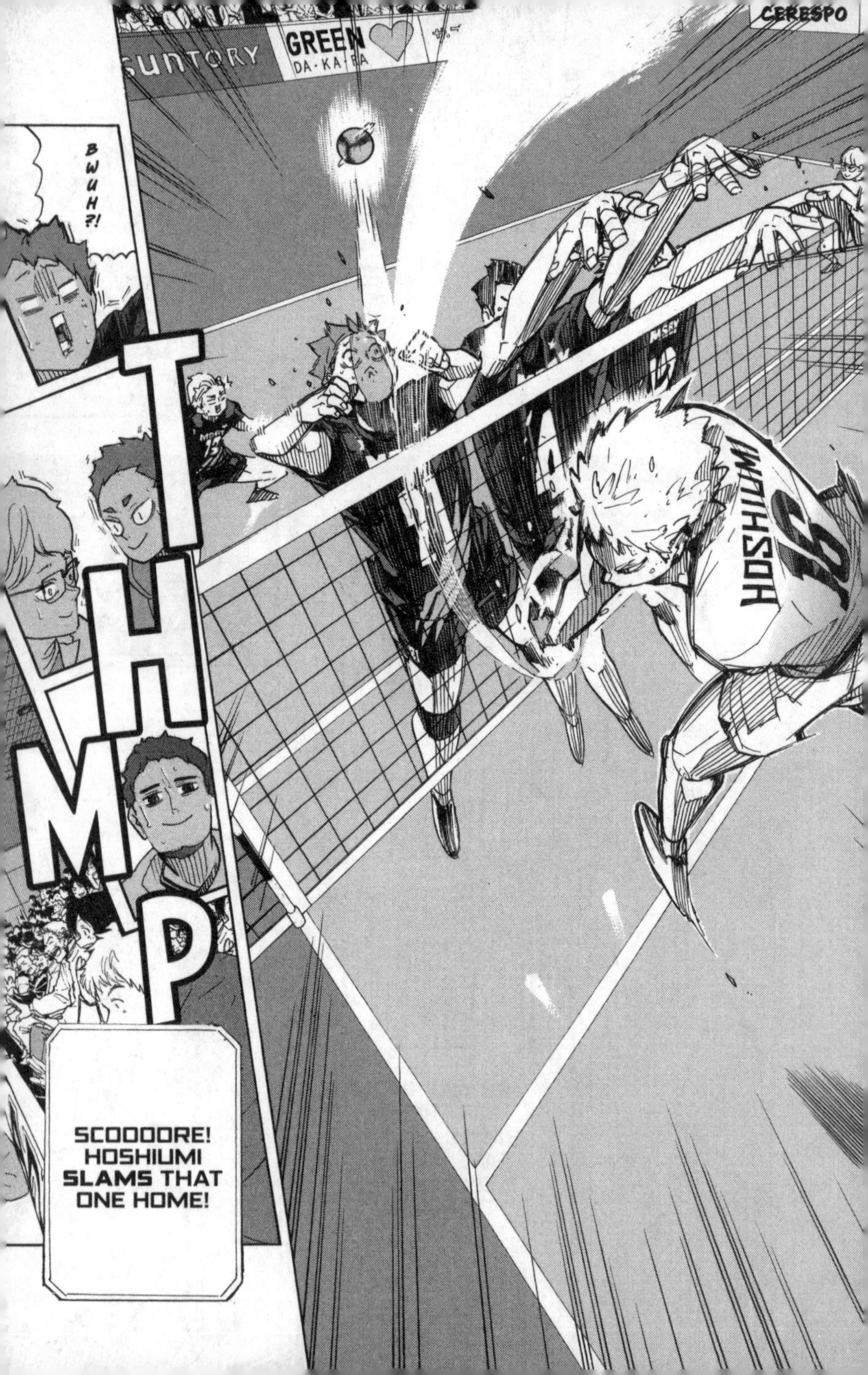
CERESPO
GREEN
DA-KA-RA
SUNTORY
HOSHIUMI
18
BWUH?!
THMP
SCOOOORE! HOSHIUMI SLAMS THAT ONE HOME!

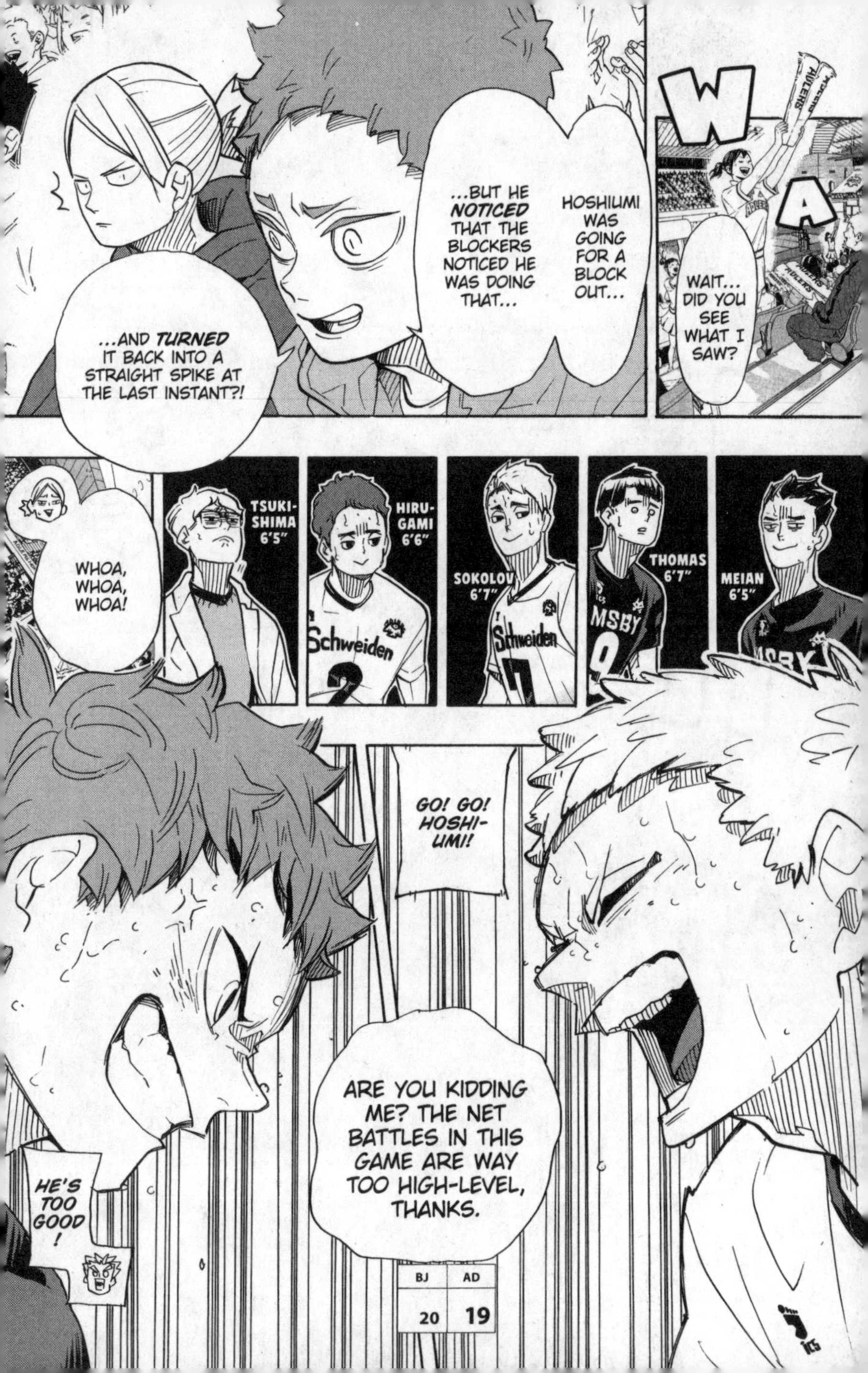
W
A
WAIT… DID YOU SEE WHAT I SAW?
HOSHIUMI WAS GOING FOR A BLOCK OUT…
…BUT HE NOTICED THAT THE BLOCKERS NOTICED HE WAS DOING THAT…
…AND TURNED IT BACK INTO A STRAIGHT SPIKE AT THE LAST INSTANT?!
MEIAN 6'5"
THOMAS 6'7"
SOKOLOV 6'7"
HIRU-GAMI 6'6"
TSUKI-SHIMA 6'5"
WHOA, WHOA, WHOA!
GO! GO! HOSHI-UMI!
ARE YOU KIDDING ME? THE NET BATTLES IN THIS GAME ARE WAY TOO HIGH-LEVEL, THANKS.
HE'S TOO GOOD!
BJ AD
20 19

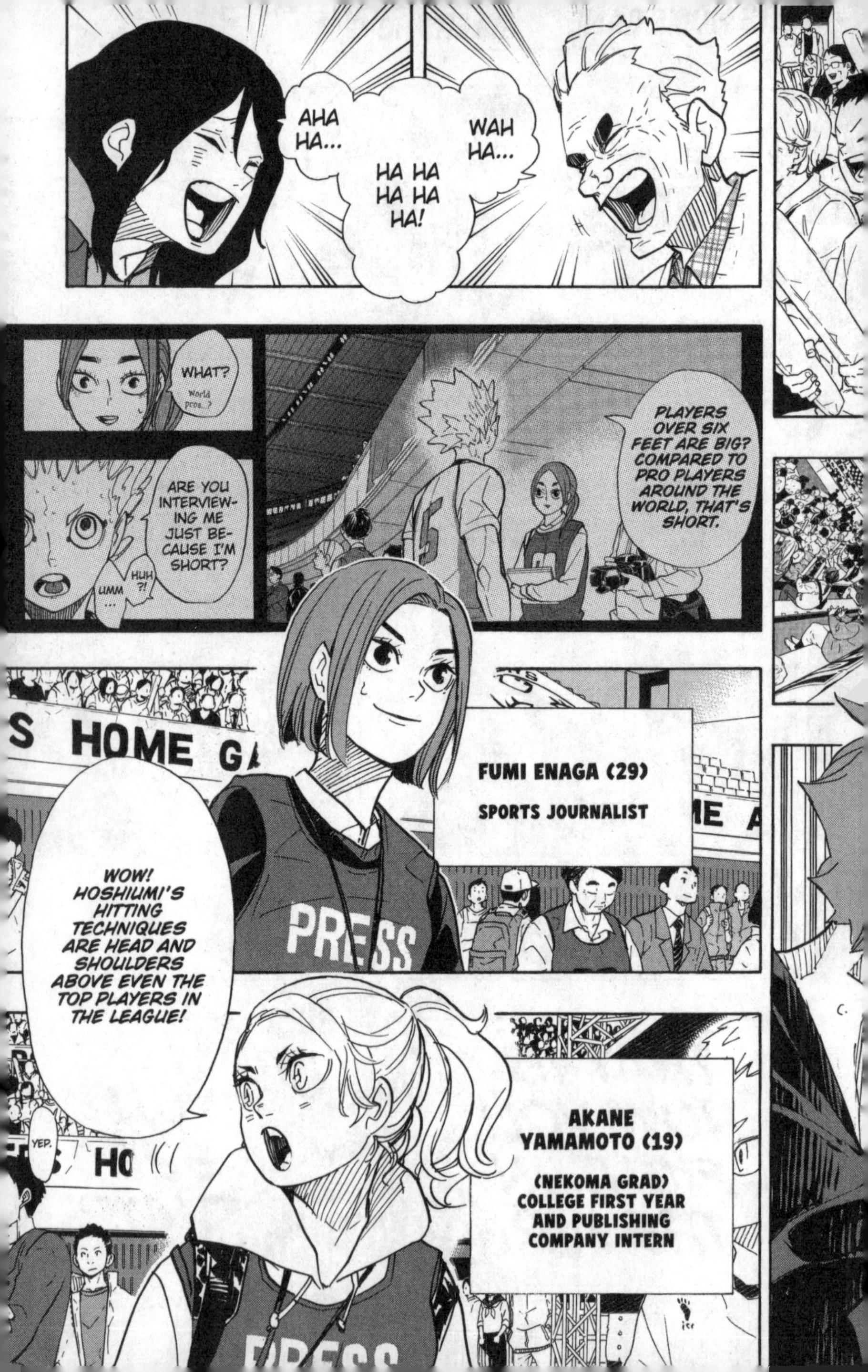
WAH HA...
AHA HA...
HA HA HA HA HA!
PLAYERS OVER SIX FEET ARE BIG? COMPARED TO PRO PLAYERS AROUND THE WORLD, THAT'S SHORT.
WHAT?
World pros...?
ARE YOU INTERVIEWING ME JUST BECAUSE I'M SHORT?
HUH?!
UMM...
FUMI ENAGA (29)
SPORTS JOURNALIST
S HOME GA
PRESS
AKANE YAMAMOTO (19)
(NEKOMA GRAD) COLLEGE FIRST YEAR AND PUBLISHING COMPANY INTERN
WOW! HOSHIUMI'S HITTING TECHNIQUES ARE HEAD AND SHOULDERS ABOVE EVEN THE TOP PLAYERS IN THE LEAGUE!
YEP.

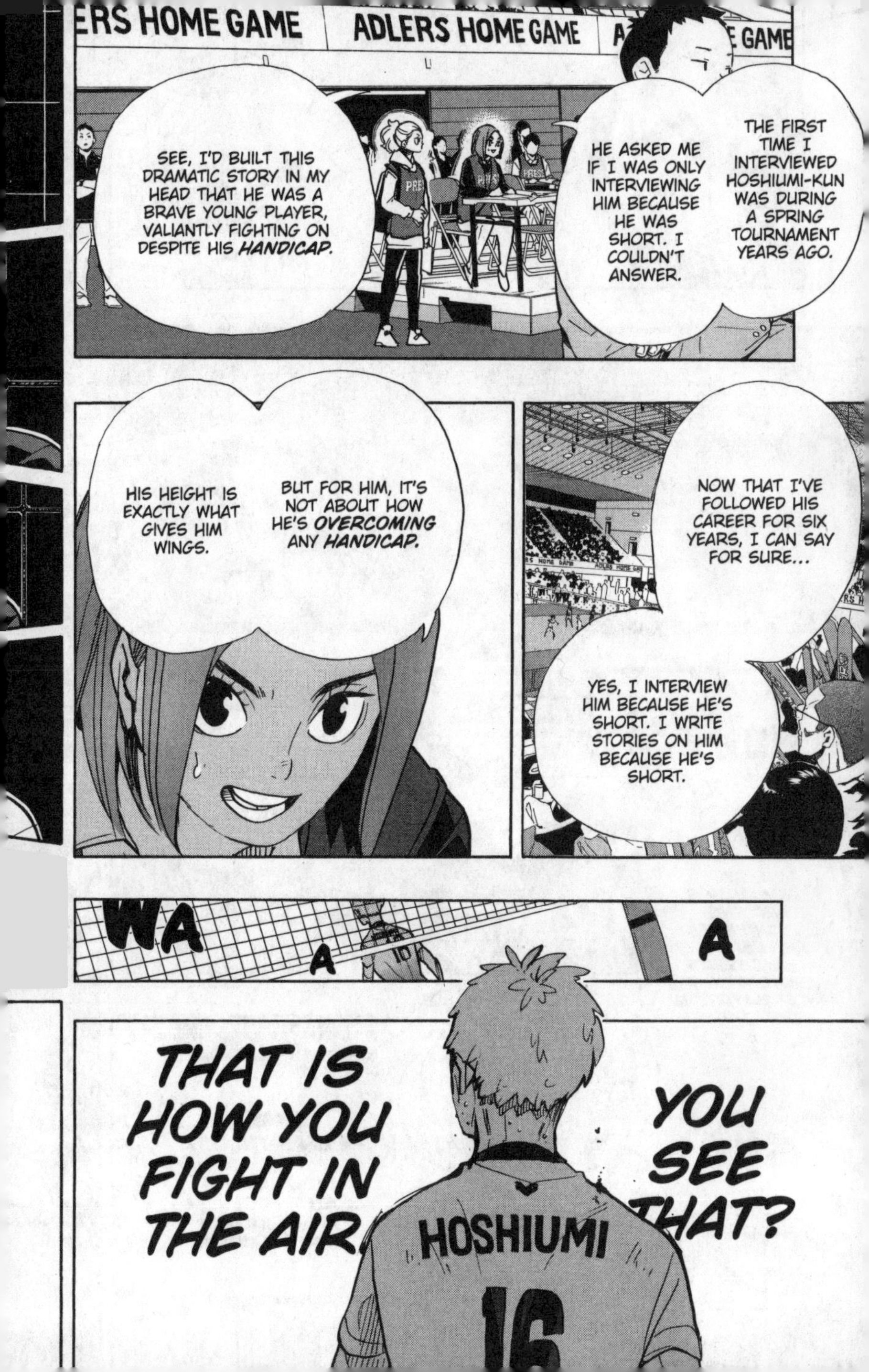
ADLERS HOME GAME
THE FIRST TIME I INTERVIEWED HOSHIUMI-KUN WAS DURING A SPRING TOURNAMENT YEARS AGO.
HE ASKED ME IF I WAS ONLY INTERVIEWING HIM BECAUSE HE WAS SHORT. I COULDN'T ANSWER.
SEE, I'D BUILT THIS DRAMATIC STORY IN MY HEAD THAT HE WAS A BRAVE YOUNG PLAYER, VALIANTLY FIGHTING ON DESPITE HIS *HANDICAP.*
NOW THAT I'VE FOLLOWED HIS CAREER FOR SIX YEARS, I CAN SAY FOR SURE...
YES, I INTERVIEW HIM BECAUSE HE'S SHORT. I WRITE STORIES ON HIM BECAUSE HE'S SHORT.
BUT FOR HIM, IT'S NOT ABOUT HOW HE'S *OVERCOMING* ANY *HANDICAP.*
HIS HEIGHT IS EXACTLY WHAT GIVES HIM WINGS.
WA
A
A
YOU SEE THAT?
THAT IS HOW YOU FIGHT IN THE AIR.
HOSHIUMI
16

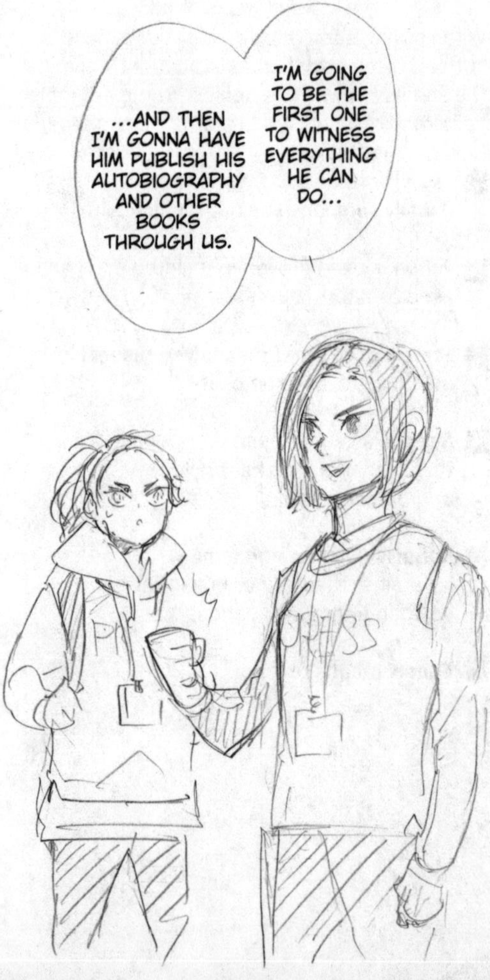
I'M GOING TO BE THE FIRST ONE TO WITNESS EVERYTHING HE CAN DO...
...AND THEN I'M GONNA HAVE HIM PUBLISH HIS AUTOBIOGRAPHY AND OTHER BOOKS THROUGH US.

EDITOR'S NOTES

The English edition of Haikyu!! maintains the honorifics used in the original Japanese version. For those of you who are new to these terms, here's a brief explanation to help with your reading experience!

When saying someone's name in Japanese, a suffix is often attached to indicate how familiar the speaker is with the person. Some are more polite and respectful, while others are endearing.

1. ***-kun*** is often used for young men or boys, usually someone you are familiar with.

2. ***-chan*** is used for young children and can be used as a term of endearment.

3. ***-san*** is used for someone you respect or are not close to, or to be polite.

4. ***Senpai*** is used for someone who is older than you or in a higher position or grade in school.

5. ***Kohai*** is used for someone who is younger than you or in a lower position or grade in school.

6. ***Sensei*** means teacher.

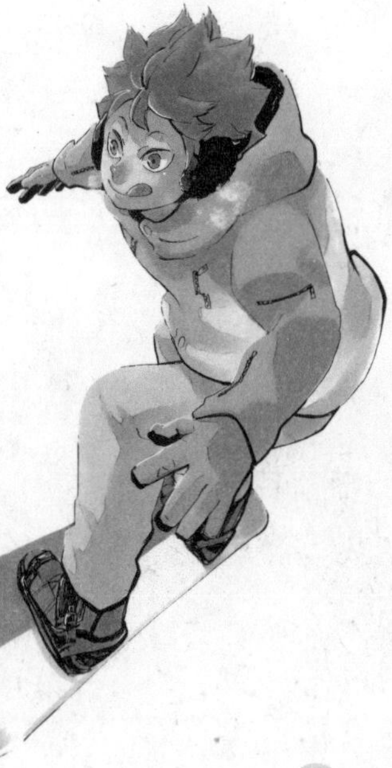

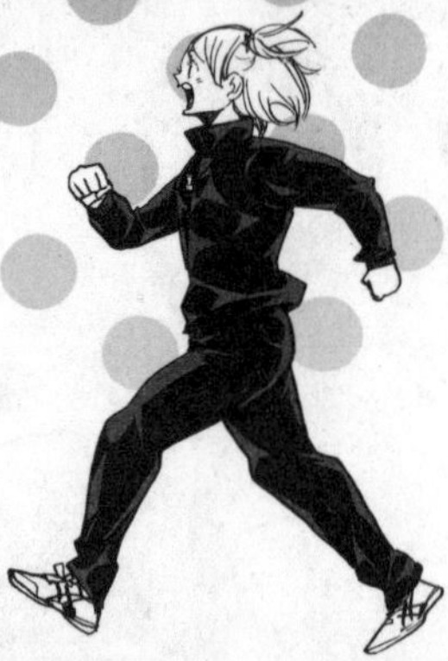

You're Reading the WRONG WAY!

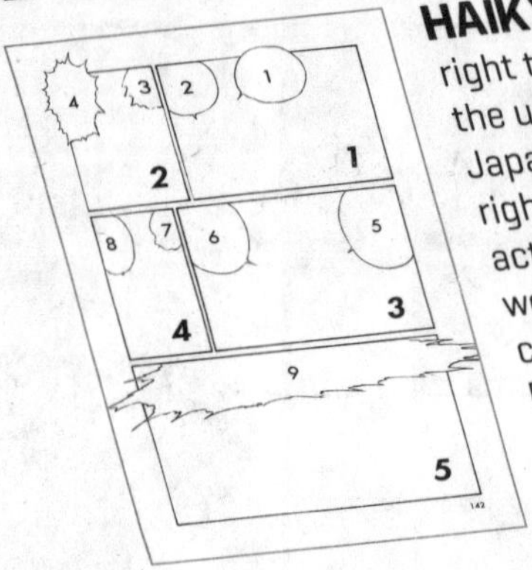

1
2
3
4
1
2
5
6
7
8
3
4
9
5
142

HAIKYU!! reads from right to left, starting in the upper-right corner. Japanese is read from right to left, meaning that action, sound effects and word-balloon order are completely reversed from English order.

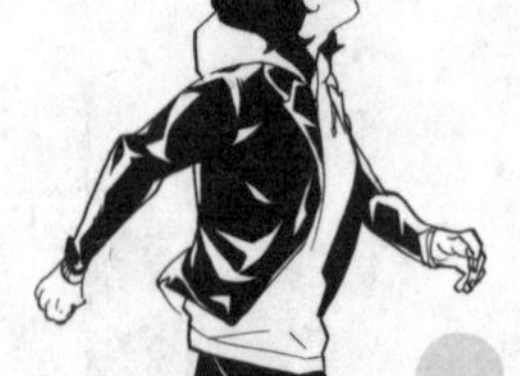

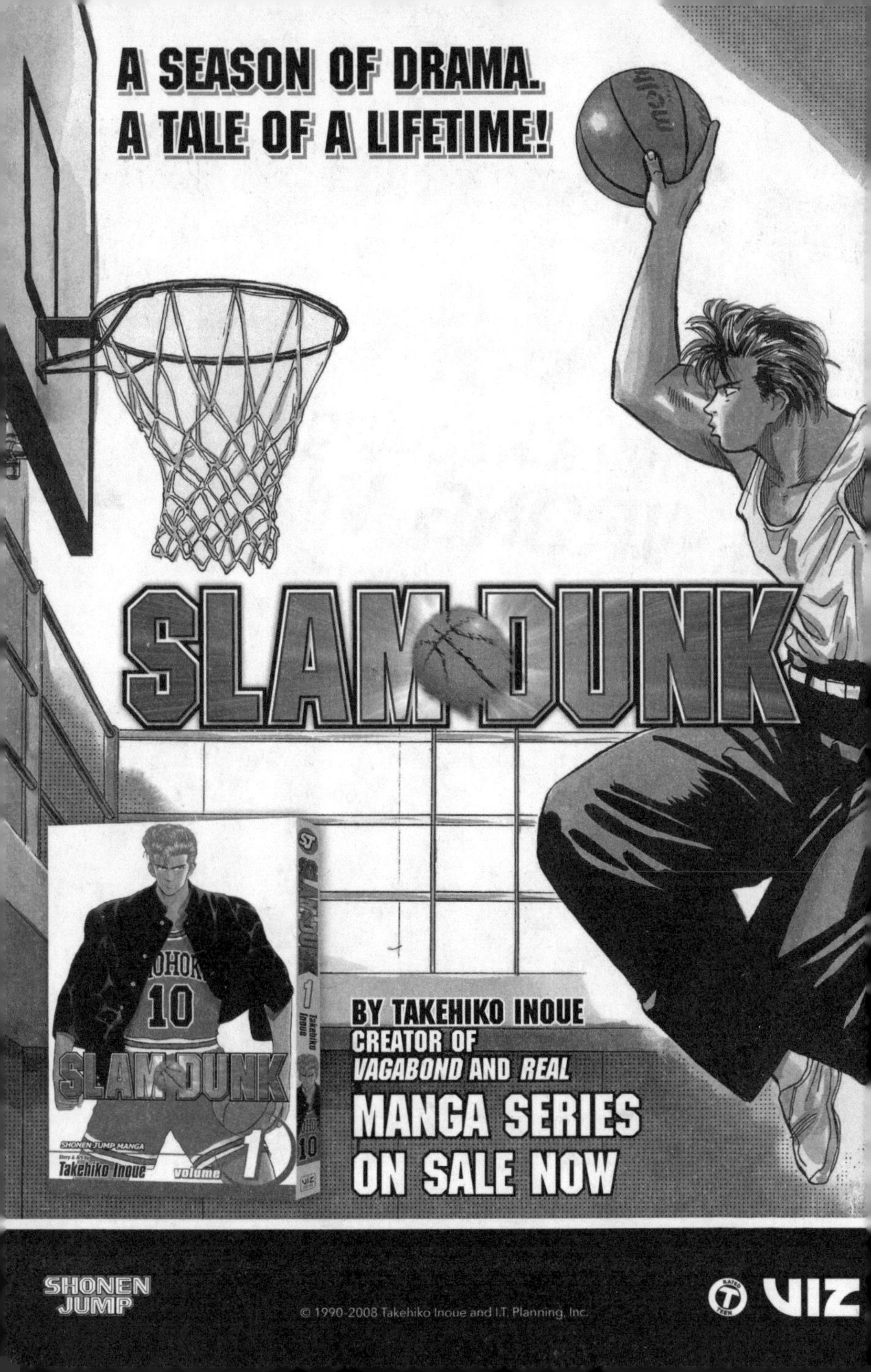
A SEASON OF DRAMA.
A TALE OF A LIFETIME!
SLAM DUNK
SLAM DUNK
SHONEN JUMP MANGA
Takehiko Inoue
volume 1
BY TAKEHIKO INOUE
CREATOR OF
VAGABOND AND REAL
MANGA SERIES
ON SALE NOW
SHONEN JUMP
© 1990-2008 Takehiko Inoue and I.T. Planning, Inc.
VIZ

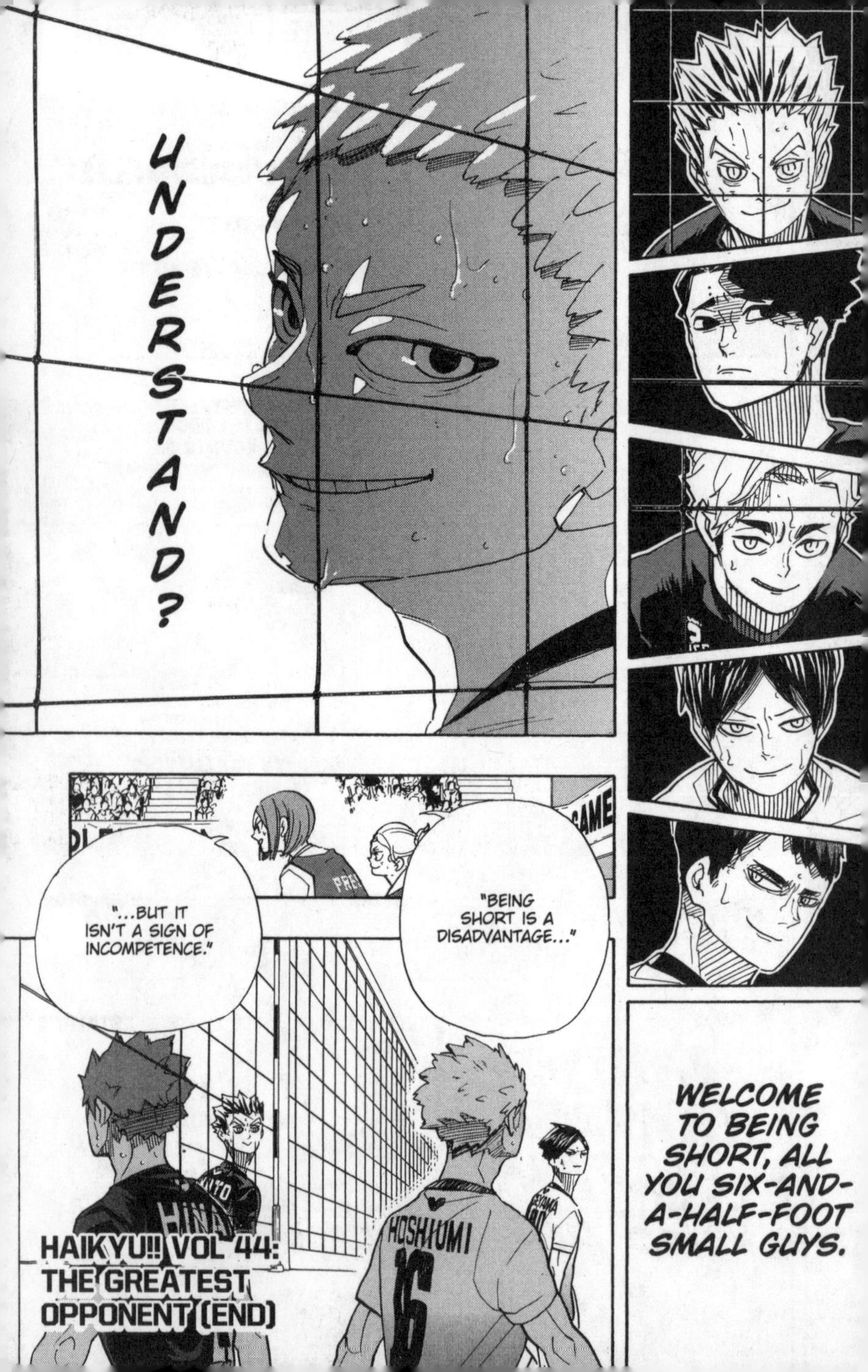
UNDERSTAND?
"BEING SHORT IS A DISADVANTAGE..."
"...BUT IT ISN'T A SIGN OF INCOMPETENCE."
WELCOME TO BEING SHORT, ALL YOU SIX-AND-A-HALF-FOOT SMALL GUYS.
HAIKYU!! VOL 44: THE GREATEST OPPONENT (END)

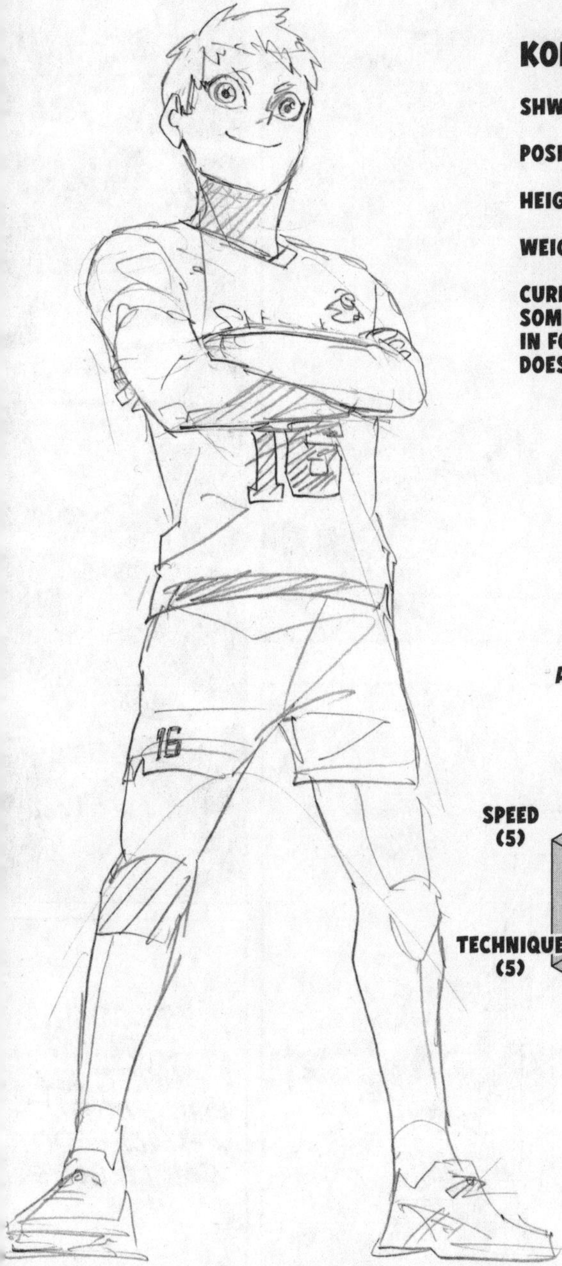

KORAI HOSHIUMI (23)

SHWEIDEN ADLERS

POSITION: OUTSIDE HITTER

HEIGHT: 5'8"

WEIGHT: 154 LBS.

CURRENT WORRY:
SOMETIMES THE FOOD
IN FOREIGN COUNTRIES
DOESN'T AGREE WITH HIM.

ABILITY PARAMETERS
(5-POINT SCALE)

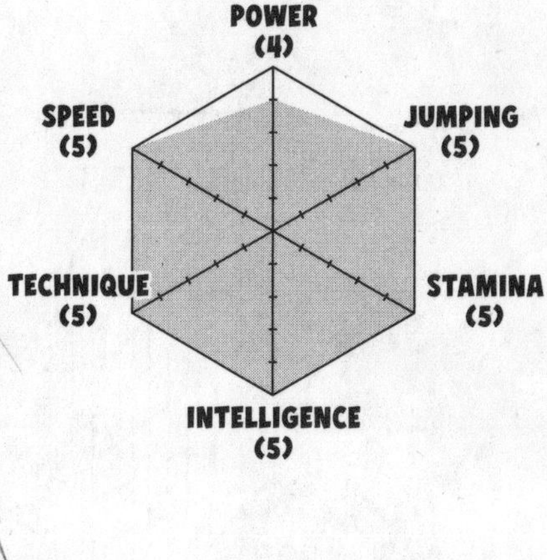
POWER (4)
JUMPING (5)
STAMINA (5)
INTELLIGENCE (5)
TECHNIQUE (5)
SPEED (5)